GREENBERG'S
POCKET PRICE GUIDE

LIONEL®
TRAINS
1901-2000

Editor: Kent J. Johnson

KALMBACH
BOOKS

Twentieth Edition

For more information, visit our website at http://books.kalmbach.com

Manufactured in the United States of America

Lionel® and American Flyer are the registered trademarks of Lionel LLC, Chesterfield, Michigan

Cover design: Kristi Ludwig

Cover photo: Provided by Erv Tarnow, model no. 18130 Santa Fe F-3 diesel locomotive AB set was produced in 1996. In the background model no. 700E 4-6-4 scale Hudson steam locomotive was produced between 1937 and 1942, and provided here by Jack Sommerfeld.

CONTENTS

This handy reference is divided into eight major sections: Prewar 1901–1942, Postwar 1945–1969, Modern Era (MPC) 1970–1986, Modern Era (LTI) 1987–1995, Modern Era (Lionel LLC) 1996–2000, Special Production, Large Scale, and Catalogs. In the first four sections and in the Large Scale section, production is listed numerically, using the item's catalog number. In the Prewar section, equipment is further described by gauge—Standard, O, OO, or 2⅞. The gauge type is within the parentheses.

Steam locomotives in all sections include value with tender, even if tenders are not listed in detail. Be advised that the value of steam locomotives, particularly those of the Prewar period, may be significantly affected by the type of tender the item came with. For detailed information on tenders, consult the relevant comprehensive guides.

FOREWORD

IT'S SUPPLY VS. DEMAND AND MORE

While the toy train prices in this Guide all come back to the contributors' observations of the laws of supply and demand in the toy train market, perhaps the simple statement that the price at which a train is sold is a function of supply and demand doesn't go far enough.

As reason suggests, the *supply* of a particular train affects its price on the market depending on whether the piece is scarce or widely available. Scarcity is a function of the number of pieces initially manufactured (a.k.a. rarity) and, increasingly, the current supply of the piece in the better condition categories (e.g., Like New). The *area* or *location* in which the piece is being bought or sold can also affect the supply of toy trains from which a collector can choose. For example, we might expect a Mickey Mouse Handcar to cost more in Sasketchewan than in New Jersey.

Demand, at the simplest level, is determined by the number of persons interested in acquiring a certain piece. There are a number of factors (mostly human) which can influence the demand for a toy train. When we begin to review the factors which influence collectors' demand for certain pieces, we can see that the market behaves in interesting (and sometimes strange) ways:

• The *aesthetic appeal* of a piece can increase or decrease demand among collectors. For example, the supply of mint, in-the-box, Lionel Scout sets is probably quite low in the current market. However, this usually won't make them worth more to collectors than a 700E in almost any condition because of the demand for the more popular Hudson.

• Related to aesthetic appeal, an unusual *provenance*, or "story" behind a piece can significantly influence its demand by collectors. For example, there are a number of trains that are at least as scarce as the Postwar Girls Train. However, the Girls Train has a great story behind it and, thus, tends to be in greater demand among collectors.

• Interestingly enough, the *area* or *location* in which the piece is being bought or sold can also affect demand. We might expect a piece bearing the roadname of the Providence and Worcester RR to be worth more to the residents of those two New England cities than to a resident of, say, Amarillo, Texas.

• Finally, the age of the piece can help determine demand, in part, because collectors tend to be more interested in trains from their own "era." This factor (perhaps the most important) bears further discussion.

COLLECTING IS A FUNCTION OF NOSTALGIA

One member of the Internet discussion group I monitored wondered how it could be possible that a reasonably common Modern-MPC Era diesel engine commands three times the purchase price of a somewhat scarce Prewar electric engine. It's an interesting observation (and a frustrating one if you happen to be a Prewar Lionel collector).

I had a hunch that toy train collecting isn't the only pastime to be affected by the presence of "baby boomers" in one segment of the market but not in another. I checked a current issue of a widely read car collectors' guide, and noted that prices for both Fords and Chevrolets produced between 1955–57 were uniformly two to three times as high as prices for Fords and Chevrolets produced between 1928–32. Do you think it's a function of rarity or aesthetic preeminence that a Thunderbird two-seater goes for $45,000 while a nice, clean Model A goes for about $15,000? I'll argue that it's *neither*. I believe that the collectors who grew up wanting the T-Bird all want one now, which has driven up the price of these models in the current market. One final observation is that paying $15,000 for a drive-it-on-weekends-only Model A sounds like a bargain. Can you think of any Lionel Prewar items that might also be fun to own at bargain prices?

Happy collecting!

—*Steven J. Serenska*

INTRODUCTION

This **Pocket Price Guide** lists all major Lionel items numerically for the years 1901–1942 and 1945–2000 (there was no Lionel production during World War II). This list of items includes Lionel products tentatively planned for production in 2000. Subsequent additions and deletions to the 2000 product line will be reported in the 2001 edition of this pocket guide.

The values quoted in this guide are for the most common variety of each item. Some rare variations are worth considerably more, and a few of the more important ones are cited. For more detailed information about variations, please consult these comprehensive guides: *Greenberg's Guide to Lionel Trains: 1901–1942, Volumes I, II,* and *III; Greenberg's Guide to Lionel Trains: 1945–1969, Volumes I, III, IV, V, VI,* and *VII; Greenberg's Guide to Lionel Trains: 1970–1991, Volumes I and II; and Greenberg's Guide to Lionel Paper and Collectibles.*

Dates cited in this guide are cataloged dates. If there is no catalog date, production dates are listed, if known. Lionel trains are frequently marked with "Built" or "New" dates. These dates often reflect the dates that Lionel's artists picked up from prototype photographs or the date when the artists prepared their drawings. These dates may or may not have any relation to catalog dates or actual production dates. In some cases, Lionel numbered cars with a number different from the catalog number. In these cases we also list this number, enclosed in parentheses, and refer the reader to the published catalog number for the price.

In recent years, reproductions of Prewar and Postwar Lionel trains and train parts have become a major concern for collectors. Today it is difficult to find a Prewar or Postwar Lionel item that has not had parts reproduced or remanufactured for it. Collectors need to be aware of this—while many reproductions are marked or exhibit distinct differences from the original to indicate that they are indeed reproductions, many others are virtually identical to the originals. In some reported cases reproduction markings have been removed. Very close and careful study of an item is advised before making a purchase.

Also, collectors should be aware that counterfeit reproductions of some popular Lionel Postwar items do appear from time to time in the marketplace. These counterfeits often are extremely difficult to detect. If you have any doubts at all about an item's authenticity, you should seek the assistance of a knowledgeable and reputable collector.

We have provided several columns for items listed in Sections 1, 2, 3, 4, 5, 7, and 8. The first two columns give the current market values for each piece. In the Prewar and Postwar sections, values are denoted by Good and Excellent. In the Modern Era sections, the Large Scale section, and the Catalog section, values are given for Excellent and New. The "Cond/$" column is for noting the condition and your cost in acquiring the item.

We are constantly striving to improve **Greenberg's Pocket Price Guide**. If you find any missing items or detect any misinformation, please write to us. If you have recommendations for improving a listing, we would also like to hear from you. Send comments, new information, or corrections to:

EDITOR—LIONEL POCKET GUIDE (10-8700)
BOOKS DIVISION, KALMBACH PUBLISHING CO.
P. O. BOX 1612
21027 CROSSROADS CIRCLE
WAUKESHA, WI 53187-1612

HOW VALUES WERE DETERMINED

The values presented in this Pocket Price Guide are meant to serve only as a *guide* to collectors. They are an averaged reflection of prices for items bought and sold across the country, and are intended to assist the collector in making informed decisions concerning purchases and sales.

Values listed herein are based on values obtained at train meets held throughout the nation during the Spring and Summer of 1999, and from private transactions reported by members of our nationwide review panel. Values in your area may be consistent with values published in this guide, or higher or lower, depending upon the relative availability, scarcity, or desirability of a particular item. General economic conditions in your area may also affect values. Even regional preferences for specific road names may be a factor.

If you are selling a train to an individual who is planning to resell it—a retailer, for example—you will NOT obtain the values reported in this book. Rather, you may expect to receive about 50 percent of these prices. For your item to be of interest to such a buyer, it must be purchased for considerably less than the price listed here. But, if you are dealing one-to-one with another private collector, values may be expected to be more consistent with this guide.

Our studies of train values indicate that mail order and retail store prices are generally higher than prices found at train meets because of the cost and effort of running a retail establishment or producing and distributing a price list, as well as packing and shipping trains.

WE STRONGLY RECOMMEND THAT NOVICE COLLECTORS SEEK THE ADVICE AND ASSISTANCE OF FRIENDS OR ASSOCIATES WHO HAVE EXPERIENCE IN BUYING, SELLING, AND TRADING TRAINS.

NOTABLE FEATURES IN THIS EDITION

This edition lists Lionel production from 1970 to 2000 (which we define as Modern Era) in three subsections. The first Modern Era section covers 1970–1986, when Lionel Electric Trains were manufactured by various subsidiaries of General Mills—most notably Model Products Corporation (MPC) and the Fundimensions toy division. The second Modern Era section lists items manufactured by Richard Kughn's Lionel Trains, Inc. (LTI), from 1987 through pre-announced 1996 production. Finally, the third Modern Era section lists items manufactured or announced by Lionel LLC, for 1996–2000. The enormous volume of production since 1970—and especially since 1987—made it both logical and necessary to better define the distinct entities that have manufactured Lionel trains in this period.

This edition involved the participation of many people who generously gave of their time and knowledge. We appreciate their contributions to this publication and to our enjoyment of the hobby.

—*Kent J. Johnson, Editor*

CLASSIC LIONEL PRODUCTS

By Bob Keller
Associate Editor
Classic Toy Trains Magazine

With 100 years of toy train production under its belt, Lionel's history has both its hits and its misses. Hits include some superb locomotives, such as the scale Hudson and Fairbanks Morse Train Master, and accessories, like the Intermodal Crane, that push the envelope of realistic operation.

Some of the misses include trains, such as the space and military cars of the 60s, that totally misunderstood the market, and today's Road Runner and Wile Coyote Ambush Shack—cute, but where would you place it on a layout for maximum impact?

Regardless, all of the products made by Lionel, whether successes or failures, have had one goal in mind: to increase the pleasure of running our toy trains. Here, then, are several notable Lionel products sure to please collectors and operators.

MODERN ERA
WHAT RICHARD KUGHN HAS WROUGHT: The Reading T-1 (1989). One of the fateful events in modern toy train history was when Lionel owner Richard Kughn contacted Mike Wolf (eventual founder of M.T.H. Electric Trains) regarding development and production of a scale-like model of a Reading Railroad T-1-class 4-8-4 Northern, no. 2100.

Developed and produced by Samhongsa in Korea, this locomotive would be the largest O gauge steam locomotive made by Lionel to date. Unlike any previous large Modern Era steamer, it wouldn't be a rehash of Postwar tooling. It would be completely new. The model sold briskly and ran smoothly. It is well regarded by collectors and operators. The engine was reissued in a most prototypical fashion as well. A later version was made, decorated as the Chessie Steam Special, emulating the real railroad publicity and safety awareness train, which also used a repainted Reading T-1 for power.

MODERN ERA
BELLS AND WHISTLES—FOR LESS: The no. 2380 Geep (1996). In an attempt to get deeper market penetration at a lower price point, Lionel LLC loaded the no. 2380s with all the right stuff: Pullmor motor, Railsounds, Command Control, and a terrific-looking strobe light. These are features that hobbyists would have paid more for just a year earlier. The result? A success. Hobbyists who hadn't experienced Command Control because it was featured only on high-end power were able to sample the system's features, and they liked what they saw—and heard.

MODERN ERA

WHAT WE REALLY SAW AT THE GRADE CROSSING: The SD40 (1980 to date). This locomotive was the second original MPC diesel offered in the Modern Era. The first, the U36, was an attempt to produce something new, but it was an aesthetic failure. While it may have evoked the image of a General Electric U-boat, it was far too shrunken a model for all but the most whimsical layouts.

The same can't be said for the SD-40. While the SD-40 had one foot in the toy realm, it had the other firmly planted in realism. It duplicated the major reference points and successfully managed to suggest the image of a "kid with sneakers that are too large," as an author in *Trains* Magazine once described the SD-40.

SD-40s are top-of-the-line Lionel engines and are popular for good reason. Well made, smooth running, and realistic, they come in a variety of popular road names ranging from Santa Fe to Milwaukee Road and Conrail.

POSTWAR

MOTHER OF ALL MODEL RAILROAD ENGINES: The Santa Fe no. 2343 F-3 (1950–1952). What can be said about the Santa Fe F-3 diesel? Well, it is easily recognized and admired by people who otherwise wouldn't know a tank car from a cow catcher. How did it get to be that way? Lawrence Cowen, J. L.'s son, and Lionel, of course.

Seeking to capture the spirit of modern railroading, Cowen selected the General Motors F-3 to hold the place of honor in the Lionel catalog. Needing a colorful paint scheme, Lawrence approached the Santa Fe railroad, which offered $7,000 to help defray the cost of developing the model. The railroad saw the advantage to having its image in the living rooms and basements of tens of thousands of potential Santa Fe travelers or freight customers throughout the country.

The first Santa Fe F-3, the no. 2333, was fielded in 1948, but this wasn't the best of the Postwar F-3s. That honor goes to the no. 2343. Released in 1950, this engine came equipped with Magne-Traction, which notably improved performance over the earlier version. The no. 2343 was well built and to this day is a consistently reliable operator. Despite later cost-cutting compromises, such as the loss of detail, the no. 2343 is the most desirable

POSTWAR

HIGH-QUALITY SWITCHERS: The nos. 622/623/624, 6220, 6250 (1949–55). During the Postwar era most youngsters didn't start out with top-of-the-line steam or diesel engines, they began a little lower on the toy train food chain: a no. 248 or 2018 steamer, a 44-tonner, or if you were in the right place at the right time, one of the better Lionel GM switchers.

Like many Lionel products of the Postwar era, the GM switchers started out as a high-quality product and then spent the rest of their catalog lifespan being issued in progressively cheaper forms. The early switchers had die-cast metal frames and very accurate truck sideframes based on General Motors prototypes. They also had wire handrails and grab irons, a plastic radio antenna, a die-cast simulated fuel tank, and a warning bell that rang continuously.

Lionel LLC reintroduced the elements of better-quality engines in the no. 622 New York Central switcher in 1998 and a no. 6250 Seaboard switcher in 1999.

of the Santa Fe F-3s offered by Lionel in either the Postwar or Modern Era.

In the Modern Era the Santa Fe F-3 has been reissued by MPC as the single-motor no. 8652 in 1976, by LTI as the twin-motored no. 18100 in 1991 (part of the highly desirable no. 11711 streamliner set), and by Lionel LLC as the twin-motored no. 18130, which was also equipped with Railsounds and Command Control.

POSTWAR

BULLET-NOSED WONDER: The no. 746 N&W J 4-8-4 Northern (1957–1960).
Coming very late in the steam era, this model of a Norfolk & Western J-class 4-8-4 Northern was actually a very good representation of the real thing. The J was based on an idea and prototype made from a no. 726 Berkshire submitted by John Van Dyke, a Portsmouth, Virginia, Lionel enthusiast. Even today the smooth lines of the model suggest speed and power. Known for good operation (and a collectible stripe variation), the J continues to be a popular locomotive and represents a bright spot on the eve of the Lionel Corp.'s declining years.

In the Modern Era Fundimensions produced the no. 8100 (1981), which bears the road number 611; it was the last operational J-class engine. LTI offered model no. 18040 with Railsounds, bearing the road number 612; Lionel LLC offered the J-class engine, complete with Railsounds and Command Control, as part of the no. 11909 Warhorse set in 1996. The outfit featured a heavily weathered locomotive and coal train consist.

PREWAR

TOP OF THE LINE: The no. 700E Scale Hudson (1937–1942). This locomotive changed everything that came after it. J. L. Cowen and Co. created the first scale model of a U.S. steam locomotive and heightened the expectations of hobbyists who wanted the realistic prototypical detail on their locomotives that tin litho, stamped-steel, or less-intricate die-casting could not provide.

The scope of detail of the scale Hudson was unrivaled until the Modern Era. The engine took $75,000 and nearly two years to develop from American Locomotive Company blueprints. The Hudson was constructed to NMRA standards to run on the more-realistic T-rail track, and the product, with more than 1,300 model rivets on the tender alone, delivered unprecedented accuracy.

The 700E is the locomotive ideal of the Prewar period. This is a highly desirable—and collectible—locomotive on its own merits. Many want to own this engine, but few who do are bold enough to run it.

PREWAR

PREWAR LEGEND: The 400E 4-4-4 (1931–1939). If one were to pick a single Standard gauge engine to represent the Prewar era, it would have to be the no. 400E 4-4-4. The 400E is truly a piece in which you can feel the quality and effort that went into its creation: the locomotive was big, it was heavy, it had a terrific focused headlight and a red firebox glow.

Produced in at least six color combinations, no matter what the scheme, the name and number plates and brass trim wonderfully accented the model. The 400E headed up countless Standard gauge sets, including what is possibly the most famous of them all, the *Blue Comet.*

Although there may be Standard gauge pieces that are more difficult to find, the 400E is the keystone to a good Standard gauge collection or operating fleet. Though the model was nicely reproduced by Samhongsa for LTI, the original 400E has high marks as a runner and is in demand.

PREWAR

SLEEKEST OF THE SLEEK: The no. 250E *Hiawatha* 4-4-2 (1935-1942). A certain generation of hobbyists from the upper Midwest equate the word "speed" with the name *Hiawatha*. The striking prototype *Hiawatha* ran on the Milwaukee Road and set speed records for the run between Chicago and St. Paul, Minnesota. Ever with an eye on innovative trains that could boost the bottom line, Lionel engineers entered a crash program to develop a *Hi* for the 1935 season.

The engine is a good representation of the prototype and is close to scale in dimension. The 250E was the first successful die-cast metal engine made by Lionel, though it had a complementary tender made of sheet-metal. To keep costs down, designers suggested both freight and passenger versions be offered; the latter utilized cars designed for the M-10000.

Arguably, the 250E was Lionel's top steamer until nudged aside by the scale Hudson. Though good runners, originals are tough to find in top shape because of chipping and peeling paint. Superbly reproduced by Samhongsa for Lionel Trains Inc. in 1988, the reproduction duplicated the quality of the original, yet with enhanced decoration. The 250E is a good choice to collect or to run.

ACCESSORIES

GREAT EXPECTATIONS: Lionel Railsounds and Command Control. If Lionel has an edge in the battle for the toy train market, it is in technology. Railsounds and Trainmaster Command Control have raised the expectations of what hobbyists expect from sound and control systems.

Although many firms offer sound-equipped locomotives or aftermarket sound systems, Lionel's Railsounds is the most innovative and realistic sound system on the market today. Engine sounds are recorded from specific locomotives, and the sounds vary depending on whether the engine is at rest, accelerating, decelerating, or at speed.

As with Railsounds, Command Control has revolutionized a segment of the hobby. Even in its least-ambitious form, Trainmaster offers operators better speed control and lower starting speeds. At the other end, you can activate otherwise "hidden" sound features in Railsounds, turn lights on and off, adjust rpm and engine sounds, and lash Command-equipped engines into multiple-unit power packages.

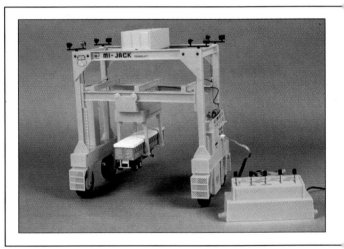

ACCESSORIES

EVERYONE WANTED ONE: The no. 313 Bascule Bridge (1940–42, 1946–49). This is one of those unforgettable accessories that just about every kid who saw it in action wanted. Imagine, a heavy metal bridge that lifted, lowered, and stopped your train for safe operation! Of course you did not need it to actually bridge anything deeper than some blue paint on your tabletop, but it was a good-looking accessory that mimicked many bascule bridges that dotted rivers and canals throughout the nation. The no. 313 is highly regarded as a rugged and reliable accessory. Demand for the no. 313 increased as more hobbyists shifted to operation rather than simply collecting their trains.

Lionel LLC took the cue and offered an improved version of the no. 313 in 1998. The bridge is made of steel, like the original, mounts a can motor, and comes in two color choices.

ACCESSORIES

THE FIRST TRULY MODERN ACCESSORY: No. 12741 Intermodal Crane (1990–1991). Hats off to Lionel for creating the first Modern Era accessory that actually reflected a change in how prototype railroads did business. Not another accessory to saw wood. Not another accessory to move logs. Not another accessory to dump coal at your local fuel dealer. This accessory helped load and unload the hottest cargo on today's rails: intermodal containers. If this product has a down side, it is simply that you need a lot of space to make the crane, containers, and rolling stock look at home.

THE TOP 10 MOST ACTIVELY TRADED LIONEL TRAINS

Lionel Prewar

The 814 Boxcar and 812 Gondola and several 200-series freight cars remained among the most actively traded trains from the Lionel Prewar era. The scale freight cars (headed by a semi-scale 0-6-0) were also actively traded.

1. **814**	Boxcar (O), *26–42*				
	(A) Cream, orange roof	46	105	____	[5]
	(B) Cream, maroon roof	115	140	____	[5]
	(C) Yellow, brown roof	115	115	____	[5]
2. **812**	Gondola (O), *26–42*	33	65	____	[5]
3. **2817**	Caboose (O), *36–42*				
	(A) Light red body and roof	85	140	____	[5]
	(B) Flat red, tuscan roof	145	235	____	[5]
4. **2957**	Caboose (O), *40–42**	190	470	____	[5]
5. **227**	Steam 0-6-0 (O), *39–42*				
	(A) With 2227B tender w/bell	600	1250	____	[5]
	(B) With 2227T tender w/o bell	600	1150	____	[5]
6. **219**	Crane (Std.), *26–40**				
	(A) Peacock, red boom	130	235	____	[4]
	(B) Yellow, light green boom	270	400	____	[4]
	(C) Ivory, light green boom	270	435	____	[4]
	(D) Cream, red boom	130	305	____	[4]
	(E) White, green boom	300	470	____	[4]
7.(tie) **817**	Caboose (O), *26–42*				
	(A) Peacock, dark green roof	45	80	____	[4]
	(B) Red, peacock roof	45	80	____	[4]
	(C) Light red body and roof	45	80	____	[4]
2955	Sunoco Tank Car (O), *40–42**				
	(A) "SHELL" decal	225	560	____	[4]
	(B) "SUNOCO" decal	340	780	____	[4]
9. **514**	Boxcar (Std.), *29–40*				
	(A) Cream yellow, orange roof	85	155	____	[4]
	(B) Yellow, brown roof	115	270	____	[4]
10.(tie) **218**	Dump Car (Std.), *26–38**	150	250	____	[4]
2954	Boxcar (O), *40–42**	200	495	____	[4]

Lionel Postwar

The 3927 Track Cleaner car and the ZW transformer were the most actively traded items in the Lionel Postwar era. Since the 397 Coal Loader is also on the Top 10 list, we might wonder if the increased buying and selling of these items is due to the absence of direct equivalents in current Lionel production. The usual suspects—the Berkshire, the Santa Fe and NYC F-3s, and the Lackawanna Train Master—rounded out the rest of the Postwar Top 10.

1. **3927**	Lionel Lines Track Cleaner, *56–60*	46	95	____	[5]
2. **ZW**	Transformer, 275 watts, *50–66*	135	270	____	[5]
3. **2321**	Lackawanna Train Master, *54–56*				
	(A) Gray roof	295	425	____	[5]
	(B) Maroon roof	420	680	____	[5]
4. **736**	Steam 2-8-4 , *50–66*	255	370	____	[4]
5. **2343**	Santa Fe F-3 AA units, *50–52*	220	450	____	[4]

6. **60**	Lionelville Trolley, *55–58*	100	185	____	4
7. **397**	Diesel Coal Loader, *48–57*	85	140	____	4
8. **773**	Steam 4-6-4 Hudson , *50*	730	1250	____	4
9. (tie)					
2344	NYC F-3 AA units, *50–52*	250	495	____	3
3656	Armour Operating Cattle Car, *49–55*				
	(A) Black letters, Armour sticker	75	190	____	3
	(B) White letters, Armour sticker	35	60	____	3
	(C) No "ARMOUR" sticker, black	25	70	____	3
	(D) White lettering	25	70	____	3

Lionel Modern-MPC

With the exception of the NYC Woodside Caboose, the Lionel Modern-MPC Top 10 Most Actively Traded list is made up entirely of motive power. In fact, positions 10-20 are also made up of steam and diesel engines, with the exception of the 9308 Aquarium Car. Can we surmise that we all have enough Wheaties boxcars and aqua GN hoppers in our collections?

1. **8850**	Penn Central GG-1, *78 u, 79*	360	410	____	5
2. **(8406)**	NYC 4-6-4 "783", *84*	660	750	____	5
3. (tie)					
8003	Chessie System 2-8-4, *80*	640	640	____	5
8477	NYC GP-9, *84 u*	245	285	____	5
5. **8753**	Pennsylvania GG-1, *77 u*	495	570	____	5
6. **8002**	Union Pacific 2-8-4, *80*	520	550	____	4
7. **(8307)**	Southern Pacific 4-8-4, *83*	910	1050	____	4
8. **8687**	Jersey Central Train Master, *86*	365	415	____	4
9. **6907**	NYC Woodside Caboose, *86 u*	125	135	____	4
10. **8951**	SP Train Master, *79*	415	480	____	4

Lionel Modern-LTI

The 11711 Santa Fe F-3 set maintained its widespread presence in the marketplace. This set was seen in the market almost three times as often as the similar 2343 Set from the Postwar era. The scale steam locos produced by LTI in 1990-91 continued to be widely traded as did the LTI GG-1s.

1. **(11711)**	Santa Fe F-3 ABA set "8100", "8101", "8102", *91*	700	800	____	5
2. (tie)					
(18007)	Southern Pacific 4-8-4 "4410", *91*	570	730	____	2
(18303)	Amtrak GG-1 "8303", *89*	350	400	____	2
4. **(18005)**	NYC 4-6-4 "5340" w/ display case, *90*	990	1350	____	2
5. **(18043)**	Chesapeake &Ohio 4-6-4 "490", *95*	1050	1250	____	2
6. **(18040)**	N&W 4-8-4 "612", *95*	1100	1200	____	2
7. **(18000)**	PRR 0-6-0 "8977" *89, 91*	580	660	____	2
8. **(18606)**	NYC 2-6-4 "8606", *89*	155	175	____	2
9. **(18301)**	Southern Train Master "8301", *88*	310	360	____	2
10. **(18313)**	Pennsylvania GG-1 "4907", *96*	—	360	____	2

In summary, it appears as though big ticket items (i.e., nicer steam engines, GG-1s, Train Masters, etc.) dominate the trading activity among Modern collectors. Lionel Prewar and Postwar collectors appear to buy and sell accessories and freight cars more often, however, and seem to trade most in items which are not available in current production.

—SJS

HOW TO READ THIS GUIDE

This Pocket Price Guide lists prices for Prewar and Postwar trains as GOOD and EXCELLENT. Modern Era (1970–2000) trains, Large Scale trains, and catalogs are priced EXCELLENT and NEW. Prices for restored pieces fall between Good and Excellent, depending on the item. New pieces bring a substantial premium over Excellent pieces. Fair pieces bring substantially less than Good and Excellent pieces.

In the toy train field there is a great deal of concern with exterior appearance and less concern with operation. If operation is important to you, ask the seller if the train runs. If the seller indicates that he does not know whether the equipment operates, you should test it. Most train meets provide test tracks for this purpose.

PRODUCT NUMBER
- **(#)** Numbers that have been put in parentheses by us do not appear on the actual items.
- **[#]** means decorations which make this item unique were not done by Lionel.
- **No Number** means item may have lettering, but lacks an item number.
- **(no letters)** means no lettering or number appears on the item.
- ***** means excellent reproductions have been made.

2343 Santa Fe F-3 AA units, *50–52*
2343C Santa Fe F-3 B unit, *50–55*
    (A) Screen roof vents
    (B) Louver roof vents
2344 NYC F-3 AA units, *50–52*
2344C NYC F-3 B unit, *50–55*
2345 Western Pacific F-3 AA units, *52*
2346 B&M GP-9, *65–66*

CONDITION

Trains and related items are usually classified by condition relating to appearance. The following definitions apply for this guide:

- **FAIR**—well-scratched, chipped, dented, rusted, or warped condition.
- **GOOD**—scratched, small dents, and dirty.
- **VERY GOOD**—few scratches, no dents, rust or warpage; very clean.
- **EXCELLENT**—minute scratches or nicks; no dents or rust; exceptionally clean.
- **LIKE NEW**—free of blemishes, nicks or scratches; original condition throughout, with vibrant colors; only faint signs of handling or use; price includes original box.
- **NEW**—brand new, absolutely unmarred, all original and unused, in original packaging with all paperwork provided by the manufacturer.
- **CP (C**urrent **P**roduction) means that the item is now being advertised, manufactured, or is currently available from retail stores.
- **NRS (N**o **R**ecorded **S**ales) means that we do not know the current market value of the item. The item may be very scarce and bring a substantial premium over items in its general class, or it may be relatively common but unnoticed. Usually NRS listings occur when an older and previously unknown item is first reported, although we are still discovering relatively common variations that have not been previously reported. If you have confirmable information about the value of an NRS item, please write to us.
- **NM (N**ot **M**anufactured) means that the item may have been cataloged or otherwise advertised, but it was not produced.

Good	Exc	
220	450	4
100	195	1
100	195	1
250	495	3
115	240	1
910	1450	2
150	270	1

ACTIVE TRADING INDEX

The Active Trading Index is a measurement of how often a particular train is offered for sale on the open market. The Greenberg's Toy Train Active Trading Index is based on a five-point scale: an Active Trading Index value of "5" indicates that a train has appeared for sale in various advertisements, lists, and at shows/auctions with a frequency that places it in the top 20% of all toy trains. (To borrow a little terminology from the stock and bond markets, we can say that pieces with an Active Trading Index of "5" are among the most actively traded among collectors.) An Active Trading Index value of "4" indicates that the piece was offered for sale less frequently (i.e., in the next 20%), and so on, down to an Active Trading Index of "1."

Section 1
PREWAR 1901–1942

		Good	Exc	Cond/$
001	Steam 4-6-4 (OO), *38–42*	175	360	___[1]
1	Bild-A-Motor, *28–31*	60	135	___[1]
1	Trolley (Std.), *06–14*			
	(A) Cream body, orange band/roof	1900	4750	___[1]
	(B) White body, blue band/roof	1750	4750	___[1]
	(C) Cream body, blue band/roof	1300	3150	___[1]
	(D) Cream body, blue band/roof	2150	5550	___[1]
	(E) Blue, cream band, blue roof	1450	3150	___[1]
1/111	Trolley Trailer (Std.), *06–14*	1000	2700	___[1]
002	Steam 4-6-4 (OO), *39–42*	160	315	___[1]
2	Bild-A-Motor, *28–31*	100	180	___[1]
2	Countershafting, *04–11*		NRS	___
2	Trolley (Std.), *06–16**			
	(A) Yellow, red band	1200	2250	___[1]
	(B) Red, yellow band	1200	2250	___[1]
2/200	Trolley Trailer (Std.), *06–16*	1000	1800	___[1]
003	Steam 4-6-4 (OO), *39–42*			
	(A) With 003W whistling tender	190	395	___[1]
	(B) With 003T non-whistling tender	175	360	___[1]
3	Trolley (Std.), *06–13*			
	(A) Cream, orange band	1400	3150	___[1]
	(B) Cream, dark olive green band	1400	3150	___[1]
	(C) Orange, dark olive green band	1400	3150	___[1]
	(D) Dark green, cream windows	1400	3150	___[1]
	(E) Green, cream window, "BAY SHORE"	1650	3700	___[1]
3/300	Trolley Trailer (Std.), *06–13*	1300	3500	___[1]
004	Steam 4-6-4 (OO), *39–42*			
	(A) With 004W whistling tender	205	340	___[1]
	(B) With 004T non-whistling tender	190	315	___[1]
4	Electric 0-4-0 (O), *28–32**			
	(A) Orange, black frame	550	900	___[1]
	(B) Gray, apple green stripe	580	1050	___[1]

		Good	Exc	Cond/$
4	Trolley (Std.), *06–12*			
	(A) Cream, dark olive green band	3000	4950	___ [1]
	(B) Green or olive green, cream roof	3000	4950	___ [1]
4U	No. 4 Kit form (O), *28–29*	1050	1400	___ [1]
5	Electric (2⅞") (See 100)			
5	Steam 0-4-0, no tender, Early (Std.), *06–07*			
	(A) "N.Y.C. & H.R.R."	1000	1450	___ [3]
	(B) "PENNSYLVANIA"	1400	2300	___ [3]
	(C) "N.Y.C. & H.R.R.R." (3 Rs)	1250	2050	___ [3]
	(D) "B. & O. R.R."	1500	2400	___ [3]
5	Steam 0-4-0, w/ tender, Early Special (Std.), *06–09*	1250	1650	___ [1]
5	Steam 0-4-0, no tender, Later (Std.), *10–11*	750	1150	___ [1]
5	Steam 0-4-0, w/ tender, Later Special (Std.), *10–11*	800	1350	___ [1]
5/51	Steam 0-4-0, w/ tender, Latest (Std.), *12–23*	800	1100	___ [1]
6	Steam 4-4-0 (Std.), *06–23*	750	1100	___ [2]
6	Steam 0-4-0 Special (Std.), *08–09*	2050	2950	___ [1]
7	Steam 4-4-0 (Std.), *10–23**	1850	2300	___ [1]
8	Electric 0-4-0 (Std.), *25–32*			
	(A) Maroon, brass windows/trim	235	250	___ [2]
	(B) Olive green or mojave w/brass	155	205	___ [2]
	(C) Red, brass or cream window	195	250	___ [2]
	(D) Peacock, orange windows	520	750	___ [2]
8	Trolley (Std.), *08–14**			
	(A) Cream, orange band/roof	3000	5400	___ [1]
	(B) Dark green, cream windows	3000	5400	___ [1]
8E	Electric 0-4-0 (Std.), *26–32*			
	(A) Mojave, brass windows/trim	175	240	___ [1]
	(B) Red, brass or cream window	130	205	___ [1]
	(C) Peacock, orange windows	370	590	___ [1]
	(D) Pea green, cream stripe	465	670	___ [1]
9	Electric 0-4-0 (Std.), *29**	1200	2150	___ [1]
9	Trolley (Std.), *09*	3000	5400	___ [1]

		Good	Exc	Cond/$
9E	Electric 0-4-0 (Std.), *28–35**			
	(A) 0-4-0	700	1250	___ [1]
	(B) 2-4-2, two-tone green	880	1600	___ [1]
	(C) 2-4-2, gun-metal gray	820	1300	___ [1]
9U	Electric 0-4-0 Kit (Std.), *28–29*	1450	3000	___ [1]
9	Motor Car (Std.), *09–12*		NRS	___
10	Electric 0-4-0 (Std.), *25–29**			
	(A) Mojave, brass trim	150	215	___ [3]
	(B) Gray, brass trim	125	205	___ [3]
	(C) Peacock, brass inserts	125	205	___ [3]
	(D) Red, cream stripe	580	880	___ [3]
10	Interurban (Std.), *10–16*			
	(A) Maroon	3000	5750	___ [1]
	(B) Dark olive green	1200	2150	___ [1]
10E	Electric 0-4-0 (Std.), *26–30*			
	(A) Olive green, black frame		NRS	___
	(B) Peacock, dark green or black frame	345	470	___ [2]
	(C) State brown, dark green frame	435	630	___ [2]
	(D) Gray, black frame	165	220	___ [2]
	(E) Red, cream stripe	610	880	___ [2]
011	Switches, pair (O), *33–37*	20	41	___ [1]
11	Flatcar, Early (Std.), *06–11*	150	360	___ [1]
11	Flatcar, Later (Std.), *11–16*	50	90	___ [1]
11	Flatcar, Latest (Std.), *16–18*	50	90	___ [1]
11	Flatcar, Lionel Corp. (Std.), *18–26*	50	80	___ [1]
012	Switches, pair (O), *27–33*	21	38	___ [1]
12	Gondola, Early (Std.), *06–11*	600	720	___ [1]
12	Gondola, Later(Std), *11–16*	50	90	___ [1]
12	Gondola, Latest (Std.), *16–18*	45	70	___ [1]
12	Gondola, Lionel Corp. (Std.), *18–26*	50	70	___ [1]
013	(2) 012 Switches and 439 Panel Board, *27–33*	100	160	___ [1]
13	Cattle Car, Early (Std.), *06–11*	300	450	___ [1]
13	Cattle Car, Later (Std.), *11–16*	150	225	___ [1]
13	Cattle Car, Latest (Std.), *16–18*	65	115	___ [1]
13	Cattle Car, Lionel Corp. (Std.), *18–26*	65	115	___ [1]

		Good	Exc	Cond/$
0014	Boxcar (OO), *38–42*			
	(A) Yellow, "Lionel Lines"	80	145	____[1]
	(B) Tuscan body, "PENNSYLVANIA"	50	90	____[1]
14	Boxcar, Early (Std.), *06–11*	200	450	____[1]
14	Boxcar, Later (Std.), *11–16*	75	100	____[1]
14	Boxcar, Latest (Std.), *16–18*	75	100	____[1]
14	Boxcar, Lionel Corp. (Std.), *18–26*	75	100	____[1]
0015	Tank Car (OO), *38–42*			
	(A) Silver, "SUN OIL"	40	70	____[1]
	(B) Black, "SHELL"	40	70	____[1]
15	Oil Car, Early (Std.), *06–11*	200	360	____[1]
15	Oil Car, Later (Std.), *11–16*	75	115	____[1]
15	Oil Car, Latest (Std.), *16–18*	75	115	____[1]
15	Oil Car, Lionel Corp. (Std.), *18–26*	75	115	____[1]
0016	Hopper Car (OO), *38–42*			
	(A) Gray	75	145	____[1]
	(B) Black	75	125	____[1]
16	Ballast (Dump) Car, Early (Std.), *06–26*	250	405	____[1]
16	Ballast (Dump) Car, Later (Std.), *11–16*	100	180	____[1]
16	Ballast (Dump) Car, Latest (Std.), *16–18*	100	180	____[1]
16	Ballast (Dump) Car, Lionel Corp. (Std.), *18–26*	100	180	____[1]
0017	Caboose (OO), *38–42*	45	80	____[1]
17	Caboose, Early (Std.), *06–11*	225	450	____[1]
17	Caboose, Later (Std.), *11–16*	70	135	____[1]
17	Caboose, Latest (Std.), *16–18*	70	135	____[1]
17	Caboose, Lionel Corp. (Std.), *18–26*	50	90	____[1]
18	Pullman (Std.), *08*			
	(A) Dark olive green, unremovable roof	700	2160	____[1]
	(B) Dark olive green, removable roof	90	195	____[1]
	(C) Yellow-orange, removable roof	275	865	____[1]
	(D) Orange, removable roof	80	180	____[1]
	(E) Mojave, removable roof	275	865	____[1]
18	Pullman (Std.), *11–13*		NRS	____
18	Pullman (Std.), *13–15*	150	270	____[1]
18	Pullman (Std.), *15–18*	150	270	____[1]
18	Pullman (Std.), *18–22*	80	135	____[1]

		Good	Exc	Cond/$
18	Pullman (Std.), *23–26*	270	530	1
19	Combine (Std.), *08*			
	(A) Dark olive green, unremovable roof	1100	2590	1
	(B) Dark olive green, removable roof	80	125	1
	(C) Yellow-orange, removable roof	225	375	1
	(D) Orange, removable roof	100	180	1
	(E) Mojave, removable roof	275	865	1
19	Combine (Std.), *11–13*		NRS	
19	Combine (Std.), *13–15*	200	270	1
19	Combine (Std.), *15–18*	200	270	1
19	Combine (Std.), *18–22*	80	135	1
19	Combine (Std.), *23–26*	265	520	1
020	90° Crossover (O), *15–42*	2	5	1
020X	45° Crossover (O), *17–42*	3	8	1
20	90° Crossover (Std.), *??-??, 09–32*	4	9	1
20	Direct Current Reducer, *06*	—	270	1
20X	45° Crossover (Std.), *28–32*	5	9	1
021	Switches, pair (O), *15–37*	20	45	1
21	Switches, pair (Std.), *15–25*	45	80	3
21	90° Crossover (Std.), *06*	10	18	1
022	Switches, pair, Remote (O), *38–42*	35	65	1
22	Switches, pair (Std.), *06–25*	45	90	2
023	Bumper (O), *15–33*	15	36	1
23	Bumper (Std.), *06–23*	20	45	1
0024	PRR Boxcar (OO), *39–42*	45	80	1
24	Railway Station (Std.), *06*		NRS	
025	Bumper (O), *28–42*	19	26	1
0025	Tank Car (OO), *39–42*			
	(A) Black, "SHELL"	40	80	1
	(B) Silver, "SUNOCO"	40	80	1
25	Open Station (Std.), *06*		NRS	
25	Bumper (Std.), *27–42*	30	45	1
26	Passenger Bridge (Std.), *06*		NRS	
0027	Caboose (OO), *39–42*	40	80	1
27	Lighting set, *11–23*	15	41	1
27	Station (Std.), *09–12*		NRS	
28	Double Station w/ dome, *09–12*		NRS	

		Good	Exc	Cond/$
29	Day Coach (Std.), *07–22*			
	(A) Dark olive green, 9-window	1500	3000	[1]
	(B) Maroon, 10-window body	1200	1500	[1]
	(C) Dark green, 10-window body	3000	4500	[1]
	(D) Dark olive green, 10-window	675	1000	[1]
	(E) Dark green, 10-window body	500	900	[1]
29	(See no. 3 Trolley)			
31	Combine (Std.), *21–25*			
	(A) Maroon	70	90	[1]
	(B) Orange	115	170	[1]
	(C) Dark olive green	70	90	[1]
	(D) Brown	75	95	[1]
32	Mail Car (Std.), *21–25*			
	(A) Maroon	85	110	[1]
	(B) Orange	105	160	[1]
	(C) Dark olive green	65	85	[1]
	(D) Brown	70	90	[1]
32	Miniature Figures, *09–18*	75	135	[1]
33	Electric 0-6-0, Early (Std.), *13*			
	(A) Dark olive green, NYC in oval	90	175	[3]
	(B) Black, NYC LINES in oval	440	950	[3]
	(C) Dark olive green, NYC	440	950	[3]
	(D) "PENNSYLVANIA RAILROAD"	580	1250	[3]
33	Electric 0-4-0, Later (Std.), *13–24*			
	(A) Dark olive green or black, NYC	85	145	[1]
	(B) Black, lettered "C & O"	395	720	[1]
	(C) Maroon, red, or peacock	340	620	[1]
34	Electric 0-6-0, Early (Std.), *12*	450	810	[1]
34	Electric 0-4-0 (Std.), *13*	200	385	[1]
35	Blvd. Lamp, 6⅛" high, *40–42*	25	50	[3]
35	Pullman (Std.), *12–13*			
	(A) Dark blue	470	900	[1]
	(B) Dark olive green	150	205	[1]
35	Pullman (Std.), *14–16*			
	(A) Dark olive green, maroon windows	50	70	[1]
	(B) Maroon, green windows	85	105	[1]
	(C) Orange, maroon windows	125	170	[1]

		Good	Exc	Cond/$
35	Pullman (Std.), *15–18*	50	70	___[1]
35	Pullman (Std.), *18–23*			
	(A) Dark olive green, maroon windows	36	50	___[1]
	(B) Maroon, green windows	30	45	___[1]
	(C) Orange, maroon windows	110	195	___[1]
	(D) Brown, green windows	36	50	___[1]
35	Pullman (Std.), *24*	40	55	___[1]
35	Pullman (Std.), *25–26*	40	55	___[1]
36	Observation (Std.), *12–13*			
	(A) Dark blue	315	810	___[1]
	(B) Dark olive green	125	180	___[1]
36	Observation (Std.), *14–16*			
	(A) Dark olive green, maroon windows	70	95	___[1]
	(B) Maroon, green windows	50	70	___[1]
	(C) Orange, maroon windows	180	290	___[1]
	(D) Brown, green windows	60	75	___[1]
36	Observation (Std.), *15–18*	60	80	___[1]
36	Observation (Std.), *18–23*			
	(A) Dark olive green, maroon windows	40	55	___[1]
	(B) Maroon, green windows	40	55	___[1]
	(C) Orange, maroon windows	120	205	___[1]
	(D) Brown, green windows	40	55	___[1]
36	Observation (Std.), *24*	40	55	___[1]
36	Observation (Std.), *25–26*	40	55	___[1]
38	Electric 0-4-0 (Std.), *13–24*			
	(A) Black	95	115	___[1]
	(B) Red	475	680	___[1]
	(C) Mojave or pea green	405	540	___[1]
	(D) Dark green	270	360	___[1]
	(E) Brown	270	315	___[1]
	(F) Red, cream trim	405	540	___[1]
	(G) Maroon	170	270	___[1]
	(H) Gray	110	125	___[1]
40	(See no. 4 Trolley)			
41	Accessory Contactor, *37–42*	1	2.50	___[1]
042	Switches, pair (O), *38–42*	25	45	___[1]

		Good	Exc	Cond/$
42	Electric 0-4-4-0, square hood, Early (Std.), *12**	1200	2000	___[3]
42	Electric 0-4-4-0, round hood, Later (Std.), *13–23*			
	(A) Black or gray	280	475	___[1]
	(B) Maroon	1250	2050	___[1]
	(C) Dark gray	375	600	___[1]
	(D) Dark green or mojave	500	800	___[1]
	(E) Peacock	1100	1800	___[1]
	(F) Olive or dark olive green	750	1200	___[1]
043/43	Bild-A-Motor Gear set, *29*	NRS	115	___[1]
43	Boat, Runabout, *33–36, 39–41*	375	550	___[1]
0044	Boxcar (OO), *39–42*	38	70	___[1]
0044K	Boxcar Kit (OO), *39–42*	75	120	___[1]
44	Boat, Speedster, *35–36*	370	590	___[2]
0045	Tank Car (OO), *39–42*			
	(A) Black, "SHELL"	40	80	___[1]
	(B) Silver, "SUNOCO"	40	80	___[1]
0045K	Tank Car Kit (OO), *39–42*	75	120	___[1]
45/045/45N	Automatic Gateman, *35–42*	40	70	___[1]
0046	Hopper Car (OO), *39–42*	45	80	___[1]
0046K	Hopper Car Kit (OO), *39–42*			
	(A) "SOUTHERN PACIFIC"	75	135	___[1]
	(B) "READING"		NRS	___
46	Crossing Gate, *39–42*	60	90	___[1]
0047	Caboose (OO), *39–42*	35	70	___[1]
0047K	Caboose Kit (OO), *39–42*	75	135	___[1]
47	Crossing Gate, *39–42*	60	115	___[1]
48W	Whistle Station, *37–42*	30	65	___[1]
49	Lionel Airport, *37–39*	160	410	___[1]
50	Airplane, *36–39*	110	255	___[2]
50	Electric 0-4-0 (Std.), *24*			
	(A) Dark green or dark gray	125	225	___[1]
	(B) Maroon	315	600	___[1]
	(C) Mojave	155	300	___[1]
50	Cardboard Train, Cars, Accessory (O), *43**	200	360	___[1]

		Good	Exc	Cond/$
51	Steam 0-4-0, 5 Late eight-wheel (Std.), *12–23*	800	1150	___[1]
51	Lionel Airport, *36, 38*	155	395	___[1]
52	Lamp Post, *33–41*	45	85	___[1]
53	Electric 0-4-4-0, Early (Std.), *12–14*	1200	2450	___[1]
53	Electric 0-4-0, Later (Std.), *15–19*			
	(A) Maroon	500	900	___[1]
	(B) Mojave	670	1350	___[1]
	(C) Dark olive green	560	1150	___[1]
53	Electric 0-4-0, Latest (Std.), *20–21*	200	450	___[1]
53	Lamp Post, *31–42*	35	70	___[1]
53	Electric 0-6-6-0, Early (Std.), *11*		NRS	___
54	Electric 0-4-4-0, Early (Std.), *12**	2500	4050	___[1]
54	Electric 0-4-4-0, Late (Std.), *13–23*	1800	2700	___[1]
54	Lamp Post, *29–35*	45	80	___[1]
55	Airplane w/ stand, *37–39*	165	450	___[1]
56	Lamp Post, removable lens and cap, *24–42*	30	75	___[1]
57	Lamp Post w/ street names, *22–42*	47	95	___[3]
58	Lamp Post, 7⅜" high, *22–42*	25	50	___[2]
59	Lamp Post, 8¾" high, *20–36*	40	85	___[1]
60/060	Telegraph Post (Std./O), *29–42*	10	20	___[1]
60	Electric 0-4-0, F.A.O.S. (Std.), *15 u*		NRS	___
61	Electric 0-4-4-0, F.A.O.S. (Std.), *15 u*		NRS	___
61	Lamp Post, one globe, *14–36*	45	75	___[1]
62	Electric 0-4-0, F.A.O.S. (Std.), *24–32 u*		NRS	___
62	Semaphore, *20–32*	25	50	___[1]
63	Lamp Post, two globes, *33–42*	120	200	___[1]
63	Semaphore, *15–21*	25	50	___[1]
64	Lamp Post, *40–42*	33	65	___[1]
64	Semaphore, 6¾" high, *15–21*	30	60	___[1]
65	Semaphore, one-arm, *15–26*	30	60	___[1]
65	Whistle Contoller, *35*	5	7	___[1]
66	Semaphore, two-arm, *15–26*	35	70	___[1]
66	Whistle Controller, *36–39*	6	9	___[1]
67	Lamp Post, *15–32*	70	110	___[1]
67	Whistle Controller, *36–39*	4	8	___[1]

		Good	Exc	Cond/$
68/068	Crossing Sign, *25–42*	10	15	___1
69/069/69N	Electric Warning Signal, *21–42*	35	75	___1
70	Outfit: (2) 62s (1) 59 (1) 68, *21–32*	55	120	___1
071	(6) 060 Telegraph Poles (Std.), *24–42*	70	160	___1
71	(6) 60 Telegraph Poles (Std.), *29–42*	70	160	___1
0072	Switches, pair (OO), *38–42*	130	205	___1
0074	Boxcar (OO), *39–42*	40	80	___1
0075	Tank Car (OO), *39–42*	50	100	___1
076/76	Block Signal, *23–28*	25	75	___1
76	Warning Bell and Shack, *39–42*	80	160	___1
0077	Caboose (OO), *39–42*	40	70	___1
77/077/77N	Automatic Crossing Gate, *23–39*	25	50	___1
78/078	Train Signal (Std.), *24–32*	40	100	___1
79	Flashing Signal, *28–40*	90	105	___1
80	Automobile, *12–16*	720	1450	___1
80/080/80N	Semaphore (Std), *26–42*	50	130	___1
81	Automobile, *12–16*	720	1450	___1
81	Controlling Rheostat, *27–33*	2	5	___1
82/082/82N	Semaphore, *27–42*	55	110	___1
83	Flashing Traffic Signal, *27–42*	50	135	___1
084	Semaphore, *28–32*	60	100	___1
84	Semaphore, *27–32*	55	85	___1
84	(2) Automobiles, *12–16*	1400	2900	___1
85	Telegraph Pole (Std.), *29–42*	15	27	___1
85	(2) Automobiles, *12–16*	1400	2900	___1
86	(6) Telegraph Poles, *29–42*	65	140	___1
87	Flashing Crossing Signal, *27–42*	60	120	___1
88	Battery Rheostat, *15–27*	2	5	___1
88	Rheostat Controller, *33–42*	3	5	___1
89	Flag Pole, *23–34*	35	70	___1
90	Flag Pole, *27–42*	35	75	___1
91	Circuit Breaker, *30–42*	25	45	___1
092	Signal Tower, *23–27*	100	160	___1
92	Floodlight Tower, *31–42**	105	200	___3
93	Water Tower, *31–42*	50	80	___1
94	High Tension Tower, *32–42**	115	235	___1
95	Controlling Rheostat, *34–42*	2	5	___1

		Good	Exc	Cond/$
96	Coal Elevator, manual, *38–40*	200	270	___[1]
097	Telegraph set (O), *N/A*	50	75	___[1]
97	Coal Elevator, *38–42*	130	220	___[2]
98	Coal Bunker, *38–40*	200	405	___[1]
99/099/99N	Train Control, *32–42*	45	150	___[1]
100	Electric Loco (2⅞"), *03–05**	3000	5400	___[1]
100	Trolley (Std.), *10–16*			
	(A) Blue, white windows	1300	2700	___[1]
	(B) Blue, cream windows	1850	3600	___[1]
	(C) Red, cream windows	1300	2700	___[1]
100	(2) Bridge Apprch. (Std.), *20–31*	20	36	___[1]
100	Wooden Gondola (2⅞"), *01*		NRS	___
101	Bridge Span (2) Approaches (Std.), *20–31*	50	90	___[1]
101	Summer Trolley (Std.), *10–13*	1300	2700	___[1]
102	(2) Bridge Spans (2) Approaches (Std.), *20–31*	50	115	___[1]
103	Bridge (Std.), *13–16*	50	70	___[1]
103	(3) Bridge Spans (2) Approaches (Std.), *20–31*	60	145	___[1]
104	Bridge Span (Std.), *20–31*	20	41	___[1]
104	Tunnel (Std.), *09–14*	50	135	___[1]
105	Bridge (Std.), *11–14*	40	70	___[1]
105	(2) Bridge Apprchs. (O), *20–31*	50	70	___[1]
106	Bridge Span, (2) Approaches (O), *20–31*	30	65	___[1]
107	DC Reducer, 110V, *23–32*		NRS	___
108	(2) Bridge Spans, (2) Approaches (O), *20–31*	50	90	___[1]
109	(3) Bridge Spans, (2) Approaches (O), *20–32*	50	115	___[1]
109	Tunnel (Std.), *13–14*	30	70	___[1]
110	Bridge Span (O), *20–31*	12	23	___[1]
111	Box of 50 Bulbs, *20–31*	50	90	___[1]
112	Gondola, Early (Std.), *10–12*	200	360	___[1]
112	Gondola, Later (Std.), *12–16*	40	65	___[1]
112	Gondola, Latest (Std.), *16–18*	40	65	___[1]
112	Gondola, Lionel Corp. (Std.), *18–26*	40	65	___[1]

		Good	Exc	Cond/$
112	Station, *31–35*	160	290	___ [1]
113	Cattle Car, Later (Std.), *12–16*	50	70	___ [2]
113	Cattle Car, Latest (Std.), *16–18*	50	70	___ [1]
113	Cattle Car, Lionel Corp. (Std.), *18–26*	40	55	___ [1]
113	Station, *31–34*	150	295	___ [1]
114	Boxcar, Later (Std.), *12–16*	50	90	___ [1]
114	Boxcar, Latest (Std.), *16–18*	40	70	___ [1]
114	Boxcar, Lionel Corp. (Std.), *18–26*	40	70	___ [1]
114	Station, *31–34*	550	1250	___ [1]
115	Station, *35–42**	175	310	___ [1]
116	Station, *35–42**	600	1350	___ [3]
116	Ballast Car, Early and Later (Std.), *10–16*	75	100	___ [1]
116	Ballast Car, Latest (Std.), *16–18*	50	90	___ [1]
116	Ballast Car, Lionel Corp. (Std.), *18–26*	50	90	___ [1]
117	Caboose, Early (Std.), *12*	60	70	___ [2]
117	Caboose, Later (Std.), *12–16*	50	70	___ [1]
117	Caboose, Latest (Std.), *16–18*	50	70	___ [1]
117	Caboose, Lionel Corp. (Std.), *18–26*	40	65	___ [1]
117	Station, *36–42*	100	250	___ [1]
118	Tunnel, 8" long (O), *22–32*	20	55	___ [1]
118L	Tunnel, 8" long, *27*	20	55	___ [1]
119	Tunnel, 12" long, *20–42*	20	55	___ [1]
119L	Tunnel, 12" long, *27–33*	20	55	___ [1]
120	Tunnel, 17" long, *22–27*	25	70	___ [1]
120L	Tunnel, *27–42*	60	110	___ [1]
121	Station (Std.), *09–16*			
	(A) 14" x 10" x 9"		NRS	___
	(B) 13" x 9" x 13"	150	300	___ [1]
121	Station (Std.), *20–26*	75	150	___ [1]
121X	Station (Std.), *17–19*	110	255	___ [1]
122	Station (Std.), *20–30*	75	145	___ [1]
123	Station (Std.), *20–23*	75	205	___ [1]
123	Tunnel, 18½" long (O), *33–42*	75	170	___ [1]
124	Station, "Lionel City", *20–36**			
	(A) Tan or gray base, pea green	90	180	___ [3]
	(B) Pea green base, red roof	200	360	___ [3]

125	Station, "Lionelville", 23–25	85	195	___[1]
125	Track Template, 38	1	4	___[1]
126	Station, "Lionelville", 23–36	75	160	___[1]
127	Station, "Lionel Town", 23–36	80	140	___[2]
128	124 Station and Terrace, 31–34*	900	1900	___[1]
128	115 Station and Terrace, 35–42*	900	1900	___[1]
129	Terrace, 28–42*	600	1100	___[1]
130	Tunnel, 26" long, 20–36	100	450	___[1]
130L	Tunnel, 26" long, 27–33	150	450	___[1]
131	Corner Display, 24–28	125	295	___[1]
132	Corner Grass Plot, 24–28	125	295	___[1]
133	Heart-Shaped Plot, 24–28	125	295	___[1]
134	Oval-Shaped Plot, 24–28	125	295	___[1]
134	Station, "Lionel City", w/ stop, 37–42	200	340	___[1]
135	Circular Plot, 24–28	125	295	___[1]
136	Large Elevation, 24–28		NRS	___
136	Station, "Lionelville", w/ stop, 37–42	75	180	___[1]
140L	Tunnel, 37" long, 27–32	400	900	___[1]
150	Electric 0-4-0, Early (O), 17	90	160	___[1]
150	Electric 0-4-0, Late (O), 18–25			
	(A) Brown, brown or olive windows	95	150	___[1]
	(B) Maroon, dark olive windows	90	135	___[1]
152	Electric 0-4-0 (O), 17–27			
	(A) Dark green	90	135	___[2]
	(B) Gray	115	160	___[2]
	(C) Mojave	340	680	___[2]
	(D) Peacock	340	680	___[2]
152	Crossing Gate, 40–42	18	40	___[1]
153	Block Signal, 40–42	23	45	___[2]
153	Electric 0-4-0 (O), 24–25			
	(A) Dark green	100	160	___[1]
	(B) Gray	100	160	___[1]
	(C) Mojave	100	160	___[1]
154	Electric 0-4-0 (O), 17–23	100	180	___[1]
154	Highway Signal, 40–42	17	39	___[1]

		Good	Exc	Cond/$
155	Freight Shed, *30–42**			
	(A) Yellow base, orange floor	180	320	[1]
	(B) White base, terra-cotta floor	240	400	[1]
156	Electric 4-4-4 (O), *17–23*			
	(A) Dark green	475	810	[1]
	(B) Maroon	540	890	[1]
	(C) Olive green	600	1050	[1]
	(D) Gray	670	1200	[1]
156	Electric 0-4-0 (O), *17–23*	400	720	[1]
156	Station Platform, *39–42*	75	130	[1]
156X	Electric 0-4-0 (O), *23–24*			
	(A) Maroon	380	495	[1]
	(B) Olive green	440	550	[1]
	(C) Gray	530	710	[1]
	(D) Brown	470	600	[1]
157	Hand Truck, *30–32*	25	41	[1]
158	Electric 0-4-0 (O), *19–23*			
	(A) Gray, red windows	75	205	[1]
	(B) Black	95	250	[1]
158	(2) 156s and (1) 136, *40–42*	110	245	[1]
159	Block Actuator, *40*	10	27	[1]
161	Baggage Truck, *30–32**	40	75	[1]
162	Dump Truck, *30–32**	40	75	[1]
163	(2) 157 (1) 162 (1) 161, boxed, *30–42**	200	360	[1]
164	Log Loader, *40–42*	150	270	[3]
165	Magnetic Crane, *40–42*	200	295	[3]
166	Whistle Controller, *40–42*	3	5	[1]
167	Whistle Controller, *40–42*	4	9	[1]
167X	Whistle Controller (OO), *40–42*	5	11	[1]
169	Controller, *40–42*	2	5	[1]
170	DC Reducer, 220V, *14–38*	2	5	[1]
171	DC to AC Inverter, 110V, *36–42*	2	5	[1]
172	DC to AC Inverter, 229V, *39–42*	2	5	[1]
180	Pullman (Std.), *11–13*			
	(A) Maroon body and roof	125	180	[1]
	(B) Brown body and roof	125	235	[1]
180	Pullman (Std.), *13–15*	80	160	[1]

		Good	Exc	Cond/$
180	Pullman (Std.), *15–18*	80	160	____[1]
180	Pullman (Std.), *18–22*	80	135	____[1]
181	Combine (Std.), *11–13*			
	(A) Maroon, dark olive doors	125	180	____[1]
	(B) Brown, dark olive doors	125	180	____[1]
	(C) Yellow-orange, orange door	350	495	____[1]
181	Combine (Std.), *13–15*	80	160	____[1]
181	Combine (Std.), *15–18*	80	160	____[1]
181	Combine (Std.), *18–22*	80	135	____[1]
182	Observation (Std.), *11–13*			
	(A) Maroon, dark olive doors	125	180	____[1]
	(B) Brown, dark olive doors	125	180	____[1]
	(C) Yellow-orange, orange door	350	495	____[1]
182	Observation (Std.), *13–15*	80	160	____[1]
182	Observation (Std.), *15–18*	80	160	____[1]
182	Observation (Std.), *18–22*	80	135	____[1]
183	Pullman (Std.), *N/A*		NM	____
184	Bungalow, Illuminated, *23–32**	65	115	____[2]
184	Combine (Std.), *11*		NM	____
185	Bungalow, *23–24*	50	115	____[1]
185	Observation (Std.), *11*		NM	____
186	(5) 184 Bungalows, *23–32*	165	520	____[1]
186	Log Loader Outfit, *40–41*	130	340	____[1]
187	(5) 185 Bungalows, *23–24*	165	580	____[1]
188	Elevator and Car set, *38–41*	115	370	____[1]
189	Villa, Illuminated, *23–32**	120	205	____[2]
190	Observation (Std.), *08*			
	(A) Dark olive green, unremovable roof	1125	2590	____[1]
	(B) Dark olive green, removable roof	100	180	____[1]
	(C) Yellow-orange, removable roof	280	540	____[1]
	(D) Orange, removable roof	100	180	____[1]
	(E) Mojave, removable roof	345	865	____[1]
190	Observation (Std.), *11–13*		NRS	____
190	Observation (Std.), *13–15*	200	295	____[1]
190	Observation (Std.), *15–18*	200	295	____[1]
190	Observation (Std.), *18–22*	80	135	____[1]
190	Observation (Std.), *23–26*	255	530	____[1]

		Good	Exc	Cond/$
191	Villa, Illuminated, *23–32**	160	285	[2]
192	Villa set, Illuminated: (1) 189; (1) 191; (2) 184, *27–32*		NRS	
193	Accessory set, boxed, *27–29*	150	325	[1]
194	Accessory set, boxed, *27–29*	100	325	[1]
195	Terrace, *27–30*	350	740	[1]
196	Accessory set, *27*	200	335	[1]
200	Electric Express (2⅞"), *03*	4000	5400	[1]
200	Turntable, *28–33**	85	190	[1]
200	Wooden Gondola (2⅞"), *01–02*		NRS	
200	Trailer, matches no. 2 Trolley (Std.), *11–16*	—	3250	[1]
200	Electric Express (2⅞"), *03–05**	4000	6300	[1]
201	Steam 0-6-0 (O), *40–42*			
	(A) With 2201B tender w/ bell	375	760	[1]
	(B) With 2201T tender w/o bell	345	690	[1]
202	Summer Trolley (Std.), *10–13*			
	(A) "ELECTRIC RAPID TRANSIT"	1300	2700	[1]
	(B) "PRESTON ST."	3250	4500	[1]
203	Armored 0-4-0 (O), *17–21*	1100	1800	[2]
203	Steam 0-6-0 (O), *40–42*			
	(A) With 2203B tender w/ bell	400	590	[1]
	(B) With 2203T tender w/o bell	365	550	[1]
204	Steam 2-4-2 (O), *40–42 u*			
	(A) Black locomotive	60	110	[1]
	(B) Gun-metal gray locomotive	80	165	[1]
205	(3) Merch. Containers, *30–38**	150	340	[1]
206	Sack of Coal, *38–42*	5	16	[1]
208	Tool set, boxed, *34–42**	50	110	[1]
0209	Barrels, *34–42*	5	14	[1]
209	Wooden Barrels, *34–42*	8	19	[1]
210	Switches, pair (Std.), *26, 34–42*	30	70	[1]
211	Flatcar (Std.), *26–40**	75	125	[2]
212	Gondola (Std.), *26–40**			
	(A) Gray or green	100	205	[3]
	(B) Maroon	75	135	[3]

		Good	Exc	Cond/$
213	Cattle Car (Std.), *26–40**			
	(A) Mojave, maroon roof	180	400	___ 3
	(B) Terra-cotta, green or maroon roof	130	280	___ 3
214	Boxcar (Std.), *26–40**			
	(A) Terra-cotta, green roof	195	295	___ 2
	(B) Cream body, orange roof	150	270	___ 2
	(C) Yellow, brown roof	300	495	___ 2
214R	Refrigerator Car (Std.), *29–40**			
	(A) Ivory or white, peacock roof	325	495	___ 2
	(B) White, light blue nickel roof	435	720	___ 2
215	Tank Car (Std.), *26–40**			
	(A) Pea green	150	215	___ 1
	(B) Ivory	220	360	___ 1
	(C) Silver	315	720	___ 1
216	Hopper Car (Std.), *26–38**			
	(A) Brass plates	195	335	___ 3
	(B) Nickel plates	445	1100	___ 3
217	Caboose (Std.), *26–40**			
	(A) Orange, maroon roof	250	510	___ 4
	(B) Red, peacock roof	120	240	___ 4
	(C) Red body/roof, white door	150	320	___ 4
217	Lighting set, *14–23*		NRS	___
218	Dump Car (Std.), *26–38**	150	250	___ 4
219	Crane (Std.), *26–40**			
	(A) Peacock, red boom	130	235	___ 4
	(B) Yellow, light green boom	270	400	___ 4
	(C) Ivory, light green boom	270	435	___ 4
	(D) Cream, red boom	130	305	___ 4
	(E) White, green boom	300	470	___ 4
220	Floodlight Car (Std.), *31–40**			
	(A) Terra-cotta base	225	385	___ 2
	(B) Green base	340	485	___ 2
220	Switches, pair (Std.), *26**	25	90	___ 1
222	Switches, pair (Std.), *26–32*	40	100	___ 1
223	Switches, pair (Std.), *32–42*	40	100	___ 1

		Good	Exc	Cond/\$
224/224E	Steam 2-6-2 (O), *38–42*			
	(A) Black loco, die-cast 2224 tender	155	290	___[1]
	(B) Black loco, plastic 2224 tender	115	205	___[1]
	(C) Gun-metal, die-cast 2224 tender	385	950	___[1]
	(D) Gun-metal loco, 2689 tender	115	205	___[1]
225	222 Switches, 439 Panel, *29–32*	75	170	___[3]
225/225E	Steam 2-6-2 (O), *38–42*			
	(A) Black, 2235 or 2245 tender	205	365	___[1]
	(B) Black, 2235 plastic tender	190	325	___[1]
	(C) Gun-metal, 2225 or 2265 tender	190	325	___[1]
	(D) Gun-metal, 2235 diecast tender	285	730	___[1]
226/226E	Steam 2-6-4 (O), *38–41*	345	670	___[1]
227	Steam 0-6-0 (O), *39–42*			
	(A) With 2227B tender w/bell	600	1250	___[5]
	(B) With 2227T tender w/o bell	600	1150	___[5]
228	Steam 0-6-0 (O), *39–42*			
	(A) With 2228B tender w/bell	600	1250	___[2]
	(B) With 2228T tender w/o bell	600	1150	___[2]
229	Steam 2-4-2 (O), *39–42*			
	(A) Black or gun-metal w/2689W	155	280	___[1]
	(B) Black or gun-metal w/2689T	120	200	___[1]
	(C) Black w/2666W whistle tender	155	280	___[1]
	(D) Black w/2666T non-whistle tender	120	200	___[1]
230	Steam 0-6-0 (O), *39–42*	1000	1800	___[1]
231	Steam 0-6-0 (O), *39*	1000	1800	___[1]
232	Steam 0-6-0 (O), *40–42*	1000	1800	___[1]
233	Steam 0-6-0 (O), *40–42*	1000	1800	___[1]
238	Steam 4-4-2 (O), *39–40 u*	270	440	___[1]
238E	Steam 4-4-2 (O), *36–38*			
	(A) W/265W or 2225W whistle tender	275	360	___[2]
	(B) W/265 or 2225T non-whistling tender	275	360	___[2]
248	Electric 0-4-0 (O), *27–32*	100	160	___[2]
249/249E	Steam 2-4-2 (O), *36–39*			
	(A) Gun-metal, 265T or 265W tender	100	200	___[1]
	(B) Black, 265W tender	110	210	___[1]
250	Electric 0-4-0, Early (O), *26*	125	220	___[1]

		Good	Exc	Cond/$
250	Electric 0-4-0, Late (O), *34*			
	(A) Yellow-orange, terra-cotta frame	145	245	___1
	(B) Terra-cotta body, maroon frame	160	275	___1
250E	Steam 4-4-2 Hiawatha (O), *35–42**	580	1150	___1
251	Electric 0-4-0 (O), *25–32*			
	(A) Gray body, red windows	190	340	___2
	(B) Red body, ivory stripe	215	410	___2
	(C) Red body, w/o ivory stripe	200	380	___2
251E	Electric 0-4-0 (O), *27–32*			
	(A) Red body, ivory stripe	225	425	___1
	(B) Red body, w/o ivory stripe	205	385	___1
	(C) Gray, red trim	195	350	___1
252	Electric 0-4-0 (O), *26–32*			
	(A) Peacock or olive green	95	195	___2
	(B) Terra-cotta or yellow-orange	125	255	___2
252E	Electric 0-4-0 (O), *33–35*			
	(A) Terra-cotta	145	250	___1
	(B) Yellow-orange	125	205	___1
253	Electric 0-4-0 (O), *24–32*			
	(A) Maroon	180	430	___3
	(B) Dark green	105	195	___3
	(C) Mojave	105	235	___3
	(D) Terra-cotta	180	430	___3
	(E) Peacock	95	195	___3
	(F) Red	210	475	___3
253E	Electric 0-4-0 (O), *31–36*			
	(A) Green	150	205	___1
	(B) Terra-cotta	190	305	___1
254	Electric 0-4-0 (O), *24–32*	170	245	___2
254E	Electric 0-4-0 (O), *27–34*	175	250	___2
255E	Steam 2-4-2 (O), *35–36*	400	770	___1
256	Electric 0-4-4-0 (O), *24–30**			
	(A) Rubber-stamped lettering	470	1250	___2
	(B) (A) w/o outline and "LIONEL..."	425	770	___2
	(C) "LIONEL" & "256" on brass	450	1050	___2

		Good	Exc	Cond/$
257	Steam 2-4-0 (0), *30–35 u*			
	(A) Black tender	145	305	[1]
	(B) Black crackle-finish tender	240	435	[1]
258	Steam 2-4-0, Early (0), *30–35 u*			
	(A) With four-wheel 257 tender	85	170	[1]
	(B) With eight-wheel 258 tender	100	195	[1]
258	Steam 2-4-2, Late (0), *41 u*			
	(A) Black	60	90	[1]
	(B) Gun-metal	85	135	[1]
259	Steam 2-4-2 (0), *32*	60	105	[1]
259E	Steam 2-4-2 (0), *33–42*	60	105	[2]
260E	Steam 2-4-2 (0), *30–35 **			
	(A) Black, green or black frame	385	520	[2]
	(B) Dark gun-metal body and frame	440	640	[2]
261	Steam 2-4-2 (0), *31*	150	215	[1]
261E	Steam 2-4-2 (0), *35*	170	250	[1]
262	Steam 2-4-2 (0), *31–32*	150	205	[3]
262E	Steam 2-4-2 (0), *33–36*			
	(A) Gloss black, copper/brass trim	100	210	[2]
	(B) Satin black, nickel trim	125	265	[2]
263E	Steam 2-4-2 (0), *36–39 **			
	(A) Gun-metal gray	310	600	[1]
	(B) Two-tone blue, from Blue Comet	415	950	[1]
264E	Steam 2-4-2 (0), *35–36*			
	(A) Red, "RED COMET"	145	285	[2]
	(B) Black	220	380	[2]
265E	Steam 2-4-2 (0), *35–40*			
	(A) Black or gun-metal	170	330	[2]
	(B) Light blue, "BLUE STREAK"	460	800	[2]
267E/267W	Sets: 616, (2) 617s, 618, *35–41*	300	495	[1]
270	Bridge, 10" long (0), *31–42*	23	65	[1]
270	Lighting set, *15–23*		NRS	
271	(2) 270 Spans (0), *31–33, 35–40*	50	115	[1]
271	Lighting set, *15–23*		NRS	
272	(3) 270 Spans (0), *31–33, 35–40*	50	115	[1]
280	Bridge, 14" long (Std.), *31–42*	50	115	[1]
281	(2) Bridge Spans (Std.), *31–33, 35–40*	65	160	[1]

		Good	Exc	Cond/$
282	(3) Bridge Spans (Std.), *31–33, 35–40*	85	185	_____ [1]
289E	Steam 2-4-2 (O), *37 u*	120	305	_____ [1]
300	Electric Trolley Car (2⅞"), *01–05*	2000	3600	_____ [2]
300	Hell Gate Bridge (Std.), *28–42**			
	(A) Cream towers, green trusses	800	1350	_____ [1]
	(B) Ivory towers, aluminum truss	700	1600	_____ [1]
300	(See no. 3 Trolley)			
301	Batteries, set of 4 (2⅞"), *03–05*		NRS	_____
302	Plunge Battery (2⅞"), *01–02*		NRS	_____
303	Summer Trolley, *10–13*	1500	3150	_____ [1]
303	Carbon Cylinders (2⅞"), *02*		NRS	_____
304	Composite Zincs (2⅞"), *02*		NRS	_____
306	Glass Jars (2⅞"), *02*		NRS	_____
308	(5) Signs (O), *40–42*	25	70	_____ [1]
309	Electric Trolley Trailer (2⅞"), *01–05*	2500	4050	_____ [2]
309	Pullman (Std.), *26–39*			
	(A) Maroon body/roof, mojave windows	100	160	_____ [1]
	(B) Mojave body/roof, maroon windows	100	160	_____ [1]
	(C) Light brown body, dark brown roof	120	185	_____ [1]
	(D) Medium blue body, dark blue roof	170	260	_____ [1]
	(E) Apple green body, dark green roof	170	260	_____ [1]
	(F) Pale blue body, silver roof	100	160	_____ [1]
	(G) Maroon body, terra-cotta roof	130	185	_____ [1]
310	Baggage (Std.), *26–39*			
	(A) Maroon body/roof, mojave window	100	160	_____ [1]
	(B) Mojave body/roof, maroon window	100	160	_____ [1]
	(C) Light brown body, dark brown roof	115	185	_____ [1]
	(D) Medium blue body, dark blue roof	170	260	_____ [1]
	(E) Apple green body, dark green roof	170	260	_____ [1]
	(F) Pale blue body, silver roof	100	160	_____ [1]
310	Rails and Ties, complete section (2⅞"), *01–02*	5	14	_____ [1]

		Good	Exc	Cond/$
312	Observation (Std.), *24–39*			
	(A) Maroon body/roof, mojave windows	100	160	[1]
	(B) Mojave body/roof, maroon windows	100	160	[1]
	(C) Light brown body, dark brown roof	120	185	[1]
	(D) Medium blue body, dark blue roof	170	260	[1]
	(E) Apple green body, dark green roof	170	260	[1]
	(F) Pale blue body, silver roof	100	160	[1]
	(G) Maroon body, terra-cotta roof	130	185	[1]
313	Bascule Bridge (O), *40–42*			
	(A) Silver bridge	235	495	[2]
	(B) Gray bridge	250	590	[2]
314	Girder Bridge (O), *40–42*	15	32	[1]
315	Trestle Bridge (O), *40–42*	25	70	[1]
316	Trestle Bridge (O), *40–42*	20	45	[1]
318	Electric 0-4-0 (Std.), *24–32*			
	(A) Gray, dark gray, or mojave	150	250	[3]
	(B) Pea green	150	250	[3]
	(C) State brown	250	395	[3]
318E	Electric 0-4-0, *26–35*			
	(A) Gray, mojave, or pea green	150	250	[1]
	(B) State brown	275	440	[1]
	(C) Black	550	990	[1]
319	Pullman (Std.), *24–27*	105	175	[1]
320	Baggage (Std.), *25–27*	100	175	[1]
320	Switch and Signal (2⅞"), *02–05*		NRS	
322	Observation (Std.), *24–27, 29–30 u*	100	175	[1]
330	Crossing, 90° (2⅞"), *02–05*		NRS	
332	Baggage (Std.), *26–33*			
	(A) Red body and roof, cream door	75	115	[1]
	(B) Peacock body/roof, orange door	75	115	[1]
	(C) Gray body/roof, maroon doors	75	115	[1]
	(D) Olive green body/roof, red doors	85	135	[1]
	(E) State brown body, dark brown roof	165	375	

		Good	Exc	Cond/$
337	Pullman (Std.), *25–32*			
	(A) Red body/roof, cream doors	95	190	[1]
	(B) Mojave body/roof, maroon doors	95	190	[1]
	(C) Olive green body/roof, red doors	105	225	[1]
	(D) Olive green body/roof, maroon doors	95	190	[1]
	(E) Pea green body/roof, cream doors	210	500	[1]
338	Observation (Std.), *25–32*			
	(A) Red body/roof, cream doors	95	190	[1]
	(B) Mojave body/roof, maroon doors	95	190	[1]
	(C) Olive green body/roof, red doors	105	225	[1]
	(D) Olive green body/roof, maroon doors	95	190	[1]
339	Pullman (Std.), *25–33*			
	(A) Peacock body/roof, orange doors	55	100	[1]
	(B) Gray body/roof, maroon doors	55	100	[1]
	(C) State brown body, dark brown roof	120	330	[1]
	(D) Peacock body, dark green roof	75	130	[1]
	(E) Mojave body, maroon roof/doors	145	230	[1]
340	Suspension Bridge (2⅞"), *02–05**		NRS	
341	Observation (Std.), *25–33*			
	(A) Peacock body/roof, orange doors	50	70	[1]
	(B) Gray body/roof, maroon doors	50	70	[1]
	(C) State brown body, dark brown roof	110	240	[1]
	(D) Peacock body, dark green roof	65	95	[1]
	(E) Mojave body, maroon roof/doors	135	165	[1]
350	Track Bumper (2⅞"), *02–05*		NRS	
370	Jars and Plates (2⅞"), *02–03*		NRS	
380	Electric 0-4-0 (Std.), *23–27*	245	335	[1]
380	Elevated Pillars (2⅞"), *04–05**	30	70	[1]
380E	Electric 0-4-0 (Std.), *26–29*			
	(A) Mojave	445	630	[1]
	(B) Maroon	295	400	[1]
	(C) Dark green	370	460	[1]
381	Electric 4-4-4 (Std.), *28–29**	1800	2500	[1]
381E	Electric 4-4-4 (Std.), *28–36**			
	(A) State green, apple green sub-frame	1500	2500	[1]
	(B) State green, red sub-frame	1900	2850	[1]

		Good	Exc	Cond/$
381U	Electric 4-4-4 Kit (Std.), *28–29*	1600	3600	___¹
384	Steam 2-4-0 (Std.), *30–32**	410	600	___¹
384E	Steam 2-4-0 (Std.), *30–32**	405	590	___¹
385E	Steam 2-4-2 (Std.), *33–39**	330	570	___²
390	Steam 2-4-2 (Std.), *29**	415	720	___¹
390E	Steam 2-4-2 (Std.), *29–31**			
	(A) Black, w/ or w/o orange stripe	445	670	___²
	(B) Two-tone blue, cream-orange stripe	590	1200	___²
	(C) Two-tone green, orange or green stripe	990	2050	___²
392E	Steam 4-4-2 (Std.), *32–39**			
	(A) Black, 384 tender	750	1250	___¹
	(B) Black, large 12-wheel tender	1050	1800	___¹
	(C) Gun-metal gray	880	1600	___¹
400	Express Trail Car (2⅞"), *03–05**	3500	5850	___¹
400E	Steam 4-4-4 (Std.), *31–39**			
	(A) Black or dark gun-metal	1400	2150	___³
	(B) Medium blue boiler	1400	2150	___³
	(C) Crackle black finish	1400	2150	___³
402	Electric 0-4-4-0 (Std.), *23–27*	300	495	___¹
402E	Electric 0-4-4-0 (Std.), *26–29*	300	495	___¹
404	Summer Trolley (Std.), *10*		NRS	___
408E	Electric 0-4-4-0 (Std.), *27–36**			
	(A) Apple green or mojave, red pilots	700	1150	___¹
	(B) Two-tone brown, brown pilots	2100	2650	___¹
	(C) Dark green, red pilots	1850	3400	___¹
412	Pullman, "California" (Std.), *29–35**			
	(A) Light green body, dark green roof	590	1750	___¹
	(B) Light brown body, dark brown roof	620	2100	___¹
413	Pullman, "Colorado" (Std.), *29–35**			
	(A) Light green body, dark green roof	590	1750	___¹
	(B) Light brown body, dark brown roof	620	2100	___¹
414	Pullman, "Illinois" (Std.), *29–35**			
	(A) Light green body, dark green roof	590	2050	___¹
	(B) Light brown body, dark brown roof	590	1750	___¹
416	Observation, "New York" (Std.), *29–35**			
	(A) Light green body, dark green roof	590	1750	___¹
	(B) Light brown body, dark brown roof	620	2100	___¹

		Good	Exc	Cond/$
418	Pullman (Std.), *23–32**	205	280	1
419	Combination (Std.), *23–32**	205	280	1
420	Pullman, "Faye" (Std.), *30–40**	510	880	1
421	Pullman, "Westphal" (Std.), *30–40**	540	880	1
422	Observation, "Tempel" (Std.), *30–40**	510	880	1
424	Pullman, "Liberty Belle" (Std.), *31–40**			
	(A) Brass trim	325	495	1
	(B) Nickel trim	350	590	1
425	Pullman, "Stephen Girard" (Std.), *31–40**			
	(A) Brass trim	325	495	1
	(B) Nickel trim	350	590	1
426	Observation, "Coral Isle" (Std.), *31–40**			
	(A) Brass trim	325	495	1
	(B) Nickel trim	350	590	1
427	Diner (Std.), *30*		NM	
428	Pullman (Std.), *26–30**			
	(A) Dark green body and roof	250	385	1
	(B) Orange body/roof, apple green window	390	890	1
429	Combine (Std.), *26–30**			
	(A) Dark green body and roof	250	385	1
	(B) Orange body/roof, apple green window	390	890	1
430	Observation (Std.), *26–30**			
	(A) Dark green body and roof	250	385	1
	(B) Orange body/roof, apple green window	390	890	1
431	Diner (Std.), *27–32**			
	(A) Mojave body, screw-mounted roof	350	540	1
	(B) Mojave body, hinged roof	465	720	1
	(C) Dark green body, orange windows	410	720	1
	(D) Orange body, apple green windows	410	720	1
	(E) Apple green body, red window	410	720	1
435	Power Station, *26–38**	130	250	1
436	Power Station, *26–37**			
	(A) "POWER STATION" plates	120	230	2
	(B) "EDISON SERVICE" plate	240	540	2
437	Switch/Signal Tower, *26–37**	210	430	1

		Good	Exc	Cond/$
438	Signal Tower, *27–39**			
	(A) Mojave base, orange house	215	425	____3
	(B) Gray base, ivory house	325	640	____3
	(C) Black base, white house	325	640	____3
439	Panel Board, *28–42**	75	120	____1
440/0440/440N	Signal Bridge, *32–42**	190	465	____1
440C	Panel Board, *32–42*	75	120	____1
441	Weighing Station (Std.), *32–36*	550	1550	____1
442	Landscape Diner, *38–42*	130	175	____1
444	Roundhouse (Std.), *32–35**	1100	2300	____1
444-18	Roundhouse Clip, *33*		NRS	____
450	Electric 0-4-0, Macy's (O), *30 u*			
	(A) Red, black frame	295	700	____1
	(B) Apple green, dark green frame	415	880	____1
450	Set: 450; matching 605; (2) 606s, *30 u*	750	1800	____1
455	Electric Range, *30, 32–33*	320	880	____1
490	Observation (Std.), *23–32**	195	260	____1
500	Dealer Display, *27–28*		NRS	____
500	Electric Derrick Car (2⅞"), *03–04**	5000	6750	____1
501	Dealer Display, *27–28*		NRS	____
502	Dealer Display, *27–28*		NRS	____
503	Dealer Display, *27–28*		NRS	____
504	Dealer Display, *24–28*		NRS	____
505	Dealer Display, *24–28*		NRS	____
506	Dealer Display, *24–28*		NRS	____
507	Dealer Display, *24–28*		NRS	____
508	Dealer Display, *24–28*		NRS	____
509	Dealer Display, *24–28*		NRS	____
510	Dealer Display, *27–28*		NRS	____
511	Flatcar (Std.), *27–40*	45	70	____3
512	Gondola (Std.), *27–39*			
	(A) Peacock	38	70	____2
	(B) Green	50	90	____2
513	Cattle Car (Std.), *27–38*			
	(A) Olive green	70	135	____3
	(B) Orange	70	135	____3
	(C) Cream, maroon roof	70	135	____3

		Good	Exc	Cond/$
514	Boxcar (Std.), *29–40*			
	(A) Cream yellow, orange roof	85	155	4
	(B) Yellow, brown roof	115	270	4
514	Refrigerator Car (Std.), *27–28*			
	(A) White, peacock roof	240	540	1
	(B) Cream, peacock roof	215	340	1
	(C) Ivory, peacock roof	285	800	1
	(D) Cream, green roof	265	680	1
514R	Refrigerator Car (Std.), *29–40*			
	(A) Ivory, peacock roof, brass plates	140	180	1
	(B) Ivory, light blue roof, nickel plates	440	600	1
	(C) White, light blue roof, brass plates	140	180	1
515	Tank Car (Std.), *27–40*			
	(A) Ivory or terra-cotta	90	160	2
	(B) Light tan	110	160	2
	(C) Silver	90	160	2
	(D) Orange, red "SHELL" decal	340	520	2
516	Hopper Car (Std.), *28–40*	165	245	2
517	Caboose (Std.), *27–40*			
	(A) Pea green, red roof	50	100	3
	(B) Red body and roof	105	155	3
	(C) Red, black roof, orange windows	355	610	3
520	Floodlight Car (Std.), *31–40*			
	(A) Terra-cotta base	95	185	2
	(B) Green base	95	215	2
529	Pullman (O), *26–32*			
	(A) Olive green body and roof	25	45	1
	(B) Terra-cotta body and roof	25	60	1
530	Observation (O), *26–32*			
	(A) Olive green body and roof	25	45	1
	(B) Terra-cotta body and roof	25	60	1
550	Miniature Figures, boxed (Std.), *32–36**	135	230	1
551	Engineer (Std.), *32*	25	45	1
552	Conductor (Std.), *32*	25	45	1
553	Porter (Std.), *32*	25	45	1
554	Male Passenger (Std.), *32*	25	45	1
555	Female Passenger (Std.), *32*	25	45	1

		Good	Exc	Cond/$
556	Red Cap Figure (Std.), *32*	25	45	___[1]
600	Derrick Trailer (2⅞"), *03–04**	5000	8550	___[1]
600	Pullman, Early (O), *15–23*			
	(A) Dark green	65	170	___[1]
	(B) Maroon or brown	48	85	___[1]
600	Pullman, Late (O), *33–42*			
	(A) Light red or gray; red roof	50	90	___[1]
	(B) Light blue, aluminum roof	70	120	___[1]
601	Observation, Late (O), *33–42*			
	(A) Light red body and roof	50	90	___[1]
	(B) Light gray, red roof	50	90	___[1]
	(C) Light blue body, aluminum roof	70	120	___[1]
601	Pullman, Early (O), *15–23*	50	70	___[1]
602	Baggage, Lionel Lines, Late (O), *33–42*			
	(A) Light red or gray; red roof	60	110	___[1]
	(B) Light blue body, aluminum roof	90	150	___[1]
602	Baggage, NYC (O), *15–23*	30	45	___[1]
602	Observation (O), *22 u*	30	36	___[1]
603	Pullman, Early (O), *22 u*	40	70	___[1]
603	Pullman, Later (O), *20–25*	20	45	___[1]
603	Pullman, Latest (O), *31–36*			
	(A) Light red body and roof	45	85	___[1]
	(B) Red body, black roof	35	60	___[1]
	(C) Stephen Girard green, dark green roof	35	60	___[1]
	(D) Maroon body/roof, "MACY SPCL"	60	125	___[1]
604	Observation, Later (O), *20–25*	35	60	___[1]
604	Observation, Latest (O), *31–36*			
	(A) Light red body and roof	44	85	___[1]
	(B) Red body, black roof	35	60	___[1]
	(C) Yellow-orange body, terra-cotta roof	35	60	___[1]
	(D) Stephen Girard green, dark green roof	35	60	___[1]
	(E) Maroon body and roof	70	150	___[1]

		Good	Exc	Cond/$
605	Pullman (O), *25–32*			
	(A) Gray, "LIONEL LINES"	85	170	___[1]
	(B) Gray, "ILLINOIS CENTRAL"	85	170	___[1]
	(C) Red, "LIONEL LINES"	170	255	___[1]
	(D) Red, "ILLINOIS CENTRAL"	255	340	___[1]
	(E) Orange, "LIONEL LINES"	170	255	___[1]
	(F) Orange, "ILLINOIS CENTRAL"	300	430	___[1]
	(G) Olive green, "LIONEL LINES"	255	340	___[1]
606	Observation (O), *25–32*			
	(A) Gray, "LIONEL LINES"	130	215	___[1]
	(B) Gray, "ILLINOIS CENTRAL"	85	170	___[1]
	(C) Red, "LIONEL LINES"	170	255	___[1]
	(D) Red, "ILLINOIS CENTRAL"	255	340	___[1]
	(E) Orange, "LIONEL LINES"	170	255	___[1]
	(F) Orange, "ILLINOIS CENTRAL"	170	255	___[1]
	(G) Olive green, "LIONEL LINES"	255	340	___[1]
607	Pullman (O), *26–27*			
	(A) Peacock, "LIONEL LINES"	50	70	___[3]
	(B) Peacock, "ILLINOIS CENTRAL"	75	115	___[3]
	(C) Two-tone green, "LIONEL LINES"	50	75	___[3]
	(D) Red, "LIONEL LINES"	75	110	___[3]
608	Observation (O), *26–37*			
	(A) Peacock, "LIONEL LINES"	50	70	___[2]
	(B) Peacock, "ILLINOIS CENTRAL"	75	115	___[2]
	(C) Two-tone green, "LIONEL LINES"	50	75	___[2]
	(D) Red, "LIONEL LINES"	75	110	___[2]
609	Pullman (O), *37*	50	70	___[1]
610	Pullman, Early (O), *15–25*			
	(A) Dark green body and roof	50	65	___[3]
	(B) Maroon body and roof	60	95	___[3]
	(C) Mojave body and roof	60	95	___[3]

		Good	Exc	Cond/$
610	Pullman, Late (O), *26–30*			
	(A) Olive green body and roof	60	75	___ [1]
	(B) Mojave body and roof	50	75	___ [1]
	(C) Terra-cotta body, maroon roof	100	155	___ [1]
	(D) Pea green body and roof	70	115	___ [1]
	(E) Light blue body, aluminum roof	130	260	___ [1]
	(F) Light red, aluminum finish roof	100	155	___ [1]
611	Observation (O), *37*	50	85	___ [1]
612	Observation, Early (O), *15–25*			
	(A) Dark green body and roof	50	60	___ [1]
	(B) Maroon body and roof	70	90	___ [1]
	(C) Mojave body and roof	70	90	___ [1]
612	Observation, Late (O), *26–30*			
	(A) Olive green body and roof	50	75	___ [1]
	(B) Mojave body and roof	50	75	___ [1]
	(C) Terra-cotta body, maroon roof	100	155	___ [1]
	(D) Pea green body and roof	70	115	___ [1]
	(E) Light blue body, aluminum roof	130	260	___ [1]
	(F) Light red, aluminum finish roof	100	155	___ [1]
613	Pullman (O), *31–40**			
	(A) Terra-cotta, maroon/terra-cotta roof	70	140	___ [1]
	(B) Light red, light red/aluminum roof	175	350	___ [1]
	(C) Blue, two-tone blue roof	105	210	___ [1]
614	Observation (O), *31–40**			
	(A) Terra-cotta, maroon/terra-cotta roof	70	140	___ [1]
	(B) Light red, light red/aluminum roof	175	350	___ [1]
	(C) Blue, two-tone blue roof	105	210	___ [1]
615	Baggage (O), *33–40**	110	190	___ [1]
616E/616W	Diesel only (O), *35–41*	80	190	___ [1]
616E/616W	Set: 616, (2) 617s, 618	300	550	___ [1]
617	Coach (O), *35–41*			
	(A) Blue and white	55	85	___ [1]
	(B) Chrome, gun-metal skirts	55	85	___ [1]
	(C) Chrome, chrome skirts	55	85	___ [1]
	(D) Silver finish	55	85	___ [1]

		Good	Exc	Cond/$
618	Observation (O), *35–41*			
	(A) Blue and white	55	85	[1]
	(B) Chrome, gun-metal skirts	55	85	[1]
	(C) Chrome, chrome skirts	55	85	[1]
	(D) Silver finish	55	85	[1]
619	Combine (O), *36–38*			
	(A) Blue, white window band	100	205	[1]
	(B) Chrome, chrome skirts	100	205	[1]
620	Floodlight Car (O), *37–42*	50	85	[1]
629	Pullman (O), *24–32*			
	(A) Dark green body and roof	30	40	[1]
	(B) Orange body and roof	30	40	[1]
	(C) Red body and roof	20	32	[1]
	(D) Light red body and roof	40	55	[1]
630	Observation, *24–32*			
	(A) Dark green body and roof	30	40	[1]
	(B) Orange body and roof	30	40	[1]
	(C) Red body and roof	20	32	[1]
	(D) Light red body and roof	40	55	[1]
636W	Diesel only (O), *36–39*	90	175	[1]
636W	Set: 636W, (2) 637s, 638, *36–39*	295	510	[1]
637	Coach (O), *36–39*	70	105	[1]
638	Observation (O), *36–39*	70	105	[1]
651	Flatcar (O), *35–40*	25	50	[1]
652	Gondola (O), *35–40*	25	50	[1]
653	Hopper Car (O), *34–40*	35	65	[1]
654	Tank Car (O), *34–42*			
	(A) Orange or aluminum finish	35	60	[1]
	(B) Gray	42	75	[1]
655	Boxcar (O), *34–42*			
	(A) Cream, maroon roof	35	60	[1]
	(B) Cream, tuscan roof	47	75	[1]
656	Cattle Car (O), *35–40*			
	(A) Light gray, vermilion roof	40	75	[1]
	(B) Burnt orange, tuscan roof	65	115	[1]

		Good	Exc Cond/$
657	Caboose (O), _34–42_		
	(A) Red body and roof	20	35 ____ [2]
	(B) Red, tuscan roof	24	44 ____ [2]
659	Dump Car (O), _35–42_	40	75 ____ [1]
700	Electric 0-4-0 (O), _15–16_	360	690 ____ [1]
700	Window Display (2⅞"), _03–05_		NRS ____
700E	Steam 4-6-4, Scale Hudson, 5344	1900	3650 ____ [3]
	(O), _37–42*_		
700K	Steam 4-6-4, unbuilt (O), _38–42_	4000	5400 ____ [1]
701	Electric 0-4-0 (O), _15–16_	390	660 ____ [2]
701	Steam 0-6-0 (See 708)		
702	Baggage (O), _17–21_	115	305 ____ [1]
703	Electric 4-4-4 (O), _15–16_	1400	2350 ____ [1]
706	Electric 0-4-0 (O), _15–16_	375	630 ____ [1]
708	Steam 0-6-0, "8976" on boiler front	1500	2900 ____ [2]
	(O), _39–42*_		
710	Pullman (O), _24–34_		
	(A) Red, "LIONEL LINES"	200	300 ____ [2]
	(B) Orange, "LIONEL LINES"	150	225 ____ [2]
	(C) Orange, "NEW YORK CENTRAL"	200	225 ____ [2]
	(D) Orange, "ILLINOIS CENTRAL"	300	450 ____ [2]
	(E) Two-tone blue, "LIONEL LINES"	300	415 ____ [2]
	(F) Orange, "NEW YORK CENTRAL"	200	260 ____ [2]
711	R.C. Switches, pair (O72), _35–42_	75	155 ____ [1]
712	Observation (O), _24–34_		
	(A) Red, "LIONEL LINES"	185	355 ____ [1]
	(B) Orange, "LIONEL LINES"	140	265 ____ [1]
	(C) Orange, "NEW YORK CENTRAL"	185	310 ____ [1]
	(D) Orange, "ILLINOIS CENTRAL"	280	530 ____ [1]
	(E) Two-tone blue, "LIONEL LINES"	280	485 ____ [1]
	(F) Orange, "NEW YORK CENTRAL"	185	310 ____ [1]
714	Boxcar (O), _40–42*_	300	540 ____ [1]
714K	Boxcar, unbuilt (O), _40–42_	—	900 ____ [1]
715	Tank Car (O), _40–42*_		
	(A) "S.E.P.S. 8124" decal	340	610 ____ [2]
	(B) "S.U.N.X. 715" decal	435	880 ____ [2]
715K	Tank Car, unbuilt (O), _40–42_	—	720 ____ [1]

No.	Description	Good	Exc	Cond/$
716	Hopper Car (O), *40–42**	400	750	1
716K	Hopper, unbuilt (O), *40–42*	—	990	1
717	Caboose (O), *40–42**	390	590	1
717K	Caboose, unbuilt (O), *40–42*	—	810	1
720	90° Crossing (O72), *35–42*	20	39	1
721	Manual Switches, pair (O72), *35–42*	45	90	1
730	90° Crossing (O72), *35–42*	20	36	1
731	R.C. Switches, pair, T-rail (O72), *35–42*	95	160	1
751E/751W	Set: 752; (2) 753s; 754 (O), *34–41**	600	990	1
752E	Diesel only (O), *34–41*			
	(A) Yellow and brown	180	340	2
	(B) Aluminum finish	180	340	2
753	Coach (O), *36–41*			
	(A) Yellow and brown	95	180	2
	(B) Aluminum Finish	95	180	2
754	Observation (O), *36–41*			
	(A) Yellow and brown	95	180	2
	(B) Aluminum Finish	95	180	2
760	16-piece Curved Track (O72), *35–42*	35	70	1
761	Curved Track (O72), *34–42*	1	2.50	1
762	Straight Track (O72), *34–42*	1	2.50	1
762	Inside Straight Track (O72), *34–42*	2	5	1
763E	Steam 4-6-4 (O), *37–42*			
	(A) Gun-metal, 263 or 2263W tender	1200	2650	3
	(B) Gun-metal, 2226X or 2226WX	1200	2650	3
	(C) Black, 2226WX tender	1200	2650	3
771	Curved Track, T-rail (O72), *35–42*	3	9	2
772	Straight Track, T-rail (O72), *35–42*	4	12	1
773	Fishplate Outfit (O72), *36–42*	25	32	1
782	Hiawatha Combine (O), *35–41**	185	405	1
783	Hiawatha Coach (O), *35–41**	185	405	1
784	Hiawatha Observation (O), *35–41**	185	405	1
792	Rail Chief Combine (O), *37–41**	290	800	1
793	Rail Chief Coach (O), *37–41**	290	800	1
794	Rail Chief Observation (O), *37–41**	290	800	1

		Good	Exc	Cond/$
800	Boxcar (O), *15–26*			
	(A) Light orange, brown-maroon roof	45	70	[1]
	(B) Orange body/roof, "PENN RR"	30	50	[1]
800	Boxcar (2⅞"), *04–05**	2500	4050	[1]
801	Caboose (O), *15–26*	35	45	[1]
802	Stock Car (O), *15–26*	43	60	[1]
803	Hopper Car, Early (O), *23–28*	29	43	[1]
803	Hopper Car, Late (O), *29–34*	35	60	[1]
804	Tank Car (O), *23–28*	32	55	[2]
805	Boxcar (O), *27–34*			
	(A) Pea green, terra-cotta roof	35	60	[1]
	(B) Pea green, maroon roof	44	115	[1]
	(C) Orange, maroon roof	44	95	[1]
806	Stock Car (O), *27–34*			
	(A) Pea green, terra-cotta roof	42	75	[1]
	(B) Orange; various color roof	35	60	[1]
807	Caboose (O), *27–40*			
	(A) Peacock, dark green roof	20	35	[1]
	(B) Red, peacock roof	20	35	[1]
	(C) Light red body and roof	23	40	[1]
809	Dump Car (O), *31–41*			
	(A) Orange bin	40	75	[1]
	(B) Green bin	40	85	[1]
810	Crane (O), *30–42*			
	(A) Terra-cotta cab, maroon roof	190	200	[3]
	(B) Cream cab, vermilion roof	125	180	[3]
811	Flatcar (O), *26–40*			
	(A) Maroon	40	70	[1]
	(B) Aluminum finish	47	100	[1]
812	Gondola (O), *26–42*	33	65	[5]
813	Stock Car (O), *26–42*			
	(A) Orange, pea green roof	65	140	[3]
	(B) Orange, maroon roof	50	120	[3]
	(C) Cream, maroon roof	100	225	[3]
	(D) Tuscan body and roof	NRS	2250	[3]

		Good	Exc	Cond/$
814	Boxcar (O), *26–42*			
	(A) Cream, orange roof	46	105	5
	(B) Cream, maroon roof	115	140	5
	(C) Yellow, brown roof	115	115	5
814R	Refrigerator Car (O), *29–42*			
	(A) Ivory, peacock roof	100	190	2
	(B) White, light blue roof	120	265	2
	(C) Flat white, brown roof	600	900	2
815	Tank Car (O), *26–42*			
	(A) Pea green, maroon frame	250	510	3
	(B) Pea green, black frame	70	155	3
	(C) Aluminum, black frame	50	115	3
	(D) Orange-yellow, black frame	150	255	3
816	Hopper Car (O), *27–42*			
	(A) Olive green	85	155	3
	(B) Red body	65	135	3
	(C) Black body	370	680	3
817	Caboose (O), *26–42*			
	(A) Peacock, dark green roof	45	80	4
	(B) Red, peacock roof	45	80	4
	(C) Light red body and roof	45	80	4
820	Boxcar (O), *15–26*			
	(A) Orange, "ILLINOIS CENTRAL"	45	80	3
	(B) Orange, "UNION PACIFIC"	65	105	3
820	Floodlight Car (O), *31–42*			
	(A) Terra-cotta	100	175	1
	(B) Green	100	175	1
	(C) Light green	100	175	1
821	Stock Car (O), *15–16, 25–26*	45	85	1
822	Caboose (O), *15–26*	35	70	1
831	Flatcar (O), *27–34*	24	40	1
840	Industrial Power Station, *28–40**	1200	3050	2
900	Ammunition Car (O), *17–21*	120	340	1
900	Box Trail Car (2⅞"), *04–05**	2000	3600	1
901	Gondola (O), *19–27*	27	44	1
902	Gondola (O), *27–34*	24	39	1
910	Grove of Trees, *32–42*	70	155	1

		Good	Exc	Cond/$
911	Country Estate, *32–42*	175	360	1
912	Suburban Home, *N/A*	175	360	1
913	Landscaped Bungalow, *40–42*	140	285	1
914	Park Landscape, *32–35*	90	205	1
915	Tunnel, *32, 34–35*	160	435	1
916	Tunnel, 29¼" long, *35*	95	180	1
917	Scenic Hillside, *32–36*	90	205	1
918	Scenic Hillside, *32–36*	90	205	1
919	Park Grass, bag, *32–42*	7	15	1
920	Village, *32–33*	600	1600	1
921	Scenic Park, 3 pieces, *32–33*	980	2600	1
921C	Park Center, *32–33*	400	1050	1
922	Terrace, *32–36*	80	155	1
923	Tunnel, 40¼" long, *33–42*	90	225	1
924	Tunnel, 30" long (O72), *35–42*	50	135	1
925	Lubricant, *35–42*	1	2.50	1
927	Flag Plot, *37–42*	70	135	1
1000	Passenger Car (2⅞"), *05* *	4500	6750	1
1000	Trolley Trailer (Std.), *10–16*	1400	2250	1
1010	Electric 0-4-0, Winner (O), *31–32*	75	135	1
1010	Interurban Trailer (Std.), *10–16*	1000	1800	1
1011	Pullman, Winner (O), *31–32*	50	70	1
1011	Interurban (Std.), *10*		NM	
1012	Station, *32*	50	70	1
1012	(See no. 1011 Interurban)			
1015	Steam 0-4-0 (O), *31–32*	100	205	1
1017	Winner Station, *33*	25	70	1
1019	Observation (O), *31–32*	50	70	1
1020	Baggage (O), *31–32*	65	110	1
1021	90° Crossover (O27), *32–42*	1	4	1
1022	Tunnel, 18¾" long (O), *35–42*	15	32	1
1023	Tunnel, 19" long, *34–42*	20	41	1
1024	Switches, pair (O27), *37–42*	4	15	1
1025	Bumper (O27), *40–42*	11	23	1
1027	Transformer, Tin Station, *34*	50	115	1
1028	Transformer, 40 watts, *39*	3	11	1
1030	Electric 0-4-0 (O), *32*	75	135	1

		Good	Exc	Cond/$
1035	Steam 0-4-0 (O), *32*	75	115	____[1]
1045	Watchman, *38–42*	15	60	____[1]
1050	Passenger Car Trailer (2⅞"), *05**	5000	7200	____[1]
1100	Handcar, Mickey Mouse, *35–37**			
	(A) Red base	400	630	____[1]
	(B) Apple green base, orange shoes	500	880	____[1]
	(C) Orange base	600	1200	____[1]
1100	Summer Trolley Trailer (Std.), *10–13*		NRS	____
1103	Handcar, Peter Rabbit (O), *35–37**	400	990	____[1]
1105	Handcar, Santa Claus (O), *35–35**			
	(A) Red base	580	1250	____[1]
	(B) Green base	630	1400	____[1]
1107	Transformer, Tin Station, *33*	25	70	____[1]
1107	Handcar, Donald Duck (O), *36–37**			
	(A) White dog house w/red roof	475	1200	____[1]
	(B) White dog house w/green roof	450	1100	____[1]
	(C) Orange dog house w/green roof	640	1850	____[1]
1121	Switches, pair (O27), *37–42*	15	32	____[1]
1506L	Steam 0-4-0 (O), *33–34*	95	125	____[1]
1506M	Steam 0-4-0 (O), *35*	250	430	____[1]
1508	Steam 0-4-0, Commodore Vanderbilt w/ Mickey in 1509 Stoker Tender, *35*	335	540	____[1]
1511	Steam 0-4-0 (O), *36–37*	110	160	____[1]
1512	Gondola (O), *31–33, 36–37*	25	41	____[1]
1514	Boxcar (O), *31–37*	25	41	____[1]
1515	Tank Car (O), *33–37*	25	41	____[1]
1517	Caboose (O), *31–37*	25	41	____[1]
1518	Mickey Mouse Diner (O), *35*	105	235	____[1]
1519	Mickey Mouse Band (O), *35*	105	235	____[1]
1520	Mickey Mouse Animal (O), *35*	105	235	____[1]
1536	Circus: 1508, 1509, 1518, 1519, 1520, *15–20*	700	1550	____[1]
1550	Switches, pair, windup, *33–37*	2	5	____[1]
1555	90° Crossover, windup, *33–37*	1	2.50	____[1]
1560	Station, *33–37*	15	34	____[1]
1569	Accessory set, 8 pieces, *33–37*	35	70	____[1]

		Good	Exc Cond/$
1588	Steam 0-4-0 (O), *36–37*	150	250 ___[1]
1630	Pullman (O), *38–42*		
	(A) Aluminum windows	35	70 ___[1]
	(B) Light gray windows	47	80 ___[1]
1631	Observation (O), *38–42*		
	(A) Aluminum windows	35	70 ___[1]
	(B) Light gray windows	47	80 ___[1]
1651E	Electric 0-4-0 (O), *33*	120	225 ___[1]
1661E	Steam 2-4-0 (O), *33*	75	160 ___[1]
1662	Steam 0-4-0 (O27), *40–42*	185	305 ___[2]
1663	Steam 0-4-0 (O27), *40–42*	200	385 ___[1]
1664/1664E Steam 2-4-2 (O27), *38–42*			
	(A) Gun-metal	55	90 ___[1]
	(B) Black	55	85 ___[1]
1666/1666E Steam 2-6-2 (O27), *38–42*			
	(A) Gun-metal	115	155 ___[1]
	(B) Black	95	145 ___[1]
1668/1668E Steam 2-6-2 (O27), *37–41*			
	(A) Gun-metal	70	120 ___[1]
	(B) Black	70	120 ___[1]
1673	Coach (O), *36–37*		
	(A) Aluminum windows	35	75 ___[1]
	(B) Light gray windows	47	90 ___[1]
1674	Pullman (O), *36–37*	35	75 ___[1]
1675	Observation (O), *36–37*	30	70 ___[1]
1677	Gondola (O), *33–35, 39–42*		
	(A) "IVES/R.R. LINES", light blue	40	60 ___[1]
	(B) "LIONEL", blue or red	20	36 ___[1]
1679	Boxcar (O), *33–42*		
	(A) Cream, "IVES" on side	23	38 ___[1]
	(B) Cream, "LIONEL" on side	23	38 ___[1]
	(C) Cream or yellow, "BABY RUTH"	23	38 ___[1]
1680	Tank Car (O), *33–42*		
	(A) Aluminum, "IVES TANK LINES"	80	95 ___[2]
	(B) Aluminum, no "IVES" lettering	20	35 ___[2]

		Good	Exc	Cond/$
1681	Steam 2-4-0 (O), *34–35*			
	(A) Black, red frame	55	115	[1]
	(B) Red, red frame	110	145	[1]
1681E	Steam 2-4-0 (O), *34–35*			
	(A) Black, red frame	65	130	[1]
	(B) Red, red frame	130	165	[1]
1682	Caboose (O), *33–42*			
	(A) Vermilion, "IVES" on side	34	70	[3]
	(B) Red or tuscan, "LIONEL"	17	40	[3]
1684	Steam 2-4-2 (O27), *41–42*	45	70	[1]
1685	Coach (O), *33–37 u*			
	(A) Gray, maroon roof	240	495	[1]
	(B) Red, maroon roof	170	335	[1]
	(C) Blue, silver roof	170	315	[1]
1686	Baggage (O), *33–37 u*			
	(A) Gray, maroon roof	240	495	[1]
	(B) Red, maroon roof	170	335	[1]
	(C) Blue, silver roof	170	315	[1]
1687	Observation (O), *33–37 u*			
	(A) Gray, maroon roof	170	315	[1]
	(B) Red, maroon roof	170	315	[1]
	(C) Blue, silver roof	170	315	[1]
1688/1688E Steam 2-4-2 (O27), *36–46*		50	85	[1]
1689E	Steam 2-4-2 (O27), *36–37*			
	(A) Gun-metal	75	115	[1]
	(B) Black	60	100	[1]
1690	Pullman (O), *33–40*	35	60	[1]
1691	Observation (O), *33–40*	35	60	[1]
1692	Pullman (O27), *39 u*	45	70	[1]
1693	Observation (O27), *39 u*	45	70	[1]
1700E	Diesel, power unit only (O27), *35–37*	45	70	[1]
1700E	Set: 1700 (2) 1701s, 1702 (O27), *35–37 u*			
	(A) Aluminum and light red	140	250	[1]
	(B) Chrome and light red	140	250	[1]
	(C) Orange and gray	140	250	[1]

		Good	Exc	Cond/$
1701	Coach (O27), *35–37*			
	(A) Chrome sides and roof	20	45	[1]
	(B) Silver sides and roof	30	55	[1]
	(C) Orange and gray	70	135	[1]
1702	Observation (O27), *35–37*			
	(A) Chrome sides and roof	20	45	[1]
	(B) Silver sides and roof	30	55	[1]
	(C) Orange and gray	70	135	[1]
1703	Observation w/hooked coupler, *35–37 u*	35	75	[1]
1717	Gondola (O), *33–40 u*	26	41	[1]
1717X	Gondola (O), *40 u*	25	45	[1]
1719	Boxcar (O), *33–40 u*	30	50	[1]
1719X	Boxcar (O), *41–42 u*	30	50	[1]
1722	Caboose (O), *33–42 u*	25	50	[1]
1722X	Caboose (O), *39–40 u*	26	41	[1]
1766	Pullman (Std.), *34–40**			
	(A) Terra-cotta, maroon roof, brass trim	300	650	[1]
	(B) Red, maroon roof, nickel tram	300	540	[1]
1767	Baggage Car (Std.), *34–40**			
	(A) Terra-cotta, maroon roof, brass trim	295	850	[1]
	(B) Red, maroon roof, nickel trim	295	700	[1]
1768	Observation (Std.), *34–40**			
	(A) Terra-cotta, maroon roof, brass trim	300	650	[1]
	(B) Red, maroon roof, nickel trim	300	540	[1]
1811	Pullman (O), *33–37*	30	65	[1]
1812	Observation (O), *33–37*	30	65	[1]
1813	Baggage Car (O), *33–37*	60	135	[1]
1816/1816W Diesel (O), *35–37*		100	235	[1]
1817	Coach (O), *35–37*	22	50	[1]
1818	Observation (O), *35–37*	22	50	[1]
1835E	Steam 2-4-2 (Std.), *34–39*	520	790	[1]
1910	Electric 0-6-0, Early (Std.), *10–11*	800	1800	[1]
1910	Electric 0-6-0, Late (Std.), *12*	550	1350	[1]
1910	Pullman (Std.), *09–10 u*	1000	1800	[1]
1911	Electric 0-4-0, Early (Std.), *10–12*	1000	2000	[1]
1911	Electric 0-4-0, Late (Std.), *13*	700	1100	[1]
1911	Electric 0-4-4-0, Special (Std.), *11–12*	1000	2500	[1]

		Good	Exc	Cond/$
1912	Electric 0-4-4-0 (Std.), *10–12* *			
	(A) NY, New Haven & Hartford	1800	3200	____ [1]
	(B) "NEW YORK CENTRAL LINES"	1500	2700	____ [1]
1912	Electric 0-4-4-0 Special (Std.), *11* *	2500	4500	____ [1]
2200	Summer Trolley Trailer (Std.), *10–13*	1100	2250	____ [1]
2600	Pullman (O), *38–42*	70	135	____ [1]
2601	Observation (O), *38–42*	70	135	____ [1]
2602	Baggage Car (O), *38–42*	75	155	____ [1]
2613	Pullman (O), *38–42* *			
	(A) Blue, two-tone blue roof	100	270	____ [1]
	(B) State green, two-tone green roof	200	440	____ [1]
2614	Observation (O), *38–42* *			
	(A) Blue, two-tone blue roof	100	270	____ [1]
	(B) State green, two-tone green roof	200	440	____ [1]
2615	Baggage Car (O), *38–42* *			
	(A) Blue, two-tone blue roof	115	270	____ [1]
	(B) State green, two-tone green roof	200	420	____ [1]
2620	Floodlight Car (O), *38–42*	40	90	____ [1]
2623	Pullman (O), *41–42*			
	(A) "IRVINGTON"	170	335	____ [1]
	(B) "MANHATTAN"	155	295	____ [1]
2624	Pullman (O), *41–42*	750	1700	____ [1]
2630	Pullman (O), *38–42*	30	70	____ [1]
2631	Observation (O), *38–42*	30	70	____ [1]
2640	Pullman Illuminated (O), *38–42*			
	(A) Light blue, aluminum roof	30	70	____ [2]
	(B) State green, dark green roof	30	75	____ [2]
2641	Observation Illuminated (O), *38–42*			
	(A) Light blue, aluminum roof	30	70	____ [1]
	(B) State green, dark green roof	30	75	____ [1]
2642	Pullman (O), *41–42*	30	65	____ [1]
2643	Observation (O), *41–42*	30	65	____ [1]
2651	Flatcar (O), *38–42*	30	50	____ [1]
2652	Gondola (O), *38–41*	30	50	____ [1]
2653	Hopper Car (O), *38–42*			
	(A) Stephen Girard green	35	60	____ [1]
	(B) Black	60	100	____ [1]

		Good	Exc	Cond/$
2654	Tank Car (O), *38–42*			
	(A) Aluminum finish, "SUNOCO"	35	60	3
	(B) Orange, "SHELL"	35	60	3
	(C) Light gray, "SUNOCO"	35	60	3
2655	Boxcar (O), *38–42*			
	(A) Cream, maroon roof	35	65	2
	(B) Cream, tuscan roof	35	70	2
2656	Stock Car (O), *38–41*			
	(A) Light gray, red roof	45	75	1
	(B) Burnt orange, tuscan roof	75	115	1
2657	Caboose (O), *40–41*	21	33	3
2657X	Caboose (O), *40–41*	25	41	1
2659	Dump Car (O), *38–41*	40	70	1
2660	Crane (O), *38–42*	70	110	1
2672	Caboose (O27), *41–42*	19	30	1
2677	Gondola (O27), *39–41*	20	32	1
2679	Boxcar (O27), *38–42*	17	30	1
2680	Tank Car (O27), *38–42*			
	(A) Aluminum finish, "SUNOCO"	15	41	1
	(B) Orange, "SHELL"	15	41	1
2682	Caboose (O27), *38–42*	15	27	2
2682X	Caboose (O27), *38–42*	20	32	1
2717	Gondola (O), *38–42 u*	20	40	1
2719	Boxcar (O), *38–42 u*	25	50	1
2722	Caboose (O), *38–42 u*	25	50	1
2755	Tank Car (O), *41–42*	40	80	1
2757	Caboose (O), *41–42*	21	32	1
2757X	Caboose (O), *41–42*	25	36	1
2758	Automobile Boxcar (O), *41–42*	38	60	1
2810	Crane (O), *38–42*	150	205	1
2811	Flatcar (O), *38–42*	65	115	1
2812	Gondola (O), *38–42*			
	(A) Green	40	85	2
	(B) Dark orange	40	85	2
2813	Stock Car (O), *38–42*	110	220	1

		Good	Exc	Cond/$
2814	Boxcar (O), *38–42*			
	(A) Cream, maroon roof	85	205	___ [3]
	(B) Orange, brown roof	85	205	___ [3]
2814R	Refrigerator Car (O), *38–42*			
	(A) White, light blue roof, nickel plates	150	250	___ [1]
	(B) White, brown roof, no plates	375	660	___ [1]
2815	Tank Car (O), *38–42*			
	(A) Aluminum finish	80	160	___ [2]
	(B) Orange	135	250	___ [2]
2816	Hopper Car (O), *35–42*			
	(A) Red	110	205	___ [2]
	(B) Black	110	205	___ [2]
2817	Caboose (O), *36–42*			
	(A) Light red body and roof	85	140	___ [5]
	(B) Flat red, tuscan roof	145	235	___ [5]
2820	Floodlight Car (O), *38–42*			
	(A) Stamped nickel searchlight	105	225	___ [3]
	(B) Gray die-cast searchlights	105	225	___ [3]
2954	Boxcar (O), *40–42**	200	495	___ [4]
2955	Sunoco Tank Car (O), *40–42**			
	(A) "SHELL" decal	225	560	___ [4]
	(B) "SUNOCO" decal	340	780	___ [4]
2956	Hopper Car (O), *40–42**	200	530	___ [2]
2957	Caboose (O), *40–42**	190	470	___ [5]
3300	Summer Trolley Trailer (Std.), *10–13*	1400	2250	___ [1]
3651	Operating Lumber Car (O), *39–42*	20	44	___ [1]
3652	Operating Gondola (O), *39–42*	25	55	___ [1]
3659	Operating Dump Car (O), *39–42*	21	32	___ [2]
3811	Operating Lumber Car (O), *39–42*	35	70	___ [1]
3814	Operating Merchandise Car (O), *39–42*	110	215	___ [2]
3859	Operating Dump Car (O), *38–42*	42	95	___ [1]
4351	(See 14, 17, 117)			
4400	(See no. 404 Summer Trolley)			
5344	(See 700E)			
5906	(See 14, 17)			
8118	(See 14)			
8976	(See 227, 228, 229, 230, 706, 708)			

		Good	Exc	Cond/$
19050	(See 14)			
51906	(See 17)			
54078	(See 14, 114)			
62976	(See 114)			
65784	(See 12, 16, 112)			
76399	(See 16, 112)			
98237	(See 14, 114)			
342715	(See 17)			
A	Miniature Motor, *04*	50	95	[1]
A	Transformer, 40, 60 watts, *27–37*	8	23	[1]
B	New Departure Motor, *06–16*	75	135	[1]
B	Transformer, 50, 75 watts, *16–38*	6	23	[1]
C	New Departure Motor, *06–16*	100	180	[1]
D	New Departure Motor, *06–14*	100	180	[1]
E	New Departure Motor, *06–14*	100	180	[1]
F	New Departure Motor, *06–14*	100	180	[1]
G	Battery Fan Motor, *06–14*	100	180	[1]
K	Power Motor, *05*	100	180	[1]
K	Transformer, 150, 200 watts, *13–38*	29	110	[1]
L	Power Motor, *05*	50	100	[1]
L	Transformer, 50, 75 watts, *13–38*	7	22	[1]
M	Battery Motor, *15–20*	30	80	[1]
N	Transformer, 50 watts, *41–42*	7	23	[1]
Q	Transformer, 50, 75 watts, *14–15*	15	41	[1]
R	Battery Motor, *15–20*	30	75	[1]
R	Transformer, 100 watts, *38–42*	25	55	[1]
S	Transformer, 50, 80 watts, *14–17*	17	35	[1]
T	Transformer, 75, 100,150 watts, *19–28*	10	28	[1]
U	Transformer, Aladdin, *32–33*	6	16	[1]
V	Transformer, 150 watts, *39–42*	65	135	[1]
W	Transformer, 75 watts, *32–33*	7	23	[1]
Y	Battery Motor, *15–20*	40	80	[1]
Z	Transformer, 250 watts, *39–42*	155	230	[1]

Other Transformers and Rheostats made by Lionel

		Good	Exc	Cond/$
106	Rheostat, *11–14*	3	9	[1]
1029	25 watts, *36*	6	18	[1]
1030	40 watts, *35–38*	6	23	[1]
1031	Rheosat, circa 1938, *38*	2	4	[1]
1036	Rheostat, circa 1941, *40*	2	5	[1]
1037	Tranformer, 40 watts, *40–42*	7	23	[1]
1038	Rheostat, circa 1940, *40*	2	4	[1]
1039	Transformer, 35 watts, *37–40*	7	18	[1]
1040	Transformer, 60 watts, *37–39*	12	27	[1]
1041	Transformer, 60 watts, *39–42*	12	27	[1]

Track, Lockons, and Contactors

	Good	Exc	Cond/$
O Straight	0.25	0.70	[1]
O Curve	0.25	0.70	[1]
O72 Straight	1	2	[1]
O72 Curve	1	2	[1]
O27 Straight	0.10	0.45	[1]
O27 Curve	0.10	0.45	[1]
Standard Straight	0.60	2	[1]
Standard Curve	0.60	2	[1]
O Gauge Lockon	0.10	0.45	[1]
Standard Gauge Lockon	0.25	0.90	[1]
UTC Lockon	0.25	0.70	[1]
145C Contactor	0.50	2	[1]
153C Contactor	0.50	2.50	[1]

Section 2
POSTWAR 1945–1969

		Good	Exc	Cond/$
011-11	Fiber Pins (O), *46–50*	0.10	0.15	___ [1]
011-43	Insulating Pins, dz. (O), *61*	1	1.50	___ [1]
020	90° Crossover (O), *45–61*	5	9	___ [1]
020X	45° Crossover (O), *46–59*	7	10	___ [1]
022	R.C. Switches, pair (O), *45–69*	27	45	___ [1]
022-500	Adapter set (O), *57–61*	1	2.50	___ [1]
022A	R.C. Switches, pair (O), *47*	65	110	___ [1]
025	Bumper (O), *46–47*	7	17	___ [1]
026	Bumper, *48–50*	9	17	___ [1]
027C-1	Track Clips, dz. (O27), *47, 49*	0.55	0.90	___ [1]
30	Water Tower, *47–50*	60	105	___ [2]
31	Curved Track (Super O), *57–66*	1	1.50	___ [1]
31-7	Power Blade Con. (Super O), *57–61*	—	0.45	___
31-15	Ground Rail Pin (Super O), *57–66*	—	0.80	___
31-45	Power Blade Connection (Super O), *61–66*	—	0.80	___
32	Straight Track (Super O), *57–66*	0.75	2	___ [1]
32-10	Insulating Pin (Super O)	—	0.45	___
32-20	Power Blade Ins. (Super O)	—	0.25	___
32-25	Insulating Pin (Super O)	—	0.25	___
32-30	Ground Pin (Super O)	—	0.25	___
32-31	Power Pin (Super O)	—	0.25	___
32-32	Insulating Pin (Super O)	—	0.25	___
32-33	Ground Pin (Super O)	—	0.25	___
32-34	Power Pin (Super O)	—	0.25	___
32-45	Power Blade Insulators, dz. (Super O)	1	2	___ [1]
32-55	Insulating Pins, dz. (Super O)	1	2	___ [1]
33	Half Curved Track (Super O), *57–66*	1	2	___ [1]
34	Half Straight Track (Super O), *57–66*	1	2	___ [1]
35	Boulevard Lamp, *45–49*	15	32	___ [1]
36	Remote Control set (Super O), *57–66*	10	14	___ [1]
37	Uncoupling Track set (Super O), *57–66*	7	14	___ [1]
38	Water Tower, *46–47*	165	345	___ [1]
38	Accessory Adapter Track (Super O)	5	11	___ [1]
39	Operating set (Super O), *57*	4	8	___ [1]

		Good	Exc	Cond/$
39-5	Operating set (Super O), *57–58*	4	8	[1]
39-10	Operating set (Super O), *58*	4	8	[1]
39-15	Operating set, w/ blade (Super O), *57–58*	4	8	[1]
39-20	Operating set (Super O), *57–58*	4	8	[1]
39-25	Operating set (Super O), *61–66*	4	8	[1]
39-35	Operating set (Super O), *59*	4	8	[1]
40	Hookup Wire, *50–51, 53–63*	4	15	[1]
40-25	Conductor Wire, *56–59*	5	18	[1]
40-50	Cable Reel, *60–61*	4	7	[1]
41	Contactor (Super O)	0.50	1.50	[3]
41	U.S. Army Switcher, *55–57*	85	125	[1]
42	Picatinny Arsenal Switcher, *57*	150	265	[1]
042/42	Manual Switches, pr. (O), *46–59*	15	32	[1]
43	Power Track (Super O), *59–66*	4	7	[1]
44	U.S. Army Mobile Launcher, *59–62*	110	205	[1]
44-80	Missiles, *59–60*	10	18	[1]
45	U.S. Marines Mobile Launcher, *60–62*	125	250	[1]
45	Automatic Gateman, *46–49*	28	45	[1]
45N	Automatic Gateman, *45*	30	50	[1]
48	Insl. Straight Track (Super O), *57–66*	4	8	[1]
49	Insl. Curved Track (Super O), *57–66*	4	8	[1]
50	Lionel Gang Car, *54–64*	30	55	[3]
51	Navy Yard Switcher, *56–57*	100	170	[1]
52	Fire Car, *58–61*	85	170	[2]
53	Rio Grande Snowplow, *57–60*			
	(A) Backwards "a" in Rio Grande	180	295	[2]
	(B) Correctly printed "a"	355	610	[2]
54	Ballast Tamper, *58–61, 66, 68–69*	90	175	[2]
54-6446	(See 6446 or 6446-25)			
55	Tie-jector, *57–61*	135	205	[3]
55-150	Ties, *57–60*	5	15	[1]
56	Lamp Post, *46–49*	20	41	[2]
56	M&StL Mine Transport, *58*	265	495	[1]
57	AEC Switcher, *59–60*	385	690	[1]
58	Lamp Post, *46–50*	20	45	[2]
58	GN Snowplow, *59–61*	330	590	[1]
59	Minuteman Switcher, *62–63*	300	540	[1]

		Good	Exc	Cond/$
60	Lionelville Rapid Transit Trolley, *55–58*	100	185	[4]
61	Ground Lockon (Super O), *57–66*	0.25	0.45	[1]
62	Power Lockon (Super O), *57–66*	0.25	0.45	[1]
64	Street Lamp, *45–49*	21	42	[1]
65	Lionel Lines Handcar, *62–66*	150	315	[1]
68	Executive Inspection Car, *58–61*	165	255	[2]
69	Lionel Maintenance Car, *60–62*	180	310	[1]
70	Yard Light, *49–50*	23	45	[1]
71	Lamp Post, *49–59*	8	17	[2]
75	Goose Neck Lamp, set of 2, *61–63*	12	21	[1]
76	Blvd. Street Lamp, *59–66, 68–69*	10	17	[1]
80	Controller	11	20	[1]
88	Controller, *46–60*	4	7	[1]
89	Flagpole, *56–58*	18	50	[1]
90	Controller	3	5	[1]
91	Circuit Breaker, *57–60*	12	24	[1]
92	Circuit Breaker, *59–66, 68–69*	8	14	[1]
93	Water Tower, *46–49*	21	37	[1]
96C	Controller	3	5	[1]
97	Coal Elevator, *46–50*	125	215	[2]
100	Multivolt-DC/AC Trans. *58–66*		NRS	
108	Trestle set	25	36	[1]
109	Partial Trestle set		NRS	
110	Graduated Trestle set, *55–69*	10	20	[2]
111	Elevated Trestle set, *56–69*	8	18	[1]
111-100	Two Elevated Trestle Piers, *60–63*	10	18	[1]
112	R.C. Switches, pr. (Super O), *57–66*	50	70	[1]
114	Newsstand w/ horn, *57–59*	50	115	[1]
115	Passenger Station, *46–49*	175	315	[1]
118	Newsstand w/ whistle, *57–58*	45	100	[1]
119	Landscaped Tunnel, *57–58*		NRS	
120	90° Crossing (Super O), *57–66*	5	9	[1]
121	Landscaped Tunnel, *59–66*		NRS	
122	Lamp Assortment	—	205	[1]
123	Lamp Assortment, *55–59*	75	160	[1]
123-60	Lamp Assortment, *60–63*	—	205	[1]
125	Whistle Shack, *50–55*	22	40	[2]

		Good	Exc	Cond/$
128	Animated Newsstand, *57–60*	80	175	2
130	60° Crossing (Super O)	7	13	1
131	Curved Tunnel, *59–66*		NRS	
132	Passenger Station, *49–55*	45	90	3
133	Passenger Station, *57, 61–62, 66*	30	80	1
137	Passenger Station (See Prewar section), *46*			
138	Water Tower, *53–57*	75	120	1
140	Automatic Banjo Signal, *54–66*	23	37	2
142	Man. Switches, pr. (Super O), *57–66*	25	50	1
145C	Contactor, *50–60*	1	5	1
145	Automatic Gateman, *50–66*	23	37	2
147	Whistle Controller, *61–66*	1	4	1
148	Dwarf Trackside Signal, *57–60*	18	41	1
150	Telegraph Pole set, *47–50*	25	55	1
151	Auto. Semaphore, *47–69*	18	38	2
152	Auto. Crossing Gate, *45–49*	13	29	1
153	Auto. Block Control, Signal, *45–59*	14	30	2
153C	Contactor	1	5	1
154	Auto. Highway Signal, *45–69*	12	32	2
155	Blinking Light Signal w/ bell, *55–57*	30	60	1
156	Station Platform, *46–49*	33	70	1
157	Station Platform, *52–59*	20	41	1
160	Unloading Bin, *52–57*	1	2.50	1
161	Mail Pickup set, *61–63*	32	75	1
163	Single Target Block Signal, *61–69*	15	26	1
164	Log Loader, *46–50*	100	220	1
167	Whistle Controller, *45–46*	5	11	1
175	Rocket Launcher, *58–60*	110	265	1
175-50	Extra Rocket, *59–60*	5	18	1
182	Magnetic Crane, *46–49*	115	215	1
192	Oper. Control Tower, *59–60*	100	195	1
193	Industrial Water Tower, *53–55*	75	115	1
195	Floodlight Tower, *57–69*	30	55	2
195-75	Eight-Bulb Extension, *58–60*	16	28	1
196	Smoke Pellets, *46–47*	—	50	1
197	Rotating Radar Antenna, *57–59*	50	90	1

		Good	Exc	Cond/$
199	Microwave Relay Tower, *58–59*	30	75	___ [1]
202	UP Alco A unit, *57*	60	100	___ [1]
204	Santa Fe Alco AA units, *57*	100	160	___ [1]
205	Missouri Pacific Alco AA units, *57–58*	70	130	___ [2]
206	Artificial Coal, large bag, *46–68*	—	14	___ [1]
207	Artificial Coal, small bag	—	9	___ [1]
208	Santa Fe Alco AA units, *58–59*	90	180	___ [1]
209	New Haven Alco AA units, *58*	300	620	___ [1]
209	Wooden Barrels, set of 4, *46–50*	8	18	___ [1]
210	Texas Special Alco AA units, *58*	100	165	___ [1]
211	Texas Special Alco AA units, *62–66*	80	145	___ [1]
212	USMC Alco A unit, *58–59*	75	135	___ [1]
212	Santa Fe Alco AA units, *64–66*	80	140	___ [1]
212T	USMC dummy A unit, *58–59 u*	285	520	___ [1]
213	Railroad Lift Bridge, *50*		NM	___
213	M&StL Alco AA units, *64*	75	160	___ [1]
214	Plate Girder Bridge, *53–69*	8	19	___ [1]
215	Santa Fe Alco units, *65 u*			
	(A) AB units	80	160	___ [1]
	(B) Double A units (usually w/ 212T)	80	160	___ [1]
216	Burlington Alco A unit, *58*	95	300	___ [1]
216	M&StL Alco AA units, (usually w/ 213T), *64 u*	90	180	___ [1]
217	B&M Alco AB units, *59*	75	165	___ [1]
218	Santa Fe Alco units, *59–63*			
	(A) Double A units	70	155	___ [1]
	(B) AB units	70	150	___ [1]
219	Missouri Pacific Alco AA units, *59 u*	70	135	___ [1]
220	Santa Fe Alco units, *60–61*			
	(A) A unit only	75	115	___ [1]
	(B) AA units	100	205	___ [1]
221	2-6-4, 221T/221W Tender, *46–47*			
	(A) Gray die-cast body	75	135	___ [2]
	(B) Black die-cast body	75	135	___ [2]
221	Rio Grande Alco A unit, *63–64*	45	70	___ [1]
221	USMC Alco A unit, *63–64 u*	105	255	___ [1]
221	Santa Fe Alco A unit, *63–64 u*	175	385	___ [1]

		Good	Exc	Cond/$
222	Rio Grande Alco A unit (adv. cat.), *62*	35	70	[1]
223	218C Santa Fe Alco AB units, *63*	85	165	[1]
224	Steam 2-6-2, 2466T/2466W Tender, *45–46*	90	125	[1]
224	U.S. Navy Alco AB units, *60*	110	195	[1]
225	C&O Alco A unit, *60*	65	105	[1]
226	B&M Alco AB units, *60 u*	85	180	[1]
227	CN Alco A unit, *60 u*	80	145	[1]
228	CN Alco A unit, *61 u*	70	125	[1]
229	M&StL Alco units, *61–62*			
	(A) A unit only, *61*	60	110	[1]
	(B) AB units, *62*	95	205	[1]
230	C&O Alco A unit, *61*	55	90	[1]
231	Rock Island Alco A unit, *61–63*	60	105	[2]
232	New Haven Alco A unit, *62*	65	125	[1]
233	Steam 2-4-2, 233W Tender, *61–62*	50	90	[1]
235	Steam 2-4-2, 1130T/1060T Tender, *60 u*	48	110	[1]
236	Steam 2-4-2, 1130T/1050T Tender, *61–62*			
	(A) 1050T slope-back tender	18	41	[1]
	(B) 1130T tender	18	41	[1]
237	Steam 2-4-2, *63–66*			
	(A) w/ 1060T Tender	25	55	[1]
	(B) w/ 234W Tender	45	90	[1]
238	Steam 2-4-2, 234W Tender, *63–64*	55	115	[1]
239	Steam 2-4-2, 234W Tender, *65–66*	45	70	[1]
240	Steam 2-4-2, 242T, *64 u*	135	230	[1]
241	Steam 2-4-2 w/ 234W Tender, *65 u*	70	135	[1]
242	Steam 2-4-2 w/ 1060T Tender or 1062T Tender, *62–66*	20	45	[1]
243	Steam 2-4-2, 243W Tender, *60*	75	125	[1]
244	Steam 2-4-2, 244T/1130T Tender, *60–61*	25	36	[1]
245	Steam 2-4-2, w/ 1060T Tender, *59–60 u*	35	65	[1]
246	Steam 2-4-2, 244T/1130T Tender, *59–61*	25	41	[1]
247	Steam 2-4-2, 247T Tender, *59*	30	60	[1]
248	Steam 2-4-2, 1130T Tender, *58*	30	60	[1]
249	Steam 2-4-2, 250T Tender, *58*	20	45	[1]
250	Steam 2-4-2, 250T Tender, *57*	20	45	[1]

		Good	Exc	Cond/$
251	Steam 2-4-2, 1062T Tender, *66 u*			
	(A) Slope-back tender	140	270	1
	(B) 250T-type tender	140	270	1
252	Crossing Gate, *50–62*	18	26	2
253	Block Control Signal, *56–59*	15	27	1
256	Illuminated Freight Station, *50–53*	22	41	2
257	Freight Station w/ diesel horn, *56–57*	35	80	1
260	Bumper, *51–69*			
	(A) Die-cast	8	14	2
	(B) Black plastic	19	34	2
262	Highway Crossing Gate, *62–69*	25	70	1
264	Operating Fork Lift Platform, includes 6264, *57–60*	175	295	1
270	Metal Bridge (O)	18	35	1
282	Gantry Crane, *54–57*	100	175	2
282R	Gantry Crane, *56–57*	125	210	1
299	Code Transmitter Beacon set, *61–63*	65	125	1
308	Railroad Sign set, *45–49*	16	28	1
309	Yard Sign set, die-cast, *50–59*	11	20	1
310	Billboard set, *50–68*	10	18	1
313	Bascule Bridge, *46–49*	290	520	2
313-82	Fiber Pins, *46–60*	—	0.05	
313-121	Fiber Pins, dozen, *61*	—	1.50	1
314	Scale Model Girder Bridge, *45–50*	12	22	1
315	Trestle Bridge, *46–48*	50	90	1
316	Trestle Bridge, *49*	15	36	1
317	Trestle Bridge, *50–56*	15	32	1
321	Trestle Bridge, *58–64*	11	32	1
332	Arch-Under Bridge, *59–66*	20	45	1
334	Operating Dispatching Board, *57–60*	125	235	1
342	Culvert Loader, *56–58*	130	250	2
345	Culvert Unloader, *57–59*	175	315	1
346	Manual Culvert Unloader, *65*	70	155	1
347	Cannon Firing Range set, *64 u*	150	450	1
348	Manual Culvert Unloader, *66–69*	70	165	1
350	Engine Transfer Table, *57–60*	175	315	1
350-50	Transfer Table Extension, *57–60*	75	160	1

		Good	Exc	Cond/$
352	Ice Depot, includes 6352, *55–57*	130	225	3
353	Trackside Control Signal, *60–61*	14	35	1
356	Operating Freight Station, *52–57*	40	85	2
362	Barrel Loader, *52–57*	46	105	3
362-78	Wooden Barrels, *52–57*	5	14	1
364	Conveyor Lumber Loader, *48–57*	85	115	3
364C	On/Off Switch, *48–64*	3	6	1
365	Dispatching Station, *58–59*	65	115	1
375	Turntable, *62–64*	155	255	1
390C	Switch, d.p.d.t., *60–64*	5	9	1
394	Rotary Beacon, *49–53*	21	34	3
395	Floodlight Tower, *49–56*	21	37	1
397	Diesel Operating Coal Loader, *48–57*	85	140	4
400	B&O RDC Passenger, *56–58*	160	240	3
404	B&O RDC Baggage-Mail, *57–58*	180	295	1
410	Billboard Blinker, *56–58*	25	41	1
413	Countdown Control Panel, *62*	40	70	1
415	Diesel Fueling Station, *55–57*	80	125	1
419	Heliport Control Tower, *62*	150	340	1
443	Missile Launch Platform, w/ 943 Ammo Dump, *60–62*	15	36	1
445	Switch Tower, lighted, *52–57*	33	60	2
448	Missile Firing Range set, w/ 6448, *61–63*	75	135	1
450	Signal Bridge, two-track, *52–58*	27	55	2
450L	Signal Light Head	15	32	1
452	Signal Bridge, single-track, *61–63*	65	115	1
455	Operating Oil Derrick, *50–54*	130	200	3
456	Coal Ramp w/ 3456 Hopper, *50–55*	95	195	2
460	Piggyback Transportation, includes 3460, *55–57*	75	125	1
460P	Piggyback Platform, *55–57*	30	80	1
461	Platform w/ Truck and Trailer, *66*	70	140	1
462	Derrick Platform set, *61–62*	150	270	1
464	Lumber Mill, *56–60*	85	160	1
465	Sound Dispatching Station, *56–57*	50	105	1
470	Missile Launching Platform w/ 6470, *59–62*	85	115	2
480-25	Conversion Coupler, *50–60*	1	2.50	1

		Good	Exc	Cond/$
480-32	Conv. Magnetic Coupler, *61–69*	1	2.50	___¹
494	Rotary Beacon, *54–66*	25	45	___¹
497	Coaling Station, *53–58*	105	170	___²
520	Lionel Lines Box Cab Electric, *56–57*	70	120	___¹
600	MKT NW-2 Switcher, *55*			
	(A) Black frame and end rails	85	150	___²
	(B) Gray frame and yellow end rails	220	360	___²
601	Seaboard NW-2 Switcher, *56*	80	160	___¹
602	Seaboard NW-2 Switcher, *57–58*	85	165	___²
610	Erie NW-2 Switcher, *55*			
	(A) Black frame	85	145	___¹
	(B) Yellow frame	285	540	___¹
611	Jersey Central NW-2 Switcher, *57–58*	125	190	___¹
613	UP NW-2 Switcher, *58*	125	375	___¹
614	Alaska NW-2 Switcher, *59–60*			
	(A) Plastic bell, no brake	120	180	___¹
	(B) No bell, yellow brake/air	135	205	___¹
	(C) (B) w/ "BUILT BY LIONEL"	165	285	___¹
616	Santa Fe NW-2 Switcher, *61–62*	100	175	___²
617	Santa Fe NW-2 Switcher, *63*	130	250	___¹
621	Jersey Central NW-2 Switcher, *56–57*	75	145	___¹
622	Santa Fe NW-2 Switcher, *49–50*			
	(A) Large "GM" decal on cab	190	320	___²
	(B) Small "GM" decal on cab	150	295	___²
623	Santa Fe NW-2 Switcher, *52–54*	100	195	___³
624	C&O NW-2 Switcher, *52–54*	95	190	___³
625	LV GE 44-ton Switcher, *57–58*	75	130	___¹
626	B&O GE 44-ton Switcher, *59*	120	315	___¹
627	LV GE 44-ton Switcher, *56–57*	70	110	___²
628	NP GE 44-ton Switcher, *56–57*	85	145	___³
629	Burlington GE 44-ton Switcher, *56*	115	300	___¹
633	Santa Fe NW-2 Switcher, *62*	100	185	___¹
634	Santa Fe NW-2 Switcher, *63, 65–66*			
	(A) w/ safety stripes	80	160	___¹
	(B) w/o safety stripes	50	110	___¹
635	UP NW-2 Switcher, *65 u*	65	115	___¹

		Good	Exc	Cond/$
637	Steam 2-6-4, 2046W/736W Tender, *59–63*			
	(A) 2046W "LIONEL LINES" tender	60	145	[1]
	(B) 736W "PENNSYLVANIA" tender	60	145	[1]
638-2361	Van Camp's Pork & Beans Boxcar, *62 u*	24	43	[1]
645	Union Pacific NW-2 Switcher, *69*	60	115	[1]
646	Steam 4-6-4, 2046W Tdr., *54–58*	125	220	[1]
665	Steam 4-6-4, 2046W/6026W/736W	100	205	[2]
	Tender, *54–59, 66*			
670	Pennsylvania Turbine, 6-8-6, *52*		NM	
671	Steam 6-8-6, *46–49*			
	(A) 671W Tender	120	205	[3]
	(B) 2671W Tender	120	220	[3]
671R	Steam 6-8-6, 4424W/4671 Tender, *46–49*	130	280	[1]
671RR	Steam 6-8-6, 2046W-50 Tender, *52*	130	235	[1]
671S	Smoke Conversion Kit	—	39	[1]
674	Steam 2-6-4, *52*		NM	
675	Steam 2-6-2, 2466W/2466WX/6466WX			
	Tender, *47–49; 2–6–4, 52*			
	(A) 2-6-2, disc drivers	80	160	[1]
	(B) 2-6-4, spoked drivers	90	170	[1]
681	Steam Turbine, 6-8-6,	110	205	[2]
	2046W-50/2671W Tender, *50–51, 53*			
682	Steam 6-8-6, 2046W-50 Tender, *54–55*	220	390	[1]
685	Steam 4-6-4, 6026W Tender, *53*	110	220	[1]
703	Steam 4-6-4, Hudson, *46*		NM	
703-10	Special Smoke Bulb, *46*	—	32	[1]
725	Steam 2-8-4, Berkshire, *52*		NM	
726	Steam 2-8-4 Berkshire			
	(A) 2426W Tender, *46*	280	410	[2]
	(B) 2426W Tender, *47–49*	265	385	[2]
726RR	Steam 2-8-4 Berkshire, 2046W Tender, *52*	210	345	[1]
726S	Smoke Conversion Kit		NRS	
736	Steam 2-8-4, 2671WX/2046W/736W	255	370	[4]
	Tender, *50–66*			
746	N&W Steam 4-8-4, *57–60*			
	(A) Long stripe Tender	550	1050	[3]
	(B) Short stripe Tender	500	950	[3]

		Good	Exc	Cond/$
760	Curved Track, 16 sec. (O72), *54–57*	16	28	[1]
773	Steam 4-6-4 Hudson, 2426W Tender, *50*	730	1250	[4]
773	Steam 4-6-4 Hudson, *64–66*			
	(A) w/ 773W Tender	500	900	[1]
	(B) w/ 736W Tender	465	740	[1]
902	Elevated Trestle set, *60*		NRS	
909	Smoke Fluid, *57–68*	—	10	[1]
919	Artificial Grass, *46–64*	—	14	[1]
920	Scenic Display set, *57–58*	50	90	[1]
920-2	Tunnel Portals, pair, *58–59*	21	33	[1]
920-3	Green Grass, *57*	—	14	[1]
920-4	Yellow Grass, *57*	—	14	[1]
920-5	Artificial Rock, *58*	2	5	[1]
920-8	Lichen, *58*	1	5	[1]
925	Lionel Lubricant, lg. tube, *46–69*	1	5	[1]
926	Lionel Lubricant, sm. tube, *55*	1	2	[1]
926-5	Instruction Booklet, *46–48*	1	5	[1]
927	Lubricating Kit, *50–59*	10	23	[1]
928	Maint. & Lubricating Kit, *60–63*	24	50	[1]
943	Ammo Dump, *59–61*	25	45	[1]
950	U.S. Railroad Map, *58–66*	20	45	[1]
951	Farm set, *58*	15	41	[1]
952	Miniature Figure set, *58*	18	41	[1]
953	Miniature Figure set, *60–62*	20	45	[1]
954	Swimming Pool/Playground set, *59*	16	35	[1]
955	Highway set, *58*	15	37	[1]
956	Stockyard set, *59*	15	32	[1]
957	Farm Building and Animal set, *58*	20	41	[1]
958	Vehicle set, *58*	13	33	[1]
959	Barn set, *58*	15	37	[1]
960	Barnyard set, *59–61*	12	34	[1]
961	School set, *59*	12	35	[1]
962	Turnpike set, *58*	20	50	[1]
963	Frontier set, *59–60*	20	55	[1]
963-100	Frontier set w/ box for Halloween General set	95	185	[1]
964	Factory set, *59*	16	38	[1]

		Good	Exc	Cond/$
965	Farm set, *59*	15	35	1
966	Firehouse set, *58*	15	37	1
967	Post Office set, *58*	15	37	1
968	TV Transmitter set, *58*	12	32	1
969	Construction set, *60*	13	34	1
970	Ticket Booth, *58–60*	40	110	1
971	Lichen Package, *60–64*	5	9	1
972	Landscape Tree Assortment, *61–64*	7	11	1
973	Complete Landscaping set, *60–64*	10	23	1
974	Scenery set, *62–63*	5	14	1
980	Ranch set, *60*	15	41	1
981	Freight Yard set, *60*	12	37	1
982	Suburban Split Level set, *60*	12	37	1
983	Farm set, *60–61*	12	37	1
984	Railroad set, *61–62*	12	37	1
985	Freight Area set, *61*	13	35	1
986	Farm set, *62*	19	34	1
987	Town set, *62*	19	34	1
988	Railroad Structure set, *62*	19	33	1
1001	Steam 2-4-2, 1001T Tender, *48*	22	41	1
1002	Lionel Gondola, *48–52*			
	(A) Black w/ white lettering	5	9	1
	(B) Blue w/ white lettering	6	11	1
	(C) Silver w/ black lettering	100	295	1
	(E) Red w/ white lettering	110	315	1
	(D) Yellow w/ black lettering	100	305	1
	(F) Light blue w/ black lettering		NRS	
X1004	PRR Baby Ruth Boxcar, *48–52*	5	11	1
1005	Sunoco 1-D Tank Car, *48–50*	6	10	1
1007	LL SP-Type Caboose, *48–52*	4	8	1
1008	Camtrol Uncoupling Unit (O27), *57–62*	0.50	0.90	1
1008-50	Camtrol w/ track (O27), *48*	0.25	0.90	1
1010	Transformer, 35 watts, *61–66*	8	18	1
1011	Transformer, 25 watts, *48–49*	8	18	1
1012	Transformer, 35 watts, *50–54*	7	14	1
1013	Curved Track (O27), *45–69*	0.10	0.25	1
1013-17	Steel Pins (O27), *46–60*	—	0.05	

		Good	Exc	Cond/$
1013-42	Steel Pins (027), *61–68*	—	0.70	____
1014	Transformer, 40 watts, *55*	11	22	____[1]
1015	Transformer, 45 watts, *56–60*	8	23	____[1]
1016	Transformer, 35 watts, *59–60*	6	22	____[1]
1018	Straight Track (027), *45–69*	0.15	0.35	____[1]
1018	½ Straight Track (027), *55–69*	0.15	0.35	____[1]
1019	R.C. Track set (027), *46–48*	2	7	____[1]
1020	90° Crossing (027), *55–69*	2	5	____[1]
1021	90° Crossing (027), *45–54*	2	5	____[1]
1022	Man. Switches, pr. (027), *53–69*	10	18	____[1]
1023	45° Crossing (027), *56–69*	2	5	____[1]
1024	Man. Switches, pr. (027), *46–52*	7	14	____[1]
1025	Illuminated Bumper (027), *46–47*	6	13	____[1]
1025	Transformer, 45 watts, *61–69*	12	23	____[1]
1026	Transformer, 25 watts, *61–64*	5	13	____[1]
1032	Transformer, 75 watts, *48*	25	45	____[1]
1033	Transformer, 90 watts, *48–56*	27	45	____[2]
1034	Transformer, 75 watts, *48–54*	17	30	____[1]
1035	Transformer, 60 watts, *47*	22	41	____[1]
1037	Transformer, 40 watts, *46–47*	10	25	____[1]
1041	Transformer, 60 watts, *45–46*	13	25	____[1]
1042	Transformer, 75 watts, *47–48*	18	43	____[1]
1043	Transformer			
	(A) 50 watts, black, *53–57*	13	24	____[1]
	(B) 60 watts, ivory, *57–58*	55	105	____[1]
1044	Transformer, 90 watts, *57–69*	40	70	____[1]
1045	Operating Watchman, *46–50*	15	41	____[1]
1047	Operating Switchman, *59–61*	50	155	____[1]
1050	Steam 0-4-0, 1050 Tender, *59 u*	55	155	____[1]
1053	Transformer, 60 watts, *56–60*	18	37	____[1]
1055	Texas Special Alco A unit (adv. cat.), *59–60*	35	60	____[1]
1060	Steam 2-4-2, 1050T/1060T Tender (adv. cat.), *60–62*	12	28	____[1]
1061	Steam 0-4-0, 1061T Tender, *64; 2–4–2, 69*			
	(A) Slope-back "LIONEL LINES"	13	30	____[1]
	(B) 1130T "SOUTHERN PACIFIC"	13	30	____[1]

		Good	Exc	Cond/$
1062	Steam 2-4-2, 1062T Tender, *63–64*			
	(A) 0-4-0 wheel arrangement	12	27	[1]
	(B) 2-4-2 wheel arrangement	12	27	[1]
1063	Transformer, 75 watts, *60–64*	16	45	[1]
1065	Union Pacific Alco A unit (adv. cat.), *61*	33	75	[1]
1066	Union Pacific Alco A unit, *64 u*	50	90	[1]
1073	Transformer, 60 watts, *61–66*	18	45	[1]
1101	Steam 2-4-2, 1001T Tender, *48*	20	38	[1]
1101	Transformer, 25 watts, *48*	8	14	[1]
1110	Steam 2-4-2, 1001T Tender, *49, 51–52*	15	27	[1]
1120	Steam 2-4-2, 1001T Tender, *50*	15	27	[1]
1121	R.C. Switches, pr. (O27), *46–51*	12	27	[1]
1122	R.C. Switches, pr. (O27), *52–53*	12	28	[2]
1122E	R.C. Switches, pr. (O27), *53–69*	15	32	[1]
1122-34	R.C. Switches, pair, *52–53*	14	34	[1]
1122-500	Gauge Adapter (O27), *57–66*	0.25	0.90	[1]
1130	Steam 2-4-2, 6066T/1130T Tender, *53–54*			
	(A) Plastic body	20	36	[1]
	(B) Die-cast body	33	65	[1]
1615	Steam 0-4-0, 1615T Tender, *55–57*			
	(A) No grab-irons	95	180	[2]
	(B) Grab-irons on chest/tender	175	320	[2]
1625	Steam 0-4-0, 1625T Tender, *58*	100	205	[1]
1640-100	Presidential Kit, *60*	60	160	[1]
1654	Steam 2-4-2, 1654W Tender, *46–47*	35	70	[1]
1655	Steam 2-4-2, 6654W Tender, *48–49*	35	70	[1]
1656	Steam 0-4-0, 6403B Tender, *48–49*	140	295	[2]
1665	Steam 0-4-0, 2403B Tender, *46*	150	320	[1]
1666	Steam 2-6-2, 2466W/2466WX Tender, *46–47*	50	120	[2]
1862	General 4-4-0, 1862T Tender, *59–62*			
	(A) Gray smoke stack	100	205	[1]
	(B) Black smoke stack	100	205	[1]
1865	Western & Atlantic Coach, *59–62*	22	39	[1]
1866	Western & Atlantic Baggage, *59–62*	22	39	[1]
1872	General 4-4-0, 1872T Tender, *59–62*	100	270	[1]
1875	Western & Atlantic Coach, *59–62*	125	220	[1]

		Good	Exc	Cond/$
1875W	W&A Coach w/ whistle, *59–62*	85	160	[1]
1876	Western & Atlantic Baggage, *59–62*	30	75	[1]
1877	Flatcar w/ fence and horses, *59–62*	40	70	[1]
1882	General 4-4-0, 1882T Tender, *60 u*	200	380	[1]
1885	Western & Atlantic Coach, *60 u*	95	250	[1]
1887	Flatcar w/ fences and horses, *60 u*	80	160	[1]
2001	Track Make-up Kit (O27), *63*		NRS	
2002	Track Make-up Kit (O27), *63*		NRS	
2003	Track Make-up Kit (O27), *63*		NRS	
2016	Steam 2-6-4, 6026W Tender, *55–56*	48	110	[1]
2018	Steam 2-6-4, *56–59, 61*			
	(A) 6026T Tender	40	70	[1]
	(B) 6026W Tender	60	105	[1]
	(C) 1130T Tender	43	75	[1]
2020	Steam 6-8-6, 2020W/6020W Tender, *46–49*	110	190	[1]
2023	Union Pacific Alco AA units, *50–51*			
	(A) Yellow body	145	255	[3]
	(B) Silver body	150	270	[3]
	(C) Gray nose and side frames		NRS	
2024	C&O Alco A, *69*	30	65	[1]
2025	Steam 2-6-2, 2-6-4, with	70	125	[1]
	2466W/6466W Tender, *47–49, 52*			
2026	Steam 2-6-2, 2-6-4, *48–49, 51–53*			
	(A) 6466W or 6466WX	60	115	[2]
	(B) 6466T or 6066T	40	75	[2]
2028	Pennsylvania GP-7, *55*			
	(A) Gold lettering	165	295	[2]
	(B) Yellow lettering	140	260	[2]
	(C) Tan frame	275	540	[2]
2029	Steam 2-6-4, 234W Tdr., *64–69*			
	(A) 243W "LIONEL LINES" tender	70	115	[1]
	(B) 243W "PENNSYLVANIA" tender	220	285	[1]
	(C) (A) w/"HAGERSTOWN, MAR..."	90	135	[1]
2031	Rock Island Alco AA units, *52–54*	135	285	[2]
2032	Erie Alco AA Units, *52–54*	115	205	[3]
2033	Union Pacific Alco AA units, *52–54*	155	275	[2]
2034	Steam 2-4-2, 6066T Tender, *52*	25	45	[1]

		Good	Exc	Cond/$
2035	Steam 2-6-4, 6466W Tender, *50–51*	60	145	___ [1]
2036	Steam 2-6-4, 6466W Tender, *50*	65	130	___ [1]
2037	Steam 2-6-4, black engine, *54–55, 57–63*			
	(A) w/ 6026T, 1130T	45	80	___ [2]
	(B) w/ 6026W, 233W, 234W	60	115	___ [2]
2037-500	Steam 2-6-4, pink engine, w/ 1130T-500 Tender, *57–58*	360	720	___ [1]
2041	Rock Island Alco AA units, *69*	60	110	___ [1]
2046	Steam 4-6-4, 2046W Tender, *50–51, 53*	125	185	___ [2]
2055	Steam 4-6-4, 2046W/ 6026W Tender, *53–55*	70	160	___ [2]
2056	Steam 4-6-4, 2046W Tender, *52*	105	195	___ [1]
2065	Steam 4-6-4, 2046W/6026W Tender, *54–56*	105	205	___ [2]
2240	Wabash F-3 AB units, *56*	425	720	___ [2]
2242	New Haven F-3 AB units, *58–59*	480	1050	___ [1]
2243	Santa Fe F-3 AB units, *55–57*	220	315	___ [2]
2243C	Santa Fe F-3 B units, *55–57*	100	230	___ [1]
2245	Texas Special F-3 AB units, *54–55*			
	(A) B unit w/ portholes, *54*	255	460	___ [2]
	(B) B unit w/o portholes, *55*	400	720	___ [2]
2257	Lionel SP-Type caboose, *47*			
	(A) Red, no stack	5	9	___ [1]
	(B) Tuscan, w/ stack	50	185	___ [1]
2257	Caboose, red w/ plastic stack	—	___	
2321	Lackawanna Train Master, *54–56*			
	(A) Gray roof	295	425	___ [5]
	(B) Maroon roof	420	680	___ [5]
2322	Virginian Train Master, *65–66*			
	(A) Unpainted blue stripe	340	610	___ [3]
	(B) Painted blue stripe	400	770	___ [3]
2328	Burlington GP-7, *55–56*	235	340	___ [3]
2329	Virginian Rectifier, *58–59*	335	650	___ [1]
2330	Pennsylvania GG-1, green, *50*	600	1050	___ [2]
2331	Virginian Train Master, *55–58*			
	(A) Black stripe/gold lettering, *55*	550	990	___ [3]
	(B) Blue stripe/yellow lettering, *56–58*	345	640	___ [3]
	(C) Blue and yellow, gray mold	650	1150	___ [3]

		Good	Exc	Cond/$
2332	Pennsylvania GG-1, *47–49*			
	(A) Black	880	1750	___ 3
	(B) Green	310	570	___ 3
2333	Santa Fe F-3 AA units, *48–49*	275	430	___ 2
2333	NYC F-3 AA units, *48–49*			
	(A) Rubber-stamped lettering	405	770	___ 1
	(B) Heat-stamped lettering	285	610	___ 1
2337	Wabash GP-7, *58*	110	235	___ 1
2338	Milwaukee Road GP-7, *55–56*			
	(A) Orange band around shell	900	1700	___ 3
	(B) Interrupted orange band	145	245	___ 3
2339	Wabash GP-7, *57*	175	305	___ 1
2340	Pennsylvania GG-1, *55*			
	(A) Tuscan	700	1200	___ 2
	(B) Dark green	570	950	___ 2
2341	Jersey Central Train Master, *56*			
	(A) High gloss orange	1000	2000	___ 1
	(B) Dull orange	950	1700	___ 1
2343	Santa Fe F-3 AA units, *50–52*	220	450	___ 4
2343C	Santa Fe F-3 B unit, *50–55*			
	(A) Screen roof vents	100	195	___ 1
	(B) Louver roof vents	100	195	___ 1
2344	NYC F-3 AA units, *50–52*	250	495	___ 3
2344C	NYC F-3 B unit, *50–55*	115	240	___ 1
2345	Western Pacific F-3 AA units, *52*	910	1450	___ 2
2346	B&M GP-9, *65–66*	150	270	___ 1
2347	C&O GP-7, *65 u*	1400	2600	___ 1
2348	M&StL GP-9, *58–59*	160	380	___ 2
2349	Northern Pacific GP-9, *59–60*	195	445	___ 2
2350	New Haven EP-5, *56–58*			
	(A) White "N" painted nose	370	680	___ 3
	(B) White "N" decal nose	215	385	___ 3
	(C) Orange "N" painted nose	900	1550	___ 3
	(D) Orange "N" decal nose	500	900	___ 3
	(E) White "N" orange paint through doors	395	750	___ 3
2351	Milwaukee Road EP-5, *57–58*	200	430	___ 1

		Good	Exc	Cond/$
2352	Pennsylvania EP-5, *58–59*			
	(A) Tuscan body	225	445	1
	(B) Chocolate brown body	220	475	1
2353	Santa Fe F-3 AA units, *53–55*	325	550	3
2354	NYC F-3 AA units, *53–55*	235	520	2
2355	Western Pacific F-3 AA units, *53*	780	1400	1
2356	Southern F-3 AA units, *54–56*	460	750	2
2356C	Southern F-3 B unit, *54–56*	160	290	1
2357	Lionel SP-Type Caboose, *47–48*			
	(A) Red w/ red stack	120	235	1
	(B) Tuscan w/ Tuscan stack	15	27	1
2358	Great Northern EP-5, *59–60*	425	900	1
2359	Boston & Maine GP-9, *61–62*	155	280	1
2360	Penn GG-1, *56–58, 61–63*			
	(A) Tuscan, 5 gold stripes	600	1250	2
	(B) Dark green, 5 gold stripes	580	1100	2
	(C) Tuscan, single gold stripe, heat-stamped lettering	490	880	2
	(D) Tuscan, single gold stripe, decal lettering	480	790	2
2363	Illinois Central F-3 AB units, *55–56*			
	(A) Black lettering	450	990	2
	(B) Brown lettering	450	990	2
2365	C&O GP-7, *62–63*	120	285	1
2367	Wabash F-3 AB units, *55*	425	860	2
2368	B&O F-3 AB units, *56*	720	1500	1
2373	CP F-3 AA units, *57*	1050	1900	1
2378	Milwaukee Road F-3 AB units, *56*			
	(A) w/ roof line stripes	1050	1600	2
	(B) w/o roof line stripes	970	1500	2
2379	Rio Grande F-3 AB units, *57–58*	520	860	2
2383	Santa Fe F-3 AA units, *58–66*	200	430	3
2400	Maplewood Pullman, green, *48–49*	60	115	1
2401	Hillside Obs., green, *48–49*	60	115	1
2402	Chatham Pullman, green, *48–49*	60	115	1
2404	Santa Fe Vista Dome, *64–65*	30	65	1
2405	Santa Fe Pullman, *64–65*	30	65	1

		Good	Exc	Cond/$
2406	Santa Fe Observation, *64–65*	30	65	[1]
2408	Santa Fe Vista Dome, *66*	35	70	[1]
2409	Santa Fe Pullman, *66*	35	70	[1]
2410	Santa Fe Observation, *66*	35	70	[1]
2411	Lionel Lines Flatcar, *46–48*			
	(A) w/ pipes, *46*	50	80	[1]
	(B) w/ logs, *47–48*	15	27	[1]
2412	Santa Fe Vista Dome, *59–63*	25	75	[1]
2414	Santa Fe Pullman, *59–63*	25	75	[1]
2416	Santa Fe Observation, *59–63*	23	55	[1]
2419	DL&W Work Caboose, *46–47*	25	55	[1]
2420	DL&W Work Caboose, w/ light, *46–48*	44	95	[1]
2421	Maplewood Pullman, *50–53*			
	(A) Gray roof	40	75	[2]
	(B) Silver roof	40	65	[2]
2422	Chatham Pullman, *50–53*			
	(A) Gray roof	36	70	[1]
	(B) Silver roof	35	65	[1]
2423	Hillside Observation, *50–53*			
	(A) Gray roof	40	70	[1]
	(B) Silver roof	35	60	[1]
2429	Livingston Pullman, *52–53*			
	(A) Gray roof	42	90	[1]
	(B) Aluminum roof, no stripe	50	115	[1]
2430	Blue Pullman, *46–47*	25	60	[1]
2431	Blue Observation, *46–47*	25	60	[1]
2432	Clifton Vista Dome, *54–58*	30	65	[2]
2434	Newark Pullman, *54–58*	30	65	[1]
2435	Elizabeth Pullman, *54–58*	35	70	[1]
2436	Mooseheart Observation, *57–58*	23	55	[1]
2436	Summit Observation, *54–56*	23	50	[2]
2440	Green Pullman, *46–47*	20	50	[1]
2441	Green Observation, *46–47*	20	50	[1]
2442	Clifton, Vista Dome, red stripe, *56*	45	90	[1]
2442	Brown Pullman, *46–48*			
	(A) Silver lettering	20	75	[1]
	(B) White lettering	25	65	[1]

		Good	Exc	Cond/$
2443	Brown Observation, *46–48*			
	(A) Silver lettering	20	75	[1]
	(B) White lettering	25	65	[1]
2444	Newark Pullman, *56*	37	75	[1]
2445	Elizabeth Pullman, *56*	75	205	[1]
2446	Summit Observation, *56*	40	90	[1]
2452	Pennsylvania Gondola, *45–47*	8	16	[1]
2452X	Pennsylvania Gondola, *46–47*	5	14	[1]
X2454	Pennsylvania Boxcar, *46*			
	(A) Brown door	75	160	[1]
	(B) Orange door	100	180	[1]
X2454	Baby Ruth Boxcar, "PRR" logo, *46–47*	8	21	[1]
2456	Lehigh Valley Hopper, *48*	8	22	[1]
2457	PRR Caboose, metal, N5, *45–47*			
	(A) Red, white lettering	15	27	[1]
	(B) Brown, white lettering	15	27	[1]
(2458)	Automobile Boxcar (O), Postwar trucks, "2758", *41–42*	38	65	[1]
X2458	Pennsylvania Boxcar, *46–48*	15	43	[1]
2460	Bucyrus Erie Crane, 12-wheel, *46–50*			
	(A) Gray cab	85	175	[2]
	(B) Black cab	35	70	[2]
2461	Transformer Car, die-cast, *47–48*			
	(A) Red transformer	40	100	[1]
	(B) Black transformer	30	75	[1]
2465	Sunoco 2-D Tank Car, *46–48*			
	(A) "GAS/SUNOCO/OILS" in diamond	40	90	[1]
	(B) "SUNOCO" in diamond	10	18	[1]
	(C) "SUNOCO" goes past diamond	10	18	[1]
2472	PRR Caboose, metal, N5, *46–47*	10	23	[1]
2481	Plainfield Pullman, yellow, *50*	100	250	[1]
2482	Westfield Pullman, yellow, *50*	100	250	[1]
2483	Livingston Observation, yellow, *50*	85	205	[1]
2521	President McKinley Obs., *62–66*	60	115	[1]
2522	President Harrison V. D., *62–66*	80	135	[1]
2523	President Garfield Pullman, *62–66*	80	135	[1]

		Good	Exc	Cond/$
2530	REA Baggage, *54–60*			
	(A) Large doors	260	420	3
	(B) Small doors	100	180	3
2531	Silver Dawn Observation, *52–60*	60	110	2
2532	Silver Range Vista Dome, *52–60*	55	95	1
2533	Silver Cloud Pullman, *52–59*	60	110	1
2534	Silver Bluff Pullman, *52–59*	60	110	1
2541	Alexander Hamilton Obs., *55–56**	90	180	2
2542	Betsy Ross Vista Dome, *55–56**	90	180	1
2543	William Penn Pullman, *55–56**	90	180	1
2544	Molly Pitcher Pullman, *55–56**	90	180	1
2550	B&O RDC Baggage/Mail, *57–58*	200	495	1
2551	Banff Park Observation, *57**	125	250	2
2552	Skyline 500 Vista Dome, *57**	125	250	2
2553	Blair Manor Pullman, *57**	200	360	1
2554	Craig Manor Pullman, *57**	150	315	1
2555	Sunoco 1-D Tank Car "2755", *46–48*	16	37	1
2559	B&O RDC Passenger, *57–58*	150	290	2
2560	Lionel Lines Crane, 8-wheel, *46–47*			
	(A) Black boom	20	50	1
	(B) Brown boom	20	50	1
	(C) Green boom	20	50	1
2561	Vista Valley Observation, *59–61**	100	225	1
2562	Regal Pass Vista Dome, *59–61**	125	295	1
2563	Indian Falls Pullman, *59–61**	125	295	1
2625	Madison Pullman, *46–47**	100	210	3
2625	Manhattan Pullman, *46–47**	100	215	1
2625	Irvington Pullman, *46–50**			
	(A) No silhouettes	95	205	1
	(B) w/ silhouettes	115	270	1
2627	Madison Pullman, *48–50**			
	(A) No silhouettes	95	205	1
	(B) w/ silhouettes	95	235	1
2628	Manhattan Pullman, *48–50**			
	(A) No silhouettes	100	205	1
	(B) w/ silhouettes	115	250	1
2671	TCA Tender, *68*	—	70	1

		Good	Exc	Cond/$
2855	SUNX 1-D Tank Car, *46–47*			
	(A) Black	65	180	___[1]
	(B) Black, "GAS/OILS" omitted	50	210	___[1]
	(C) Gray	50	185	___[1]
2856	B&O Scale Hopper Car, *46–47*		NM	___
2857	NYC Scale Caboose, *46*		NM	___
(3309)	Turbo Missile Launch Car, *63–64*			
	(A) Red body	23	50	___[1]
	(B) Olive body	100	295	___[1]
3330	Flatcar w/ Submarine Kit, *60–62*	60	135	___[1]
3330-100	Oper. Submarine Kit, *60–61*	50	90	___[1]
(3349)	Turbo Missile Launch Car, *62–65*			
	(A) Red body	25	45	___[1]
	(B) Olive drab body	75	250	___[1]
3356	Operating Horse Car only, *56–60, 64–66*	40	70	___[2]
3356	Operating Horse Car and Corral set, *56–60, 64–66*	70	125	___[1]
3356-100	(9) Black Horses, *56–59*	6	19	___[1]
3356-150	Horse Car Corral	30	75	___[1]
3357	Hydraulic Maintenance Car, *62–64*	25	55	___[1]
3359	Lionel Lines Two-bin Dump, *55–58*	20	50	___[1]
3360	Operating Burro Crane, *56–57*	120	205	___[3]
3361	Operating Log Dump Car, *55–58*	20	36	___[1]
3362	Flatcar w/ helium tanks or logs, *61–63*	14	38	___[1]
3362/3364	Log Dump Car, *65–69*	15	32	___[1]
3366	Circus Car Corral set, *59–62*	55	100	___[1]
3366	Circus Car only, *59–62*	150	240	___[1]
3366-100	(9) White Horses, *59–60*	27	55	___[1]
3370	W&A Outlaw Car, *61–64*	20	55	___[1]
3376	Bronx Zoo Car, *60–66, 69*			
	(A) Blue w/ white lettering	20	50	___[1]
	(B) Green w/ yellow lettering	35	100	___[1]
	(C) Blue w/ yellow lettering	115	290	___[1]
3386	Bronx Zoo Car (adv. cat.), *60*	25	55	___[1]
3409	Helicopter Car (adv. cat.), *61*	45	100	___[1]
3410	Helicopter Car, *61–63*	40	85	___[1]
(3413)	Mercury Capsule Car, *62–64*	65	130	___[1]

		Good	Exc	Cond/$
3419	Helicopter Car, *59–65*	45	100	___ 3
3424	Wabash Operating Boxcar, *56–58*	35	85	___ 3
3424-100	Low Bridge Signal set	10	36	___ 1
3428	U.S. Mail Oper. Boxcar, *59–60*	45	100	___ 1
3429	USMC Helicopter Car, *60*	195	410	___ 1
3434	Poultry Dispatch car, *59–60, 64–66*	50	90	___ 1
3435	Traveling Aquarium Car, *59–62*			
	(A) Gold circle	420	950	___ 2
	(B) Tank 1, Tank 2	280	770	___ 2
	(C) Gold lettering	155	305	___ 2
	(D) Yellow rubber stamp	100	225	___ 2
3444	Erie Operating Gondola, *57–59*	38	65	___ 2
3451	Operating Log Dump Car, *46–48*	15	32	___ 1
3454	PRR Operating Merchandise Car, *46–47*			
	(A) Red lettering		NRS	___
	(B) Blue lettering	65	115	___ 2
3456	N&W Operating Hopper Car, *50–55*	15	50	___ 1
3459	LL Operating Dump Car, *46–48*			
	(A) Aluminum bin	100	265	___ 2
	(B) Black bin	19	43	___ 2
	(C) Green bin	27	65	___ 2
3460	Flatcar w/ trailers, *55–57*	25	60	___ 1
3461	Lionel Operating Log Car, *49–55*			
	(A) Black car	15	36	___ 2
	(B) Green car	30	55	___ 2
3462	Automatic Milk Car, *47–48*	20	50	___ 1
3462P	Milk Car Platform	5	14	___ 1
X3464	ATSF Operating Boxcar, *49–52*	10	23	___ 1
X3464	NYC Operating Boxcar, *49–52*	10	23	___ 1
3469	LL Operating Dump Car, *49–55*	16	44	___ 2
3470	Target Launcher, *62–64*			
	(A) Dark blue car	30	70	___ 1
	(B) Light blue car	60	140	___ 1
3472	Automatic Milk Car, *49–53*	22	55	___ 2
3474	Western Pacific Boxcar, *52–53*	20	50	___ 1
3482	Automatic Milk Car, *54–55*	20	50	___ 1

		Good	Exc	Cond/$
3484	Pennsylvania Operating Boxcar, *53*			
	(A) White lettering	15	45	[2]
	(B) Gold lettering	15	45	[2]
3484-25	ATSF Operating Boxcar, *54*			
	(A) White lettering	33	90	[1]
	(B) Black lettering	33	90	[1]
3494-1	NYC Pacemaker Boxcar, *55*	40	95	[1]
3494-150	MP Operating Boxcar, *56*	55	100	[1]
3494-275	State of Maine Operating Boxcar, *56–58*	55	105	[2]
3494-550	Monon Operating Boxcar, *57–58*	120	395	[1]
3494-625	Soo Operating Boxcar, *57–58*	125	380	[1]
3509	Satellite Car, *61*	25	50	[1]
(3510)	Satellite Car (adv. cat.), *62*	40	140	[1]
3512	Fireman and Ladder Car, *59–61*			
	(A) Black rooftop ladder	60	110	[1]
	(B) Silver rooftop ladder	75	185	[1]
3519	Satellite Car, *61–64*	27	60	[2]
3520	Searchlight Car, *52–53*	25	50	[1]
3530	GM Generator Car, *56–58*			
	(A) Orange generator	65	135	[2]
	(B) Gray generator	65	135	[2]
3530-50	Searchlight w/ pole and base	30	70	[1]
3535	A E C Security Car, *60–61*	35	115	[1]
3540	Operating Radar Car, *59–60*	44	140	[2]
3545	Lionel TV Car, *61–62*	50	155	[1]
3559	Operating Coal Dump Car, *46–48*	14	34	[1]
3562-1	ATSF Operating Barrel Car, black, *54*			
	(A) Black body, black trough	75	180	[1]
	(B) Black body, yellow trough	75	180	[1]
	(C) Gray body, red lettering	75	180	[1]
3562-25	ATSF Operating Barrel Car, gray, *54*			
	(A) Red lettering	125	295	[1]
	(B) Blue lettering	20	50	[1]
3562-50	ATSF Oper. Barrel Car, yellow, *55–56*			
	(A) Painted	35	75	[1]
	(B) Unpainted	20	50	[1]

		Good	Exc	Cond/$
3562-75	ATSF Operating Barrel Car, orange, *57–58*	35	60	[1]
3619	Helicopter Boxcar, *62–64*			
	(A) Light yellow	30	80	[1]
	(B) Dark yellow	40	135	[1]
3620	Searchlight Car, *54–56*			
	(A) Gray searchlight	25	41	[2]
	(B) Orange generator/light	50	120	[2]
3650	Extension Searchlight Car, *56–59*			
	(A) Light gray	41	65	[3]
	(B) Dark gray	65	130	[3]
3656	Armour Operating Cattle Car, *49–55*			
	(A) Black letters, Armour sticker lettering	75	190	[3]
	(B) White letters, Armour sticker	35	60	[3]
	(C) No "ARMOUR" sticker, black	25	70	[3]
	(D) White lettering	25	70	[3]
3656	Stockyard w/ cattle	25	70	[1]
3662	Automatic Milk Car, *55–60, 64–66*	30	65	[1]
3665	Minuteman Operating Car, *61–64*			
	(A) Medium blue roof	75	155	[2]
	(B) Dark blue roof	55	110	[2]
3666	Minuteman Boxcar w/ missile, *64 u*	170	450	[1]
3672	Bosco Operating Boxcar, *59–60*			
	(A) Unpainted	85	220	[1]
	(B) Painted	100	250	[1]
3820	Flatcar w/ submarine, *60–62*	60	170	[1]
3830	Flatcar w/ submarine, *60–63*	50	110	[2]
3854	Operating Merchandise Car, *46–47*	180	385	[1]
3927	Lionel Lines Track Cleaner, *56–60*	46	95	[5]
3927-50	Track Cleaning Fluid, *57–69*	3	10	[1]
3927-75	Track Cleaning Pads, *57–69*	5	19	[1]
4357	PRR SP-Type Caboose, elec., *48–49*	55	150	[1]
4452	PRR Gondola, electronic, *46–49*	40	70	[1]
4454	Baby Ruth PRR Boxcar, elec., *46–49*	60	160	[1]
4457	PRR N5 Caboose, electronic, *46–47*	45	150	[1]
4681	Steam 6-8-6, electronic, *50*		NM	

		Good	Exc	Cond/$
4776-18	(See 2457, 2472)			
5159	Maintenance Kit, *63–65*	2	5	1
5159-50	Maintenance and Lube Kit, *66–69*	2	5	1
5160	Viewing Stand	50	130	1
5459	LL Dump Car, electronic, *46–49*	55	160	1
6002	NYC Gondola, *50*	4	9	1
X6004	Baby Ruth PRR Boxcar, *50*	4	7	1
6007	Lionel Lines SP-Type Caboose, *50*	3	7	1
6009	R.C. Uncoupling Track, *53–54*	1	4	1
6012	Lionel Gondola, *51–56*	2	7	1
6014	Airex Boxcar, *60 u*	25	50	2
6014	Bosco PRR Boxcar, *58*			
	(A) White body	35	60	1
	(B) Red body	4	7	1
	(C) Orange body	4	7	1
6014	Chun King Boxcar, *57 u*	60	110	1
6014	Frisco Boxcar, *57, 63–69*			
	(A) White body	4	8	1
	(B) Red body	4	7	1
	(C) White w/ coin slot	25	45	1
	(D) Orange body	20	36	1
X6014	Baby Ruth PRR Boxcar, *51–56*			
	(A) White	5	9	1
	(B) Red	10	27	1
6014-150	Wix Boxcar, *59 u*	80	145	1
6015	Sunoco 1-D Tank Car, *54–55*			
	(A) Painted tank	35	80	1
	(B) Unpainted tank	4	8	1
6017	Lionel Lines SP-Type Caboose, *51–62*	2	6	2
6017	Lionel SP-Type Caboose, *56*	14	34	1
6017-50	USMC SP-Type Caboose, *58*	20	45	1
6017-85	LL SP-Type Caboose, gray, *58*	19	43	1
6017-100	B&M SP-Type Caboose, *59, 62, 65–66*			
	(A) Purplish blue	255	475	1
	(B) Medium or light blue	10	37	1
6017-185	ATSF SP-Type Caboose, *59–60*	10	32	1
6017-200	U.S. Navy SP-Type Caboose, *60*	35	75	1

		Good	Exc	Cond/$
6017-225	ATSF SP-Type Caboose, c. 63 u	15	41	1
6017-235	ATSF SP-Type Caboose, *62*	28	50	1
6019	RCS Track set (O27), *48–66*	2	6	1
6024	Nabisco Shredded Wheat Boxcar, *57*	12	22	1
6024	RCA Whirlpool Boxcar, *57 u*	30	65	1
6025	Gulf 1-D Tank Car, *56–58*			
	(A) Gray, blue lettering	5	14	1
	(B) Orange, blue lettering	5	14	1
	(C) Black, red "GULF" emblem	5	14	1
6027	Alaska SP-Type Caboose, *59*	25	70	1
6029	Remote Control Uncoupling Track, *55–63*	1	4	1
6032	Lionel Gondola, black (O27), *52–54*	2	5	1
X6034	Baby Ruth PRR Boxcar, *53–54*			
	(A) Orange, blue lettering	5	11	1
	(B) Red, white lettering	5	11	1
	(C) Orange, black lettering	5	11	1
6035	Sunoco 1-D Tank Car, *52–53*	3	6	1
6037	Lionel Lines SP-Type Caboose, *52–54*	2	5	1
6042	Lionel Gondola, *59–61, 62–64 u*	2	5	1
6044	Airex Boxcar, orange lettering, *59–60 u*			
	(A) Medium blue	6	16	1
	(B) Teal blue	40	75	1
	(C) Dark blue/purple	80	250	1
6044-1X	Nestles/McCall's Boxcar (no lettering), *62–63 u*	450	810	1
6045	LL 2-D Tank Car (adv. cat.), *59–64*			
	(A) Gray	15	23	1
	(B) Orange	15	37	1
6045	Cities Service 2-D Tank, *60 u*	12	32	1
6047	Lionel Lines SP-Type Caboose, *62*	2	4	1
6050	Lionel Savings Bank Boxcar, *61*	12	26	1
6050	Swift Refrigerator Car, *62–63*	10	18	1
6050	Libby's Boxcar, *63 u*			
	(A) Green stems on tomatoes	18	41	1
	(B) Green stems missing	18	41	1
6057	LL SP-Type Caboose, *59–62*	3	8	1
6057-50	LL SP-Type Caboose, orange, *62*	12	23	1

		Good	Exc	Cond/$
6058	C&O SP-Type Caboose, *61*			
	(A) Blue lettering	18	45	___[1]
	(B) Black lettering	18	50	___[1]
6059	M&StL SP-Type Caboose, *61–69*			
	(A) Painted, red	11	20	___[1]
	(B) Unpainted, red	4	7	___[1]
	(C) Unpainted, maroon	6	11	___[1]
6062	NYC Gondola, w/ cable reels, *59–62*	8	12	___[1]
6062-50	NYC Gondola, w/ 2 canisters, *69*	5	18	___[1]
(6067)	Caboose (no lett.), SP-Type, *62*	3	5	___[1]
6076	ATSF Hopper, *63 u*	10	20	___[1]
6076	LV Hopper, red, black or gray body			
	(A) Gray body	7	13	___[1]
	(B) Black body	7	13	___[1]
	(C) Red body	7	13	___[1]
	(D) Yellow body	7	13	___[1]
(6076)	Hopper, no lettering, gray or yellow body			
	(A) Yellow Body	50	90	___[1]
	(B) Gray body	10	18	___[1]
6110	Steam 2-4-2, 6001T Tender, *50–51*	15	32	___[1]
(6111)	Flatcar w/ logs, *55–57*	6	13	___[1]
6112	Lionel Gondola, *56–58*			
	(A) Black body	3	7	___[1]
	(B) Blue body	4	9	___[1]
	(C) White body	11	24	___[1]
6119	DL&W Work Caboose, red, *55–56*	9	21	___[1]
6119-25	DL&W Work Caboose, orange, *56–59*	10	27	___[1]
6119-50	DL&W Caboose, brown, *56*	15	50	___[1]
6119-75	DL&W Caboose, gray, *57*	12	32	___[1]
6119-100	DL&W Work Caboose, red/gray, *57–66, 69*	12	35	___[1]
(6119-125)	Rescue Unit Work Caboose (no number), olive drab, *63–64 u.*	60	130	___[1]
(6120)	Work Caboose (no lettering), yellow (adv. cat.), *61–62*	7	23	___[1]
(6121)	Flatcar (various colors) w/ pipes, *56–57*	5	14	___[1]
6130	ATSF Work Caboose, *61, 65–69*	11	29	___[1]

		Good	Exc	Cond/$
6139	R.C. Uncoupling Track (O27), *63*	1	4	___1
6142	Lionel Gondola; green, blue or black, *63–66, 69*	2	5	___1
6149	Remote Control Uncoupling Track (O27), *64–69*	1	5	___1
(6151)	Flatcar (various colors) w/ patrol truck, *58*			
	(A) Yellow car	40	110	___1
	(B) Orange car	40	110	___1
	(C) Cream car	40	110	___1
6162	NYC Gondola, *59–68*			
	(A) Blue body	5	11	___1
	(B) Red body	43	115	___1
6162-60	Alaska Gondola, *59*	25	60	___1
6167	LL SP-Type Caboose, red, *63*	3	7	___1
(6167)	Unstamped SP-Type Caboose w/o end rails			
	(A) Red body	3	9	___1
	(B) Yellow body	10	23	___1
	(C) Brown body	15	36	___1
6167-85	UP SP-Type Caboose, *69*	10	27	___1
6175	Flatcar w/ rocket, red or black body, *58–61*			
	(A) Black car	25	65	___1
	(B) Red car	25	65	___1
6176	LV Hopper, yellow, gray or black body, *64–66, 69*			
	(A) Yellow	3	8	___1
	(B) Gray	3	8	___1
	(C) Black	3	8	___1
(6176)	Hopper (no lettering)			
	(A) Yellow	6	16	___1
	(B) Gray	5	14	___1
	(C) Olive	30	70	___1
6219	C&O Work Caboose, *60*	30	70	___1
6220	Santa Fe NW-2 Switcher, *49–50*			
	(A) Large "GM" decal on cab	125	265	___2
	(B) Small "GM" decal on cab	125	265	___2

		Good	Exc	Cond/$
6250	Seaboard NW-2 Switcher, *54–55*			
	(A) Decals	125	265	[3]
	(B) Rubber-stamped	110	255	[3]
6257	Lionel SP-Type Caboose, *48–56, 63–64*	3	7	[1]
6257-100	Lionel Lines SP-Type Caboose	6	15	[1]
6257-25	Lionel SP-Type Caboose	3	6	[1]
6257-50	Lionel SP-Type Caboose	3	5	[1]
6257X	Lionel SP-Type Caboose	13	29	[1]
6262	Flatcar w/ wheels, *56–57*			
	(A) Black, *56–57*	30	55	[1]
	(B) Red, *56*	160	405	[1]
6264	Flatcar w/ lumber for Fork Lift set, *57–60*	22	55	[1]
6311	Flatcar w/ three pipes, *55*	15	36	[1]
6315	Gulf 1-D Chemical Tank Car, *56–59, 68–69*			
	(A) Early, painted	35	65	[2]
	(B) Late, unpainted	30	55	[2]
	(C) Late, unpainted w/ built date	40	70	[2]
6315	Lionel Lines 1-D Tank Car, *63–66*	15	32	[1]
6342	NYC Gondola, *56–58, 64–66*	10	24	[1]
6343	Barrel Ramp Car, *61–62*	15	36	[1]
6346	Alcoa Quad Hopper, *56*	20	45	[1]
6352	PFE Reefer from 352 Ice Depot, *55–57*	43	95	[1]
6356	NYC Stock Car, 2 level, *54–55*	15	36	[1]
6357	Lionel SP-Type Caboose, *48–61*	7	19	[1]
6357-50	ATSF SP-Type Caboose	320	810	[1]
6361	Flatcar w/ timber, *60–61, 64–69*	25	65	[1]
6362	Truck Car w/ three trucks, *55–56*			
	(A) Shiny orange	20	45	[2]
	(B) Dull orange	85	135	[2]
6376	LL Circus Stock Car, *56–57*	30	65	[1]
(6401)	Flatcar, no load, gray	2	7	[1]
(6402)	Flatcar w/ reels or boat, *62, 64–66, 69*			
	(A) w/ reels	6	14	[1]
	(B) w/ boat	25	60	[1]

		Good	Exc	Cond/$
6404	Black Flatcar w/ brown auto, *60*			
	(A) With red auto	—	245	[1]
	(B) With yellow auto	0.05	610	[1]
	(C) With brown auto	0.05	1050	[1]
	(D) With green auto	0.05	1050	[1]
6405	Maroon Flatcar w/ trailer, *61*	15	41	[1]
(6406)	Flatcar w/ yellow auto, *61*			
	(A) Maroon w/ red auto	35	75	[1]
	(B) Maroon w/ yellow auto	70	260	[1]
	(C) Gray w/ dark brown car		435	[1]
(6407)	Flatcar w/ rocket, *63*	140	445	[1]
(6408)	Flatcar w/ pipes, *63*	11	20	[1]
(6409)	Flatcar w/ pipes, *63*	11	20	[1]
6411	Flatcar w/ logs, *48–50*	15	27	[1]
6413	Mercury Project Car, *62–63*			
	(A) Powder blue car	70	125	[1]
	(B) Aquamarine car	95	150	[1]
6414	Evans Auto Loader w/ four cars, *55–66*			
	(A) Early premium cars w/ windows, chrome bumpers and rubber tires; red, yellow, blue and white	42	95	[3]
	(B) Four cheap cars, w/o trim, two red, two yellow	300	540	[3]
	(C) Four red cars w/ gray bumpers	50	160	[3]
	(D) Four yellow cars w/ gray bumpers	150	360	[3]
	(E) Dark yellow, gray bumpers		NRS	
	(F) Dark brown, chrome bumpers		NRS	
	(G) Four green cars w/ gray bumpers	405	890	[3]
	(H) Medium green, chrome bumpers		NRS	
6415	Sunoco 3-D Tank Car, *53–55, 64–66, 69*	10	26	[2]
6416	Boat Loader Car, *61–63*	80	180	[1]
6417	PRR Porthole Caboose, *53–57*			
	(A) w/ "NEW YORK ZONE"	10	32	[2]
	(B) w/o "NEW YORK ZONE"	100	210	[2]
6417-3	(See 6417-25)			
6417-25	Lionel Lines N5C Caboose, *54*	15	37	[1]

		Good	Exc	Cond/$
6417-50	LV N5C Caboose, *54*			
	(A) Tuscan	350	900	___1
	(B) Gray	50	125	___1
6417-51	(See 6417-50)			
6417-53	(See 6417-25)			
6418	(See 214)			
6418	Flatcar w/ steel girders, *55–57*	45	90	___1
6419	DL&W Work Caboose, early frame, *48–50, 52–57*	15	35	___2
6419-25	DL&W Work Caboose, *54–55*	13	27	___1
6419-50	DL&W Work Caboose, late frame, *56–57*	15	45	___1
6419-57	(See 6419-100)			
6419-75	DL&W Work Caboose, late frame, *56–57*	15	45	___1
6419-100	N&W Work Caboose, *57–58*	45	120	___1
6420	DL&W Work Caboose, w/ light, *48–50*	30	75	___1
6424	Flatcar w/ two autos, *56–59*	22	45	___2
6425	Gulf 3-D Tank Car, *56–58*	15	37	___1
6427	Lionel Lines N5C caboose, *54–60*	12	28	___1
6427-60	Virginian N5C Caboose, *58*	120	300	___1
6427-500	PRR N5C Girls' Caboose, *57–58**	125	270	___1
6428	U.S. Mail Boxcar, *60–61, 65–66*	16	29	___1
6429	DL&W Work Caboose, AAR trucks, *63*	130	290	___1
6430	Flat. w/ Cooper-Jarrett vans, *56–58*			
	(A) Gray vans	20	55	___1
	(B) White vans	20	55	___1
6431	Flatcar w/ vans, *66*	80	205	___1
6434	Poultry Dispatch, *58–59*	35	65	___2
6436-1	LV Quad Hopper, black, *55*	15	32	___1
6436-25	LV Quad Hopper, maroon, *55–57*	16	29	___1
6436-57	(See 6436-500)			
6436-110	LV Quad Hopper, red, *63–68*			
	(A) w/o cover	18	28	___1
	(B) w/ cover and "NEW 3-55"	70	135	___1
6436-500	LV Girls' Hopper, lilac, "643657", *57–58**	75	205	___1

		Good	Exc	Cond/$
6436-1969	TCA Quad Hopper, *69*	50	75	___[1]
6437	Pennsylvania N5C Caboose, *61–68*	16	29	___[1]
6440	Flatcar with vans, *61–63*	25	85	___[1]
6440	Green Pullman, *48–49*	20	41	___[1]
6441	Green Observation, *48–49*	20	41	___[1]
6442	Brown Pullman, *49*	30	55	___[1]
6443	Brown Observation, *49*	30	55	___[1]
6445	Fort Knox Gold Reserve, *61–63*	60	125	___[1]
(6446)	N&W Quad Hopper "546446", black or gray, *54–55*	18	41	___[1]
6446-25	N&W Quad Hopper "644625", black or gray, *55–57*			
	(A) Black, white lettering	17	65	___[1]
	(B) Gray, black lettering	17	65	___[1]
6446-60	See 6436-110(B)			
6447	Pennsylvania N5C Caboose, *63*	125	315	___[1]
6448	Target Car, *61–64*			
	(A) Red, white lettering	17	35	___[1]
	(B) White, red lettering	17	35	___[1]
6452	Pennsylvania Gondola, black, *48–49*	6	16	___[1]
X6454	(A) Baby Ruth PRR Boxcar, *48*	60	180	___[1]
X6454	(B) NYC Boxcar, orange, *48*	45	140	___[1]
X6454	(C) NYC Boxcar, brown, *48*	17	50	___[1]
X6454	(D) NYC Boxcar, tan, *48*	16	28	___[1]
X6454	(E) ATSF Boxcar, *48*	15	36	___[1]
X6454	(F) SP Boxcar, *49–52*	15	41	___[1]
X6454	(G) Erie Boxcar, *49–52*	22	45	___[1]
X6454	(H) PRR Boxcar, *49–52*	22	55	___[1]
6456	Lehigh Valley Short Hopper, *48–55*			
	(A) Black	7	12	___[1]
	(B) Maroon	5	12	___[1]
	(C) Gray	15	32	___[1]
	(D) Enamel red, yellow lettering	50	110	___[1]
	(E) Enamel red, white lettering	205	460	___[1]
	(F) Enamel gray, maroon letter		NRS	___
6457	Lionel SP-Type Caboose, *49–52*	14	28	___[1]

		Good	Exc	Cond/$
6460	Bucyrus Erie black cab Crane, 8-wheel, *52–54*			
	(A) Black cab	18	50	2
	(B) Red cab	29	80	2
6460-25	Bucyrus Erie red cab Crane, 8-wheel, w/ box, *54*	40	85	1
6461	Transformer Car, *49–50*	25	70	1
6462	NYC Gondola, *49–57*			
	(A) Black	8	11	1
	(B) Green	7	16	1
	(C) Red	5	14	1
6462-500	NYC Girls' Gondola, pink, *57–58**	65	155	1
6463	Rocket Fuel 2-D Tank, *62–63*	10	37	1
6464-1	WP Boxcar, *53–54*			
	(A) Blue lettering	35	75	2
	(B) Red lettering	450	1150	2
	(C) Orange, silver lettering		NRS	
6464-25	GN Boxcar, *53–54*	39	85	1
6464-50	M&StL Boxcar, *53–56*	39	70	2
6464-75	RI Boxcar, *53–54, 69*	38	70	2
6464-100	WP Boxcar, *54–55*			
	(A) Silver body, yellow feather	60	115	1
	(B) Orange body, blue feather	355	760	1
	(C) Orange, blue feather, "1954"		NRS	
	(D) (C) w/ "6464-100"		NRS	
6464-125	NYC Boxcar, *54–56*	38	105	1
6464-150	MP Boxcar, *54–55, 57*	35	115	2
6464-175	Rock Island Boxcar, *54–55*			
	(A) Blue lettering	50	90	1
	(B) Black lettering	450	950	1
6464-200	Pennsylvania Boxcar, *54–55, 69*	70	120	1
6464-225	SP Boxcar, *54–56*	50	90	1
6464-250	WP Boxcar, *66*	90	160	1
6464-275	State of Maine Boxcar, *55, 57–59*			
	(A) Striped doors	48	85	3
	(B) Solid doors	55	135	3

6464-300 Rutland Boxcar, *55–56*

	Good	Exc	Cond/$
(A) Rubber-stamped	40	75	_____ [1]
(B) Split door	310	650	_____ [1]
(C) Solid shield	850	2250	_____ [1]
(D) Heat-stamped	50	135	_____ [1]

6464-325 B&O Sentinel Boxcar, *56*　　280　520 _____ [1]

6464-350 MKT Katy Boxcar, *56*　　115　250 _____ [1]

6464-375 Central of Georgia Boxcar, *56–57, 66*

(A) Unpainted, maroon body	45	110	_____ [2]
(B) Painted, red body	800	1550	_____ [2]

6464-400 B&O Time-saver Boxcar, *56–57, 69*

(A) Lettered "BLT 5-54"	40	100	_____ [2]
(B) Lettered "BLT 2-56"	95	230	_____ [2]

6464-425 New Haven Boxcar, *56–58*　　28　65 _____ [2]

6464-450 Great Northern Boxcar, *56–57, 66*　　60　110 _____ [2]

6464-475 B&M Boxcar, *57–60, 65–66, 68*　　33　60 _____ [2]

6464-500 Timken Boxcar, yellow and white,　　60　115 _____ [2]
charcoal lettering (Also see 6464-500 in
MPC) 57-58, *69*

6464-510 NYC Pacemaker Boxcar, *57–58*　　310　560 _____ [1]

6464-515 MKT Boxcar, *57–58*　　260　530 _____ [1]

6464-525 M&StL Boxcar, *57–58, 64–66*

(A) Red, white lettering	30	60	_____ [1]
(B) Maroon, white lettering	—	730	_____ [1]

6464-650 D&RGW Boxcar, *57–58, 66*

(A) Unpainted yellow body	50	115	_____ [1]
(B) (A) w/o black stripe	150	195	_____ [1]
(C) Painted yellow body & roof	500	900	_____ [1]

6464-700 Santa Fe Boxcar, *61, 66*　　50　115 _____ [1]

6464-725 New Haven Boxcar, *62–66, 68*

(A) Orange body	30	55	_____ [2]
(B) Black body	70	205	_____ [2]

6464-825 Alaska Boxcar, *59–60*　　115　255 _____ [1]

6464-900 NYC Boxcar, *60–66*　　45　90 _____ [1]

6464-1965 TCA Pittsburgh Boxcar, *65*　　—　245 _____ [1]

6464-1970 (See MPC)

6464-1971 (See MPC)

		Good	Exc	Cond/$
6465	Sunoco 2-D Tank Car, *48–56*	4	12	[2]
6465	Cities Service 2-D Tank, *60–62*	12	26	[1]
6465	Gulf 2-D Tank Car, *58*			
	(A) Black tank	25	60	[1]
	(B) Gray tank	10	23	[1]
6465	LL 2-D Tank Car, *59, 63–64*			
	(A) Black tank	10	27	[1]
	(B) Orange tank	5	14	[1]
6467	Bulkhead Flatcar, *56*	20	50	[1]
6468	B&O Auto Boxcar, *53–55*			
	(A) Tuscan	140	290	[1]
	(B) Blue	20	45	[1]
6468-25	NH Auto Boxcar, *56–58*			
	(A) Black "N" over white "H"	41	155	[1]
	(B) White "N" over black "H"	215	470	[1]
(6469)	Lionel Liquefied Gases Car, *63*	55	135	[1]
6470	Explosives Boxcar, *59–60*	12	31	[1]
6472	Refrigerator Car, *50–53*	20	40	[1]
6473	Horse Transport Car, *62–69*	9	24	[1]
6475	Heinz 57 Vat Car, post-factory alteration	50	90	[1]
6475	Libby's Crushed Pineapple Vat Car, *63 u*	22	65	[1]
6475	Pickles Vat Car, *60–62*	18	37	[1]
6476	LV Hopper, red, black, and gray body, *57–69*			
	(A) Red body	4	9	[1]
	(B) Gray body	4	9	[1]
	(C) Black body	4	9	[1]
6476-1	LV Hopper, gray, TTOS, *69*	25	70	[1]
6476-135	LV Hopper, yellow, *64–66, 68*	6	11	[1]
6476-160	LV Hopper, black, *69*	7	15	[1]
6476-185	LV Hopper, yellow, *69*	6	13	[1]
6477	Bulkhead Car w/ pipes, *57–58*	20	60	[1]
6480	Explosives Boxcar, red (adv. cat.), *61*	25	44	[1]
6482	Refrigerator Car, *57*	30	45	[1]
(6500)	Flatcar w/ Bonanza plane, *62, 65*			
	(A) Plane w/ red top/wings	365	700	[1]
	(B) Plane w/ white top/wings	280	485	[1]

		Good	Exc	Cond/$
(6501)	Flatcar w/ jet boat, *62–63*	65	115	[1]
(6502)	Flatcar w/ bridge girder, *62*	20	45	[1]
6511	Flatcar w/ pipes, *53–56*	16	34	[2]
(6512)	Cherry Picker Car, *62–63*	32	80	[1]
6517	LL Bay Window Caboose, *55–59*			
	(A) Underscored	30	70	[2]
	(B) Not underscored	20	55	[2]
6517-75	Erie B/W Caboose, *66*	180	425	[1]
6517-1966	TCA B/W Caboose, *66*	90	185	[1]
6518	Transformer Car, *56–58*	49	115	[1]
6519	Allis-Chalmers Flatcar, *58–61*			
	(A) Dark/medium orange base	35	70	[1]
	(B) Dull light orange base	40	100	[1]
6520	Searchlight Car, *49–51*			
	(A) Tan diesel generator	200	450	[2]
	(B) Green diesel generator	155	280	[2]
	(C) Maroon or orange diesel gen.	25	55	[2]
	(D) Orange generator, gray light	25	55	[2]
6530	Fire Fighting Car, red, *60–61*			
	(A) Red, white lettering	40	70	[1]
	(B) Black, white lettering	—	570	[1]
6536	M&StL Quad Hopper, *58–59, 63*	20	45	[1]
6544	Missile Firing Car, *60–64*			
	(A) White-lettered console	45	100	[1]
	(B) Black-lettered console	175	375	[1]
6555	Sunoco 1-D Tank Car, *49–50*	15	35	[1]
6556	MKT Stock Car, *58*	70	215	[1]
6557	Lionel SP-Type Caboose, smoke, *58–59*	80	215	[3]
6560	Bucyrus Erie Crane w/ stack, 8-wheel, *55–58, 68–69*			
	(A) Reddish-orange or black cab, early construction	65	165	[2]
	(B) Gray cab	40	75	[2]
	(C) Red cab	20	40	[2]
	(D) Dark blue (Hagerstown)	40	85	[2]
6560-25	Bucyrus Erie Crane, 8-whl., *56*	47	105	[1]

		Good	Exc	Cond/$
6561	Reel Car, *53–56*			
	(A) Orange reels	20	50	____ [2]
	(B) Gray reels	25	60	____ [2]
6562	NYC Gondola w/ canisters, black, red, or gray, *56–58*			
	(A) Gray body, 1956	15	36	____ [1]
	(B) Red body, 1956, 1958	15	36	____ [1]
	(C) Black body, 1957	15	36	____ [1]
6572	REA Refrig. Car, *58–59, 63*	47	95	____ [1]
6630	IRBM Rocket Launcher (adv. cat.), *61*	30	95	____ [1]
6636	Alaska Quad Hopper, *59–60*	15	41	____ [1]
6640	USMC Rocket Launcher, *60*	85	205	____ [1]
6646	Lionel Lines Stock Car, *57*	16	38	____ [1]
6650	IRBM Rocket Launcher, *59–63*	23	50	____ [2]
6650-80	Missile, *60*	3	9	____ [1]
6651	USMC Cannon Car, *64 u*	60	145	____ [1]
6656	Lionel Lines Stock Car, *49–55*			
	(A) With brown "ARMOUR" decal	55	105	____ [1]
	(B) Without decal	8	18	____ [1]
6657	Rio Grande SP-Type Caboose, *57–58*	50	160	____ [2]
6660	Flatcar w/ crane, *58*	30	70	____ [1]
6670	Flatcar w/ crane, *59–60*	20	65	____ [1]
6672	Santa Fe Refrigerator Car, *54–56*			
	(A) Blue lettering, two lines	25	60	____ [2]
	(B) Black lettering, two lines	22	65	____ [2]
	(C) Blue lettering, three lines	70	205	____ [2]
6736	Detroit & Mack. Quad Hopper, *60–62*	15	40	____ [2]
6800	Flatcar w/ airplane, *57–60*			
	(A) Yellow plane w/ black top	75	160	____ [2]
	(B) Black plane w/ yellow top	75	160	____ [2]
6801	Flatcar w/ boat, *57–60*			
	(A) Boat with blue hull	45	100	____ [2]
	(B) Brownish-yellow boat hull	45	100	____ [2]
	(C) Boat with white hull	45	100	____ [2]
6802	Flatcar w/ bridge, *58–59*	15	27	____ [1]
6803	Flatcar w/ tank and truck, *58–59*	70	185	____ [1]
6804	Flatcar w/ USMC trucks, *58–59*	75	190	____ [1]

		Good	Exc	Cond/$
6805	Atomic Disposal Flatcar, *58–59*	43	115	[1]
6806	Flatcar w/ USMC trucks, *58–59*	70	160	[1]
6807	Lionel Flatcar w/ boat, *58–59*	60	140	[1]
6808	Flatcar w/ USMC trucks, *58–59*	100	225	[1]
6809	Flatcar w/ USMC trucks, *58–59*	85	190	[1]
6810	Flatcar w/ trailer, *58*	21	42	[1]
6812	Track Maintenance Car, *59*			
	(A) Dark yellow-gold superstructure	18	80	[2]
	(B) Black base and gray top	18	80	[2]
	(C) Gray base, black top	18	80	[2]
	(D) Cream base and top	18	80	[2]
	(E) Light yellow base and top	18	80	[2]
6814	Lionel Rescue Caboose, *59–61*	30	105	[1]
6816	Flatcar w/ bulldozer, *59–60*			
	(A) Red car	200	360	[1]
	(B) Black car	260	590	[1]
6816-100	Allis-Chalmers Tractor, *59–60*	50	155	[1]
6817	Flatcar w/ scraper, *59–60*			
	(A) Red car	200	380	[2]
	(B) Black car	340	630	[2]
6817-100	Allis-Chalmers Scraper, *59–60*	75	180	[1]
6818	Transformer Car, *58*	23	50	[1]
6819	Flatcar w/ helicopter, *59–60*	25	65	[1]
6820	Flatcar w/ missile transport helicopter, *60–61*			
	(A) Light blue-painted flatcar	80	205	[1]
	(B) Darker blue flatcar	50	135	[1]
6821	Flatcar w/ crates, *59–60*	20	32	[1]
6822	Searchlight Car, *61–69*			
	(A) Black base, gray light	20	41	[2]
	(B) Gray base, black light	20	41	[2]
6823	Flatcar w/ IRBM missiles, *59–60*	25	55	[1]
6824	USMC Work Caboose, *60*	60	160	[1]
6825	Flatcar w/ bridge, *59–62*	20	41	[1]
6826	Flatcar w/ trees, *59–60*	50	110	[2]
6827	Flatcar w/ steam shovel, *60–63*	65	145	[1]
6827-100	Harnischfeger Shovel, *60*	55	95	[1]
6828	Flatcar w/ crane, *60–63, 66*	90	175	[1]

		Good	Exc Cond/$
6828-100	Harnischfeger Crane, *60*	47	95 ___ [1]
6830	Flatcar w/ submarine, *60–61*	50	105 ___ [1]
6844	Flatcar w/ missiles, *59–60*		
	(A) Black plastic flatcar	20	70 ___ [1]
	(B) Red plastic flatcar	300	590 ___ [1]
63132	(See 3464)		
64173	(See 6427 LL)		
65400	(See 2454 or 6454)		
81000	(See 6417 PRR)		
96743	(See 6454)		
159000	(See 3464)		
336155	(See 3361)		
477618	(See 2457 or 2472)		
536417	(See 6417 PRR)		
546446	(See 6446)		
576419	(See 6419-100)		
576427	(See 6427-500)		
641751	(See 6417-50)		
A	Transformer, 90 watts, *47–48*	25	70 ___ [1]
CTC	Lockon (O and O27), *47–69*	—	0.90 ___
ECU-1	Electronic Control Unit, *46*	22	65 ___ [1]
KW	Transformer, 190 watts, *50–65*	85	135 ___ [3]
LTC	Lockon (O and O27), *50–69*	—	5 ___ [1]
LW	Transformer, 125 watts, *55–56*	80	105 ___ [2]
OC	Curved Track (O), *45–61*	—	1.50 ___ [1]
OC½	Half Sec. Curve Track (O), *45–66*	—	1.50 ___ [1]
OCS	Curved Insulated Track (O), *46–50*		NRS ___
OS	Straight Track (O), *45–61*	—	1.50 ___ [1]
OSS	Straight Insulated Track, *46–50*		NRS ___
OTC	Lockon Track (O and O27)	—	5 ___ [1]
Q	Transformer, 75 watts, *46*	20	60 ___ [1]
R	Transformer, 110 watts, *46–47*	30	70 ___ [1]
RW	Transformer, 110 watts, *48–54*	42	80 ___ [1]
RCS	Remote Control Track (O), *45–48*	6	10 ___ [1]
SP	Smoke Pellets, bottle, *48–69*	5	14 ___ [1]
SW	Transformer, 130 watts, *61–66*	60	115 ___ [1]
TW	Transformer, 175 watts, *53–60*	90	155 ___ [1]

		Good	Exc	Cond/$
TOC	Curved Track (O), *62–66, 68–69*	—	2	___[1]
TOC½	Half Sec. Str. Trk. (O), *62–66*	—	2	___[1]
TOS	Straight Track (O), *62–69*	—	2	___[1]
UCS	Remote Control Track (O), *45–69*	7	14	___[1]
UTC	Lockon (O, O27, Standard), *45*	—	1.50	___[1]
V	Transformer, 150 watts, *46–47*	75	130	___[1]
VW	Transformer, 150 watts, *48–49*	70	145	___[1]
Z	Transformer, 250 watts, *45–47*	100	205	___[1]
ZW	Transformer, 250 watts, *48–49*	115	255	___[5]
ZW	Transformer, 275 watts, *50–66*	135	270	___[1]
No Number	SP-Type Caboose, (see 6067, 6167)	—	___	
No Number	Work Caboose, (see 6119-125, 6120)	—	___	
No Number	Flatcar (see 6401, 6402, 6406)	—	___	
No Number	Gondola (see 6142)	—	___	
No Number	Hopper (see 6176)	—	___	
No Number	Turbo Missile Car (see 3309, 3349)	—	___	
No Number	Rolling Stock (see 3413, 3510, 6111, 6121, 6151, 6407, 6408, 6409, 6469, 6500, 6501, 6502, 6512)	—	___	

Section 3
MODERN ERA 1970–1986
MPC/Fundimensions Production

		Exc	New	Cond/$
3	(See 8104, 8630, 8701)			
[4]	Midwest TCA C&NW F-3 A Unit, shell only, *77 u*		NRS	_____
[00005]	Midwest TCA Covered Quad Hopper, *78 u*		NRS	_____
[10]	METCA Jersey Central F-3 A Unit, shell only, *71 u*		NRS	_____
[303]	LOTS Stauffer Chemical 1-D Tank Car, *85 u*	60	75	_____[1]
484	(See 8587)			
491	(See 7203)			
(0511)	TCA St. Louis Baggage Car "1981", *81 u*	55	70	_____[1]
0512	Toy Fair Reefer, *81 u*	95	120	_____[1]
550	(See 8378)			
(550C)	Curved Track 31" (O), *70*	0.85	1.50	_____[1]
(550S)	Straight Track (O), *70*	0.85	1.50	_____[1]
577	(See 9562)			
578	(See 9563)			
579	(See 9564)			
580	(See 9565)			
581	(See 9566)			
582	(See 9567)			
611	(See 8100)			
634	Santa Fe NW-2, *70 u*	55	100	_____[1]
659	(See 8101)			
665E	Johnny Cash "Blue Train" 4-6-4, *71 u*		NRS	_____
672	(See 8610)			
779	(See 8215)			
0780	LRRC Boxcar, *82 u*	70	90	_____[1]
0781	LRRC Flatcar w/ trailers, *83 u*	95	120	_____[1]
0782	LRRC 1-D Tank Car, *85 u*	50	65	_____[1]
783	(See 8406)			
0784	LRRC Covered Quad Hopper, *84 u*	75	90	_____[1]
784	(See 8606)			
[1018-1979]	TCA Mortgage Burning Hi-cube Boxcar, *79 u*	40	50	_____[1]

		Exc	New	Cond/$
(1050)	New Englander set, *80–81*	175	215	___ [1]
(1051)	T&P Diesel set, *80*		NM	___
(1052)	Chesapeake Flyer set, *80*	155	175	___ [1]
(1053)	The James Gang set, *80–82*	220	240	___ [1]
(1070)	The Royal Limited set, *80*	360	405	___ [1]
(1071)	Mid Atlantic Limited set, *80*	315	350	___ [1]
(1072)	Cross Country Express set, *80–81*	295	385	___ [1]
(1076)	Lionel Clock, *76–77 u*	200	300	___ [1]
(1081)	Wabash Cannonball set, *70–72*	120	140	___ [1]
(1082)	Yard Boss set, *70*	140	195	___ [1]
(1083)	Pacemaker set, *70*	120	140	___ [1]
(1084)	Grand Trunk & Western set, *70*	140	165	___ [1]
(1085)	Santa Fe Express Diesel Freight set, *70*	195	220	___ [1]
(1085)	Santa Fe Twin Diesel set, *71*	195	220	___ [1]
(1086)	The Mountaineer set, *70*		NM	___
(1087)	Midnight Express set, *70*		NM	___
(1091)	Sears Special set, *70 u*		NRS	___
(1092)	79N97081C Sears set, *70 u*		NRS	___
(1092)	79C97105C Sears 6-unit set, *71 u*		NRS	___
(1100)	Happy Huff n' Puff, *74–75 u*	50	60	___ [1]
(1150)	L.A.S.E.R. Train set, *81–82*	180	210	___ [1]
(1151)	Union Pacific Thunder Freight set, *81–82*	175	205	___ [1]
(1153)	JCPenney Thunderball Freight set, *81 u*	185	210	___ [1]
(1154)	Reading Yard King set, *81–82*	215	240	___ [1]
(1155)	Cannonball Freight set, *82*	85	100	___ [1]
(1157)	Lionel Leisure Wabash Cannonball set, *81 u*		NRS	___
(1158)	Maple Leaf Limited set, *81*	430	475	___ [1]
(1159)	Toys "R" Us Midnight Flyer set, *81 u*	150	165	___ [1]
(1160)	Great Lakes Limited set, *81*	360	405	___ [1]
(T-1171)	Canadian National Steam Loco set, *71 u*	210	240	___ [1]
(T-1172)	Yardmaster set, *71 u*		NRS	___
(T-1173)	Grand Trunk & Western set, *71–73 u*	205	230	___ [1]
(T-1174)	Canadian National set, *71–73 u*	270	315	___ [1]
(1182)	The Yardmaster set, *71–72*	95	120	___ [1]
(1183)	The Silver Star set, *71–72*	85	110	___ [1]
(1184)	The Allegheny set, *71*	135	175	___ [1]
(1186)	Cross Country Express set, *71–72*	190	235	___ [1]

		Exc	New	Cond/$
(1187)	Illinois Central set (SSS), *71*	405	495	___[1]
(1190)	Sears Special no. 1 set, *71 u*		NRS	___
(1195)	JCPenney Special set, *71 u*		NRS	___
(1198)	Unnamed set, *71 u*		NRS	___
(1199)	Ford-Autolite Allegheny set, *71 u*	205	230	___[1]
(1200)	Gravel Gus, *75 u*		NRS	___
[1203]	NETCA B&M NW-2, shell only, *72 u*	—	65	___[1]
[1223]	LOTS Seattle & North Coast Hi-cube Boxcar, *86 u*	125	150	___[1]
(1250)	New York Central set (SSS), *72*	360	450	___[1]
(1252)	Heavy Iron set, *82–83*	110	160	___[1]
(1253)	Quicksilver Express set, *82–83*	210	255	___[1]
(1254)	Black Cave Flyer set, *82*	85	120	___[1]
(1260)	Continental Limited set, *82*	360	450	___[1]
(1261)	49N95211 Sears Black Cave Flyer set, *82 u*		NRS	___
(1262)	Toys "R" Us Heavy Iron set, *82 u*		NRS	___
(1263)	XU671-0701A JCPenney Overland Freight set, *82 u*		NRS	___
(1264)	Nibco Express set, *82 u*	185	230	___[1]
(1265)	Tappan Special set, *82 u*	145	180	___[1]
(T-1272)	Yardmaster set, *72–73 u*		NRS	___
(T-1273)	Silver Star set, *72–73 u*		NRS	___
(1280)	Kickapoo Valley & Northern set, *72*	65	85	___[1]
(1284)	Allegheny set, *72*	165	195	___[1]
(1285)	Santa Fe Twin Diesel set, *72*	110	165	___[1]
(1287)	Pioneer Dockside Switcher set, *72*	110	110	___[1]
[1287]	Midwest TCA C&NW Reefer, *84 u*		NRS	___
(1290)	Sears set, *72 u*		NRS	___
(1291)	Sears set, *72 u*		NRS	___
(1300)	Gravel Gus Junior, *75 u*		NRS	___
(1350)	Canadian Pacific set (SSS), *73*	720	900	___[1]
(1351)	Baltimore & Ohio set, *83–84*	195	235	___[1]
(1352)	Rocky Mountain Freight set, *83–84*	85	110	___[1]
(1353)	Southern Streak set, *83–85*	85	110	___[1]
(1354)	Northern Freight Flyer set, *83–85*	225	270	___[1]
(1355)	Commando Assault Train set, *83–84*	165	220	___[1]

		Exc	New	Cond/$
(1359)	Train Display Case for set 1355, *83 u*	75	100	1
(1361)	Gold Coast Limited set, *83*	590	710	1
(1362)	Lionel Leisure BN Express set, *83 u*		NRS	
(1380)	U.S. Steel Industrial Switcher set, *73–75*	65	85	1
(1381)	Cannonball set, *73–75*	65	85	1
(1382)	Yardmaster set, *73–74*	110	140	1
(1383)	Santa Fe Freight set, *73–75*	110	145	1
(1384)	Southern Express set, *73–76*	85	140	1
(1385)	Blue Streak Freight set, *73–74*	110	140	1
(1386)	Rock Island Express set, *73–74*	140	165	1
(1387)	Milwaukee Road Special set, *73*	180	250	1
(1388)	Golden State Arrow set, *73–75*	215	240	1
(1390)	Sears 7-unit set, *73 u*		NRS	
(1392)	79C95224C Sears 8-unit set, *73 u*		NRS	
(1393)	79C95223C Sears 6-unit set, *73 u*		NRS	
(1395)	JCPenney set, *73 u*		NRS	
(1400)	Happy Huff n' Puff Junior, *75 u*		NRS	
(1402)	Chessie System set, *84–85*	140	165	1
(1403)	Redwood Valley Express set, *84–85*	195	235	1
(1450)	D&RGW set (SSS), *74*	360	450	1
(1451)	Erie-Lackawanna Limited set, *84*	540	630	1
(1460)	Grand National set, *74*	250	270	1
(1461)	Black Diamond set, *74 u, 75*	110	140	1
(1463)	Coca-Cola Special set, *74 u, 75*	170	235	1
(1487)	Broadway Limited set, *74–75*	205	255	1
(1489)	Santa Fe Double Diesel set, *74–76*	165	195	1
(1492)	79N96185C Sears 7-unit set, *74 u*		NRS	
(1493)	79N96185C Sears 7-unit set, *74 u*		NRS	
(1499)	JCPenney Great Express set, *74 u*		NRS	
(1501)	Midland Freight set, *85–86*	85	110	1
(1502)	Yard Chief set, *85–86*	215	240	1
(1506)	Sears Chessie System set, *85 u*		NRS	
(1512)	JCPenney Midland Freight set, *85 u*		NRS	
(1549)	Toys "R" Us Heavy Iron set, *85–89 u*	190	—	1
(1552)	Burlington Northern Limited set, *85*	540	680	1
(1560)	North American Express set, *75*	205	250	1
(1562)	Fast Freight Flyer set, *85 u*	140	165	1

		Exc	New	Cond/$
(1577)	Liberty Special set, *75 u*	190	240	[1]
(1579)	Milwaukee Road set (SSS), *75*	360	430	[1]
(1581)	Thunderball Freight set, *75–76*	85	110	[1]
(1582)	Yard Chief set, *75–76*	130	180	[1]
(1584)	Norfolk & Western "Spirit of America" set, *75*	225	250	[1]
(1585)	75th Anniversary Special set, *75–77*	205	250	[1]
(1586)	Chesapeake Flyer set, *75–77*	165	195	[1]
(1587)	Capitol Limited set, *75*	225	250	[1]
(1594)	Sears set, *75 u*		NRS	
(1595)	79C9716C Sears 6-unit set, *75 u*		NRS	
(1602)	Nickel Plate Special set, *86–91*	165	175	[1]
(1606)	Sears Nickel Plate Special set, *86 u*		NRS	
(1608)	American Express General set, *86 u*	225	270	[1]
(1615)	Cannonball Express set, *86–90*	95	105	[1]
(1632)	Santa Fe Work Train set (SSS), *86*	225	260	[1]
(1652)	B&O Freight set, *86*	185	240	[1]
(1658)	Town House TV and Appliances set, *86 u*	90	110	[1]
(1660)	Yard Boss set, *76*	110	130	[1]
(1661)	Rock Island Line set, *76–77*	105	140	[1]
(1662)	Black River Freight set, *76–78*	85	110	[1]
(1663)	Amtrak Lake Shore Limited set, *76–77*	190	240	[1]
(1664)	Illinois Central Freight set, *76–77*	270	360	[1]
(1665)	NYC Empire State Express set, *76*	405	450	[1]
(1672)	Northern Pacific set (SSS), *76*	270	340	[1]
(1685)	True Value Freight Flyer set, *86–87 u*	90	110	[1]
(1686)	Kay Bee Toys Freight Flyer set, *86 u*		NRS	
(1693)	Toys "R" Us Rock Island Line set, *76 u*		NRS	
(1694)	Toys "R" Us Black River Freight set, *76 u*		NRS	
(1696)	Sears set, *76 u*		NRS	
(1698)	True Value Rock Island Line set, *76 u*		NRS	
(1760)	Trains n' Truckin' Steel Hauler set, *77–78*	100	110	[1]
(1761)	Trains n' Truckin' Cargo King set, *77–78*	110	195	[1]
(1762)	Wabash Cannonball, *77*	140	195	[1]
(1764)	Heartland Express set, *77*	205	250	[1]
(1765)	Rocky Mountain Special set, *77*	225	270	[1]
(1766)	B&O Budd Car set (SSS), *77*	315	360	[1]

		Exc	New	Cond/$
1776	Seaboard U36B, *74–76*	100	150	___1
1776	(See 8559, 8665, 9170)			
(1790)	Lionel Leisure Steel Hauler set, *77 u*		NRS	___
(1791)	Toys "R" Us Steel Hauler set, *77 u*		NRS	___
(1792)	True Value Rock Island Line set, *77 u*		NRS	___
(1793)	Toys "R" Us Black River Freight set, *77 u*		NRS	___
(1796)	JCPenney Cargo Master set, *77 u*		NRS	___
(1860)	Workin' on the Railroad Timberline set, *78*	65	85	___1
(1862)	Workin' on the Railroad Logging Empire set, *78*	85	110	___1
(1864)	Santa Fe Double Diesel set, *78–79*	165	195	___1
(1865)	Chesapeake Flyer set, *78–79*	165	195	___1
(1866)	Great Plains Express set, *78–79*	250	270	___1
(1867)	Milwaukee Road Limited set, *78*	295	340	___1
(1868)	M&StL set (SSS), *78*	205	250	___1
(1892)	JCPenney Logging Empire set, *78 u*		NRS	___
(1893)	Toys "R" Us Logging Empire set, *78 u*		NRS	___
(1960)	Midnight Flyer set, *79–81*	65	90	___1
(1962)	Wabash Cannonball set, *79*	100	120	___1
(1963)	Black River Freight set, *79–81*	85	100	___1
(1964)	Radio Control Express set, *79 u*		NM	___
(1965)	Smokey Mountain Line set, *79*		NRS	___
(1970)	Southern Pacific Limited set, *79 u*	450	540	___1
1970	(See 8615)			
(1971)	Quaker City Limited set, *1979*	425	475	___1
[1971-1976]	Rocky Mountain TCA Reefer, *76 u*		NRS	___
1973	TCA Bicentennial Observation Car (O27), *76 u*	40	60	___1
1973	(See 9123)			
1974	TCA Bicentennial Passenger Car (O27), *76 u*	40	60	___1
1975	TCA Bicentennial Passenger Car (O27), *76 u*	40	60	___1
1976	TCA Seaboard U36B, *76 u*	150	200	___1
[1976]	Southern TCA Florida East Coast F-3 ABA, shells only, *76 u*		NRS	___

		Exc	New	Cond/$
[1979]	IETCA Boxcar, *79 u*	—	14	___¹
[1980]	IETCA SP-Type Caboose, *80 u*	—	14	___¹
[1980]	Atlantic TCA Flatcar w/ trailers, *80 u*	25	30	___¹
1980	(See 8068, 9544)			
[1981]	IETCA Quad Hopper, *81 u*	—	14	___¹
[1981]	LCOL Boxcar, *81 u*	—	23	___¹
1981	(See 0511)			
[1982]	IETCA 3-D Tank Car, *82 u*	—	14	___¹
1982	(See 7205)			
[1983]	IETCA Reefer, *83 u*	—	14	___¹
[1983]	TTOS Phoenix 3-D Tank Car, *83 u*		NRS	___
[1983]	Great Lakes TCA Churchill Downs Boxcar, *83 u*		NRS	___
[1983]	Great Lakes TCA Churchill Downs Reefer, *83 u*		NRS	___
1983	(See 7206)			
[1984]	TTOS Sacramento Northern Boxcar, *84 u*	80	100	___¹
1984	(See 7212)			
[1984-30X]	Ft. Pitt TCA Heinz Ketchup Boxcar, *84 u*		NRS	___
[1985]	TTOS Snowbird Covered Quad Hopper, *85 u*	40	50	___¹
[1986]	IETCA Bunk Car, *86 u*	—	14	___¹
[1986]	Southern TCA Bunk Car, *86 u*	—	27	___¹
[1986]	LCOL Work Caboose, shell only, *86 u*	—	16	___¹
(1990)	Mystery Glow Midnight Flyer set, *79 u*		NRS	___
(1991)	JCPenney Wabash Cannonball Deluxe Express set, *79 u*		NRS	___
(1993)	Toys "R" Us Midnight Flyer set, *79 u*		NRS	___
2110	Graduated Trestle set (22), *70–88*	10	15	___¹
2111	Elevated Trestle set (10), *70–88*	10	15	___¹
(2113)	Tunnel Portals (2), *84–87*	10	15	___¹
(2115)	Dwarf Signal, *84–87*	13	15	___¹
(2117)	Block Target Signal, *84–87*	20	25	___¹
(2122)	Extension Bridge w/ rock piers, *76–87*	25	35	___¹
2125	Whistling Freight Shed, *71*	40	50	___¹
2126	Whistling Freight Shed, *76–87*	25	30	___¹
2127	Diesel Horn Shed, *76–87*	25	30	___¹
(2128)	Operating Switchman, *83–86*	30	35	___¹
2129	Illuminated Freight Station, *83–86*	30	35	___¹

		Exc	New	Cond/$
(2133)	Lighted Freight Station, *72–78, 80–84*	33	44	1
2140	Automatic Banjo Signal, *70–84*	20	25	1
(2145)	Automatic Gateman, *72–84*	30	45	1
(2151)	Operating Semaphore, *78–82*	20	25	1
(2152)	Automatic Crossing Gate, *70–84*	25	30	1
2154	Automatic Highway Flasher, *70–87*	20	25	1
2156	Illuminated Station Platform, *70–71*	30	40	1
2162	Automatic Crossing Gate and Signal, *70–87, 94, 96*		CP	
(2163)	Block Target Signal, *70–78*	20	25	1
(2170)	Street Lamps (3), *70–87*	15	20	1
(2171)	Gooseneck Street Lamps (2), *80–81, 83–84*	20	25	1
(2175)	Sandy Andy Gravel Loader kit, *76–79*	40	65	1
(2180)	Road Signs (16), *77–96*		CP	
(2181)	Telephone Poles (10), *77–96*		CP	
(2195)	Floodlight Tower, *70–71*	45	60	1
(2199)	Microwave Tower, *72–75*	30	40	1
(2214)	Girder Bridge, *70–71, 72 u, 73–87*	5	10	1
2256	Station Platform, *73–81*	15	20	1
[2256]	TCA Station Platform, *75 u*	25	35	1
(2260)	Illuminated Bumper, *70–71, 72 u, 73*	24	38	1
(2280)	Non-illuminated Bumpers (3), *73–84*	3	5	1
2282	Die-cast Bumpers (2), *83 u*	20	25	1
2283	Die-cast Bumpers (2), *84–96*		CP	
(2290)	Illuminated Bumpers (2), *75 u, 76–86*	10	12	1
(2292)	Station Platform, *85–87*	6	10	1
(2300)	Operating Oil Drum Loader, *83–87*	100	125	1
(2301)	Operating Sawmill, *80–84*	85	110	2
2302	Union Pacific Manual Gantry Crane, *80–82*	20	25	2
2303	Santa Fe Manual Gantry Crane, *80–81, 83 u*	20	25	1
2305	Getty Operating Oil Derrick, *81–84*	145	165	2
(2306)	Operating Ice Station w/ 6700 PFE Ice Car, *82–83*	150	200	2
(2307)	Lighted Billboard, *82–86*	20	25	1

		Exc	New	Cond/$
2308	Animated Newsstand, *82–83*	130	160	2
(2309)	Mechanical Crossing Gate, *82–92*	4	8	1
(2310)	Mechanical Crossing Gate, *73–77*	3	5	1
(2311)	Mechanical Semaphore, *82–92*	4	8	1
(2312)	Mechanical Semaphore, *73–77*	3	5	1
(2313)	Floodlight Tower, *75–86*	20	25	1
(2314)	Searchlight Tower, *75–84*	20	25	1
(2315)	Operating Coaling Station, *83–84*	125	175	1
2316	N&W Operating Gantry Crane, *83–84*	145	165	1
2317	Operating Drawbridge, *75 u, 76–81*	100	125	2
(2318)	Operating Control Tower, *83–86*	60	75	1
2319	Illuminated Watchtower, *75–78, 80*	30	35	1
2320	Flagpole kit, *83–87*	10	15	1
2321	Operating Sawmill, *84, 86–87*	100	120	1
2323	Operating Freight Station, *84–87*	80	100	1
2324	Operating Switch Tower, *84–87*	65	75	1
(2390)	Lionel Mirror, *82 u*	65	100	1
2494	Rotary Beacon, *72–74*	40	50	1
(2709)	Rico Station kit, *81–96*		CP	
2710	Billboards (5), *70–84*	4	8	1
(2714)	Tunnel, *75 u, 76–77*	40	50	1
(2717)	Short Extension Bridge, *77–87*	3	5	1
(2718)	Barrel Platform kit, *77–84*	3	5	1
(2719)	Watchman's Shanty kit, *77–87*	3	5	1
(2720)	Lumber Shed kit, *77–84, 87*	3	5	1
(2721)	Operating Log Mill kit, *78*	3	5	1
(2722)	Barrel Loader kit, *78*	3	5	1
(2729)	Water Tower kit, *85*		NM	
(2783)	Freight Station kit, *84*	7	12	1
(2784)	Freight Platform kit, *81–90*	6	9	1
(2785)	Engine House kit, *73–77*	27	36	1
(2786)	Freight Platform kit, *73–77*	4	7	1
(2787)	Freight Station kit, *73–77, 83*	7	10	1
(2788)	Coal Station kit, *75 u, 76–77*	20	35	1
(2789)	Water Tower kit, *75–77, 80*	20	25	1
(2791)	Cross Country set, *70–71*	25	35	1
(2792)	Whistle Stop set, *70–71*	25	35	1

		Exc	New	Cond/$
(2792)	Layout Starter Pak, *80–84*	10	25	1
(2793)	Alamo Junction set, *70–71*	25	35	1
(2796)	Grain Elevator kit, *76 u, 77*	60	70	1
(2797)	Rico Station kit, *76–77*	30	45	1
(2900)	Lockon, *70–96*		CP	
(2901)	Track Clips (12) (O27), *71–96*		CP	
(2905)	Lockon and Wire, *74–96*		CP	
2909	Smoke Fluid, *70–96*		CP	
2910	OTC Contactor, *84–86, 88*	4	8	1
(2911)	Smoke Pellets, *70–73*	10	15	1
2925	Lubricant, *70–71, 72 u, 73–75*	—	2	1
(2927)	Maintenance kit, *70, 78–96*		CP	
2928	Oil, *71*	—	2	1
2951	Track Layout Book, *70–86*	1	2	1
2952	Train and Accessory Manual, *70–74*	1	2	1
2953	Train and Accessory Manual, *75–86*	1	2	1
(2960)	Lionel 75th Anniversary Book, *75 u, 76*	10	20	1
(2980)	Magnetic Conversion Coupler, *70–71*	1	2	1
(2985)	The Lionel Train Book, *86–96*		CP	
3100	Great Northern 4-8-4 (FARR no. 3), *81*	510	630	3
[3764]	LOTS Kahn Boxcar, *81 u*	60	75	1
4044	Transformer, 45-watt, *70–71*	3	5	1
4045	Safety Transformer, *70–71*	3	4	1
4050	Safety Transformer, *72–79*	3	4	1
4060	AC/DC Power Master Transformer, *80–93*	15	25	1
4065	DC Hobby Transformer, *81–83*	3	4	1
4090	Power Master Transformer, *70–84*	40	55	1
4125	Transformer, 25-watt, *72*	3	4	1
4150	Trainmaster Transformer, *72–73, 75–77*	6	12	1
4250	Trainmaster Transformer, *74*	6	12	1
4449	(See 8307)			
4501	(See 8309)			
4651	Trainmaster Transformer, *78–79*	2	3	1
4690	MW Transformer, *86–89*	75	95	1
4851	DC Transformer, *85–91, 94–96*		CP	
4870	DC Hobby Transformer and Throttle Controller, *77–78*	3	4	1

		Exc	New	Cond/$
4935	(See 8150)			
(5012)	Curved Track 27", card of 4 (O27), *70–96*		CP	
(5013)	Curved Track 27" (O27), *70–78*	0.50	0.55	[1]
(5014)	Half-Curved Track 27" (O27), *70–96*		CP	
(5017)	Straight Track, card of 4 (O27), *70–96*		CP	
(5018)	Straight Track (O27), *70–78*	0.50	0.75	[1]
(5019)	Half-Straight Track (O27), *70–96*		CP	
5020	90° Crossover (O27), *70–96*		CP	
(5021)	Left Manual Switch 27" (O27), *70–96*		CP	
(5022)	Right Manual Switch 27" (O27), *70–96*		CP	
5023	45° Crossover (O27), *70–96*		CP	
(5025)	Manumatic Uncoupler, *71–72*	1	2	[1]
(5027)	Pair Manual Switches 27" (O27), *74–84*	15	25	[1]
(5030)	Track Expander set (O27), *71–84*	20	30	[1]
(5031)	Ford-Autolite Layout Expander set, *71 u*		NRS	
(5033)	Curved Track 27" (O27), *79–96*		CP	
(5038)	Straight Track (O27), *79–96*		CP	
(5041)	Insulator Pins (12) (O27), *70–96*		CP	
(5042)	Steel Pins (12) (O27), *70–96*		CP	
(5090)	Three Pair Manual Switches 27" (O27), *78–84*	60	80	[1]
(5113)	Curved Track 54" (O27), *79–96*		CP	
5121	Left Remote Switch 27" (O27), *70–96*		CP	
5122	Right Remote Switch 27" (O27), *70–96*		CP	
(5125)	Pair Remote Switches 27" (O27), *71–83*	25	35	[1]
5132	Right Remote Switch 31" (O), *80–94*	25	35	[1]
5133	Left Remote Switch 31" (O), *80–94*	25	35	[1]
(5149)	Remote Uncoupling Section (O27), *70–96*		CP	
(5193)	Three Pair Remote Switches 27" (O27), *78–83*	90	110	[1]
5484	(See 8476)			
(5500)	Straight Track (O), *71–96*		CP	
(5501)	Curved Track 31" (O), *71–96*		CP	
(5502)	Remote Uncoupling Section (O), *71–72*	8	10	[1]
(5504)	Half-Curved Track 31" (O), *83–96*		CP	
(5505)	Half-Straight Track (O), *83–96*		CP	
5520	90° Crossover (O), *71–72*	7	10	[1]

		Exc	New	Cond/$
5530	Remote Uncoupling Section (O), *81–96*		CP	
5540	90° Crossover (O), *81–96*		CP	
(5543)	Insulator Pins (12) (O), *70–96*		CP	
5545	45° Crossover (O), *83–96*		CP	
(5551)	Steel Pins (12) (O), *70–96*		CP	
(5572)	Curved Track 72" (O), *79–96*		CP	
5600	Curved Track (TT), *73–74*	1	2	[1]
5601	Curved Track, card of 4 (TT), *73–74*	6	10	[1]
5602	Curved Track Ballast, card of 4 (TT), *73–74*	6	10	[1]
5605	Straight Track (TT), *73–74*	1	2	[1]
5606	Straight Track, card of 4 (TT), *73–74*	6	10	[1]
5607	Straight Track Ballast, card of 4 (TT), *73–74*	6	10	[1]
5620	Left Manual Switch (TT), *73–74*	5	15	[1]
5625	Left Remote Switch (TT), *73–74*	10	20	[1]
5630	Right Manual Switch (TT), *73–74*	5	15	[1]
5635	Right Remote Switch (TT), *73–74*	10	20	[1]
5640	Left Switch Ballast, card of 2 (TT), *73–74*	6	10	[1]
5650	Right Switch Ballast, card of 2 (TT), *73–74*	6	10	[1]
5655	Lockon (TT), *73–74*	1	2	[1]
5660	Terminal Track w/ lockon (TT), *74*	2	4	[1]
5700	Oppenheimer Reefer, *81*	40	50	[1]
[5700]	Ozark TCA Oppenheimer Reefer, *81 u*	50	100	[1]
5701	Dairymen's League Reefer, *81*	27	32	[1]
5702	National Dairy Despatch Reefer, *81*	26	31	[1]
5703	North American Despatch Reefer, *81*	27	45	[1]
5704	Budweiser Reefer, *81–82*	47	75	[1]
5705	Ball Glass Jars Reefer, *81–82*	38	43	[1]
5706	Lindsay Brothers Reefer, *81–82*	29	34	[1]
5707	American Refrigerator Reefer, *81–82*	27	32	[1]
5708	Armour Reefer, *82–83*	25	32	[2]
5709	REA Reefer, *82–83*	33	38	[2]
5710	Canadian Pacific Reefer, *82–83*	25	30	[1]
[5710]	NETCA CP Reefer, *82 u*	25	30	[1]
[5710]	LCAC CP Reefer, *83 u*		NRS	
5711	Commercial Express Reefer, *82–83*	22	27	[1]
5712	Lionel Lines Reefer, *82 u*	200	245	[2]
5713	Cotton Belt Reefer, *83–84*	20	25	[1]

		Exc	New	Cond/$
5714	Michigan Central Reefer, *83–84*	19	29	___[1]
[5714]	LCAC Michigan Central Reefer, *85 u*		NRS	___
5715	Santa Fe Reefer, *83–84*	25	35	___[1]
5716	Central Vermont Reefer, *83–84*	25	30	___[1]
[5716]	NETCA Central Vermont Reefer, *83 u*	25	30	___[1]
5717	Santa Fe Bunk Car, *83*	27	36	___[2]
5718	(See 9849)			
5719	Canadian National Reefer, *84*	24	29	___[1]
5720	Great Northern Reefer, *84*	105	125	___[1]
5721	Soo Line Reefer, *84*	26	31	___[1]
5722	NKP Reefer, *84*	20	25	___[1]
5724	PRR Bunk Car, *84*	25	30	___[1]
[5724]	LCOL PRR Bunk Car, *84 u*	30	40	___[1]
5726	Southern Bunk Car, *84 u*	32	37	___[1]
5727	U.S. Marines Bunk Car, *84–85*	24	29	___[1]
5728	Canadian Pacific Bunk Car, *86*	20	25	___[2]
5730	Strasburg RR Reefer, *85–86*	20	30	___[1]
5731	L&N Reefer, *85–86*	20	25	___[1]
5732	Jersey Central Reefer, *85–86*	19	24	___[1]
5733	Lionel Lines Bunk Car, *86 u*	29	38	___[2]
5734	TCA REA Reefer, *85 u*	95	130	___[1]
5735	NYC Bunk Car, *85–86*	42	47	___[1]
5739	B&O Tool Car, *86*	37	42	___[1]
5745	Santa Fe Bunk Car (SSS), *86*	41	50	___[1]
5760	Santa Fe Tool Car (SSS), *86*	45	55	___[1]
5900	AC/DC Converter, *79–83*	4	6	___[1]
[6014-900]	LCCA Frisco Boxcar (O27), *75–76 u*	25	40	___[1]
6076	TTOS Santa Fe Hopper (O27), *70 u*		NRS	___
6076	LV Hopper (O27), *70 u*	20	25	___[1]
6100	Ontario Northland Covered Quad Hopper, *81–82*	30	40	___[1]
[6100]	LCAC Ontario Northland Covered Quad Hopper, *82 u*		NRS	___
6101	Burlington Northern Covered Quad Hopper, *81–82*	20	35	___[1]
[6101]	Atlantic TCA Burlington Northern Covered Quad Hopper, *82 u*	20	35	___[1]

		Exc	New	Cond/$
6102	GN Covered Quad Hopper (FARR no. 3), *81*	41	50	___[1]
6103	Canadian National Covered Quad Hopper, *81*	34	44	___[1]
6104	Southern Quad Hopper w/ coal load (FARR no. 4), *83*	60	75	___[2]
6105	Reading Operating Hopper, *82*	55	65	___[1]
6106	N&W Covered Quad Hopper, *82*	31	41	___[1]
6107	Shell Covered Quad Hopper, *82*	25	30	___[1]
6109	C&O Operating Hopper, *83*	34	50	___[1]
6110	Missouri Pacific Covered Quad Hopper, *83–84*	16	26	___[2]
6111	L&N Covered Quad Hopper, *83–84*	15	25	___[1]
[6111]	LOTS L&N Covered Quad Hopper, *83 u*	40	50	___[1]
[6111]	Southern TCA L&N Covered Quad Hopper, *83 u*	25	30	___[1]
6112	LCCA Commonwealth Edison Quad Hopper w/ coal load, *83 u*	75	90	___[1]
6113	Illinois Central Hopper (O27), *83–85*	10	15	___[1]
6114	C&NW Covered Quad Hopper, *83*	95	115	___[1]
6115	Southern Hopper (O27), *83–86*	15	20	___[1]
6116	Soo Line Ore Car, *84*	27	36	___[1]
6117	Erie Operating Hopper, *84*	38	43	___[1]
6118	Erie Covered Quad Hopper, *84*	50	55	___[1]
6122	Penn Central Ore Car, *84*	30	35	___[2]
6123	PRR Covered Quad Hopper (FARR no. 5), *84–85*	50	60	___[1]
6124	D&H Covered Quad Hopper, *84*	20	30	___[1]
[6124]	NETCA D&H Covered Quad Hopper, *84 u*	25	30	___[1]
6126	Canadian National Ore Car, *86*	23	27	___[2]
6127	Northern Pacific Ore Car, *86*	24	29	___[1]
6127	(See 5735)			
6131	Illinois Terminal Covered Quad Hopper, *85–86*	23	28	___[1]
6134	Burlington Northern 2-bay ACF Hopper (Std. O), *86 u*	150	190	___[2]

		Exc	New	Cond/$
6135	C&NW 2-bay ACF Hopper (Std. O), *86 u*	135	170	___2
6137	Nickel Plate Road Hopper (O27), *86–91*	15	20	___1
6138	B&O Quad Hopper w/ coal load, *86*	33	39	___1
6150	Santa Fe Hopper (O27), *85–86, 92 u*	12	18	___1
6177	Reading Hopper (O27), *86–90*	15	20	___1
6200	FEC Gondola w/ canisters, *81–82*	15	25	___1
6200	(See 8404)			
6201	Union Pacific Animated Gondola, *82–83*	24	34	___1
6202	WM Gondola w/ coal load, *82*	35	40	___1
(6203)	Black Cave Gondola (O27), *82*	3	5	___1
6205	CP Gondola w/ canisters, *83*	26	32	___1
6206	C&IM Gondola w/ canisters, *83–85*	20	30	___1
6207	Southern Gondola w/ canisters (O27), *83–85*	6	8	___1
6208	Chessie System Gondola w/ canisters, *83 u*	28	33	___1
6209	NYC Gondola w/ coal load (Std. O), *84–85*	42	50	___2
6210	Erie-Lackawanna Gondola w/ canisters, *84*	30	40	___1
6211	C&O Gondola w/ canisters, *84–85*	—	11	___1
[6211]	LOTS C&O Gondola w/ canisters, *86 u*	55	80	___1
6214	Lionel Lines Gondola w/ canisters, *84 u*	40	45	___1
6230	Erie-Lackawanna Reefer (Std. O), *86 u*	115	130	___1
6231	Railgon Gondola w/ coal load (Std. O), *86 u*	135	150	___2
6232	Illinois Central Boxcar (Std. O), *86 u*	130	155	___2
6233	Canadian Pacific Flatcar w/ stakes (Std. O), *86 u*	65	85	___2
6234	Burlington Northern Boxcar (Std. O), *85*	45	60	___1
6235	Burlington Northern Boxcar (Std. O), *85*	45	60	___1
6236	Burlington Northern Boxcar (Std. O), *85*	45	60	___1
6237	Burlington Northern Boxcar (Std. O), *85*	45	60	___1
6238	Burlington Northern Boxcar (Std. O), *85*	45	60	___1
6239	Burlington Northern Boxcar (Std. O), *86 u*	60	70	___2
6251	NYC Coal Dump Car, *85*	15	20	___1
6254	NKP Gondola w/ canisters, *86–91*	10	12	___1
6258	Santa Fe Gondola w/ canisters (O27), *85–86, 92 u*	—	5	___1
X6260	NYC Gondola w/ canisters, *85–86*	15	18	___1

		Exc	New	Cond/$
6272	Santa Fe Gondola w/ cable reels (SSS), *86*	20	25	[1]
6300	Corn Products 3-D Tank Car, *81–82*	25	35	[1]
6301	Gulf 1-D Tank Car, *81*	24	30	[1]
6302	Quaker State 3-D Tank Car, *81*	42	47	[1]
6304	GN 1-D Tank Car (FARR no. 3), *81*	55	65	[1]
6305	British Columbia 1-D Tank Car, *81*	46	65	[1]
6306	Southern 1-D Tank Car (FARR no. 4), *83*	60	70	[1]
6307	PRR 1-D Tank Car (FARR no. 5), *84–85*	75	90	[1]
6308	Alaska 1-D Tank Car (O27), *82–83*	26	31	[1]
6310	Shell 2-D Tank Car (O27), *83–84*	20	25	[1]
6312	C&O 2-D Tank Car (O27), *84–85*	20	30	[1]
6313	Lionel Lines 1-D Tank Car, *84 u*	50	60	[1]
6314	B&O 3-D Tank Car, *86*	40	50	[1]
6315	TCA Pittsburgh 1-D Tank Car, *72 u*	65	70	[1]
6317	Gulf 2-D Tank Car (O27), *84–85*	20	25	[1]
6323	LCCA Virginia Chemicals 1-D Tank Car, *86 u*	50	55	[1]
6325	(See 6579)			
6357	Frisco 1-D Tank Car, *83*	60	80	[2]
6401	Virginian B/W Caboose, *81*	40	50	[1]
[6401]	Sacramento-Sierra TCA Virginian B/W Caboose, *84 u*	—	36	[1]
6403	Amtrak Vista Dome Car (O27), *76–77*	30	40	[1]
6404	Amtrak Passenger Car (O27), *76–77*	30	40	[1]
6405	Amtrak Passenger Car (O27), *76–77*	30	40	[1]
6406	Amtrak Observation Car (O27), *76–77*	30	40	[1]
6410	Amtrak Passenger Car (O27), *77*	25	40	[1]
6411	Amtrak Passenger Car (O27), *77*	20	30	[1]
6412	Amtrak Vista Dome Car (O27), *77*	20	30	[1]
6420	Reading Transfer Caboose, *81–82*	15	20	[1]
6421	Joshua L. Cowen B/W Caboose, *82*	40	50	[1]
6422	DM&IR B/W Caboose, *81*	29	38	[1]
6425	Erie-Lackawanna B/W Caboose, *83–84*	35	40	[1]
6426	Reading Transfer Caboose, *82–83*	10	16	[1]
6427	Burlington Northern Transfer Caboose, *83–84*	10	18	[1]

		Exc	New	Cond/$
6428	C&NW Transfer Caboose, *83–85*	20	25	1
6430	Santa Fe SP-Type Caboose, *83–89*	6	10	1
6431	Southern B/W Caboose (FARR no. 4), *83*	50	60	1
6432	Union Pacific SP-Type Caboose, *81–82*	10	12	1
6433	Canadian Pacific B/W Caboose, *81*	60	75	1
6435	U.S. Transfer Caboose, *83–84*	10	20	1
6438	GN B/W Caboose (FARR no. 3), *81*	46	55	2
6439	Reading B/W Caboose, *84–85*	20	30	1
6441	Alaska B/W Caboose, *82–83*	40	45	1
6446-25	N&W Covered Quad Hopper, *70 u*	175	200	1
6449	Wendy's N5C Caboose, *81–82*	50	60	1
6464-500	Timken Boxcar, *70 u*	150	200	1
6464-1970	TCA Chicago Boxcar, *70 u*	125	160	1
6464-1971	TCA Disneyland Boxcar, *71 u*	205	230	1
(6476-135)	Lehigh Valley Hopper "25000" (O27), *70–71 u*		NRS	
(6478)	Black Cave SP-Type Caboose, *82*	5	10	1
6482	Nibco Express SP-Type Caboose, *82 u*	30	40	1
6483	LCCA Jersey Central SP-Type Caboose, *82 u*	30	40	1
6485	Chessie System SP-Type Caboose, *84–85*	5	10	1
6486	Southern SP-Type Caboose, *83–85*	6	8	1
6490	NKP N5C Caboose, *84 u*		NRS	
6491	Erie-Lackawanna Transfer Caboose, *85–86*	8	15	1
6493	L&C B/W Caboose, *86–87*	23	33	1
6494	Santa Fe Bobber Caboose, *85–86*	8	10	1
6496	Santa Fe Work Caboose (SSS), *86*	25	35	1
(6504)	L.A.S.E.R. Flatcar w/ helicopter (O27), *81–82*	20	30	1
(6505)	L.A.S.E.R. Radar Car, *81–82*	20	30	1
(6506)	L.A.S.E.R. Security Car, *81–82*	20	30	1
(6507)	L.A.S.E.R. Flatcar w/ cruise missile, *81–82*	20	30	1
6508	Canadian Pacific Crane Car, *81*	60	80	1
[6508]	LCOL Canadian Pacific Crane Car, *83 u*	—	41	1
(6509)	Depressed Flatcar w/ girders, *81*	75	85	2
6510	Union Pacific Crane Car, *82*	70	75	1
6515	Union Pacific Flatcar (O27), *83–84, 86*	5	10	1

		Exc	New	Cond/$
6521	NYC Flatcar w/ stakes (Std. O), *84–85*	46	60	1
6522	C&NW Searchlight Car, *83–85*	30	35	1
6524	Erie Crane Car, *84*	65	75	2
6526	U.S. Marines Searchlight Car, *84–85*	30	35	1
6529	NYC Searchlight Car, *85–86*	20	25	1
6531	Express Mail Flatcar w/ trailers, *85–86*	33	44	2
6560	Bucyrus Erie Crane Car, *71*	150	175	1
(6561)	Flatcar w/ cruise missile (O27), *83–84*	15	30	1
(6562)	Flatcar w/ fences (O27), *83–84*	15	25	1
(6564)	Flatcar w/ two U.S.M.C. tanks (O27), *83–84*	15	25	1
(6567)	LCCA ICG Crane Car "100408", *85 u*	65	85	2
(6573)	Redwood Valley Express Flatcar w/ dump bin (O27), *84–85*	8	15	1
(6574)	Redwood Valley Express Flatcar w/ crane (O27), *84–85*	8	15	1
(6575)	Redwood Valley Express Flatcar w/ fences (O27), *84–85*	8	15	1
6576	Santa Fe Flatcar w/ crane (O27), *85–86*	8	12	1
6579	NYC Crane Car, *85–86*	40	50	1
6582	TTOS Portland Flatcar w/ wood load, *86 u*	75	100	1
6585	PRR Flatcar w/ fences (O27), *86–90*	5	10	1
6587	W&ARR Flatcar w/ horses, *86 u*	20	30	1
6593	Santa Fe Crane Car (SSS), *86*	50	60	1
6670	(See 9378)			
6700	PFE Ice Car (See 2306), *82–83*			
6900	N&W E/V Caboose, *82*	80	95	2
6901	Ontario Northland E/V Caboose, *82 u*	60	80	2
6903	Santa Fe E/V Caboose, *83*	135	190	2
6904	Union Pacific E/V Caboose, *83*	115	135	1
6905	NKP E/V Caboose, *83 u*	65	85	1
6906	Erie-Lackawanna E/V Caboose, *84*	75	100	1
6907	NYC Wood-sided Caboose (Std. O), *86 u*	125	135	4
6908	PRR N5C Caboose (FARR no. 5), *84–85*	80	90	1
6910	NYC E/V Caboose, *84 u*	70	85	3
(6912)	Redwood Valley Express SP-Type Caboose, *84–85*	10	19	1
6913	Burlington Northern E/V Caboose, *85*	100	125	1

		Exc	New	Cond/$
6916	NYC Work Caboose, *85–86*	15	20	___1
6917	Jersey Central E/V Caboose, *86*	55	70	___1
6918	B&O SP-Type Caboose, *86*	10	15	___1
6919	NKP SP-Type Caboose, *86–91*	5	10	___1
6920	B&A Wood-sided Caboose (Std. O), *86 u*	105	125	___3
6921	PRR SP-Type Caboose, *86–90*	5	10	___1
6926	TCA New Orleans E/V Caboose, *86 u*	40	60	___1
7200	Quicksilver Passenger Car (O27), *82–83*	30	40	___1
7201	Quicksilver Passenger Car (O27), *82–83*	30	40	___1
7202	Quicksilver Observation Car (O27), *82–83*	30	40	___1
(7203)	N&W Dining Car "491", *82 u*	300	375	___3
(7204)	Southern Pacific Dining Car, *82 u*	350	415	___1
(7205)	TCA Denver Combination Car "1982", *82 u*	46	65	___1
(7206)	TCA Louisville Passenger Car "1983", *83 u*	46	65	___1
7207	NYC Dining Car, *83 u*	160	215	___2
(7208)	PRR Dining Car, *83 u*	145	160	___3
7210	Union Pacific Dining Car, *84*	100	125	___1
(7211)	Southern Pacific Vista Dome Car, *83 u*	280	350	___2
(7212)	TCA Pittsburgh Passenger Car "1984", *84 u*	55	70	___1
7215	B&O Passenger Car, *83–84*	50	60	___1
7216	B&O Passenger Car, *83–84*	50	60	___1
7217	B&O Baggage Car, *83–84*	50	60	___1
7220	Illinois Central Baggage Car, *85, 87*	80	100	___1
7221	Illinois Central Combination Car, *85, 87*	80	100	___1
7222	Illinois Central Passenger Car, *85, 87*	80	100	___1
7223	Illinois Central Passenger Car, *85, 87*	80	100	___1
7224	Illinois Central Dining Car, *85, 87*	80	100	___1
7225	Illinois Central Observation Car, *85, 87*	80	100	___1
7227	Wabash Dining Car (FF no. 1), *86–87*	75	90	___1
7228	Wabash Baggage Car (FF no. 1), *86–87*	70	85	___1
7229	Wabash Combination Car (FF no. 1), *86–87*	75	90	___1
7230	Wabash Passenger Car (FF no. 1), *86–87*	75	90	___1
7231	Wabash Passenger Car (FF no. 1), *86–87*	75	90	___1
7232	Wabash Observation Car (FF no. 1), *86–87*	75	90	___1
7241	W&ARR Passenger Car, *86 u*	50	60	___1
7242	W&ARR Baggage Car, *86 u*	50	60	___1
7301	Norfolk & Western Stock Car, *82*	40	50	___1

		Exc	New	Cond/$
7302	Texas & Pacific Stock Car (O27), *83–84*	15	20	1
7303	Erie Stock Car, *84*	50	60	1
7304	Southern Stock Car (FARR no. 4), *83 u*	55	60	1
7309	Southern Stock Car (O27), *85–86*	15	20	1
7312	W&ARR Stock Car (O27), *86 u*	25	30	1
7401	Chessie System Stock Car (O27), *84–85*	15	20	1
7403	LCCA LNAC Boxcar, *84 u*	30	45	1
7404	Jersey Central Boxcar, *86*	46	60	1
(7500)	Lionel 75th Anniversary U36B, *75–77*	125	150	1
7501	Lionel 75th Anniversary Boxcar, *75–77*	26	37	1
7502	Lionel 75th Anniversary Reefer, *75–77*	26	37	1
7503	Lionel 75th Anniversary Reefer, *75–77*	26	37	1
7504	Lionel 75th Anniversary Covered Quad Hopper, *75–77*	26	37	1
7505	Lionel 75th Anniversary Boxcar, *75–77*	26	37	1
7506	Lionel 75th Anniversary Boxcar, *75–77*	26	37	1
7507	Lionel 75th Anniversary Reefer, *75–77*	26	37	1
7508	Lionel 75th Anniversary N5C Caboose, *75–77*	29	38	1
7509	Kentucky Fried Chicken Reefer, *81–82*	28	33	1
7510	Red Lobster Reefer, *81–82*	26	31	1
7511	Pizza Hut Reefer, *81–82*	26	31	1
7512	Arthur Treacher's Reefer, *82*	26	31	1
7513	Bonanza Reefer, *82*	26	31	1
7514	Taco Bell Reefer, *82*	26	31	1
7515	Denver Mint Car, *81*	70	85	2
7517	Philadelphia Mint Car, *82*	65	70	1
7518	Carson City Mint Car, *83*	40	50	1
[7518]	IETCA Carson City Mint Car, *84 u*	—	36	1
7519	Toy Fair Reefer, *82 u*	70	80	1
7520	Nibco Express Boxcar, *82 u*	315	450	1
7521	Toy Fair Reefer, *83 u*	70	90	1
7522	New Orleans Mint Car, *84 u*	40	50	1
[7522]	Lone Star TCA New Orleans Mint Car w/ coin, *86 u*	—	250	1
7523	Toy Fair Reefer, *84 u*	85	95	1
7524	Toy Fair Reefer, *85 u*	100	115	1

		Exc	New	Cond/$
7525	Toy Fair Boxcar, *86 u*	100	120	1
7530	Dahlonega Mint Car, *86 u*	65	70	1
7600	Frisco "Spirit of '76" N5C Caboose, *74–76*	30	40	1
[7600]	Midwest TCA Frisco "Spirit of '76" N5C Caboose "00003", *76 u*	—	41	1
7601	Delaware Boxcar, *74–76*	20	25	1
7602	Pennsylvania Boxcar, *74–76*	25	30	1
7603	New Jersey Boxcar, *74–76*	25	30	1
7604	Georgia Boxcar, *74 u, 75–76*	25	30	1
7605	Connecticut Boxcar, *74 u, 75–76*	25	30	1
7606	Massachusetts Boxcar, *74 u, 75–76*	25	30	1
7607	Maryland Boxcar, *74 u, 75–76*	23	27	1
7608	South Carolina Boxcar, *75 u, 76*	30	40	1
7609	New Hampshire Boxcar, *75 u, 76*	50	60	1
7610	Virginia Boxcar, *75 u, 76*	175	225	1
7611	New York Boxcar, *75 u, 76*	65	90	1
7612	North Carolina Boxcar, *75 u, 76*	25	50	1
7613	Rhode Island Boxcar, *75 u, 76*	25	65	1
[7679]	VTC Boxcar, *79 u*	—	18	1
[7681]	VTC N5C Caboose, *81 u*	—	23	1
[7682]	VTC Covered Quad Hopper, *82 u*	—	27	1
[7683]	VTC Virginia Fruit Express Reefer, *83 u*	—	27	1
[7684]	VTC Vitraco Oil 3-D Tank Car, *84 u*	—	27	1
[7685]	VTC Boxcar, *85 u*	—	32	1
[7686]	VTC GP-7, *86 u*	—	115	1
7700	Uncle Sam Boxcar, *75 u*	50	55	2
7701	Camel Boxcar, *76–77*	18	23	1
7702	Prince Albert Boxcar, *76–77*	16	21	1
7703	Beechnut Boxcar, *76–77*	17	22	1
7704	Toy Fair Boxcar, *76 u*	120	130	1
7705	Canadian Toy Fair Boxcar, *76 u*	150	165	1
7706	Sir Walter Raleigh Boxcar, *77–78*	21	31	1
7707	White Owl Boxcar, *77–78*	21	31	1
7708	Winston Boxcar, *77–78*	21	31	1
7709	Salem Boxcar, *78*	21	31	1
7710	Mail Pouch Boxcar, *78*	21	31	1
7711	El Producto Boxcar, *78*	21	31	1

		Exc	New	Cond/$
7712	Santa Fe Boxcar (FARR no. 1), *79*	40	45	[1]
[7780]	TCA Museum Boxcar, *80 u*	—	27	[1]
[7781]	TCA Hafner Boxcar, *81 u*	—	27	[1]
[7782]	TCA Carlisle & Finch Boxcar, *82 u*	—	27	[1]
[7783]	TCA Ives Boxcar, *83 u*	—	27	[1]
[7784]	TCA Voltamp Boxcar, *84 u*	—	27	[1]
[7785]	TCA Hoge Boxcar, *85 u*	—	27	[1]
7800	Pepsi Boxcar, *76 u, 77*	55	65	[1]
7801	A&W Boxcar, *76 u, 77*	20	30	[1]
7802	Canada Dry Boxcar, *76 u, 77*	20	30	[1]
7803	Trains n' Truckin' Boxcar, *77 u*	25	31	[2]
7806	Season's Greetings Boxcar, *76 u*	70	90	[1]
7807	Toy Fair Boxcar, *77 u*	75	100	[1]
7808	Northern Pacific Stock Car, *77*	50	60	[1]
7809	Vernors Boxcar, *77 u, 78*	20	30	[1]
7810	Orange Crush Boxcar, *77 u, 78*	20	30	[1]
7811	Dr Pepper Boxcar, *77 u, 78*	20	30	[1]
7812	TCA Houston Stock Car, *77 u*	19	29	[1]
7813	Season's Greetings Boxcar, *77 u*	70	95	[1]
7814	Season's Greetings Boxcar, *78 u*	75	100	[1]
7815	Toy Fair Boxcar, *78 u*	75	100	[1]
7816	Toy Fair Boxcar, *79 u*	75	100	[1]
7817	Toy Fair Boxcar, *80 u*	115	140	[1]
7900	D&RGW Operating Cowboy Car (027), *82–83*	25	30	[1]
7901	Lionel Lines Cop and Hobo Car (027), *82–83*	30	35	[1]
7902	Santa Fe Boxcar (027), *82–85*	6	10	[1]
7903	Rock Island Boxcar (027), *83*	6	10	[1]
7904	San Diego Zoo Giraffe Car (027), *83–84*	44	55	[1]
(7905)	Black Cave Boxcar (027), *82*	7	10	[1]
7908	Tappan Boxcar (027), *82 u*	50	65	[1]
7909	L&N Boxcar (027), *83–84*	40	50	[1]
7910	Chessie System Boxcar (027), *84–85*	20	25	[1]
7912	Toys "R" Us Giraffe Car (027), *82–84 u*	75	90	[1]
7913	Turtleback Zoo Giraffe Car (027), *85–86*	35	40	[1]
7914	Toys "R" Us Giraffe Car (027), *85–89 u*	75	90	[1]

		Exc	New	Cond/$
7920	Sears Centennial Boxcar (O27), *85–86 u*	40	45	1
7925	Erie-Lackawanna Boxcar (O27), *86–90*	9	13	1
7926	NKP Boxcar (O27), *86–91*	8	11	1
7930	True Value Boxcar (O27), *86–87 u*	40	60	1
7931	Town House TV and Appliances Boxcar (O27), *86 u*	36	45	1
7932	Kay Bee Toys Boxcar (O27), *86–87 u*	40	50	1
8001	NKP 2-6-4, *80 u*	60	75	1
8002	Union Pacific 2-8-4 (FARR no. 2), *80*	520	550	4
8003	Chessie System 2-8-4, *80*	640	640	5
8004	Rock Island 4-4-0, *80–82*	150	170	1
8005	Santa Fe 4-4-0, *80–82*	60	75	1
8006	ACL 4-6-4, *80 u*	500	570	3
8007	NYNH&H 2-6-4, *80–81*	60	75	1
8008	Chessie System 4-4-2, *80*	75	85	1
8010	Santa Fe NW-2, *70, 71 u*	60	75	1
8020	Santa Fe Alco A Unit, *70–72, 74–76*	75	100	1
8020	Santa Fe Alco A Unit Dummy, *70*	50	70	1
8021	Santa Fe Alco B Unit, *71–72, 74–76*	50	75	1
8022	Santa Fe Alco A Unit, *71 u*	100	125	1
8025	CN Alco A Unit, *71–73 u*	100	125	1
8025	CN Alco A Unit Dummy, *71–73 u*	50	75	1
8030	Illinois Central GP-9, *70–72*	80	125	3
8031	Canadian National GP-7, *71–73 u*	70	120	1
8031	Illinois Central GP-9 Dummy, *70*		NM	
8040	NKP 2-4-2, *70–72*	30	40	1
8040	Canadian National 2-4-2, *71 u*	50	100	1
8041	NYC 2-4-2, *70*	60	75	1
8041	PRR 2-4-2, *71 u*	60	75	1
8042	GTW 2-4-2, *70, 71–73 u*	30	40	1
8043	NKP 2-4-2, *70 u*	50	75	1
8050	D&H U36C, *80*	120	170	1
8051	D&H U36C Dummy, *80*	100	120	1
[8051]	NETCA Hood's Milk Boxcar, *86 u*	45	55	1
8054/8055	Burlington F-3 AA set, *80*	400	450	1
8056	C&NW FM Trainmaster, *80*	275	300	3
8057	Burlington NW-2, *80*	125	165	1

		Exc	New	Cond/$
8059	Pennsylvania F-3 B Unit, *80 u*	365	440	[1]
8060	Pennsylvania F-3 B Unit, *80 u*	400	475	[1]
8061	Chessie System U36C, *80*	160	190	[1]
8062	Burlington F-3 B Unit, *80 u*	200	250	[1]
8062	Great Northern 4-6-4, *70*		NM	
8063	Seaboard SD-9, *80*	125	175	[2]
8064	Florida East Coast GP-9, *80*	125	175	[1]
8065	Florida East Coast GP-9 Dummy, *80*	100	125	[1]
8066	TP&W GP-20, *80–81, 83 u*	90	115	[1]
8067	Texas & Pacific Alco A Unit, *80*		NM	
(8068)	LCCA Rock Island GP-20 "1980", *80 u*	100	130	[2]
8071	Virginian SD-18, *80 u*	140	175	[2]
8072	Virginian SD-18 Dummy, *80 u*	90	120	[1]
(8100)	Norfolk & Western 4-8-4 "611", *81*	680	860	[1]
(8101)	Chicago & Alton 4-6-4 "659", *81*	390	490	[1]
8102	Union Pacific 4-4-2, *81–82*	60	75	[1]
[8103]	LCAC Toronto, Hamilton & Buffalo Boxcar, *81 u*		NRS	
(8104)	Union Pacific 4-4-0 "3", *81 u*	265	335	[1]
8111	DT&I NW-2, *71–74*	50	75	[1]
8140	Southern 2-4-0, *71 u*	25	35	[1]
8141	PRR 2-4-2, *71–72*	40	50	[1]
8142	C&O 4-4-2, *71–72*	55	65	[1]
(8150)	PRR GG-1 "4935", *81*	445	590	[3]
8151	Burlington SD-28, *81*	140	175	[2]
8152	Canadian Pacific SD-24, *81*	145	160	[2]
8153	Reading NW-2, *81–82*	125	150	[1]
8154	Alaska NW-2, *81–82*	125	170	[1]
8155	Monon U36B, *81–82*	95	120	[1]
8156	Monon U36B Dummy, *81–82*	60	75	[1]
8157	Santa Fe FM Trainmaster, *81*	360	385	[3]
8158	DM&IR GP-35, *81–82*	75	125	[1]
8159	DM&IR GP-35 Dummy, *81–82*	60	75	[1]
8160	Burger King GP-20, *81–82*	100	125	[1]
8161	L.A.S.E.R. Diesel Switcher, *81–82*	30	75	[1]
8162	Ontario Northland SD-18, *81 u*	130	155	[1]
8163	Ontario Northland SD-18 Dummy, *81 u*	100	125	[1]
8164	Pennsylvania F-3 B Unit, *81 u*	400	450	[1]

		Exc	New	Cond/$
8182	Nibco Express NW-2, *82 u*	100	150	___1
(8190)	Diesel Horn kit, *81 u*	—	41	___1
8200	"Kickapoo" Dockside 0-4-0T, *72*	30	40	___1
8203	PRR 2-4-2, *72, 74 u, 75*	30	40	___1
8204	C&O 4-4-2, *72*	60	70	___1
[8204]	LCAC Algoma Central Boxcar, *82 u*		NRS	___
8206	NYC 4-6-4, *72–75*	175	210	___1
8209	"Pioneer" Dockside 0-4-0T w/ tender, *72*	50	75	___1
8209	"Pioneer" Dockside 0-4-0T w/o tender, *73–76*	45	60	___1
8210	Joshua L. Cowen 4-6-4, *82*	395	430	___4
8212	Black Cave 0-4-0, *82*	30	50	___1
8213	D&RGW 2-4-2, *82–83, 84–91 u*	60	70	___1
8214	Pennsylvania 2-4-2, *82–83*	60	75	___1
(8215)	Nickel Plate Road 2-8-4 "779", *82 u*	510	540	___3
8250	Santa Fe GP-9, *72, 74–75*	90	120	___2
(8251-50)	Horn/Whistle Controller, *72–74*	2	3	___1
8252	D&H Alco A Unit, *72*	75	100	___1
8253	D&H Alco B Unit, *72*	50	75	___1
8254	Illinois Central GP-9 Dummy, *72*	60	75	___1
8255	Santa Fe GP-9 Dummy, *72*	75	90	___1
8258	Canadian National GP-7 Dummy, *72–73 u*	70	90	___1
8260/8262	Southern Pacific F-3 AA set, *82*	680	690	___1
8261	Southern Pacific F-3 B Unit, *82 u*	700	900	___1
8263	Santa Fe GP-7, *82*	75	100	___2
8264	CP Vulcan Switcher w/ snowplow, *82*	120	155	___2
8265	Santa Fe SD-40, *82*	355	400	___2
8266	Norfolk & Western SD-24, *82*	150	200	___1
8268	Quicksilver Alco A Unit, *82–83*	100	125	___1
8269	Quicksilver Alco A Unit Dummy, *82–83*	60	75	___1
8272	Pennsylvania EP-5, *82 u*	270	320	___1
8300	Santa Fe 2-4-0, *73–74*	20	25	___1
8302	Southern 2-4-0, *73–76*	25	30	___1
8303	Jersey Central 2-4-2, *73–74*	40	50	___1
8304	Rock Island 4-4-2, *73–75*	100	125	___1
8304	Pennsylvania 4-4-2, *74–75*	90	125	___1
8304	B&O 4-4-2, *75*	90	125	___1

		Exc	New	Cond/$
8304	C&O 4-4-2, *75–77*	90	125	___ [1]
8305	Milwaukee Road 4-4-2, *73*	100	125	___ [1]
(8307)	Southern Pacific 4-8-4 "4449", *83*	910	1050	___ [4]
8308	Jersey Central 2-4-2, *73–74 u*	40	50	___ [1]
(8309)	Southern 2-8-2 "4501" (FARR no. 4), *83*	450	500	___ [3]
8310	Nickel Plate Road 2-4-0, *73 u*	30	60	___ [1]
8310	Santa Fe 2-4-0, *74–75 u*	30	40	___ [1]
8310	Jersey Central 2-4-0, *74–75 u*	30	60	___ [1]
8311	Southern 0-4-0, *73 u*	30	40	___ [1]
8313	Santa Fe 0-4-0, *83–84*	15	20	___ [1]
8314	Southern 2-4-0, *83–85*	20	25	___ [1]
8315	B&O 4-4-0, *83–84*	85	120	___ [1]
8350	U.S. Steel Diesel Switcher, *73–75*	20	30	___ [1]
8351	Santa Fe Alco A Unit, *73–75*	60	70	___ [1]
8352	Santa Fe GP-20, *73–75*	65	105	___ [1]
8353	Grand Trunk GP-7, *73–75*	65	105	___ [1]
8354	Erie NW-2, *73, 75*	95	140	___ [2]
8355	Santa Fe GP-20 Dummy, *73–74*	75	115	___ [1]
8356	Grand Trunk GP-7 Dummy, *73–75*	60	75	___ [1]
8357	PRR GP-9, *73–75*	125	130	___ [1]
8358	PRR GP-9 Dummy, *73–75*	60	125	___ [1]
(8359)	Chessie System GP-7 "GM50", *73*	105	135	___ [3]
8360	Long Island GP-20, *73–74*	70	125	___ [1]
8361	Western Pacific Alco A Unit, *73–75*	75	100	___ [1]
8362	Western Pacific Alco B Unit, *73–75*	50	75	___ [1]
8363	B&O F-3 A Unit, *73–75*	240	290	___ [3]
8364	B&O F-3 A Unit Dummy, *73–75*	145	190	___ [1]
8365/8366	CP F-3 AA set (SSS), *73*	450	600	___ [1]
8367	Long Island GP-20 Dummy, *73–75*	90	115	___ [1]
8368	Alaska Vulcan Switcher, *83*	125	165	___ [1]
8369	Erie-Lackawanna GP-20, *83–85*	125	140	___ [1]
8370/8372	NYC F-3 AA set, *83*	450	600	___ [1]
8371	NYC F-3 B Unit, *83*	145	215	___ [2]
8374	Burlington Northern NW-2, *83–85*	115	140	___ [2]
8375	C&NW GP-7, *83–85*	150	175	___ [1]
8376	Union Pacific SD-40, *83*	295	340	___ [3]
8377	U.S. Diesel Switcher, *83–84*	60	75	___ [1]

		Exc	New	Cond/$
(8378)	Wabash FM Trainmaster "550", *83 u*	880	1050	___1
8379	PRR Fire Car, *83 u*	135	160	___2
8380	Lionel Lines SD-28, *83 u*	175	245	___3
8402	Reading 4-4-2, *84–85*	60	75	___1
8403	Chessie System 4-4-2, *84–85*	60	75	___1
(8404)	PRR 6-8-6 "6200" (FARR no. 5), *84–85*	430	530	___1
(8406)	NYC 4-6-4 "783", *84*	660	750	___5
8410	Redwood Valley Express 4-4-0, *84–85*	40	60	___1
8452	Erie Alco A Unit, *74–75*	80	100	___1
8453	Erie Alco B Unit, *74–75*	50	75	___1
8454	D&RGW GP-7, *74–75*	95	120	___1
8455	D&RGW GP-7 Dummy, *74–75*	50	75	___1
8458	Erie-Lackawanna SD-40, *84*	410	445	___2
8459	D&RGW Vulcan Rotary Snowplow, *84*	155	200	___1
8460	MKT NW-2, *74–75*	50	75	___1
8463	Chessie System GP-20, *74 u*	115	140	___1
8464/8465	D&RGW F-3 AA set (SSS), *74*	275	375	___1
8466	Amtrak F-3 A Unit, *74–76*	200	250	___2
8467	Amtrak F-3 A Unit Dummy, *74–76*	100	125	___1
8468	B&O F-3 B Unit (SSS), *74–75*	100	125	___1
8469	CP F-3 B Unit (SSS), *74*	155	210	___2
8470	Chessie System U36B, *74*	100	150	___1
8471	Pennsylvania NW-2, *74–76*	180	225	___3
8473	Coca-Cola NW-2, *74 u, 75*	100	125	___1
8474	D&RGW F-3 B Unit (SSS), *74*	100	125	___1
8475	Amtrak F-3 B Unit (SSS), *74*	100	125	___1
(8476)	TCA 4-6-4 "5484", *85 u*	295	345	___1
8477	NYC GP-9, *84 u*	245	285	___5
8480/8482	Union Pacific F-3 AA set, *84*	325	400	___1
8481	Union Pacific F-3 B Unit, *84*	180	200	___1
8485	U.S. Marines NW-2, *84–85*	100	140	___1
8490	(See 8690)			
8500	Pennsylvania 2-4-0, *75–76*	20	25	___1
8502	Santa Fe 2-4-0, *75*	20	25	___1
8506	PRR 0-4-0, *75–77*	95	115	___1
8507	Santa Fe 2-4-0, *75 u*	25	30	___1
[8507]/[8508]	LCAC CN F-3 AA set, shells only, *85 u*		NRS	___

		Exc	New	Cond/$
8512	Santa Fe 0-4-0T, *85–86*	25	35	[1]
8516	NYC 0-4-0, *85–86*	110	130	[1]
8550	Jersey Central GP-9, *75–76*	100	125	[1]
8551	Pennsylvania EP-5, *75–76*	140	165	[3]
8552/8553/8554 Southern Pacific Alco ABA set, *75–76*		200	250	[1]
8555/8557 Milwaukee Road F-3 AA set (SSS), *75*		350	450	[1]
8556	Chessie System NW-2, *75–76*	170	205	[2]
8558	Milwaukee Road EP-5, *76–77*	175	220	[1]
(8559)	N&W GP-9 "1776", *75*	100	130	[1]
8560	Chessie System U36B Dummy, *75*	75	115	[1]
8561	Jersey Central GP-9 Dummy, *75–76*	60	80	[1]
8562	Missouri Pacific GP-20, *75–76*	110	140	[2]
8563	Rock Island Alco A Unit, *75–76 u*	75	100	[1]
8564	Union Pacific U36B, *75*	120	170	[1]
8565	Missouri Pacific GP-20 Dummy, *75–76*	60	75	[1]
8566	Southern F-3 A Unit, *75–77*	245	345	[2]
8567	Southern F-3 A Unit Dummy, *75–77*	130	180	[1]
8568	Preamble Express F-3 A Unit, *75 u*	95	145	[2]
8569	Soo Line NW-2, *75–77*	60	70	[1]
8570	Liberty Special Alco A Unit, *75 u*	100	125	[1]
8571	Frisco U36B, *75–76*	75	100	[1]
8572	Frisco U36B Dummy, *75–76*	60	75	[1]
8573	Union Pacific U36B Dummy, *75 u*	175	225	[1]
8575	Milwaukee Road F-3 B Unit (SSS), *75*	95	170	[1]
8576	Penn Central GP-7, *75 u, 76–77*	125	150	[1]
8578	NYC Ballast Tamper, *85, 87*	90	115	[1]
8580/8582 Illinois Central F-3 AA set, *85, 87*		400	450	[1]
8581	Illinois Central F-3 B Unit, *85, 87*	175	200	[1]
8585	Burlington Northern SD-40, *85*	385	440	[2]
(8587)	Wabash GP-9 "484", *85 u*	260	310	[1]
8600	NYC 4-6-4, *76*	200	225	[1]
8601	Rock Island 0-4-0, *76–77*	20	25	[1]
8602	D&RGW 2-4-0, *76–78*	25	30	[1]
8603	C&O 4-6-4, *76–77*	155	230	[1]
8604	Jersey Central 2-4-2, *76 u*	40	45	[1]
(8606)	B&A 4-6-4 "784", *86 u*	990	1200	[1]

		Exc	New	Cond/$
(8610)	Wabash 4-6-2 "672", *86–87*	500	600	___[1]
(8615)	L&N 2-8-4 "1970", *86 u*	900	1100	___[1]
8616	Santa Fe 4-4-2, *86*	65	75	___[1]
8617	Nickel Plate Road 4-4-2, *86–91*	65	75	___[1]
8625	Pennsylvania 2-4-0, *86–90*	25	40	___[1]
(8630)	W&ARR 4-4-0 "3", *86 u*	125	150	___[1]
8635	Santa Fe 0-4-0 (SSS), *86*	125	150	___[1]
8650	Burlington Northern U36B, *76–77*	125	150	___[1]
8651	Burlington Northern U36B Dummy, *76–77*	90	100	___[1]
8652	Santa Fe F-3 A Unit, *76–77*	295	395	___[1]
8653	Santa Fe F-3 A Unit Dummy, *76–77*	175	200	___[1]
8654	Boston & Maine GP-9, *76–77*	110	135	___[1]
8655	Boston & Maine GP-9 Dummy, *76–77*	80	100	___[1]
8656	Canadian National Alco A Unit, *76*	150	200	___[1]
8657	Canadian National Alco B Unit, *76*	75	100	___[1]
8658	Canadian National Alco A Unit Dummy, *76*	100	200	___[1]
8659	Virginian Rectifier, *76–77*	175	235	___[3]
8660	CP Rail NW-2, *76–77*	100	125	___[1]
8661	Southern F-3 B Unit (SSS), *76*	155	180	___[1]
8662	B&O GP-7, *86*	125	140	___[1]
8664	Amtrak Alco A Unit, *76–77*	100	150	___[1]
8665	BAR "Jeremiah O'Brien" GP-9 "1776", *76 u*	85	140	___[1]
8666	Northern Pacific GP-9 (SSS), *76*	100	140	___[1]
8667	Amtrak Alco B Unit, *76–77*	75	100	___[1]
8668	Northern Pacific GP-9 Dummy (SSS), *76*	105	135	___[1]
8669	Illinois Central Gulf U36B, *76–77*	120	145	___[1]
8670	Chessie System Diesel Switcher, *76*	35	65	___[1]
8679	Northern Pacific GP-20, *86*	100	125	___[1]
8687	Jersey Central FM Trainmaster, *86*	365	415	___[4]
8690	Lionel Lines Trolley, *86*	110	155	___[2]
(8701)	W&ARR 4-4-0 "3", *77–79*	195	250	___[2]
8702	Southern 4-6-4, *77–78*	400	475	___[1]
8703	Wabash 2-4-2, *77*	25	35	___[1]
8750	Rock Island GP-7, *77–78*	100	125	___[1]
8751	Rock Island GP-7 Dummy, *77–78*	50	75	___[1]
8753	Pennsylvania GG-1, *77 u*	495	570	___[5]

		Exc	New	Cond/$
8754	New Haven Rectifier, *77–78*	170	185	[1]
8755	Santa Fe U36B, *77–78*	150	180	[1]
8756	Santa Fe U36B Dummy, *77–78*	90	100	[1]
8757	Conrail GP-9, *76 u, 77–78*	100	175	[3]
8758	Southern GP-7 Dummy, *77 u, 78*	80	100	[1]
8759	Erie-Lackawanna GP-9, *77–79*	120	150	[1]
8760	Erie-Lackawanna GP-9 Dummy, *77–79*	100	125	[1]
8761	GTW NW-2, *77–78*	125	175	[1]
8762	Great Northern EP-5, *77–78*	215	240	[1]
8763	Norfolk & Western GP-9, *76 u, 77–78*	100	125	[1]
8764	B&O Budd RDC Passenger (SSS), *77*	120	145	[1]
8765	B&O Budd RDC Baggage Dummy (SSS), *77*	75	100	[1]
8766	B&O Budd RDC Baggage (SSS), *77*	200	250	[2]
8767	B&O Budd RDC Passenger Dummy (SSS), *77*	100	125	[1]
8768	B&O Budd RDC Passenger Dummy (SSS), *77*	100	125	[1]
8769	Republic Steel Diesel Switcher, *77–78*	20	40	[1]
8770	EMD NW-2, *77–78*	75	100	[2]
8771	Great Northern U36B, *77*	100	120	[1]
8772	GM&O GP-20, *77*	95	115	[1]
8773	Mickey Mouse U36B, *77–78*	310	415	[3]
8774	Southern GP-7, *77 u, 78*	125	150	[1]
8775	Lehigh Valley GP-9, *77 u, 78*	125	150	[1]
8776	C&NW GP-20, *77 u, 78*	125	175	[2]
8777	Santa Fe F-3 B Unit (SSS), *77*	175	190	[2]
8778	Lehigh Valley GP-9 Dummy, *77 u, 78*	80	100	[1]
8779	C&NW GP-20 Dummy, *77 u, 78*	100	125	[1]
8800	Lionel Lines 4-4-2, *78–81*	100	125	[1]
8801	Blue Comet 4-6-4, *78–80*	390	465	[1]
8803	Santa Fe 0-4-0, *78*	15	25	[1]
8850	Penn Central GG-1, *78 u, 79*	360	410	[5]
8851/8852	New Haven F-3 AA set, *78 u, 79*	330	440	[1]
8854	CP Rail GP-9, *78–79*	100	150	[1]
8855	Milwaukee Road SD-18, *78*	150	175	[3]
8857	Northern Pacific U36B, *78–80*	100	125	[1]

		Exc	New	Cond/$
8858	Northern Pacific U36B Dummy, *78–80*	55	85	1
8859	Conrail Rectifier, *78–82*	175	250	2
8860	Rock Island NW-2, *78–79*	100	130	1
8861	Santa Fe Alco A Unit, *78–79*	75	100	1
8862	Santa Fe Alco B Unit, *78–79*	40	50	1
8864	New Haven F-3 B Unit (SSS), *78*	100	125	1
8866	M&StL GP-9 (SSS), *78*	75	100	2
8867	M&StL GP-9 Dummy (SSS), *78*	60	90	1
8868	Amtrak Budd RDC Baggage, *78, 80*	150	200	1
8869	Amtrak Budd RDC Passenger Dummy, *78, 80*	75	100	1
8870	Amtrak Budd RDC Passenger Dummy, *78, 80*	75	100	1
8871	Amtrak Budd RDC Baggage Dummy, *78, 80*	75	100	1
8872	Santa Fe SD-18, *78 u, 79*	100	150	1
8873	Santa Fe SD-18 Dummy, *78 u, 79*	75	100	1
8900	Santa Fe 4-6-4 (FARR no. 1), *79*	350	400	1
8902	ACL 2-4-0, *79–82, 86–90*	15	20	1
8903	D&RGW 2-4-2, *79–81*	20	25	1
8904	Wabash 2-4-2, *79, 81 u*	35	40	1
8905	"Smokey Mountain" Dockside 0-4-0T, *79*	10	20	1
8950	Virginian FM Trainmaster, *79*	405	435	3
8951	Southern Pacific FM Trainmaster, *79*	415	480	4
8952/8953	PRR F-3 AA set, *79*	—	580	1
8955	Southern U36B, *79*	125	175	1
8956	Southern U36B Dummy, *79*	100	125	1
8957	Burlington Northern GP-20, *79*	125	150	1
[8957]	Detroit-Toledo TCA Burlington Northern GP-20, *80 u*		NRS	
8958	Burlington Northern GP-20 Dummy, *79*	100	125	1
[8958]	Detroit-Toledo TCA Burlington Northern GP-20 Dummy, *80 u*		NRS	
8960	Southern Pacific U36C, *79 u*	90	110	1
8961	Southern Pacific U36C Dummy, *79 u*	70	90	1
8962	Reading U36B, *79*	125	150	3
8970/8971	PRR F-3 AA set, *79 u, 80*	400	500	1
9001	Conrail Boxcar (027), *86–87 u, 88–90*	5	10	1

		Exc	New	Cond/$
9010	GN Hopper (O27), *70–71*	6	8	1
9011	GN Hopper (O27), *70 u, 75–76, 78–83*	6	8	1
9012	TA&G Hopper (O27), *71–72*	5	7	1
9013	Canadian National Hopper (O27), *72–76*	5	7	1
9014	Trailer Train Flatcar (O27), *78–79*		NRS	
9015	Reading Hopper (O27), *73–75*	20	25	1
9016	Chessie System Hopper (O27), *75–79, 87–88, 89 u*	5	7	1
[9016]	LCCA Chessie System Hopper (O27), *79–80 u*	20	25	1
9017	Wabash Gondola w/ canisters (O27), *78–82*	4	5	1
9018	DT&I Hopper (O27), *78–79, 81–82*	5	7	1
(9019)	Unlettered Flatcar (O27), *78*	3	4	1
9020	Union Pacific Flatcar (O27), *70–77*	4	5	1
9021	Santa Fe Work Caboose, *70–71, 73–75*	10	15	1
9022	Santa Fe Bulkhead Flatcar (O27), *70–72, 75–79*	8	15	1
9023	MKT Bulkhead Flatcar (O27), *73–74*	8	12	1
9024	C&O Flatcar (O27), *73–75*	4	6	1
9025	DT&I Work Caboose, *71–74, 77–78*	8	10	1
9026	Republic Steel Flatcar (O27), *75–82*	6	8	1
9027	Soo Line Work Caboose, *75–76*	8	10	1
(9030)	"Kickapoo" Gondola (O27), *72, 79*	5	10	1
9031	NKP Gondola w/ canisters (O27), *73–75, 82–83, 84–91 u*	5	7	1
9032	Southern Pacific Gondola w/ canisters (O27), *75–78*	3	4	1
9033	PC Gondola w/ canisters (O27), *76–78, 82, 86 u, 87–90, 92 u*	3	4	1
9034	Lionel Leisure Hopper (O27), *77 u*	20	30	1
9035	Conrail Boxcar (O27), *78–82*	4	8	1
9036	Mobilgas 1-D Tank Car (O27), *78–82*	6	12	1
[9036]	LCCA Mobilgas 1-D Tank Car (O27), *78–79 u*	20	23	1
9037	Conrail Boxcar (O27), *78 u, 80*	4	8	1
9038	Chessie System Hopper (O27), *78 u, 80*	15	20	1
9039	Mobilgas 1-D Tank Car (O27), *78 u, 80*	10	15	1

		Exc	New	Cond/$
9040	General Mills Wheaties Boxcar (027), *70–72*	7	10	1
9041	Hershey's Boxcar (027), *70–71, 73–76*	10	15	1
9042	Ford-Autolite Boxcar (027), *71 u, 72, 74–76*	9	14	1
9043	Erie-Lackawanna Boxcar (027), *73–75*	10	15	1
9044	D&RGW Boxcar (027), *75–76*	6	8	1
9045	Toys "R" Us Boxcar (027), *75 u*	40	50	1
9046	True Value Boxcar (027), *76 u*	30	40	1
9047	Toys "R" Us Boxcar (027), *76 u*	35	50	1
9048	Toys "R" Us Boxcar (027), *76 u*	34	48	1
(9049)	Toys "R" Us Boxcar (027), *78 u*		NRS	
9050	Sunoco 1-D Tank Car (027), *70–71*	20	25	1
9051	Firestone 1-D Tank Car (027), *74–75, 78*	15	18	1
9052	Toys "R" Us Boxcar (027), *77 u*	30	40	1
9053	True Value Boxcar (027), *77 u*	32	45	1
9054	JCPenney Boxcar (027), *77 u*	17	26	1
9055	Republic Steel Gondola w/ canisters, *78 u*	9	11	1
9057	CP Rail SP-Type Caboose, *78–79*	10	15	1
9058	Lionel Lines SP-Type Caboose, *78–79, 83*	6	8	1
9059	Lionel Lines SP-Type Caboose, *79 u, 81 u*	8	10	1
9060	Nickel Plate Road SP-Type Caboose, *70–72*	6	8	1
9061	Santa Fe SP-Type Caboose, *70–76*	5	8	1
9062	Penn Central SP-Type Caboose, *70–72, 74–76*	5	9	1
9063	GTW SP-Type Caboose, *70, 71–73 u*	15	20	1
9064	C&O SP-Type Caboose, *71–72, 75–77*	7	10	1
9065	Canadian National SP-Type Caboose, *71–73 u*	20	25	1
9066	Southern SP-Type Caboose, *73–76*	8	10	1
(9067)	Kickapoo Valley Bobber Caboose, *72*	7	10	1
9068	Reading Bobber Caboose, *73–76*	6	8	1
[9068]	Gateway TCA Reading Bobber Caboose, *76 u*	—	23	1
9069	Jersey Central SP-Type Caboose, *73–74, 75–76 u*	6	8	1
9070	Rock Island SP-Type Caboose, *73–74*	10	15	1
9071	Santa Fe Bobber Caboose, *74 u, 77–78*	8	10	1

		Exc	New	Cond/$
9073	Coca-Cola SP-Type Caboose, *74 u, 75*	15	20	[1]
9075	Rock Island SP-Type Caboose, *75–76 u*	15	20	[1]
9076	"We The People" SP-Type Caboose, *75 u*	20	30	[1]
9077	D&RGW SP-Type Caboose, *76–83, 84–91 u*	6	8	[1]
9078	Rock Island Bobber Caboose, *76–77*	6	8	[1]
9079	GTW Hopper (O27), *77*	20	30	[1]
9080	Wabash SP-Type Caboose, *77*	10	12	[1]
9085	Santa Fe Work Caboose, *79–82*	5	6	[1]
9090	General Mills Mini-Max Car, *71*	34	40	[2]
9106	Miller Vat Car, *84–85*	25	35	[1]
9107	Dr Pepper Vat Car, *86–87*	26	36	[1]
9110	B&O Quad Hopper, *71*	25	30	[1]
9111	N&W Quad Hopper, *72–75*	20	25	[1]
9112	D&RGW Covered Quad Hopper, *73–75*	20	25	[1]
9113	Norfolk & Western Quad Hopper (SSS), *73*	25	30	[1]
[9113]	Three Rivers TCA N&W Quad Hopper, *76 u*	30	35	[1]
9114	Morton Salt Covered Quad Hopper, *74–76*	20	25	[1]
9115	Planter's Covered Quad Hopper, *74–76*	26	31	[1]
9116	Domino Sugar Covered Quad Hopper, *74–76*	20	25	[1]
9117	Alaska Covered Quad Hopper (SSS), *74–76*	25	35	[1]
9118	LCCA Corning Covered Quad Hopper, *74 u*	75	100	[1]
9119	Detroit & Mackinac Covered Quad Hopper (SSS), *75*	25	30	[1]
[9119]	Detroit-Toledo TCA Detroit & Mackinac Covered Quad Hopper, *77 u*	25	35	[1]
[9119]	North Texas TCA Detroit & Mackinac Covered Quad Hopper, *78 u*	25	35	[1]
9120	Northern Pacific Flatcar w/ trailers, *70–71*	35	45	[1]
9121	L&N Flatcar w/ bulldozer and scraper, *71–79*	40	50	[1]
9122	Northern Pacific Flatcar w/ trailers, *72–75*	33	44	[1]

		Exc	New	Cond/$
9123	C&O Auto Carrier (3-tier), *72 u, 73–74*	20	30	1
(9123)	TCA Dearborn Auto Carrier "1973" (3-tier), *73 u*	30	40	1
9124	P&LE Flatcar w/ log load, *73–74*	15	20	1
9125	Norfolk & Western Auto Carrier (2-tier), *73–77*	25	30	1
9126	C&O Auto Carrier (3-tier), *73–75*	20	30	1
9128	Heinz Vat Car, *74–76*	25	35	1
9129	N&W Auto Carrier (3-tier), *75–76*	25	30	1
9130	B&O Quad Hopper, *70*	20	25	1
9131	D&RGW Gondola w/ canisters, *73–77*	5	8	1
9132	Libby's Vat Car (SSS), *75–77*	20	25	1
9133	Burlington Northern Flatcar w/ trailers, *76–77, 80*	29	38	2
9134	Virginian Covered Quad Hopper, *76–77*	25	30	1
9135	N&W Covered Quad Hopper, *70 u, 71, 75*	20	25	1
9136	Republic Steel Gondola w/ canisters, *72–76, 79*	7	9	1
9138	Sunoco 3-D Tank Car (SSS), *78*	42	48	1
9139	PC Auto Carrier (3-tier), *76–77*	20	30	1
9140	Burlington Gondola w/ canisters, *70, 73–82, 87–89*	6	8	1
9141	Burlington Northern Gondola w/ canisters, *70–72*	8	10	1
9142	Republic Steel Gondola w/ canisters, *71*	6	8	1
[9142]	LCCA Republic Steel Gondola w/ canisters, *77–78 u*	15	20	1
9143	Canadian National Gondola w/ canisters, *71–73 u*	35	40	1
9144	D&RGW Gondola w/ canisters (SSS), *74–76*	8	12	1
9145	ICG Auto Carrier (3-tier), *77–80*	20	30	1
9146	Mogen David Vat Car, *77–81*	20	25	1
9147	Texaco 1-D Tank Car, *77–78*	34	49	1
9148	Du Pont 3-D Tank Car, *77–81*	20	25	1
9149	CP Rail Flatcar w/ trailers, *77–78*	25	40	1
9150	Gulf 1-D Tank Car, *70 u, 71*	20	25	1

		Exc	New	Cond/$
9151	Shell 1-D Tank Car, *72*	30	35	[1]
9152	Shell 1-D Tank Car, *73–76*	25	30	[1]
9153	Chevron 1-D Tank Car, *74–76*	22	32	[1]
9154	Borden 1-D Tank Car, *75–76*	40	55	[1]
9155	LCCA Monsanto 1-D Tank Car, *75 u*	60	70	[1]
9156	Mobilgas 1-D Tank Car, *76–77*	28	37	[1]
9157	C&O Flatcar w/ crane, *76–78, 81–82*	50	60	[2]
9158	PC Flatcar w/ shovel, *76–77, 80*	45	55	[1]
9159	Sunoco 1-D Tank Car, *76*	45	50	[1]
9160	Illinois Central N5C Caboose, *70–72*	17	28	[1]
9161	CN N5C Caboose, *72–74*	15	30	[1]
9162	PRR N5C Caboose (SSS), *72–76*	33	38	[2]
9163	Santa Fe N5C Caboose, *73–76*	14	24	[1]
9165	Canadian Pacific N5C Caboose (SSS), *73*	25	35	[1]
9166	D&RGW SP-Type Caboose (SSS), *74–75*	16	21	[1]
9167	Chessie System N5C Caboose, *74–76*	29	39	[1]
9168	Union Pacific N5C Caboose, *75–77*	20	25	[1]
9169	Milwaukee Road SP-Type Caboose (SSS), *75*	20	25	[1]
(9170)	N&W N5C Caboose "1776", *75*	30	35	[1]
9171	Missouri Pacific SP-Type Caboose, *75 u, 76–77*	20	25	[1]
9172	Penn Central SP-Type Caboose, *75 u, 76–77*	25	40	[1]
9173	Jersey Central SP-Type Caboose, *75 u, 76–77*	20	25	[1]
9174	NYC P&E B/W Caboose, *76*	75	85	[1]
9175	Virginian N5C Caboose, *76–77*	30	40	[1]
9176	BAR N5C Caboose, *76 u*	20	35	[1]
9177	Northern Pacific B/W Caboose (SSS), *76*	26	37	[1]
9178	ICG SP-Type Caboose, *76–77*	20	25	[1]
9179	Chessie System Bobber Caboose, *76*	6	10	[1]
9180	Rock Island N5C Caboose, *77–78*	20	39	[1]
9181	B&M N5C Caboose, *76 u, 77*	29	39	[1]
[9181]	NETCA B&M N5C Caboose, *77 u*	25	30	[1]
9182	N&W N5C Caboose, *76 u, 77–80*	26	36	[1]
9183	Mickey Mouse N5C Caboose, *77–78*	42	65	[1]

		Exc	New	Cond/$
9184	Erie B/W Caboose, *77–78*	24	34	___[1]
[9184]	North Texas TCA Erie B/W Caboose, *77 u*	20	25	___[1]
[9184]	LCOL Erie B/W Caboose, *82 u*	20	25	___[1]
9185	GTW N5C Caboose, *77*	25	35	___[1]
9186	Conrail N5C Caboose, *76 u, 77–78*	31	41	___[1]
[9186]	Atlantic TCA Conrail N5C Caboose, *79 u*	25	35	___[1]
9187	GM&O SP-Type Caboose, *77*	15	25	___[1]
9188	GN B/W Caboose, *77*	33	44	___[1]
9189	Gulf 1-D Tank Car, *77*	50	60	___[1]
9193	Budweiser Vat Car, *83–84*	125	150	___[1]
[9193]	Atlantic TCA Budweiser Vat Car, *84 u*	75	100	___[1]
9200	Illinois Central Boxcar, *70–71*	20	25	___[2]
9201	Penn Central Boxcar, *70*	18	27	___[1]
9202	Santa Fe Boxcar, *70*	33	38	___[2]
9203	Union Pacific Boxcar, *70*	32	37	___[1]
9204	Northern Pacific Boxcar, *70*	29	34	___[1]
9205	Norfolk & Western Boxcar, *70*	20	22	___[1]
9206	Great Northern Boxcar, *70–71*	20	22	___[1]
9207	Soo Line Boxcar, *71*	16	21	___[1]
9208	CP Rail Boxcar, *71*	22	24	___[1]
9209	Burlington Northern Boxcar, *71–72*	19	24	___[1]
9210	B&O DD Boxcar, *71*	18	23	___[2]
9211	Penn Central Boxcar, *71*	23	25	___[1]
9212	LCCA SCL Flatcar w/ trailers, *76 u*	30	35	___[1]
9213	M&StL Covered Quad Hopper (SSS), *78*	23	33	___[2]
9214	Northern Pacific Boxcar, *71–72*	23	27	___[1]
9215	Norfolk & Western Boxcar, *71*	20	25	___[1]
9216	Great Northern Auto Carrier (3-tier), *78*	31	48	___[1]
9217	Soo Line Operating Boxcar, *82–84*	30	35	___[1]
9218	Monon Operating Boxcar, *81*	29	34	___[1]
9219	Missouri Pacific Operating Boxcar, *83*	30	35	___[1]
9220	Borden Milk Car, *83–86*	100	110	___[2]
9221	Poultry Dispatch Operating Chicken Car, *83–85*	60	65	___[1]
9222	L&N Flatcar w/ trailers, *83–84*	28	44	___[1]
9223	Reading Operating Boxcar, *84*	31	36	___[1]

		Exc	New	Cond/$
9224	Churchill Downs Operating Horse Car, *84–86*	115	135	2
9225	Conrail Operating Barrel Car, *84*	60	65	1
9226	Delaware & Hudson Flatcar w/ trailers, *84–85*	29	34	2
9228	Canadian Pacific Operating Boxcar, *86*	22	33	1
9229	Express Mail Operating Boxcar, *85–86*	31	41	1
9230	Monon Boxcar (SSS), *71, 72 u*	17	22	2
9231	Reading B/W Caboose, *79*	29	39	1
9232	Allis-Chalmers Condenser Car, *80–81, 83 u*	50	60	1
9233	Depressed Flatcar w/ transformer, *80*	70	80	2
9234	Lionel Radioactive Waste Car, *80*	40	60	1
9235	Union Pacific Derrick Car, *83–84*	15	20	1
9236	C&NW Derrick Car, *83–85*	25	35	1
9237	UPS Operating Boxcar, *84*		NM	
9238	Northern Pacific Log Dump Car, *84*	15	20	1
9239	Lionel Lines N5C Caboose, *83 u*	50	60	1
9240	NYC Operating Hopper, *86*	36	45	1
9241	PRR Log Dump Car, *85–86*	15	20	1
9245	Illinois Central Derrick Car, *85*		NM	
9247	(See 6529)			
9250	WaterPoxy 3-D Tank Car, *70–71*	27	32	2
X9259	LCCA Southern B/W Caboose, *77 u*	35	40	1
9260	Reynolds Aluminum Covered Quad Hopper, *75–76*	20	25	1
9261	Sun-maid Raisins Covered Quad Hopper, *75 u, 76*	19	29	1
9262	Ralston Purina Covered Quad Hopper, *75 u, 76*	60	70	1
9263	PRR Covered Quad Hopper, *75 u, 76–77*	34	48	1
9264	Illinois Central Covered Quad Hopper, *75 u, 76–77*	30	35	1
[9264]	Midwest TCA Museum Express Illinois Central Covered Quad Hopper, *78 u*	25	30	1
9265	Chessie System Covered Quad Hopper, *75 u, 76–77*	30	35	1

		Exc	New	Cond/$
9266	Southern "Big John" Covered Quad Hopper, *76*	60	75	___[1]
9267	Alcoa Covered Quad Hopper (SSS), *76*	30	40	___[1]
9268	Northern Pacific B/W Caboose, *77 u*	28	37	___[1]
9269	Milwaukee Road B/W Caboose, *78*	34	49	___[1]
9270	Northern Pacific N5C Caboose, *78*	14	27	___[1]
9271	M&StL B/W Caboose (SSS), *78–79*	18	36	___[1]
9272	New Haven B/W Caboose, *78–80*	19	34	___[1]
[9272]	Detroit-Toledo TCA New Haven B/W Caboose, *79 u*	25	30	___[1]
[9272]	METCA New Haven B/W Caboose, *79 u*	25	30	___[1]
9273	Southern B/W Caboose, *78 u*	44	55	___[1]
9274	Santa Fe B/W Caboose, *78 u*	60	70	___[2]
9276	Peabody Quad Hopper, *78*	29	39	___[1]
9277	Cities Service 1-D Tank Car, *78*	50	60	___[1]
9278	Life Savers 1-D Tank Car, *78–79*	120	165	___[2]
9279	Magnolia 3-D Tank Car, *78, 79 u*	22	28	___[1]
9280	Santa Fe Operating Stock Car (O27), *77–81*	25	30	___[1]
9281	Santa Fe Auto Carrier (3-tier), *78–80*	20	25	___[1]
9282	Great Northern Flatcar w/ trailers, *78–79, 81–82*	33	41	___[2]
9283	Union Pacific Gondola w/ canisters, *77*	14	19	___[1]
9284	Santa Fe Gondola w/ canisters, *77*	20	25	___[1]
9285	ICG Flatcar w/ trailers, *77*	55	65	___[1]
9286	B&LE Covered Quad Hopper, *77*	15	25	___[1]
9287	Southern N5C Caboose, *77 u, 78*	17	28	___[1]
[9287]	Southern TCA Southern N5C Caboose, *77 u*	20	25	___[1]
9288	Lehigh Valley N5C Caboose, *77 u, 78, 80*	19	29	___[1]
9289	C&NW N5C Caboose, *77 u, 78, 80*	30	50	___[1]
[9289]	Midwest TCA Museum Express C&NW N5C Caboose, *80 u*	40	50	___[1]
9290	Union Pacific Operating Barrel Car, *83*	75	85	___[1]
9300	PC Log Dump Car, *70–75, 77*	15	20	___[1]
9301	U.S. Mail Operating Boxcar, *73–84*	30	40	___[1]

		Exc	New	Cond/$
[9301]	Sacramento-Sierra TCA U.S. Mail Operating Boxcar, *76 u*	30	45	[1]
9302	L&N Searchlight Car, *72 u, 73–78*	17	26	[1]
9303	Union Pacific Log Dump Car, *74–78, 80*	10	20	[1]
9304	C&O Coal Dump Car, *74–78*	10	20	[1]
9305	Santa Fe Operating Cowboy Car (O27), *80–82*	20	30	[1]
9306	Santa Fe Flatcar w/ horses, *80–82*	20	30	[1]
9307	Erie Animated Gondola, *80–84*	55	80	[2]
9308	Aquarium Car, *81–84*	145	175	[3]
9309	TP&W B/W Caboose, *80–81, 83 u*	25	35	[1]
9310	Santa Fe Log Dump Car, *78 u, 79–83*	10	20	[1]
9311	Union Pacific Coal Dump Car, *78 u, 79–82*	10	20	[1]
9312	Conrail Searchlight Car, *78 u, 79–83*	19	29	[1]
9313	Gulf 3-D Tank Car, *79 u*	55	65	[1]
9315	Southern Pacific Gondola w/ canisters, *79 u*	21	32	[1]
9316	Southern Pacific B/W Caboose, *79 u*	80	90	[1]
9317	Santa Fe B/W Caboose, *79*	33	47	[1]
9319	TCA Silver Jubilee Mint Car, *79 u*	180	205	[1]
9320	Fort Knox Mint Car, *79 u*	205	235	[1]
9321	Santa Fe 1-D Tank Car (FARR no. 1), *79*	36	50	[1]
9322	Santa Fe Covered Quad Hopper (FARR no. 1), *79*	65	75	[1]
9323	Santa Fe B/W Caboose (FARR no. 1), *79*	49	60	[1]
9324	Tootsie Roll 1-D Tank Car, *79–81*	47	80	[2]
9325	Norfolk & Western Flatcar w/ fences, *79–81 u*	5	10	[1]
9325	(See 9363, 9364)			
9326	Burlington Northern B/W Caboose, *79–80*	24	29	[1]
[9326]	TTOS Burlington Northern B/W Caboose, *82 u*		NRS	
9327	Bakelite 3-D Tank Car, *80*	19	28	[1]
9328	Chessie System B/W Caboose, *80*	40	45	[1]
9329	Chessie System Crane Car, *80*	55	70	[1]
(9330)	"Kickapoo" Dump Car, *72, 79*	3	8	[1]
9331	Union 76 1-D Tank Car, *79*	50	60	[1]
9332	Reading Crane Car, *79*	47	70	[1]
9333	Southern Pacific Flatcar w/ trailers, *79–80*	30	40	[1]

		Exc	New	Cond/$
9334	Humble 1-D Tank Car, *79*	25	35	1
9335	B&O Log Dump Car, *86*	15	20	1
9336	CP Rail Gondola w/ canisters, *79*	21	31	1
9338	Penn Power Quad Hopper, *79*	60	75	1
9339	Great Northern Boxcar (O27), *79–83, 85 u, 86*	7	10	1
9340	Illinois Central Gondola w/ canisters (O27), *79–81, 82 u, 83*	5	10	1
9341	ACL SP-Type Caboose, *79–82, 86 u, 87–90*	6	8	1
9344	Citgo 3-D Tank Car, *80*	44	55	2
9345	Reading Searchlight Car, *84–85*	20	25	1
9346	Wabash SP-Type Caboose, *79*	6	10	1
9347	TTOS Niagara Falls 3-D Tank Car, *79 u*	40	50	1
9348	Santa Fe Crane Car (FARR no. 1), *79 u*	55	65	2
9349	San Francisco Mint Car, *80*	105	150	2
9351	PRR Auto Carrier (3-tier), *80*	20	35	1
9352	Trailer Train Flatcar w/ C&NW trailers, *80*	65	75	1
[9352]	Trailer Train Flatcar w/ Circus trailers, *80 u*	30	40	1
9353	Crystal Line 3-D Tank Car, *80*	21	32	1
9354	Pennzoil 1-D Tank Car, *80, 81 u*	40	50	1
9355	Delaware & Hudson B/W Caboose, *80*	30	40	1
[9355]	TTOS D&H B/W Caboose, *82 u*		NRS	
9356	Life Savers Stik-O-Pep 1-D Tank Car, *80 u*		NM	
9357	Smokey Mountain Bobber Caboose, *79*	8	10	1
9358	LCCA Sands of Iowa Covered Quad Hopper, *80 u*	30	40	1
9359	National Basketball Association Boxcar (O27), *79–80 u*	20	25	1
9360	National Hockey League Boxcar (O27), *79–80 u*	20	25	1
9361	C&NW B/W Caboose, *80*	55	65	1
[9361]	TTOS C&NW B/W Caboose, *82 u*		NRS	
9362	Major League Baseball Boxcar (O27), *79–80 u*	20	25	1

		Exc	New	Cond/$
(9363)	N&W Flatcar w/ dump bin "9325" (027), *79*	5	8	___[1]
(9364)	N&W Flatcar w/ crane "9325" (027), *79*	8	10	___[1]
9365	Toys "R" Us Boxcar (027), *79 u*	40	50	___[1]
9366	Union Pacific Covered Quad Hopper (FARR no. 2), *80*	30	35	___[1]
9367	Union Pacific 1-D Tank Car (FARR no. 2), *80*	30	39	___[1]
9368	Union Pacific B/W Caboose (FARR no. 2), *80*	38	47	___[1]
9369	Sinclair 1-D Tank Car, *80*	50	60	___[1]
9370	Seaboard Gondola w/ canisters, *80*	22	27	___[1]
9371	Atlantic Sugar Covered Quad Hopper, *80*	29	39	___[1]
9372	Seaboard B/W Caboose, *80*	30	46	___[1]
9373	Getty 1-D Tank Car, *80–81, 83 u*	40	50	___[1]
9374	Reading Covered Quad Hopper, *80–81, 83 u*	50	55	___[1]
9375	Union Pacific Flatcar w/ fences (027), *80*		NM	___
9376	Soo Line Boxcar (027), *81 u*		NRS	___
9376	Texas & Pacific SP-Type Caboose, *80*		NM	___
9377	Missouri Pacific Boxcar (027), *80*		NM	___
9378	Lionel Derrick Car, *80–82*	25	30	___[1]
9379	Santa Fe Gondola w/ canisters, *80–81, 83 u*	24	34	___[1]
9380	NYNH&H SP-Type Caboose, *80–81*	10	12	___[1]
9381	Chessie System SP-Type Caboose, *80*	8	10	___[1]
9382	Florida East Coast B/W Caboose, *80*	30	40	___[1]
[9382]	TTOS Florida East Coast B/W Caboose, *82 u*		NRS	___
9383	Union Pacific Flatcar w/ trailers (FARR no. 2), *80 u*	39	43	___[2]
9384	Great Northern Operating Hopper, *81*	70	85	___[1]
9385	Alaska Gondola w/ canisters, *81*	38	47	___[1]
9386	Pure Oil 1-D Tank Car, *81*	45	55	___[1]
9387	Burlington B/W Caboose, *81*	45	60	___[1]
9388	Toys "R" Us Boxcar (027), *81 u*	40	50	___[1]
9389	Lionel Radioactive Waste Car, *81–82*	39	55	___[1]
9398	PRR Coal Dump Car, *83–84*	20	25	___[1]
9399	C&NW Coal Dump Car, *83–85*	15	20	___[1]
9400	Conrail Boxcar, *78*	15	20	___[1]

		Exc	New	Cond/$
[9427]	Sacramento-Sierra TCA Bay Line Boxcar, *81 u*	—	41	___ [1]
9428	TP&W Boxcar, *80–81, 83 u*	35	40	___ [1]
9429	"The Early Years" Boxcar, *80*	27	32	___ [1]
9430	"The Standard Gauge Years" Boxcar, *80*	23	27	___ [1]
9431	"The Prewar Years" Boxcar, *80*	23	27	___ [2]
9432	"The Postwar Years" Boxcar, *80*	80	90	___ [1]
9433	"The Golden Years" Boxcar, *80*	60	85	___ [1]
9434	Joshua Lionel Cowen "The Man" Boxcar, *80 u*	46	60	___ [2]
9435	LCCA Central of Georgia Boxcar, *81 u*	31	41	___ [1]
9436	Burlington Boxcar, *81*	39	49	___ [1]
9437	Northern Pacific Stock Car, *81*	36	60	___ [1]
9438	Ontario Northland Boxcar, *81*	20	30	___ [1]
9439	Ashley Drew & Northern Boxcar, *81*	10	20	___ [1]
9440	Reading Boxcar, *81*	50	70	___ [1]
9441	Pennsylvania Boxcar, *81*	60	80	___ [1]
9442	Canadian Pacific Boxcar, *81*	15	25	___ [1]
9443	Florida East Coast Boxcar, *81*	15	18	___ [1]
[9443]	Southern TCA Florida East Coast Boxcar, *81 u*	—	27	___ [1]
9444	Louisiana Midland Boxcar, *81*	15	20	___ [1]
[9444]	Sacramento-Sierra TCA Louisiana Midland Boxcar, *82 u*	—	41	___ [1]
9445	Vermont Northern Boxcar, *81*	15	20	___ [1]
[9445]	NETCA Vermont Northern Boxcar, *81 u*	25	30	___ [1]
9446	Sabine River & Northern Boxcar, *81*	15	20	___ [2]
9447	Pullman Standard Boxcar, *81*	18	23	___ [1]
9448	Santa Fe Stock Car, *81–82*	50	60	___ [1]
9449	Great Northern Boxcar (FARR no. 3), *81*	40	50	___ [1]
9450	Great Northern Stock Car (FARR no. 3), *81 u*	70	80	___ [2]
9451	Southern Boxcar (FARR no. 4), *83*	38	43	___ [1]
9452	Western Pacific Boxcar, *82–83*	15	20	___ [1]
[9452]	Sacramento-Sierra TCA WP Boxcar, *83 u*	—	41	___ [1]
9453	MPA Boxcar, *82–83*	14	19	___ [1]
9454	New Hope & Ivyland Boxcar, *82–83*	15	20	___ [1]
9455	Milwaukee Road Boxcar, *82–83*	15	20	___ [1]

		Exc	New	Cond/$
[9400]	NETCA Conrail Boxcar, *78 u*	28	33	___[1]
9401	Great Northern Boxcar, *78*	15	20	___[1]
[9401]	Detroit-Toledo TCA GN Boxcar, *78 u*	—	27	___[1]
9402	Susquehanna Boxcar, *78*	31	36	___[1]
9403	Seaboard Coast Line Boxcar, *78*	15	20	___[1]
[9403]	Southern TCA SCL Boxcar, *78 u*	—	23	___[1]
9404	NKP Boxcar, *78*	25	30	___[1]
9405	Chattahoochee Boxcar, *78*	16	21	___[1]
[9405]	Southern TCA Chattahoochee Boxcar, *79 u*	—	27	___[1]
9406	D&RGW Boxcar, *78–79*	15	20	___[1]
9407	Union Pacific Stock Car, *78*	33	38	___[1]
9408	Lionel Lines Circus Stock Car (SSS), *78*	36	45	___[2]
9411	Lackawanna "Phoebe Snow" Boxcar, *78*	50	60	___[1]
9412	RF&P Boxcar, *79*	20	30	___[1]
[9412]	WB&A TCA RF&P Boxcar, *79 u*	—	27	___[1]
9413	Napierville Junction Boxcar, *79*	15	20	___[1]
[9413]	LCAC Napierville Junction Boxcar, *80 u*		NRS	___
9414	Cotton Belt Boxcar, *79*	20	25	___[1]
[9414]	LOTS Cotton Belt Boxcar, *80 u*	—	45	___[1]
[9414]	Sacramento-Sierra TCA Cotton Belt Boxcar, *80 u*	—	41	___[1]
9415	Providence & Worcester Boxcar, *79*	15	20	___[1]
[9415]	NETCA Providence & Worcester Boxcar, *79 u*	25	30	___[1]
9416	MD&W Boxcar, *79, 81*	14	19	___[1]
9417	CP Rail Boxcar, *79*	35	45	___[1]
9418	FARR Boxcar, *79 u*	55	65	___[1]
9419	Union Pacific Boxcar (FARR no. 2), *80*	24	28	___[1]
9420	B&O "Sentinel" Boxcar, *80*	26	31	___[2]
9421	Maine Central Boxcar, *80*	12	20	___[1]
9422	EJ&E Boxcar, *80*	15	25	___[1]
9423	NYNH&H Boxcar, *80*	15	30	___[1]
[9423]	NETCA NYNH&H Boxcar, *80 u*	25	30	___[1]
9424	TP&W Boxcar, *80*	20	25	___[1]
9425	British Columbia DD Boxcar, *80*	23	28	___[1]
9426	Chesapeake & Ohio Boxcar, *80*	25	40	___[1]
9427	Bay Line Boxcar, *80–81*	15	20	___[1]

		Exc	New	Cond/$
9456	PRR DD Boxcar (FARR no. 5), *84–85*	33	42	1
9460	LCCA D&TS DD Boxcar, *82 u*	35	45	1
9461	Norfolk & Southern Boxcar, *82*	35	60	1
9462	Southern Pacific Boxcar, *83–84*	20	25	1
9463	Texas & Pacific Boxcar, *83–84*	17	22	1
9464	NC&StL Boxcar, *83–84*	15	20	1
9465	Santa Fe Boxcar, *83–84*	15	25	1
9466	Wanamaker Boxcar, *82 u*	75	95	1
[9466]	Atlantic TCA Wanamaker Boxcar, *83 u*		NRS	
9467	Tennessee World's Fair Boxcar, *82 u*	45	55	1
9468	Union Pacific DD Boxcar, *83*	50	55	2
9469	NYC "Pacemaker" Boxcar (Std. O), *84–85*	90	115	2
9470	Chicago Beltline Boxcar, *84*	15	20	1
9471	Atlantic Coast Line Boxcar, *84*	15	20	1
[9471]	Southern TCA Atlantic Coast Line Boxcar, *84 u*	—	27	1
9472	Detroit & Mackinac Boxcar, *84*	20	25	1
9473	Lehigh Valley Boxcar, *84*	20	25	1
9474	Erie-Lackawanna Boxcar, *84*	39	49	1
9475	D&H "I Love NY" Boxcar, *84 u*	27	43	1
[9475]	LCOL D&H "I Love New York" Boxcar, *85 u*	—	27	1
9476	PRR Boxcar (FARR no. 5), *84–85*	50	55	2
9480	MN&S Boxcar, *85–86*	17	22	1
9481	Seaboard System Boxcar, *85–86*	17	22	1
9482	Norfolk & Southern Boxcar, *85–86*	15	20	1
[9482]	Southern TCA Norfolk & Southern Boxcar, *85 u*	—	27	1
9483	Manufacturers Railway Boxcar, *85–86*	15	20	1
9484	Lionel 85th Anniversary Boxcar, *85*	21	25	2
9486	GTW "I Love Michigan" Boxcar, *86*	20	30	1
9490	Christmas Boxcar for Lionel Employees, *85 u*	—	1550	1
9491	Christmas Boxcar, *86 u*	46	65	1
9492	Lionel Lines Boxcar, *86*	29	33	2
9500	Milwaukee Road Passenger Car, *73*	40	60	1

		Exc	New	Cond/$
9501	Milwaukee Road Passenger Car, 73 u, 74–76	31	41	1
9502	Milwaukee Road Observation Car, 73	40	60	1
9503	Milwaukee Road Passenger Car, 73	40	60	1
9504	Milwaukee Road Passenger Car, 73 u, 74–76	31	41	1
9505	Milwaukee Road Passenger Car, 73 u, 74–76	31	41	1
9506	Milwaukee Road Combination Car, 74 u, 75–76	27	42	1
9507	PRR Passenger Car, 74–75	40	60	1
9508	PRR Passenger Car, 74–75	40	60	1
9509	PRR Observation Car, 74–75	50	75	1
9510	PRR Combination Car, 74 u, 75–76	30	40	2
9511	Milwaukee Road Passenger Car, 74 u	30	55	2
9512	TTOS Summerdale Junction Passenger Car, 74 u	40	50	1
9513	PRR Passenger Car, 75–76	29	49	1
9514	PRR Passenger Car, 75–76	29	49	1
9515	PRR Passenger Car, 75–76	29	49	1
9516	B&O Passenger Car, 76	30	50	1
9517	B&O Passenger Car, 75	50	75	1
9518	B&O Observation Car, 75	50	75	1
9519	B&O Combination Car, 75	50	75	1
9520	TTOS Phoenix Combination Car, 75 u	35	40	1
9521	PRR Baggage Car, 75 u, 76	90	110	2
9522	Milwaukee Road Baggage Car, 75 u, 76	95	115	1
9523	B&O Baggage Car, 75 u, 76	70	80	1
9524	B&O Passenger Car, 76	40	60	1
9525	B&O Passenger Car, 76	40	60	1
9526	TTOS Snowbird Observation Car, 76 u	35	40	1
(9527)	Milwaukee Road Campaign Observation Car, 76 u	50	75	1
(9528)	PRR Campaign Observation Car, 76 u	55	80	1
(9529)	B&O Campaign Observation Car, 76 u	55	80	1
9530	Southern Baggage Car, 77–78	45	70	1
9531	Southern Combination Car, 77–78	45	70	1

		Exc	New	Cond/$
9532	Southern Passenger Car, *77–78*	45	70	[1]
9533	Southern Passenger Car, *77–78*	45	70	[1]
9534	Southern Observation Car, *77–78*	45	70	[1]
9535	TTOS Columbus Baggage Car, *77 u*	35	40	[1]
9536	Blue Comet Baggage Car, *78–80*	42	60	[1]
9537	Blue Comet Combination Car, *78–80*	45	65	[1]
9538	Blue Comet Passenger Car, *78–80*	41	55	[1]
9539	Blue Comet Passenger Car, *78–80*	41	55	[1]
9540	Blue Comet Observation Car, *78–80*	45	65	[1]
9541	Santa Fe Baggage Car, *80–82*	20	30	[1]
(9544)	TCA Chicago Observation Car "1980", *80 u*	—	60	[1]
9545	Union Pacific Baggage Car, *84*	100	125	[1]
9546	Union Pacific Combination Car, *84*	100	125	[1]
9547	Union Pacific Observation Car, *84*	100	125	[1]
(9548)	Union Pacific "Placid Bay" Passenger Car, *84*	100	125	[1]
(9549)	Union Pacific "Ocean Sunset" Passenger Car, *84*	100	125	[1]
9551	W&ARR Baggage Car, *77 u, 78–80*	45	60	[1]
9552	W&ARR Passenger Car, *77 u, 78–80*	45	60	[1]
9553	W&ARR Flatcar w/ horses, *77 u, 78–80*	30	50	[1]
(9554)	Chicago & Alton Baggage Car, *81*	50	75	[1]
(9555)	Chicago & Alton Combination Car, *81*	50	75	[1]
(9556)	Chicago & Alton "Wilson" Passenger Car, *81*	60	90	[1]
(9557)	Chicago & Alton "Webster Groves" Passenger Car, *81*	60	90	[1]
(9558)	Chicago & Alton Observation Car, *81*	50	75	[1]
9559	Rock Island Baggage Car, *81–82*	40	60	[1]
9560	Rock Island Passenger Car, *81–82*	40	60	[1]
9561	Rock Island Passenger Car, *81–82*	40	60	[1]
(9562)	Norfolk & Western Baggage Car "577", *81*	90	115	[1]
(9563)	Norfolk & Western Combination Car "578", *81*	90	115	[1]
(9564)	Norfolk & Western Passenger Car "579", *81*	100	115	[1]

		Exc	New	Cond/$
(9565)	Norfolk & Western Passenger Car "580", *81*	95	110	[1]
(9566)	Norfolk & Western Observation Car "581", *81*	100	115	[1]
(9567)	Norfolk & Western Vista Dome Car "582", *81 u*	310	445	[3]
9569	PRR Combination Car, *81 u*	125	150	[1]
9570	PRR Baggage Car, *79*	125	150	[1]
9571	PRR Passenger Car, *79*	140	175	[1]
9572	PRR Passenger Car, *79*	140	175	[1]
9573	PRR Vista Dome Car, *79*	125	150	[1]
9574	PRR Observation Car, *79*	125	150	[1]
9575	PRR Passenger Car, *79–80 u*	125	155	[1]
9576	Burlington Baggage Car, *80*	100	115	[1]
9577	Burlington Passenger Car, *80*	100	115	[1]
9578	Burlington Passenger Car, *80*	100	115	[1]
9579	Burlington Vista Dome Car, *80*	100	115	[1]
9580	Burlington Observation Car, *80*	100	115	[1]
9581	Chessie System Baggage Car, *80*	60	75	[1]
9582	Chessie System Combination Car, *80*	60	75	[1]
9583	Chessie System Passenger Car, *80*	60	75	[1]
9584	Chessie System Passenger Car, *80*	60	75	[1]
9585	Chessie System Observation Car, *80*	60	75	[1]
9586	Chessie System Dining Car, *86 u*	100	115	[1]
9588	Burlington Vista Dome Car, *80 u*	125	140	[1]
(9589)	Southern Pacific Baggage Car, *82–83*	100	120	[1]
(9590)	Southern Pacific Combination Car, *82–83*	100	120	[1]
(9591)	Southern Pacific "Pullman" Passenger Car, *82–83*	100	120	[1]
(9592)	Southern Pacific "Chair" Passenger Car, *82–83*	100	120	[1]
(9593)	Southern Pacific Observation Car, *82–83*	100	120	[1]
9594	NYC Baggage Car, *83–84*	100	120	[2]
9595	NYC Combination Car, *83–84*	100	120	[1]
(9596)	NYC "Wayne County" Passenger Car, *83–84*	100	120	[1]

		Exc	New	Cond/$
(9597)	NYC "Hudson River" Passenger Car, *83–84*	100	120	___ 1
(9598)	NYC Observation Car, *83–84*	100	120	___ 1
(9599)	Chicago & Alton Dining Car, *86 u*	100	120	___ 1
9600	Chessie System Hi-cube Boxcar, *75 u, 76–77*	20	23	___ 1
9601	ICG Hi-cube Boxcar, *75 u, 76–77*	20	23	___ 1
[9601]	Gateway TCA ICG Hi-cube Boxcar, *77 u*	—	23	___ 1
9602	Santa Fe Hi-cube Boxcar, *75 u, 76–77*	20	23	___ 1
9603	Penn Central Hi-cube Boxcar, *76–77*	20	23	___ 1
9604	Norfolk & Western Hi-cube Boxcar, *76–77*	20	23	___ 1
9605	NH Hi-cube Boxcar, *76–77*	19	29	___ 1
9606	Union Pacific Hi-cube Boxcar, *76 u, 77*	20	23	___ 1
9607	Southern Pacific Hi-cube Boxcar, *76 u, 77*	20	23	___ 1
9608	Burlington Northern Hi-cube Boxcar, *76 u, 77*	20	23	___ 1
9610	Frisco Hi-cube Boxcar, *77*	31	46	___ 1
9611	TCA Boston Hi-cube Boxcar, *78 u*	27	32	___ 1
9620	NHL Wales Boxcar, *80*	20	25	___ 1
9621	NHL Campbell Boxcar, *80*	20	25	___ 1
9622	NBA Western Boxcar, *80*	20	25	___ 1
9623	NBA Eastern Boxcar, *80*	20	25	___ 1
9624	National League Baseball Boxcar, *80*	20	25	___ 1
9625	American League Baseball Boxcar, *80*	20	25	___ 1
9626	Santa Fe Hi-cube Boxcar, *82–84*	15	20	___ 1
9627	Union Pacific Hi-cube Boxcar, *82–83*	15	20	___ 1
9628	Burlington Northern Hi-cube Boxcar, *82–84*	15	20	___ 1
9629	Chessie System Hi-cube Boxcar, *83–84*	20	30	___ 1
9660	Mickey Mouse Hi-cube Boxcar, *77–78*	43	48	___ 1
9661	Goofy Hi-cube Boxcar, *77–78*	40	45	___ 1
9662	Donald Duck Hi-cube Boxcar, *77–78*	44	50	___ 1
9663	Dumbo Hi-cube Boxcar, *77 u, 78*	43	75	___ 1
9664	Cinderella Hi-cube Boxcar, *77 u, 78*	50	75	___ 1
9665	Peter Pan Hi-cube Boxcar, *77 u, 78*	50	80	___ 1
9666	Pinocchio Hi-cube Boxcar, *78*	125	185	___ 1
9667	Snow White Hi-cube Boxcar, *78*	345	470	___ 1
9668	Pluto Hi-cube Boxcar, *78*	150	200	___ 1

		Exc	New	Cond/$
9669	Bambi Hi-cube Boxcar, *78 u*	60	95	1
9670	Alice In Wonderland Hi-cube Boxcar, *78 u*	50	75	1
9671	Fantasia Hi-cube Boxcar, *78 u*	55	65	1
9672	Mickey Mouse 50th Anniversary Hi-cube Boxcar, *78 u*	390	465	1
9678	TTOS Hollywood Hi-cube Boxcar, *78 u*	25	30	1
9700	Southern Boxcar, *72–73*	20	25	2
9700-1976	(See 9779)			
9701	B&O DD Boxcar, *72*	15	20	1
9701	TCA B&O DD Boxcar, *72 u*	75	100	1
[9701]	LCCA B&O DD Boxcar, *72 u*		NRS	
9702	Soo Line Boxcar, *72–73*	15	20	1
9703	CP Rail Boxcar, *72*	38	48	2
9704	Norfolk & Western Boxcar, *72*	12	20	1
9705	D&RGW Boxcar, *72*	13	22	1
[9705]	Sacramento-Sierra TCA D&RGW Boxcar, *75 u*	—	45	1
9706	C&O Boxcar, *72*	15	20	1
9707	MKT Stock Car, *72–75*	15	20	2
9708	U.S. Mail Boxcar, *72–75*	19	24	1
9708	U.S. Mail Toy Fair Boxcar, *73 u*	85	100	1
9709	BAR "State of Maine" Boxcar (SSS), *72–74*	37	42	1
9710	Rutland Boxcar (SSS), *72–74*	27	32	1
9711	Southern Boxcar, *74–75*	15	20	1
9712	B&O DD Boxcar, *73–74*	30	35	1
9713	CP Rail Boxcar, *73–74*	20	25	1
9713	CP Rail Season's Greetings Boxcar, *74 u*	100	125	1
9714	D&RGW Boxcar, *73–74*	21	26	1
9715	C&O Boxcar, *73–74*	20	25	1
9716	Penn Central Boxcar, *73–74*	20	25	1
9717	Union Pacific Boxcar, *73–74*	21	26	1
9718	Canadian National Boxcar, *73–74*	20	25	1
[9718]	LCAC Canadian National Boxcar, *79 u*		NRS	
9719	New Haven DD Boxcar, *73 u*	28	39	1
9723	Western Pacific Boxcar (SSS), *73–74*	30	35	1
9723	Western Pacific Toy Fair Boxcar, *74 u*	95	110	1
[9723]	Sacramento-Sierra TCA WP Boxcar, *73 u*		NRS	

		Exc	New	Cond/$
9724	Missouri Pacific Boxcar (SSS), *73–74*	28	33	___1
9725	MKT Stock Car (SSS), *73–75*	20	25	___1
[9725]	Midwest TCA Stock Car "00002", *75 u*		NRS	___
9726	Erie-Lackawanna Boxcar (SSS), *78*	25	30	___1
[9726]	Sacramento-Sierra TCA Erie-Lack. Boxcar, *79 u*	—	41	___1
9727	LCCA TA&G Boxcar, *73 u*	175	190	___1
9728	LCCA Union Pacific Stock Car, *78 u*	35	40	___1
9729	CP Rail Boxcar, *78*	35	40	___1
9730	CP Rail Boxcar, *74–75*	26	31	___1
[9730]	Western Michigan TCA CP Rail Boxcar, *74 u*		NRS	___
[9730]	Detroit-Toledo TCA CP Rail Boxcar, *76 u*	—	32	___1
[9730]	Sacramento-Sierra TCA CP Rail Boxcar, *77 u*	—	39	___1
9731	Milwaukee Road Boxcar, *74–75*	15	20	___1
9732	Southern Pacific Boxcar, *79 u*	30	40	___1
9733	LCCA Airco Boxcar w/ tank, *79 u*	50	65	___1
9734	Bangor & Aroostook Boxcar, *79*	30	40	___1
9735	Grand Trunk Boxcar, *74–75*	15	20	___1
9737	Central Vermont Boxcar, *74–76*	16	21	___1
9738	Illinois Terminal Boxcar, *82*	46	55	___1
9739	D&RGW Boxcar (SSS), *74–76*	20	25	___1
[9739]	LCCA D&RGW Boxcar, *78 u*		NRS	___
[9739]	North Texas TCA D&RGW Boxcar, *76 u*	—	23	___1
9740	Chessie System Boxcar, *74–75*	15	20	___1
[9740]	Great Lakes TCA Chessie System Boxcar, *76 u*	—	23	___1
[9740]	WB&A TCA Chessie System Boxcar, *76 u*	—	27	___1
9742	M&StL Boxcar, *73 u*	25	30	___1
9742	M&StL Season's Greetings Boxcar, *73 u*	100	125	___1
9743	Sprite Boxcar, *74 u, 75*	15	25	___1
9744	Tab Boxcar, *74 u, 75*	15	25	___1
9745	Fanta Boxcar, *74 u, 75*	15	25	___1
9747	Chessie System DD Boxcar, *75–76*	26	31	___1
9748	CP Rail Boxcar, *75–76*	17	22	___1
9749	Penn Central Boxcar, *75–76*	17	22	___1
9750	DT&I Boxcar, *75–76*	17	22	___1

		Exc	New	Cond/$
9751	Frisco Boxcar, *75–76*	19	24	[1]
9752	L&N Boxcar, *75–76*	17	22	[1]
9753	Maine Central Boxcar, *75–76*	15	20	[1]
[9753]	NETCA Maine Central Boxcar, *75 u*	25	35	[1]
9754	NYC "Pacemaker" Boxcar (SSS), *75–77*	30	45	[1]
[9754]	METCA NYC "Pacemaker" Boxcar, *76 u*	—	32	[1]
9755	Union Pacific Boxcar, *75–76*	21	26	[1]
9757	Central of Georgia Boxcar, *74 u*	18	23	[2]
9758	Alaska Boxcar (SSS), *75–77*	30	40	[2]
9759	Paul Revere Boxcar, *75 u*	40	50	[1]
9760	Liberty Bell Boxcar, *75 u*	40	50	[1]
9761	George Washington Boxcar, *75 u*	40	50	[1]
(9762)	Toy Fair Boxcar, *75 u*	150	200	[1]
9763	D&RGW Stock Car, *76–77*	20	25	[1]
9764	GTW DD Boxcar, *76–77*	22	28	[1]
9767	Railbox Boxcar, *76–77*	25	30	[1]
[9767]	Gateway TCA Railbox Boxcar, *78 u*	—	27	[1]
9768	B&M Boxcar, *76–77*	20	25	[1]
[9768]	NETCA B&M Boxcar, *76 u*	25	30	[1]
9769	B&LE Boxcar, *76–77*	16	21	[1]
9770	Northern Pacific Boxcar, *76–77*	15	20	[2]
9771	Norfolk & Western Boxcar, *76–77*	16	21	[1]
[9771]	LCCA N&W Boxcar, *77 u*		NRS	
[9771]	TCA Museum N&W Boxcar, *77 u*	30	40	[1]
[9771]	WB&A TCA N&W Boxcar, *78 u*	—	27	[1]
9772	Great Northern Boxcar, *76*	75	85	[1]
9773	NYC Stock Car, *76*	25	30	[1]
9774	TCA Orlando Southern Belle Boxcar, *75 u*	30	40	[1]
9775	M&StL Boxcar (SSS), *76*	27	32	[1]
9776	Southern Pacific "Overnight" Boxcar (SSS), *76*	50	60	[2]
9777	Virginian Boxcar, *76–77*	20	25	[1]
9778	Season's Greetings Boxcar, *75 u*	150	175	[1]
(9779)	TCA Philadelphia Boxcar "9700-1976", *76 u*	26	32	[1]
9780	Johnny Cash Boxcar, *76 u*	27	38	[2]
9781	Delaware & Hudson Boxcar, *77–78*	22	28	[1]
9782	Rock Island Boxcar, *77–78*	20	25	[1]

9783	B&O "Time-Saver" Boxcar, *77–78*	35	40 ___ [1]
[9783]	WB&A TCA B&O "Time-Saver" Boxcar, *77 u*	—	27 ___ [1]
9784	Santa Fe Boxcar, *77–78*	23	32 ___ [1]
9785	Conrail Boxcar, *77–78*	20	25 ___ [1]
[9785]	Midwest TCA Museum Express Conrail Boxcar, *77 u*		NRS ___
[9785]	NETCA Conrail Boxcar, *78 u*	25	30 ___ [1]
[9785]	Sacramento-Sierra TCA Conrail Boxcar, *78 u*	—	32 ___ [1]
9786	C&NW Boxcar, *77–79*	19	28 ___ [1]
[9786]	Midwest TCA Museum Express C&NW Boxcar, *79 u*		NRS ___
9787	Jersey Central Boxcar, *77–79*	18	27 ___ [1]
9788	Lehigh Valley Boxcar, *77–79*	15	20 ___ [1]
[9788]	Atlantic TCA Lehigh Valley Boxcar, *78 u*	20	25 ___ [1]
9789	Pickens Boxcar, *77*	29	38 ___ [1]
9801	B&O "Sentinel" Boxcar (Std. O), *73–75*	38	48 ___ [3]
9802	Miller High Life Reefer (Std. O), *73–75*	35	40 ___ [2]
9803	Johnson Wax Boxcar (Std. O), *73–75*	26	32 ___ [3]
9805	Grand Trunk Reefer (Std. O), *73–75*	33	38 ___ [1]
9806	Rock Island Boxcar (Std. O), *74–75*	55	75 ___ [2]
9807	Stroh's Beer Reefer (Std. O), *74–76*	75	110 ___ [2]
9808	Union Pacific Boxcar (Std. O), *75–76*	55	80 ___ [2]
9809	Clark Reefer (Std. O), *75–76*	39	44 ___ [2]
9811	Pacific Fruit Express Reefer (FARR no. 2), *80*	30	40 ___ [1]
9812	Arm & Hammer Reefer, *80*	20	25 ___ [1]
9813	Ruffles Reefer, *80*	20	25 ___ [1]
9814	Perrier Reefer, *80*	31	41 ___ [1]
9815	NYC "Early Bird" Reefer (Std. O), *84–85*	65	80 ___ [2]
9816	Brach's Candy Reefer, *80*	20	25 ___ [1]
9817	Bazooka Gum Reefer, *80*	20	25 ___ [1]
9818	Western Maryland Reefer, *80*	27	36 ___ [1]
9819	Western Fruit Express Reefer (FARR no. 3), *81*	30	40 ___ [1]
9820	Wabash Gondola w/ coal load (Std. O), *73–74*	41	50 ___ [3]

		Exc	New	Cond/$
9821	Southern Pacific Gondola w/ coal load (Std. O), *73–75*	41	45	3
9822	Grand Trunk Gondola w/ coal load (Std. O), *74–75*	42	47	1
9823	Santa Fe Flatcar w/ crates (Std. O), *75–76*	75	100	1
9824	NYC Gondola w/ coal load (Std. O), *75–76*	55	80	2
9825	Schaefer Reefer (Std. O), *76–77*	50	70	1
9826	P&LE Boxcar (Std. O), *76–77*	80	100	2
9827	Cutty Sark Reefer, *84*	23	27	1
9828	J&B Reefer, *84*	23	27	1
9829	Dewar's White Label Reefer, *84*	23	27	1
9830	Johnnie Walker Red Label Reefer, *84*	23	27	1
9831	Pepsi Cola Reefer, *82*	50	70	1
9832	Cheerios Reefer, *82*	100	125	1
9833	Vlasic Pickles Reefer, *82*	20	25	1
9834	Southern Comfort Reefer, *83–84*	20	25	1
9835	Jim Beam Reefer, *83–84*	20	25	1
9836	Old Grand-Dad Reefer, *83–84*	20	25	1
9837	Wild Turkey Reefer, *83–84*	19	24	1
9840	Fleischmann's Gin Reefer, *85*	23	27	1
9841	Calvert Gin Reefer, *85*	23	27	1
9842	Seagram's Gin Reefer, *85*	23	27	1
9843	Tanqueray Gin Reefer, *85*	23	27	1
9844	Sambuca Reefer, *86*	21	26	1
9845	Baileys Irish Cream Reefer, *86*	23	27	1
9846	Seagram's Vodka Reefer, *86*	23	27	1
9847	Wolfschmidt Vodka Reefer, *86*	23	27	1
9849	Lionel Lines Reefer, *83 u*	50	60	2
9850	Budweiser Reefer, *72 u, 73–75*	38	49	2
9851	Schlitz Reefer, *72 u, 73–75*	23	27	1
9852	Miller Reefer, *72 u, 73–77*	24	28	1
9853	Cracker Jack Reefer, caramel, *72 u, 73–75*			
	(A) Caramel, *72 u*	30	35	2
	(B) White, *73–75*	23	30	2
9854	Baby Ruth Reefer, *72 u, 73–76*	20	25	1
9855	Swift Reefer, *72 u, 73–77*	24	28	2
9856	Old Milwaukee Reefer, *75–76*	23	27	1

		Exc	New	Cond/$
9858	Butterfinger Reefer, *73 u, 74–76*	21	26	[1]
9859	Pabst Reefer, *73 u, 74–75*	25	30	[1]
9860	Gold Medal Reefer, *73 u, 74–76*	20	25	[1]
9861	Tropicana Reefer, *75–77*	26	36	[1]
9862	Hamm's Reefer, *75–76*	25	30	[1]
9863	REA Reefer (SSS), *74–76*	33	39	[2]
9864	TCA Seattle Reefer, *74 u*	32	36	[1]
9866	Coors Reefer, *76–77*	38	48	[1]
9867	Hershey's Reefer, *76–77*	40	50	[1]
9868	TTOS Oklahoma City Reefer, *80 u*	40	50	[1]
9869	Santa Fe Reefer (SSS), *76*	36	45	[2]
9870	Old Dutch Cleanser Reefer, *77–78, 80*	22	28	[1]
9871	Carling Black Label Reefer, *77–78, 80*	29	34	[1]
9872	Pacific Fruit Express Reefer, *77–79*	23	28	[1]
[9872]	Midwest TCA PFE Reefer, *79 u*		NRS	
9873	Ralston Purina Reefer, *78*	30	40	[1]
9874	Miller Lite Beer Reefer, *78–79*	30	45	[2]
9875	A&P Reefer, *78–79*	25	35	[1]
9876	Central Vermont Reefer, *78*	40	50	[1]
9877	Gerber Reefer, *79–80*	50	60	[1]
9878	Good and Plenty Reefer, *79*	19	24	[1]
9879	Hills Bros. Reefer, *79–80*	20	25	[1]
9879	Kraft Reefer, *79 u*		NM	
9880	Santa Fe Reefer (FARR no. 1), *79*	38	43	[2]
9881	Rath Packing Reefer, *79 u*	38	43	[1]
9882	NYC "Early Bird" Reefer, *79*	32	41	[2]
9883	Nabisco Oreo Reefer, *79*	60	70	[1]
[9883]	TTOS Phoenix Reefer, *83 u*		NRS	
9884	Fritos Reefer, *81–82*	20	25	[1]
9885	Lipton Tea Reefer, *81–82*	20	25	[1]
9886	Mounds Reefer, *81–82*	20	25	[1]
9887	Fruit Growers Express Reefer (FARR no. 4), *83*	45	60	[1]
9888	Green Bay & Western Reefer, *83*	60	65	[1]
16800	Lionel Railroader Club Ore Car, *86 u*	75	95	[1]
25000	(See 6476-135)			
[80948]	LOTS Michigan Central Boxcar, *82 u*	100	175	[1]
[86009]	LCAC CN Bunk Car, *86 u*	—	115	[1]

		Exc	New	Cond/$
97330	(See 9733)			
100408	(See 6567)			
[121315]	LOTS PRR Hi-cube Boxcar, *84 u*	75	100	___ 1
[830005]	LCAC CN Boxcar, *83 u*		NRS	___
[840006]	LCAC Canadian Wheat Board Covered Quad Hopper, *84 u*	—	145	___ 1
79C95204C	Sears Santa Fe Diesel set, *71 u*		NRS	___
79C97101C	Sears 5-unit set, *71 u*		NRS	___
79C9715C	Sears 4-unit set, *75 u*		NRS	___
79C9717C	Sears 7-unit set, *75 u*		NRS	___
79N9552C	Sears 6-unit set, *72 u*		NRS	___
79N9553C	Sears 6-unit Diesel set, *72 u*		NRS	___
79N95223C	Sears 6-unit set, *74 u*		NRS	___
79N96178C	Sears 4-unit set, *74 u*		NRS	___
79N97082C	Sears set, *70 u*		NRS	___
79N97101C	Sears 5-unit set, *75 u*		NRS	___
79N98765C	Sears Logging Empire set, *78 u*		NRS	___
UCS	Remote Control Track (O), *70*	5	8	___ 1
No Number	B&A Hudson and Standard O cars set, *86 u*	1750	2000	___ 1
No Number	The Blue Comet set, *78–80, 87 u*	630	720	___ 1
No Number	Burlington "Texas Zephyr" set, *80, 80 u*	1150	1350	___ 1
No Number	Jersey Central set, *86*	385	430	___ 1
No Number	Chessie System Special set, *80, 86 u*	630	720	___ 1
No Number	Chicago & Alton Limited set, *81, 86 u*	630	720	___ 1
No Number	Favorite Food Freight set, *81–82*	250	295	___ 1
No Number	The General set, *77–80*	250	295	___ 1
No Number	Great Northern set (FARR no. 3), *81, 81 u*	720	810	___ 1
No Number	Illinois Central "City of New Orleans" set, *85, 87, 93*	920	1100	___ 1
No Number	Joshua Lionel Cowen set, *80, 80 u, 82*	630	650	___ 1
No Number	Lionel Lines set, *82–84 u, 86, 86–87 u, 94–95*	590	720	___ 1

	Exc	New	Cond/$
No Number Mickey Mouse Express set, *77–78, 78 u*	1450	1700	___ [1]
No Number The Mint set, *79 u, 80–83, 84 u, 86 u, 87, 91 u, 93*	1100	1250	___ [1]
No Number NYC "20th Century Limited" set, *83, 83 u, 95*	1150	1350	___ [1]
No Number N&W "Powhatan Arrow" set, *81, 81 u, 82 u, 91 u*	1800	2150	___ [1]
No Number PRR set, *79–80, 79–80 u, 81 u, 83 u*	1350	1550	___ [1]
No Number PRR set (FARR no. 5), *84–85, 89 u*	630	720	___ [1]
No Number Rock Island & Peoria set, *80–82*	225	295	___ [1]
No Number Santa Fe set (FARR no. 1), *79, 79 u*	540	680	___ [1]
No Number Southern set (FARR no. 4), *83, 83 u*	720	810	___ [1]
No Number Southern Crescent Limited set, *77–78, 87 u*	540	630	___ [1]
No Number Southern Pacific Daylight Diesel set, *82–83, 82–83 u, 90 u*	2500	2700	___ [1]
No Number The Spirit of '76 set, *74–76*	560	630	___ [1]
No Number Toys "R" Us Thunderball Freight set, *75 u*		NRS	___
No Number Union Pacific set (FARR no. 2), *80, 80 u*	630	680	___ [1]
No Number Union Pacific "Overland Route" set, *84, 92 u*	900	1150	___ [1]
No Number Wabash set (FF no. 1), *86, 87*	920	1100	___ [1]
No Number L.A.S.E.R. Playmat, *81–82*	—	9	___ [1]
No Number Cannonball Freight Playmat, *81–82*	—	9	___ [1]
No Number Station Platform, *83–84*	—	9	___ [1]
No Number Rocky Mountain Platform, *83–84*	—	9	___ [1]
No Number Commando Assault Train Playmat, *83–84*	—	9	___ [1]
No Number Black Cave Flyer Playmat, *82*	—	9	___ [1]
No Number Pacific Northwest TCA F-3 AA, shells only, *74 u*	—	70	___ [1]
No Number LCCA Lionel Lines Tender only, *76–77 u*	25	30	___ [1]

No Number Lone Star TCA Texas Special F-3 A Unit,　　　NRS _____
　　　　　shell only, *81 u*

No Number Lone Star TCA Texas Special F-3 B Unit,　　　NRS _____
　　　　　shell only, *82 u*

No Number Sacramento-Sierra TCA Lionel Lines Tender,　　NRS _____
　　　　　shell only, *84 u*

Section 4
MODERN ERA 1987–1995
Lionel Trains, Inc. (LTI) Production

4	(See 18008, 18013)
T-4	(See 12923)
6	(See 18023)
12	(See 16137, 52029)
14	(See 52032)
27	(See 18841)
29	(See 52039)
36	(See 19042)
40	(See 11737)
52	(See 18555)
65-00637	(See 18927)
74	(See 19718)
91	(See 18558)
102	(See 19538)
109	(See 11809)
0121	(See 19717)
125	(See 19724)
150	(See 18553)
154	(See 18223)
155	(See 18224)
190	(See 17899)
197	(See 18843)
200	(See 18117/18118)
200A	(See 18121)
200B	(See 18122)
D200	(See 18512)
D202	(See 18506)
D203	(See 18506)
211	(See 19136)
C217	(See 19715)
D250	(See 18512)
254	(See 18920)
260	(See 19133)

300	(See 17307, 18934/18935)
C300	(See 19719)
301	(See 16807, 17308)
302	(See 17309)
303	(See 17310)
304	(See 18934/18935)
342	(See 11903)
342B	(See 11903)
343	(See 11903)
351C	(See 11724)
366A	(See 11724)
370B	(See 11724)
371	(See 18907)
371B	(See 18108)
400	(See 18505)
401	(See 18505)
425	(See 19135)
469	(See 19132)
483	(See 18306)
484	(See 18310)
485	(See 18310)
490	(See 18043)
494	(See 19140)
495	(See 19141)
501	(See 17213)
504	(See 18504)
507	(See 19128)
537	(See 19143)
538	(See 19142)
539	(See 16539)
576	(See 19108)
577	(See 19139)
582	(See 19144)
600	(See 18824)
601	(See 19111)
612	(See 18040)
618	(See 18042)

619	(See 18041)
638	(See 18638)
639	(See 18639)
672	(See 8610)
680	(See 51229)
681	(See 51240)
684	(See 51233)
685	(See 51245)
700	(See 18046)
721	(See 18554)
725A	(See 11734)
725B	(See 11734)
736A	(See 11734)
785	(See 18002)
788	(See 19818)
789	(See 19134)
858	(See 18116)
859	(See 18116)
863	(See 18309)
868	(See 18842)
901	(See 19532)
907	(See 16566, 18024)
914	(See 17893)
1017	(See 18921)
1041	(See 16538)
1115	(See 19040)
1116	(See 19041)
1192	(See 19120)
1200	(See 19116)
1201	(See 18022)
1212	(See 19118)
1240	(See 19117)
1289	(See 17875)
1322	(See 19119)
1390	(See 18044)
1403	(See 19145)
1458	(See 52031)

		Exc	New	Cond/$
1501	(See 18003)			
1538	(See 18838)			
1552	(See 52007)			
(1602)	Nickel Plate Special set, *86–91*	135	145	___[1]
(1615)	Cannonball Express set, *86–90*	75	85	___[1]
1623	(See 19146)			
(1685)	True Value Freight Flyer set, *86–87 u*	70	90	___[1]
(1687)	Freight Flyer set, *87–90*	46	55	___[1]
1750	(See 52035)			
1754	(See 52037)			
1803	(See 19147)			
1815	(See 18815)			
1818	(See 18931)			
1821	(See 18840)			
1900	(See 18502)			
1905-95	(See 16953)			
1921	(See 52047)			
1947	(See 18830)			
1952	(See 19960)			
1960	(See 18943)			
1987	(See 16205, 16310, 16311, 16507, 18605)			
[1988]	Midwest TCA IC Boxcar, *88 u*		NRS	___
1989	(See 16110, 17879, 18614)			
1990	(See 17883, 18090, 19708)			
1992	(See 18818)			
1993	(See 16655, 18713, 19927)			
1993X	(See 52008)			
1994	(See 52043, 52050)			
1995	(See 19934, 19935, 52062)			
1996	(See (52079, 52085)			
2000	(See 18710, 18711, 18712, 19131)			
2100	(See 18006)			
2101	(See 18011, 18557)			
2110	Graduated Trestle set (22), *70–88*	10	15	___[1]
2111	Elevated Trestle set (10), *70–88*	10	15	___[1]
(2113)	Tunnel Portals (2), *84–87*	10	15	___[1]
(2115)	Dwarf Signal, *84–87*	13	15	___[1]

		Exc	New	Cond/$
(2117)	Block Target Signal, *84–87*	20	25	1
(2122)	Extension Bridge w/ rock piers, *76–87*	25	35	1
2126	Whistling Freight Shed, *76–87*	25	30	1
2127	Diesel Horn Shed, *76–87*	25	30	1
2154	Automatic Highway Flasher, *70–87*	20	25	1
2162	Automatic Crossing Gate and Signal, *70–87, 94, 96*		CP	
(2170)	Street Lamps (3), *70–87*	15	20	1
(2180)	Road Signs (16), *77–95*		CP	
(2181)	Telephone Poles (10), *77–95*		CP	
2184	(See 17218)			
(2214)	Girder Bridge, *70–71, 72 u, 73–87*	5	10	1
2283	Die-cast Bumpers (2), *84–95*		CP	
2283	(See 52039)			
(2292)	Station Platform, *85–87*	6	10	1
(2300)	Operating Oil Drum Loader, *83–87*	100	125	1
(2309)	Mechanical Crossing Gate, *82–92*	4	8	1
(2311)	Mechanical Semaphore, *82–92*	4	8	1
2320	Flagpole kit, *83–87*	10	15	1
2321	Operating Sawmill, *84, 86–87*	100	120	1
2323	Operating Freight Station, *84–87*	80	100	1
2324	Operating Switch Tower, *84–87*	60	70	1
2400	(See 18305)			
2401	(See 18304)			
2402	(See 18304)			
2403	(See 18305)			
2487	(See 18833)			
2504	(See 19150)			
2601	(See 52023)			
2626	(See 18016)			
(2709)	Rico Station kit, *81–95*		CP	
(2716)	Short Extension Bridge, *88–95*		CP	
(2717)	Short Extension Bridge, *77–87*	3	5	1
(2719)	Watchman's Shanty kit, *77–87*	3	5	1
(2720)	Lumber Shed kit, *77–84, 87*	3	5	1
(2784)	Freight Platform kit, *81–90*	6	9	1
2848	(See 12848)			

(2900)	Lockon, *70–95*		CP ____
(2901)	Track Clips (12) (O27), *71–95*		CP ____
2902	(See 12902)		
2903	(See 18630)		
(2905)	Lockon and Wire, *74–95*		CP ____
2909	Smoke Fluid, *70–95*		CP ____
2910	OTC Contactor, *84–86, 88*	4	8 ____ [1]
(2927)	Maintenance kit, *70, 78–95*		CP ____
2930	(See 12930)		
2956	(See 19721)		
(2985)	The Lionel Train Book, *86–95*		CP ____
3000	(See 18009, 33000)		
3004	(See 33004)		
3005	(See 33005)		
3010	(See 23010)		
3011	(See 23011)		
3158	(See 18034)		
3285	(See 16805)		
3400	(See 19109)		
3500	(See 19110)		
3768	(See 18028)		
4000	(See 18812, 18825)		
4002	(See 18211)		
4004	(See 18218)		
4023	(See 52030)		
04039	(See 16908)		
04040	(See 16939)		
4060	Power Master Transformer, *80–93*	—	14 ____ [1]
4060	(See 18831)		
4100	(See 18030)		
4124	(See 18514)		
4136	(See 18819)		
4410	(See 18007)		
4501	(See 18018)		
4574	(See 18306)		
4600	(See 18816)		
4690	MW Transformer, *86–89*	75	95 ____ [1]

		Exc	New	Cond/$
4851	DC Transformer, *85–91, 94–95*		CP	___
4866	(See 18308)			
4907	(See 18313)			
(5012)	Curved Track 27", card of 4 (O27), *70–95*	—	25	___ [1]
(5014)	Half-Curved Track 27" (O27), *70–95*		CP	___
(5016)	36" Straight Track (O27), *87–88*	2	3	___ [1]
(5017)	Straight Track, card of 4 (O27), *70–95*		NRS	___ [1]
(5017)	Straight Track, card of 4 (O27), *70–95*		CP	___
5017	(See 51230)			
(5019)	Half-Straight Track (O27), *70–95*		CP	___
5020	90° Crossover (O27), *70–95*		CP	___
5020	(See 51234)			
(5021)	Left Manual Switch 27" (O27), *70–95*		CP	___
(5022)	Right Manual Switch 27" (O27), *70–95*		CP	___
5023	45° Crossover (O27), *70–95*		CP	___
(5024)	35" Straight Track (O27), *88–95*		CP	___
(5033)	Curved Track 27" (O27), *79–95*		CP	___
(5038)	Straight Track (O27), *79–95*		CP	___
(5041)	Insulator Pins (12) (O27), *70–95*		CP	___
(5042)	Steel Pins (12) (O27), *70–95*		CP	___
(5044)	Curved Track Ballast 42" (O27), *88*		NM	___
(5045)	Curved Track Ballast 54" (O27), *87–88*	1	2	___ [1]
(5046)	Curved Track Ballast 27" (O27), *87–88*	1	2	___ [1]
(5047)	Straight Track Ballast (O27), *87–88*	1	2	___ [1]
(5049)	Curved Track 42" (O27), *88–95*		CP	___
5100	(See 18001)			
(5113)	Curved Track 54" (O27), *79–95*		CP	___
5121	Left Remote Switch 27" (O27), *70–95*		CP	___
5122	Right Remote Switch 27" (O27), *70–95*		CP	___
5132	Right Remote Switch 31" (O), *80–94*	25	35	___ [1]
5133	Left Remote Switch 31" (O), *80–94*	25	35	___ [1]
(5149)	Remote Uncoupling Section (O27), *70–95*		CP	___
5165	Right Remote Switch 72" (O), *87–95*		CP	___
5166	Left Remote Switch 72" (O), *87–95*		CP	___
5167	Right Remote Switch 42" (O27), *88–95*		CP	___
5168	Left Remote Switch 42" (O27), *88–95*		CP	___
5300	(See 18636)			

5340	(See 18005, 18012)			
5366	(See 52078)			
5450	(See 18026, 18027, 18029)			
(5500)	Straight Track (O), *71–95*		CP	
5500	(See 18216)			
(5501)	Curved Track 31" (O), *71–95*		CP	
(5504)	Half-Curved Track 31" (O), *83–95*		CP	
(5505)	Half-Straight Track (O), *83–95*		CP	
5512	(See 18221)			
5517	(See 18222)			
(5522)	36" 540, *87–88*	3	4	[1]
(5523)	40" Straight Track (O), *88–95*		CP	
5530	Remote Uncoupling Section (O), *81–95*		CP	
5540	90° Crossover (O), *81–95*		CP	
(5543)	Insulator Pins (12) (O), *70–95*		CP	
5545	45° Crossover (O), *83–95*		CP	
(5551)	Steel Pins (12) (O), *70–95*		CP	
(5554)	Curved Track 54" (O), *90–95*		CP	
(5560)	Curved Track Ballast 72" (O), *87–88*	1	2	[1]
(5561)	Curved Track Ballast 31" (O), *87–88*	1	2	[1]
(5562)	Straight Track Ballast (O), *87–88*	1	2	[1]
(5572)	Curved Track 72" (O), *79–95*		CP	
5658	(See 16559)			
[5731]	TCA Museum L&N Reefer, *90 u*	100	150	[1]
5800	(See 18836)			
5808	(See 18826)			
6001	(See 18107)			
6002	(See 18107)			
6003	(See 17611)			
6005	(See 18821)			
6006	(See 18210)			
6007	(See 18217)			
6061	(See 16061)			
6062	(See 16062)			
6063	(See 16063)			
6064	(See 16064)			
6065	(See 16065)			

		Exc	New	Cond/$
6066	(See 16066)			
6067	(See 16067)			
6068	(See 16068)			
6069	(See 16069)			
6070	(See 16070)			
6071	(See 16071)			
6072	(See 16072)			
6073	(See 16073)			
6074	(See 16074)			
6080	(See 16080)			
6081	(See 16081)			
6082	(See 16082)			
6083	(See 16083)			
6084	(See 16084)			
6086	(See 16086)			
6087	(See 16087)			
6088	(See 16088)			
6089	(See 16089)			
6090	(See 16090)			
6108	(See 16108)			
6137	NKP Hopper (O27), *86–91*	15	20	[1]
6150	Santa Fe Hopper (O27), *85–86, 92 u*	12	18	[1]
6177	Reading Hopper (O27), *86–90*	15	20	[1]
6200	(See 18010)			
6226	(See 16226)			
6254	NKP Gondola w/ canisters, *86–91*	10	12	[1]
6258	Santa Fe Gondola w/ canisters (O27), *85–86, 92 u*	3	5	[1]
6336	(See 16336)			
6408	(See 16408)			
6430	Santa Fe SP-Type Caboose, *83–89*	6	10	[1]
6464	(See 19248, 19249, 19250, 19258, 19269, 19275)			
6464-095	(See 52051)			
6464-100	(See 19259, 19260)			
6464-125	(See 19267, 52063)			
6464-150	(See 19268, 52064)			

		Exc	New	Cond/$
6464-225	(See 19274)			
6464-275	(See 19273)			
6464-555	(See 52081)			
6464-1895	(See 52058)			
6464-1972	(See 52086)			
6464-1993	(See 52009)			
6464-1995	(See 52057)			
6464-1996	(See 52087)			
6493	L&C B/W Caboose, *86–87*	25	40	[1]
6508	(See 16508)			
6528	(See 16528)			
6576	Santa Fe Flatcar w/fences (O27), *92 u*	8	12	[1]
6585	PRR Flatcar w/ fences (O27), *86–90*	5	10	[1]
6602	(See 16053)			
6603	(See 16054)			
6609	(See 16079)			
6616	(See 16052, 16077)			
6620	(See 16050, 16075)			
6630	(See 16051, 16076)			
6919	Nickel Plate Road SP-Type Caboose, *86–91*	5	10	[1]
6921	PRR SP-Type Caboose, *86–90*	5	10	[1]
7000	(See 51301)			
7200	(See 19415)			
7220	Illinois Central Baggage Car, *85, 87*	100	125	[1]
7221	Illinois Central Combination Car, *85, 87*	100	125	[1]
7222	Illinois Central Passenger Car, *85, 87*	100	125	[1]
7223	Illinois Central Passenger Car, *85, 87*	100	125	[1]
7224	Illinois Central Dining Car, *85, 87*	100	125	[1]
7225	Illinois Central Observation Car, *85, 87*	100	125	[1]
7227	Wabash Dining Car (FF no. 1), *86–87*	100	115	[1]
7228	Wabash Baggage Car (FF no. 1), *86–87*	100	115	[1]
7229	Wabash Combination Car (FF no. 1), *86–87*	100	115	[1]
7230	Wabash Passenger Car (FF no. 1), *86–87*	100	115	[1]
7231	Wabash Passenger Car (FF no. 1), *86–87*	100	115	[1]
7232	Wabash Observation Car (FF no. 1), *86–87*	100	115	[1]
7420	(See 18513)			

		Exc	New	Cond/$
7500	(See 18214)			
7613	(See 17613)			
7643	(See 18215)			
[7692-1]	VTC Baggage Car (O27), *92 u*	30	35	___[1]
[7692-2]	VTC Combination Car (O27), *92 u*	30	35	___[1]
[7692-3]	VTC Dining Car (O27), *92 u*	30	35	___[1]
[7692-4]	VTC Passenger Car (O27), *92 u*	30	35	___[1]
[7692-5]	VTC Vista Dome Car (O27), *92 u*	30	35	___[1]
[7692-6]	VTC Passenger Car (O27), *92 u*	30	35	___[1]
[7692-7]	VTC Observation Car (O27), *92 u*	30	35	___[1]
7694	(See 52060)			
7805	(See 16078)			
7890	(See 17303)			
7914	Toys "R" Us Giraffe Car (O27), *85–89 u*	80	105	___[1]
7925	Erie-Lackawanna Boxcar (O27), *86–90*	9	13	___[1]
7926	NKP Boxcar (O27), *86–91*	8	11	___[1]
7930	True Value Boxcar (O27), *86–87 u*	40	60	___[1]
7932	Kay Bee Toys Boxcar (O27), *86–87 u*	40	50	___[1]
8004	(See 18004)			
8014	(See 18014)			
8100	(See 11711)			
8101	(See 11711)			
8102	(See 11711)			
8103	(See 18103)			
8119	(See 18119/18120)			
8120	(See 18119/18120)			
8124	(See 51300)			
8200	(See 18200)			
8201	(See 18201)			
8203	(See 18203)			
8204	(See 18204)			
8206	(See 18206)			
8209	(See 18209)			
8212	(See 18212)			
8213	D&RGW 2-4-2, *82–83, 84–91 u*	60	70	___[1]
8223	(See 18835)			
8300	(See 18300)			

		Exc	New	Cond/$
8301	(See 18301)			
8302	(See 18302)			
8303	(See 18303)			
8311	(See 18311)			
[8389]	NLOE Long Island Boxcar, *89 u*	50	60	___1
[8390]	NLOE Long Island Covered Quad Hopper, *90 u*	40	50	___1
[8391A]	NLOE Long Island Bunk Car, *91 u*	30	35	___1
[8391B]	NLOE Long Island Tool Car, *91 u*	30	35	___1
8392	NLOE Long Island 1-D Tank Car, *92 u*	50	60	___1
8393	(See 52019, 52020)			
8394	(See 52026)			
8395	(See 52061)			
8396	(See 52076)			
8400	(See 18400)			
8404	(See 18404)			
8419	(See 18419)			
8446	(See 18832)			
8459	(See 18202)			
8500	(See 18500, 18550)			
8501	(See 18219, 18501)			
8502	(See 18220)			
8503	(See 18503)			
8578	NYC Ballast Tamper, *85, 87*	110	115	___1
8580/8582	Illinois Central F-3 AA set, *85, 87*	400	450	___1
8581	Illinois Central F-3 B Unit, *85, 87*	175	200	___1
8586	(See 18208)			
8600	(See 18600)			
8601	(See 18601)			
8602	(See 18602)			
8604	(See 18604)			
8606	(See 18606)			
8607	(See 18607)			
8608	(See 18608)			
8609	(See 18609)			
(8610)	Wabash 4-6-2 "672" (FF no. 1), *86–87*	500	600	___1
8610	(See 18610)			

8611	(See 18611)			
8612	(See 18612)			
8613	(See 18613)			
8615	(See 18615)			
8616	(See 18616)			
8617	Nickel Plate Road 4-4-2, *86–91*	65	75	[1]
8618	(See 18618)			
8620	(See 18620)			
8621	(See 18621)			
8622	(See 18622)			
8623	(See 18623)			
8625	Pennsylvania 2-4-0, *86–90*	25	40	[1]
8625	(See 18625, 18635)			
8626	(See 18626)			
8627	(See 18627)			
8628	(See 18628)			
8632	(See 18632)			
8633	(See 18627, 18633, 18637)			
8640	(See 18640)			
8641	(See 18641)			
8642	(See 18642)			
8688	(See 18213)			
8689	(See 18207)			
8699	(See 18307)			
8700	(See 18700)			
8702	(See 18702)			
8704	(See 18704)			
8705	(See 18705)			
8706	(See 18706)			
8707	(See 18707)			
8716	(See 18716)			
8800	(See 18800)			
8801	(See 18801)			
8802	(See 18802)			
8803	(See 18803)			
8804	(See 18804)			
8805	(See 18805, 18890)			

8806	(See 18806)		
8807	(See 18807)		
8808	(See 18808)		
8809	(See 18551)		
8810	(See 18810)		
8811	(See 18811)		
8813	(See 18552)		
8814	(See 18814)		
8820	(See 18820)		
8827	(See 18827)		
8834	(See 18834)		
8837	(See 18837)		
8900	(See 18900)		
8901	(See 18901/18902)		
8902	ACL 2-4-0, *79–82, 86 u, 87–90*	15	20 _____ [1]
8902	(See 18901/18902)		
8903	(See 18903/18904)		
8904	(See 18903/18904)		
8906	(See 18906)		
8908	(See 18908/18909)		
8909	(See 18908/18909)		
8910	(See 18910)		
8911	(See 18911)		
[8912]	LCAC Canada Southern Operating Hopper, *89 u*	—	115 _____ [1]
8912	(See 18912)		
8913	(See 18913)		
8915	(See 18915)		
8916	(See 18916)		
8918	(See 18918)		
8919	(See 18919)		
8922	(See 18922)		
8923	(See 18923)		
8924	(See 18924)		
8925	(See 18925)		
8926	(See 18926)		
8932	(See 18932)		

		Exc	New	Cond/$
8933	(See 18933)			
8936	(See 18936)			
8937	(See 18937)			
8977	(See 18000)			
9001	Conrail Boxcar (O27), *86–87 u, 88–90*	5	10	___ [1]
9011	(See 19011)			
9015	(See 19015)			
9016	Chessie System Hopper (O27), *75–79, 87–88, 89 u*	5	7	___ [1]
9016	(See 19016)			
9017	(See 19017)			
9018	(See 19018)			
9019	(See 19019)			
9023	(See 19023)			
9024	(See 19024)			
9025	(See 19025)			
9026	(See 19026)			
9027	(See 19027)			
9031	NKP Gondola w/ canisters (O27), *73–75, 82–83, 84–91 u*	5	7	___ [1]
9031	(See 19031)			
9032	(See 19032)			
9033	PC Gondola w/ canisters (O27), *76–78, 82, 86 u, 87–90, 92 u*	3	4	___ [1]
9033	(See 19033)			
9047	(See 19047)			
9048	(See 19048)			
9049	(See 19049)			
9050	(See 19050)			
9077	D&RGW SP-Type Caboose, *76–83, 84–91 u*	6	8	___ [1]
9100	(See 18205, 19100)			
9101	(See 19101)			
9102	(See 19102)			
9103	(See 19103)			
9104	(See 19104)			
9105	(See 19105)			

		Exc	New	Cond/$
9106	(See 19106)			
9107	Dr Pepper Vat Car, *86–87*	25	35	[1]
9121	(See 19121)			
9129	(See 19129)			
9140	Burlington Gondola w/ canisters, *70, 73–82, 87–89*	6	8	[1]
9146	(See 19821)			
9215	(See 52004)			
9240	NYC Hopper (O27), *87 u*	20	25	[1]
9288	(See 18844)			
9312	(See 18905)			
8341	ACL SP-Type Caboose, *86 u, 87–90*	7	9	[1]
9405	(See 19716)			
9486	Artrain GTW "I Love Michigan" Boxcar, *87 u*	—	360	[1]
9517	(See 52005)			
9695	(See 52077)			
9706	(See 19706)			
9790	(See 19243)			
9791	(See 19244)			
10001	(See 19251)			
10009	(See 17008)			
10131	(See 16541)			
(11700)	Conrail Limited set, *87*	500	590	[1]
(11701)	Rail Blazer set, *87–88*	—	70	[1]
(11702)	Black Diamond set, *87*	160	205	[1]
(11703)	Iron Horse Freight set, *88–91*	120	125	[1]
(11704)	Southern Freight Runner set (SSS), *87*	205	270	[1]
(11705)	Chessie System Unit Train set, *88*	450	520	[1]
(11706)	Dry Gulch Line set (SSS), *88*	205	270	[1]
(11707)	Silver Spike set, *88–89*	180	250	[1]
(11708)	Midnight Shift set, *88 u, 89*	70	90	[1]
(11710)	CP Rail Freight set, *89*	405	520	[1]
(11711)	Santa Fe F-3 ABA set "8100", "8101", "8102", *91*	700	800	[5]
(11712)	Great Lakes Express set (SSS), *90*	305	330	[1]
(11713)	Santa Fe Dash 8-40B set, *90*	450	540	[1]

		Exc	New	Cond/$
(11714)	Badlands Express set, *90–91*	55	70	[1]
(11715)	Lionel 90th Anniversary set, *90*	225	270	[1]
(11716)	Lionelville Circus Special set, *90–91*	175	220	[1]
(11717)	CSX Freight set, *90*	225	295	[1]
(11718)	Norfolk Southern Dash 8-40C Unit Train set, *92*	590	680	[1]
(11719)	Coastal Freight set (SSS), *91*	225	295	[1]
(11720)	Santa Fe Special set, *91*	55	70	[1]
(11721)	Mickey's World Tour Train set, *91, 92 u*	135	180	[1]
(11722)	Girl's Train set, *91*	540	700	[1]
(11723)	Amtrak Maintenance Train set, *91, 92 u*	250	295	[1]
(11724)	Great Northern F-3 ABA set "366A","370B","351C", *92*	810	910	[2]
(11726)	Erie-Lackawanna Freight set, *91 u*	225	270	[1]
(11727)	Coastal Limited set, *92*	90	115	[1]
(11728)	High Plains Runner set, *92*	135	150	[1]
(11729)	L&N Express set, *92*		NRS	[1]
11730	Evergreen Intermodal Container (See 12805)			
11731	Maersk Intermodal Container (See 12805)			
11732	American President Lines Intermodal Container (See 12805)			
(11733)	Feather River set (SSS), *92*	295	360	[1]
(11734)	Erie Alco ABA set "725A", "725B", "736A" (FF no. 7), *93*	260	305	[1]
(11735)	New York Central Flyer set, *93–95*		NRS	[1]
(11736)	Union Pacific Express set, *93–95*	115	135	[1]
(11737)	TCA F-3 ABA set "40", *93 u*	520	690	[1]
(11738)	Soo Line set (SSS), *93*	270	305	[1]
(11739)	Super Chief set, *93–94*	115	125	[1]
(11740)	Conrail Consolidated set, *93*	250	270	[1]
(11741)	Northwest Express set, *93*	135	160	[1]
(11742)	Coastal Limited set, *93 u*	90	115	[1]
(11743)	Chesapeake & Ohio Freight set, *94*	225	270	[1]
(11744)	NYC Passenger/Freight set (SSS), *94*	270	315	[1]
(11745)	U.S. Navy set, *94–95*	160	180	[1]
(11746)	Seaboard Freight set, *94, 95 u*	90	115	[1]
(11747)	Lionel Lines Steam set, *95*	250	270	[1]

		Exc	New	Cond/$
(11748)	Amtrak set, *95*		NRS	1
(11749)	Western Maryland set (SSS), *95*	250	270	1
(11750)	McDonald's Nickel Plate Special set, *87 u*		NRS	1
(11751)	49C95171C Sears Pennsylvania Passenger set, *87 u*	135	180	1
(11752)	JCPenney Timber Master set, *87 u*	90	135	1
(11753)	Kay Bee Toys Rail Blazer set, *87 u*	90	115	1
(11754)	Key America set, *87 u*		NRS	1
(11755)	Timber Master set, *87 u*		NRS	1
(11756)	Hawthorne Freight Flyer set, *87–88 u*	70	90	1
(11757)	Chrysler Mopar Express set, *88 u*	270	295	1
(11758)	The Desert King set (SSS), *89*	180	225	1
(11759)	JCPenney Silver Spike set, *88 u*		NRS	1
(11761)	JCPenney Iron Horse Freight set, *88 u*		NRS	1
(11762)	True Value Cannonball Express set, *89 u*	90	135	1
(11763)	United Model Freight Hauler set, *88 u*		NRS	1
(11764)	49N95178 Sears Iron Horse Freight set, *88 u*	180	225	1
(11765)	Spiegel Silver Spike set, *88 u*		NRS	1
(11767)	Shoprite Freight Flyer set, *88 u*	90	135	1
(11769)	JCPenney Midnight Shift set, *89 u*		NRS	1
(11770)	49GY95280 Sears Circus set, *89 u*	180	205	1
(11771)	K-Mart Microracers set, *89 u*	70	90	1
(11772)	Macy's Freight Flyer set, *89 u*	135	180	1
(11773)	49GY95281 Sears NYC Passenger set, *89 u*		NRS	1
(11774)	Ace Hardware Cannonball Express set, *89 u*	135	160	1
(11775)	Anheuser-Busch set, *89–92 u*	180	225	1
(11776)	Pace Iron Horse Freight set, *89 u*	135	160	1
(11777)	49N95265 Sears Lionelville Circus Special set, *90 u*	205	225	1
(11778)	49N95264 Sears Badlands Express set, *90 u*	55	70	1
(11779)	49N95267 Sears CSX Freight set, *90 u*	225	270	1
(11780)	49N95266 Sears Northern Pacific Passenger set, *90 u*	180	225	1

		Exc	New	Cond/$
(11781)	True Value Cannonball Express set, *90 u*	90	135	___ [1]
(11783)	Toys "R" Us Heavy Iron set, *90–91 u*	180	225	___ [1]
(11784)	Pace Iron Horse Freight set, *90 u*	135	160	___ [1]
(11785)	Costco Union Pacific Express set, *90 u*	160	180	___ [1]
(11789)	Sears Illinois Central Passenger set, *91 u*	180	205	___ [1]
(11793)	Santa Fe set w/ mailer, *91 u*	55	70	___ [1]
(11794)	Mickey's World Tour set w/ mailer, *91 u*	90	115	___ [1]
(11796)	Union Pacific Express set, *91 u*	160	180	___ [1]
(11797)	Sears Coastal Limited set w/ mailer, *92 u*	90	115	___ [1]
(11800)	Toys "R" Us Heavy Iron Thunder Limited set, *92–93 u*	205	250	___ [1]
(11803)	Mall Promotion Nickel Plate Special set, *92 u*		NRS	___ [1]
(11804)	K-Mart Coastal Limited set, *92 u*	90	115	___ [1]
(11809)	Village Trolley Company set, *95*		NRS	___ [1]
(11810)	Budweiser Modern Era set, *93–94 u*	160	180	___ [1]
(11811)	United Auto Workers set, *93 u*	160	205	___ [1]
(11812)	Mall Promotion Coastal Limited set, *93 u*		NRS	___ [1]
(11813)	Crayola Activity Train set, *94 u, 95*	47	70	___ [1]
(11814)	Ford Limited Edition set, *94 u*	180	205	___ [1]
(11818)	Chrysler Mopar set, *94 u*	180	205	___ [1]
(11819)	Georgia Power set, *95 u*	450	520	___ [1]
(11820)	Red Wing Shoes NYC Flyer set, *95 u*	180	225	___ [1]
(11822)	Chevrolet set, *96 u*		NRS	___ [1]
(11903)	Atlantic Coast Line F-3 ABA set "342", "342B", "343", *96*	—	630	___ [1]
(11906)	Factory Selection Special set, *95 u*		NRS	___ [1]
12000	(See 52000)			
12046	(See 52046)			
12700	Erie Magnetic Gantry Crane, *87*	165	190	___ [1]
(12701)	Operating Fueling Station, *87*	80	100	___ [1]
(12702)	Control Tower, *87*	80	100	___ [1]
(12703)	Icing Station, *88–89*	80	100	___ [1]
(12704)	Dwarf Signal, *88–93*	15	20	___ [1]
(12705)	Lumber Shed kit "832K", *88–95*		CP	___
(12706)	Barrel Loader Building kit "826K", *87–95*		CP	___
(12707)	Billboards (3), *87–95*		CP	___

		Exc	New	Cond/$
(12708)	Street Lamps (3), *88–93*	7	10	[1]
(12709)	Banjo Signal, *87–91, 95*		CP	
(12710)	Engine House kit, *87–91*	25	30	[1]
(12711)	Water Tower kit, *87–95*		CP	
(12712)	Automatic Ore Loader, *87–88*	20	25	[1]
(12713)	Automatic Gateman, *87–88, 94–95*		CP	
(12714)	Automatic Crossing Gate, *87–91, 93–95*		CP	
(12715)	Illuminated Bumpers (2), *87–95*		CP	
(12716)	Searchlight Tower, *87–89, 91–92*	25	30	[1]
(12717)	Non-illuminated Bumpers (3), *87–95*		CP	
(12718)	Barrel Shed kit, *87–95*		CP	
(12719)	Animated Refreshment Stand, *88–89*	60	65	[1]
12720	Rotary Beacon, *88–89*	40	45	[1]
(12721)	Illuminated Extension Bridge w/ rock piers, *89*	30	45	[1]
(12722)	Roadside Diner w/ smoke, *88–89*	40	50	[1]
(12723)	Microwave Tower, *88–91, 94–95*	20	25	[1]
(12724)	Double Signal Bridge, *88–90*	45	60	[1]
12725	Lionel Tractor and Trailer, *88–89*	18	23	[1]
(12726)	Grain Elevator kit, *88–91, 94–95*		CP	
(12727)	Automatic Operating Semaphore, *89–95*		CP	
(12728)	Illuminated Freight Station, *89*	30	40	[1]
(12729)	Mail Pick-up set, *88–91, 95*	15	20	[1]
(12730)	Girder Bridge, *88–95*		CP	
(12731)	Station Platform, *88–95*		CP	
(12732)	Coal Bag, *88–95*		CP	
(12733)	Watchman Shanty kit, *88–95*		CP	
(12734)	Passenger/Freight Station, *89–95*		CP	
(12735)	Diesel Horn Shed, *88–91*	20	25	[1]
(12736)	Coaling Station kit, *88–91*	20	25	[1]
(12737)	Whistling Freight Shed, *88–95*		CP	
(12739)	Lionel Gas Company Tractor and Tanker, *89*	17	22	[1]
(12740)	Log Package (3), *88–92, 94–95*		CP	
12741	Union Pacific Intermodal Crane, *89*	215	255	[1]
(12742)	Gooseneck Street Lamps (2), *89–95*		CP	
(12743)	Track Clips (12) (O), *89–95*		CP	

		Exc	New	Cond/$
(12744)	Rock Piers (2), *89–92, 94–95*		CP	
(12745)	Barrel Pack (6), *89–95*		CP	
(12746)	Operating/Uncoupling Track (O27), *89–95*		CP	
(12748)	Illuminated Station Platform, *89–95*		CP	
(12749)	Rotary Radar Antenna, *89–92, 95*	35	40	[1]
(12750)	Crane kit, *89–91*	8	10	[1]
(12751)	Shovel kit, *89–91*	8	10	[1]
(12752)	History of Lionel Trains video (VHS), *89–92, 94*	22	25	[1]
(12753)	Ore Load (2), *89–91, 95*	2	3	[1]
(12754)	Graduated Trestle set (22), *89–95*		CP	
(12755)	Elevated Trestle set (10), *89–95*		CP	
(12756)	The Making of the Scale Hudson video (VHS), *91–94*	22	25	[1]
(12759)	Floodlight Tower, *90–95*		CP	
(12760)	Automatic Highway Flasher, *90–91*	35	40	[1]
(12761)	Animated Billboard, *90–91, 93, 95*	25	30	[1]
(12762)	Freight Station w/ train control and sounds, *90–91*		NM	
(12763)	Single Signal Bridge, *90–91, 93*	30	35	[1]
(12765)	Die-cast Auto Assortment (6), *90*		NM	
(12767)	Steam Clean and Wheel Grind Shop, *92–93, 95*	275	325	[1]
(12768)	Burning Switch Tower, *90, 93*	85	100	[1]
(12770)	Arch-Under Bridge, *90–95*		CP	
(12771)	Mom's Roadside Diner w/ smoke, *90–91*	40	60	[1]
(12772)	Illuminated Extension Bridge w/ rock piers, *90–95*		CP	
(12773)	Freight Platform kit, *90–95*		CP	
(12774)	Lumber Loader kit, *90–95*		CP	
12777	Chevron Tractor and Tanker, *90–91*	10	15	[1]
12778	Conrail Tractor and Trailer, *90*	10	15	[1]
12779	Lionelville Grain Company Tractor and Trailer, *90*	10	15	[1]
(12780)	RS-1 50 Watt Transformer, *90–93*	125	175	[1]
12781	N&W Intermodal Crane, *90–91*	200	235	[1]
(12782)	Lift Bridge, *91–92*	540	690	[1]

		Exc	New	Cond/$
12783	Monon Tractor and Trailer, *91*	10	15	[1]
(12784)	Intermodal Containers (3), *91*	15	20	[1]
12785	Lionel Gravel Company Tractor and Trailer, *91*	10	15	[1]
12786	Lionel Steel Company Tractor and Trailer, *91*	10	15	[1]
12787	Family Lines Intermodal Container (See 12784)			
12788	UP Intermodal Container (See 12784)			
12789	B&M Intermodal Container (See 12784)			
(12790)	ZW-II Transformer, *91*		NM	
(12791)	Animated Passenger Station, *91*	65	75	[1]
(12794)	Lionel Tractor, *91*	10	15	[1]
(12795)	Cable Reels (2), *91–95*		CP	
(12797)	Crossing Gate and Signal, *91*		NM	
(12798)	Forklift Loader Station, *92–95*	55	65	[1]
(12800)	Scale Hudson Replacement Pilot Truck, *91 u*	15	20	[1]
(12802)	"Chat & Chew" Roadside Diner w/ smoke and lights, *92–95*	50	55	[1]
(12804)	Highway Lights (4), *92–95*		CP	
(12805)	Intermodal Containers (3), *92*	10	15	[1]
12806	Lionel Lumber Company Tractor and Trailer, *92*	10	15	[1]
(12807)	Little Caesars Tractor and Trailer, *92*	10	15	[1]
12808	Mobil Tractor and Tanker, *92*	10	15	[1]
(12809)	Animated Billboard, *92–93*	25	30	[1]
(12810)	American Flyer Tractor and Trailer "DX26925", *94*	15	20	[1]
12811	Alka Seltzer Tractor and Trailer, *92*	10	15	[1]
(12812)	Illuminated Freight Station, *93–95*		CP	
(12818)	Animated Freight Station, *92, 94–95*	65	80	[1]
12819	Inland Steel Tractor and Trailer, *92*	10	15	[1]
(12821)	Lionel Catalog video (VHS), *92*	15	20	[1]
(12826)	Intermodal Containers (3), *93*	10	15	[1]
(12827)	CSX Intermodal Container "610584" (See 12826)			
(12828)	NYC Intermodal Container (See 12826)			

		Exc	New	Cond/$
(12829)	Great Northern Container (See 12826)			
12831	Rotary Beacon, *93–95*	35	40	[1]
(12832)	Block Target Signal, *93–95*		CP	
(12833)	RoadRailer Tractor and Trailer, *93*	10	15	[1]
12834	Pennsylvania Magnetic Gantry Crane, *93*	140	155	[1]
(12835)	Operating Fueling Station, *93*	75	90	[1]
12836	Santa Fe Quantum Tractor and Trailer, *93*	10	15	[1]
(12837)	Humble Oil Tractor and Tanker, *93*	10	15	[1]
(12838)	Crate Load (2), *93–95*		CP	
(12839)	Grade Crossing (2), *93–95*		CP	
(12840)	Insulated Straight Track (O), *93–95*		CP	
(12841)	Insulated Straight Track (O27), *93–95*		CP	
(12842)	Dunkin' Donuts Tractor and Trailer, *92 u*	32	37	[1]
(12843)	Die-cast Metal Sprung Trucks (2), *93–95*		CP	
(12844)	Coil Covers (2) (O), *93–95*		CP	
(12847)	Icing Station, *94–95*	100	115	[1]
(12848)	Lionel Oil Company Oil Derrick "2848", *94*	80	105	[1]
(12849)	Lionel Controller w/ wall pack, *94, 95 u*		CP	
(12852)	Trailer Frame, *94–95*		CP	
(12853)	Coil Covers (2) (Std. O), *94–95*		CP	
(12854)	U.S. Navy Tractor and Tanker, *94–95*	30	41	[1]
(12855)	Intermodal Containers (3), *94–95*	10	15	[1]
12856	CP Rail Intermodal Container (See 12855)			
12857	Frisco Intermodal Container (See 12855)			
12858	Vermont Railways Intermodal Container (See 12855)			
(12860)	Lionel Visitor's Center Tractor and Trailer, *94 u*	15	20	[1]
(12861)	Lionel Leasing Company Tractor, *94*	5	8	[1]
(12862)	Oil Drum Loader, *94–95*	100	120	[1]
(12864)	Little Caesars Tractor and Trailer, *94*	10	15	[1]
(12865)	Wisk Tractor and Trailer, *94*	10	15	[1]
(12866)	PH-1 Power House, *94 u, 95*		CP	
(12867)	PM-1 Power Master, *94 u, 95–96*		CP	
(12868)	CAB-1 Remote Controller, *94 u, 95–96*		CP	
(12869)	Marathon Oil Tractor and Tanker, *94*	15	20	[1]
(12873)	Operating Sawmill, *95–96*		CP	

		Exc	New	Cond/$
(12874)	Street Lamps (3), *94–95*		CP	
(12875)	Lionel Railroader Club Tractor and Trailer, *94 u*	19	28	[1]
(12877)	Operating Fueling Station, *95*	75	90	[1]
(12878)	Control Tower, *95*	55	70	[1]
(12880)	Power Station Transformer, *96*		NM	
(12881)	Chrysler Mopar Tractor and Trailer, *94 u*	40	50	[1]
(12882)	Lighted Billboard, *95*	10	15	[1]
(12883)	Dwarf Signal, *95*		CP	
(12884)	Truck Loading Dock kit, *95*		CP	
(12885)	40-watt Control System, *94 u, 95*		CP	
12886	395 Floodlight Tower, *95*		CP	
(12887)	Lionel Conductor Display, *95*		NM	
(12888)	Automatic Highway Flasher, *95*		CP	
(12889)	Operating Windmill, *95*		CP	
(12890)	Big Red Button, *94 u, 95*		CP	
(12891)	Lionel Lines Refrigerator Tractor and Trailer, *95*	10	12	[1]
(12892)	Automatic Flagman, *95*		CP	
(12893)	Power Master Cable, *94 u, 95*		CP	
(12894)	Single Signal Bridge, *95*		CP	
(12895)	Double Signal Bridge, *95*		CP	
(12896)	Tunnel Portals (2), *95*		CP	
(12897)	Engine House kit, *95*		CP	
(12898)	Flagpole kit, *95*		CP	
(12899)	Searchlight Tower, *95*		CP	
(12900)	Crane kit, *95*		CP	
(12901)	Shovel kit, *95*		CP	
(12902)	Marathon Oil Derrick "2902", *94 u, 95*	115	160	[1]
(12903)	Diesel Horn Shed, *95*		CP	
(12904)	Coaling Station kit, *95*		CP	
(12905)	Factory kit, *95*		CP	
(12906)	Maintenance Shed kit, *95*		CP	
(12907)	Intermodal Containers (3), *95*	10	15	[1]
(12908)	Western Pacific Intermodal Container (See 12907)			

		Exc	New	Cond/$
(12909)	Northern Pacific Intermodal Container "33621" (See 12907)			
(12910)	CP Rail Intermodal Container "680441" (See 12907)			
(12911)	Trainmaster Command Base, *95*		CP	___
12912	Oil Pumping Station, *95*		CP	___
(12914)	SC-1 Controller, *95*		CP	___
(12917)	Operating Switch Tower, *96*		CP	___
(12921)	LRRC Illuminated Station Platform, *95 u*	25	30	___ [1]
12922	NYC Operating Gantry Crane w/ coil covers, *96*	100	120	___ [1]
(12923)	Red Wing Shoes Tractor and Trailer "T-4", *95 u*	32	37	___ [1]
(12930)	Lionelville Oil Company Oil Derrick "2930", *95 u, 96*	80	100	___ [1]
15000	D&RGW Waffle-side Boxcar, *95*	20	25	___ [1]
15001	Seaboard Waffle-side Boxcar, *95*	20	25	___ [1]
15100	Amtrak Passenger Car (027), *95*	25	32	___ [1]
15101	Reading Baggage Car (027), *96*	25	32	___ [1]
15102	Reading Combination Car (027), *96*	25	32	___ [1]
15103	Reading Passenger Car (027), *96*	25	32	___ [1]
15104	Reading Vista Dome Car (027), *96*	25	32	___ [1]
15105	Reading Full Vista Dome Car (027), *96*	25	32	___ [1]
15106	Reading Observation Car (027), *96*	25	32	___ [1]
15791	(See 17889)			
15906	RailSounds Trigger Button, *90–95*		CP	___
16000	PRR Vista Dome Car (027), *87–88*	25	35	___ [1]
16001	PRR Passenger Car (027), *87–88*	25	35	___ [1]
16002	PRR Passenger Car (027), *87–88*	25	35	___ [1]
16003	PRR Observation Car (027), *87–88*	25	35	___ [1]
16009	PRR Combination Car (027), *88*	33	39	___ [1]
16010	Virginia & Truckee Passenger Car (SSS), *88*	40	50	___ [1]
16011	Virginia & Truckee Passenger Car (SSS), *88*	40	50	___ [1]
16012	Virginia & Truckee Baggage Car (SSS), *88*	40	50	___ [1]

16013	Amtrak Combination Car (O27), *88–89*	25	40____[1]
16014	Amtrak Vista Dome Car (O27), *88–89*	25	40____[1]
16015	Amtrak Observation Car (O27), *88–89*	25	40____[1]
16016	NYC Baggage Car (O27), *89*	25	35____[1]
16017	NYC Combination Car (O27), *89*	25	35____[1]
16018	NYC Passenger Car (O27), *89*	25	35____[1]
16019	NYC Vista Dome Car (O27), *89*	25	35____[1]
16020	NYC Passenger Car (O27), *89*	25	35____[1]
16021	NYC Observation Car (O27), *89*	25	35____[1]
16021	(See 17210)		
16022	Pennsylvania Baggage Car (O27), *89*	25	40____[1]
16022	(See 17211)		
16023	Amtrak Passenger Car (O27), *89*	25	35____[1]
16023	(See 17212)		
16024	NP Dining Car (O27), *92*	40	45____[1]
16027	LL Combination Car (O27) (SSS), *90*	40	50____[1]
16028	LL Passenger Car (O27) (SSS), *90*	40	50____[1]
16029	LL Passenger Car (O27) (SSS), *90*	40	50____[1]
16030	LL Observation Car (O27) (SSS), *90*	40	50____[1]
16031	Pennsylvania Dining Car (O27), *90*	35	40____[1]
16033	Amtrak Baggage Car (O27), *90*	25	35____[1]
16034	NP Baggage Car (O27), *90–91*	20	30____[1]
16035	NP Combination Car (O27), *90–91*	20	30____[1]
16036	NP Passenger Car (O27), *90–91*	20	30____[1]
16037	NP Vista Dome Car (O27), *90–91*	20	30____[1]
16038	NP Passenger Car (O27), *90–91*	20	30____[1]
16039	NP Observation Car (O27), *90–91*	20	30____[1]
16040	Southern Pacific Baggage Car, *90–91*	25	35____[1]
16041	NYC Dining Car (O27), *91*	45	55____[1]
16042	Illinois Central Baggage Car (O27), *91*	25	35____[1]
16043	Illinois Central Combination Car (O27), *91*	25	35____[1]
16044	Illinois Central Passenger Car (O27), *91*	25	35____[1]
16045	Illinois Central Vista Dome Car (O27), *91*	25	35____[1]
16046	Illinois Central Passenger Car (O27), *91*	25	35____[1]
16047	Illinois Central Observation Car (O27), *91*	25	35____[1]
16048	Amtrak Dining Car (O27), *91–92*	40	50____[1]
16049	Illinois Central Dining Car (O27), *92*	25	35____[1]

		Exc	New	Cond/$
(16050)	C&NW Baggage Car "6620", *93*	45	55	____1
(16051)	C&NW Combination Car "6630", *93*	45	55	____1
(16052)	C&NW Passenger Car "6616", *93*	45	55	____1
(16053)	C&NW Passenger Car "6602", *93*	45	55	____1
(16054)	C&NW Observation Car "6603", *93*	45	55	____1
16055	Santa Fe Passenger Car (O27), *93–94*	30	40	____1
16056	Santa Fe Vista Dome Car (O27), *93–94*	30	40	____1
16057	Santa Fe Passenger Car (O27), *93–94*	30	40	____1
16058	Santa Fe Combination Car (O27), *93–94*	30	40	____1
16059	Santa Fe Vista Dome Car (O27), *93–94*	30	40	____1
16060	Santa Fe Observation Car (O27), *93–94*	30	40	____1
(16061)	N&W Baggage Car "6061", *94*	45	55	____1
(16062)	N&W Combination Car "6062", *94*	45	55	____1
(16063)	N&W Passenger Car "6063", *94*	45	55	____1
(16064)	N&W Passenger Car "6064", *94*	45	55	____1
(16065)	N&W Observation Car "6065", *94*	45	55	____1
(16066)	NYC Combination Car "6066" (SSS), *94*	45	55	____1
(16067)	NYC Passenger Car "6067" (SSS), *94*	45	55	____1
(16068)	UP Baggage Car "6068" (O27), *94*	40	50	____1
(16069)	UP Combination Car "6069" (O27), *94*	40	50	____1
(16070)	UP Passenger Car "6070" (O27), *94*	40	50	____1
(16071)	UP Dining Car "6071" (O27), *94*	50	65	____1
(16072)	UP Vista Dome Car "6072" (O27), *94*	40	50	____1
(16073)	UP Passenger Car "6073" (O27), *94*	40	50	____1
(16074)	UP Observation Car "6074" (O27), *94*	40	50	____1
(16075)	Missouri Pacific Baggage Car "6620", *95*	40	50	____1
(16076)	Missouri Pacific Combination Car "6630", *95*	40	50	____1
(16077)	Missouri Pacific Passenger Car "6616", *95*	40	50	____1
(16078)	Missouri Pacific Passenger Car "7805", *95*	40	50	____1
(16079)	Missouri Pacific Observation Car "6609", *95*	40	50	____1
(16080)	New Haven Baggage Car "6080" (O27), *95*	40	50	____1

		Exc	New	Cond/$
(16081)	New Haven Combination Car "6081" (O27), *95*	30	40	___[1]
(16082)	New Haven Passenger Car "6082" (O27), *95*	30	40	___[1]
(16083)	New Haven Vista Dome Car "6083" (O27), *95*	30	40	___[1]
(16084)	New Haven Full Vista Dome Car "6084" (O27), *95*	30	40	___[1]
(16086)	New Haven Observation Car "6086" (O27), *95*	30	40	___[1]
(16087)	NYC Baggage Car "6087" (SSS), *95*	40	50	___[1]
(16088)	NYC Passenger Car "6088" (SSS), *95*	40	50	___[1]
(16089)	NYC Dining Car "6089" (SSS), *95*	40	50	___[1]
(16090)	NYC Observation Car "6090" (SSS), *95*	40	50	___[1]
(16091)	NYC Passenger Cars, set of 4 (SSS), *95*	150	185	___[1]
16092	Santa Fe Full Vista Dome Car (O27), *95*	30	40	___[1]
16093	Illinois Central Full Vista Dome Car (O27), *95*	30	40	___[1]
16094	Pennsylvania Full Vista Dome Car (O27), *95*	30	40	___[1]
16095	Amtrak Combination Car (O27), *95*	25	32	___[1]
16096	Amtrak Vista Dome Car (O27), *95*	25	32	___[1]
16097	Amtrak Observation Car (O27), *95*	25	32	___[1]
16098	Amtrak Passenger Car (O27), *95*	25	32	___[1]
16099	Amtrak Vista Dome Car (O27), *95*	25	32	___[1]
16102	Southern 3-D Tank Car (SSS), *87*	30	40	___[1]
16103	Lehigh Valley 2-D Tank Car (O27), *88*	25	30	___[1]
16104	Santa Fe 2-D Tank Car (O27), *89*	22	27	___[1]
16105	D&RGW 3-D Tank Car (SSS), *89*	45	60	___[1]
(16106)	Mopar Express 3-D Tank Car, *88 u*	75	125	___[1]
16107	Sunoco 2-D Tank Car (O27), *90*	20	25	___[1]
(16108)	Racing Fuel 1-D Tank Car "6108" (O27), *89 u, 92 u*	10	15	___[1]
16109	B&O 1-D Tank Car (SSS), *91*	40	50	___[1]
(16110)	Circus Animals Operating Stock Car "1989" (O27), *89 u*	25	35	___[1]
16111	Alaska 1-D Tank Car (O27), *90–91*	20	25	___[1]

		Exc	New	Cond/$
16112	Dow Chemical 3-D Tank Car, *90*	25	35	[1]
16113	Diamond Shamrock 2-D Tank Car (O27), *91*	20	25	[1]
16114	Hooker Chemicals 1-D Tank Car (O27), *91*	15	20	[1]
16115	MKT 3-D Tank Car, *92*	20	25	[1]
16116	U.S. Army 1-D Tank Car, *91 u*	40	50	[1]
16119	MKT 2-D Tank Car (O27), *92, 93 u*	15	20	[1]
16121	C&NW Stock Car (SSS), *92*	75	90	[1]
16123	Union Pacific 3-D Tank Car, *93–95*	14	18	[1]
16124	Penn Salt 3-D Tank Car, *93*	20	25	[1]
16125	Virginian Stock Car, *93*	19	24	[1]
16126	Jefferson Lake 3-D Tank Car, *93*	25	30	[1]
16127	Mobil 1-D Tank Car, *93*	25	30	[1]
16128	Alaska 1-D Tank Car, *94*	25	30	[1]
16129	Alaska 1-D Tank Car (O27), *93 u, 94*	10	15	[1]
16130	SP Stock Car (O27), *93 u, 94*	8	10	[1]
16131	T&P Reefer, *94*	20	25	[1]
16132	Deep Rock 3-D Tank Car, *94*	25	30	[1]
16133	Santa Fe Reefer, *94*	20	25	[1]
16134	Reading Reefer, *94*	20	25	[1]
16135	C&O Stock Car, *94*	25	30	[1]
16136	B&O 1-D Tank Car, *94*	30	35	[1]
16137	Ford 1-D Tank Car "12", *94 u*	35	40	[1]
16138	Goodyear 1-D Tank Car, *95*	25	30	[1]
16140	Domino Sug, *95*	25	30	[1]
16141	Erie Stock Car, *95*	28	33	[1]
16142	Santa Fe 1-D Tank Car, *95*	30	35	[1]
16143	Reading Reefer, *95*	22	28	[1]
16144	San Angelo 3-D Tank Car, *95*	25	30	[1]
16146	Dairy Despatch Reefer, *95*	20	25	[1]
(16147)	Clearly Canadian 1-D Tank Car (O27), *94 u*	65	70	[1]
16149	Zep Chemical 1-D Tank Car (O27), *95 u*	8	11	[1]
16200	Rock Island Boxcar (O27), *87–88*	8	12	[1]
16201	Wabash Boxcar (O27), *88–91*	8	12	[1]
16203	Key America Boxcar (O27), *87 u*	50	75	[1]

		Exc	New	Cond/$
16204	Hawthorne Boxcar (O27), *87 u*	60	100	_____1
(16205)	Mopar Express Boxcar "1987" (O27), *87–88 u*	50	60	_____1
16206	D&RGW Boxcar (SSS), *89*	50	60	_____1
16207	True Value Boxcar (O27), *88 u*	50	75	_____1
16208	PRR Auto Carrier w/ autos (3-tier), *89*	35	55	_____1
16209	Disney Magic Boxcar (O27), *88 u*	85	110	_____1
16211	Hawthorne Boxcar (O27), *88 u*	50	75	_____1
16213	Shoprite Boxcar (O27), *88 u*	50	70	_____1
16214	D&RGW Auto Carrier, *90*	28	33	_____1
16215	Conrail Auto Carrier, *90*	28	33	_____1
16217	Burlington Northern Auto Carrier, *92*	25	30	_____1
16219	True Value Boxcar (O27), *89 u*	50	70	_____1
(16220)	Ace Hardware Boxcar (O27), *89 u*	50	70	_____1
(16221)	Macy's Boxcar (O27), *89 u*	50	70	_____1
16222	Great Northern Boxcar (O27), *90–91*	8	15	_____1
(16223)	Budweiser Reefer, *89–92 u*	50	60	_____1
16224	True Value "Lawn Chief" Boxcar (O27), *90 u*	50	70	_____1
16225	Budweiser Vat Car, *90–91 u*	110	140	_____1
(16226)	Union Pacific Boxcar "6226" (O27), *90–91 u*	15	20	_____1
16227	Santa Fe Boxcar (O27), *91*	15	20	_____1
16228	Union Pacific Auto Carrier, *92*	25	30	_____1
16229	Erie-Lackawanna Auto Carrier, *91 u*	40	50	_____1
16232	Chessie System Boxcar, *92, 93 u, 94, 95 u*		NRS	_____
16233	MKT DD Boxcar, *92*	20	30	_____1
16234	ACY Boxcar (SSS), *92*	40	50	_____1
16235	Railway Express Agency Reefer, *92*	27	32	_____1
16236	NYC "Pacemaker" Boxcar, *92 u*	32	37	_____1
16237	Railway Express Agency Boxcar, *92 u*	33	38	_____1
16238	NYNH&H Boxcar, *93–95*		NRS	_____
16239	Union Pacific Boxcar, *93–95*		NRS	_____
16241	Toys "R" Us Boxcar, *92–93 u*	50	60	_____1
16242	Grand Trunk Auto Carrier, *93*	35	40	_____1
16243	Conrail Boxcar, *93*	30	40	_____1
16244	Duluth, South Shore & Atlantic Boxcar, *93*	20	25	_____1

		Exc	New	Cond/$
16245	Contadina Boxcar, *93*	20	25	___[1]
16245	(See 52068)			
16247	ACL Boxcar, *94*	20	25	___[1]
16247	(See 52046)			
16248	Budweiser Boxcar, *93–94 u*	25	30	___[1]
16249	United Auto Workers Boxcar, *93 u*		NRS	___
16250	Santa Fe Boxcar (027), *93 u, 94*	8	10	___[1]
16251	Columbus & Greenville Boxcar, *94*	20	25	___[1]
(16252)	Rapid Strike Attack Force Fleet Boxcar "6106888", *94–95*	22	32	___[1]
16253	Santa Fe Auto Carrier, *94*	28	33	___[1]
16255	Wabash DD Boxcar, *95*	20	25	___[1]
16256	Ford DD Boxcar, *94 u*	35	40	___[1]
(16257)	Crayola Boxcar, *94 u, 95*		NRS	___
16258	Lehigh Valley Boxcar, *95*	20	25	___[1]
16259	Chrysler Mopar Boxcar, *94 u*	26	31	___[1]
16260	Chrysler Mopar Auto Carrier, *94 u*	55	65	___[1]
16261	Union Pacific DD Boxcar, *95*	30	35	___[1]
16264	Red Wing Shoes Boxcar, *95*	25	30	___[1]
16265	Georgia Power "Atlanta '96" Boxcar, *95 u*		NRS	___
16266	Crayola Boxcar, *95*	15	20	___[1]
16300	Rock Island Flatcar w/ fences (027), *87–88*	8	10	___[1]
16301	Lionel Barrel Ramp Car, *87*	15	20	___[1]
16303	PRR Flatcar w/ trailers, *87*	30	40	___[1]
16304	Rock Island Gondola w/ cable reels (027), *87–88*	5	10	___[1]
16305	Lehigh Valley Ore Car, *87*	90	130	___[1]
16306	Santa Fe Barrel Ramp Car, *88*	14	19	___[1]
16307	NKP Flatcar w/ trailers, *88*	27	32	___[1]
16308	Burlington Northern Flatcar w/ trailer, *88–89*	38	48	___[1]
16309	Wabash Gondola w/ canisters, *88–91*	10	15	___[1]
(16310)	Mopar Express Gondola w/ canisters "1987", *87–88 u*	30	35	___[1]
(16311)	Mopar Express Flatcar w/trailers "1987", *87–88 u*	100	150	___[1]

		Exc	New	Cond/$
16313	PRR Gondola w/ cable reels (027), 88 u, 89	8	10	[1]
16314	Wabash Flatcar w/ trailers, 89	28	33	[1]
16315	PRR Flatcar w/ fences (027), 88 u, 89	8	10	[1]
16317	PRR Barrel Ramp Car, 89	20	25	[1]
16318	Lionel Lines Depressed Flatcar w/ cable reels, 89	18	23	[1]
16320	Great Northern Barrel Ramp Car, 90	15	20	[1]
16321/16322	Sealand TTUX Flatcar set w/ trailers, 90	75	100	[1]
16323	Lionel Lines Flatcar w/ trailers, 90	27	32	[1]
16324	PRR Depressed Flatcar w/ cable reels, 90	20	25	[1]
16325	Microracers Exhibition Ramp Car, 89 u	25	35	[1]
16326	Santa Fe Depressed Flatcar w/ cable reels, 91	19	24	[1]
(16327)	"The Big Top" Circus Gondola w/ canisters, 89 u	20	25	[1]
16328	NKP Gondola w/ cable reels, 90–91	15	20	[1]
16329	SP Flatcar w/ horses (027), 90–91	20	25	[1]
16330	MKT Flatcar w/ trailers, 91	23	27	[1]
16331	Southern Barrel Ramp Car, 91		NM	
16332	Lionel Lines Depressed Flatcar w/ transformer, 91	25	30	[1]
16333	Frisco Bulkhead Flatcar w/ wood load, 91	22	28	[1]
(16334)	C&NW TTUX Flatcar set w/ trailers "16337" and "16338", 91	65	75	[1]
16335	NYC "Pacemaker" Flatcar w/ trailer (SSS), 91	80	100	[1]
(16336)	UP Gondola w/ canisters "6336", 90–91 u	20	25	[1]
16337/16338	C&NW TTUX Flatcars w/ trailers (See 16334)			
16339	Mickey's World Tour Gondola w/ canisters (027), 91, 92 u	20	25	[1]
16340	Amtrak Flatcar w/ stakes, 91		NM	
16341	NYC Depressed Flatcar w/ transformer, 92	23	28	[1]

		Exc	New	Cond/$
16342	CSX Gondola w/ coil covers, *92*	25	30	1
16343	Burlington Gondola w/ coil covers, *92*	25	30	1
16345/16346	SP TTUX Flatcar set w/ trailers, *92*	55	70	1
16347	Ontario Northland Bulkhead Flatcar w/ pulp load, *92*	30	35	1
16348	Lionel-Erie Liquefied Gas Car, *92*	33	38	1
16349	Allis Chalmers Condenser Car, *92*	36	45	1
16350	CP Rail Bulkhead Flatcar w/ wood load, *91 u*	20	25	1
16351	Lionel Flatcar w/ U.S.N. submarine, *92*	46	60	1
16352	U.S. Military Flatcar w/ cruise missile, *92*	41	55	1
16353	B&M Gondola w/ coil covers, *91 u*	30	35	1
16355	Burlington Gondola, *92, 93 u, 94–95*	10	15	1
16356	MKT Depressed Flatcar w/ cable reels, *92*	20	25	1
16357	L&N Flatcar w/ trailer, *92*	28	37	1
16358	L&N Gondola w/ coil covers, *92*	24	29	1
16359	Pacific Coast Gondola w/ coil covers (SSS), *92*	35	40	1
(16360)	N&W Maxi-Stack Flatcar set w/ containers "16361" and "16362", *93*	55	65	1
16361/16362	N&W Maxi-Stack Flatcars w/ containers (See 16360)			
(16363)	Southern TTUX Flatcar set w/ trailers "16364" and "16365", *93*	60	75	1
16364/16365	Southern TTUX Flatcars w/ trailers (See 16363)			
16367	Clinchfield Gondola w/ coil covers, *93*	19	24	1
16368	MKT Liquid Oxygen Car, *93*	20	25	1
16369	Amtrak Flatcar w/ wheel load, *92 u*	20	30	1
16370	Amtrak Flatcar w/ rail load, *92 u*	20	30	1
16371	BN I-Beam Flatcar w/ load, *92 u*	44	55	1
16372	Southern I-Beam Flatcar w/ load, *92 u*	25	33	1
16373	Erie-Lackawanna Flatcar w/ stakes, *93*	20	25	1
16374	D&RGW Flatcar w/ trailer, *93*	25	30	1
16375	NYC Bulkhead Flatcar, *93–95*	20	25	
16376	UP Flatcar w/ trailer, *93–95*	20	25	
16378	Toys "R" Us Flatcar w/ trailer, *92–93 u*	80	135	1

		Exc	New	Cond/$
16379	NP Bulkhead Flatcar w/ pulp load, *93*	15	20	[1]
16380	UP I-Beam Flatcar w/ load, *93*	30	35	[1]
16380	(See 52084)			
16381	CSX I-Beam Flatcar w/ load, *93*	28	33	[1]
16382	Kansas City Southern Bulkhead Flatcar, *93*	15	20	[1]
16383	Conrail Flatcar w/ trailer, *93*	55	65	[1]
16384	Soo Line Gondola w/ cable reels, *93*	15	20	[1]
16385	Soo Line Ore Car, *93*	60	75	[1]
16386	SP Flatcar w/ wood load, *94*	20	25	[1]
16387	Kansas City Southern Gondola w/ coil covers, *94*	20	25	[1]
16388	LV Gondola w/ canisters, *94*	20	25	[1]
16389	PRR Flatcar w/ wheel load, *94*	25	30	[1]
16390	Lionel Flatcar w/ water tank, *94*	32	42	[1]
16391	Lionel Lines Gondola, *93 u*	—	20	[1]
16392	Wabash Gondola w/ canisters (O27), *93 u, 94*	8	10	[1]
16393	Wisconsin Central Bulkhead Flatcar, *94*	15	20	[1]
16394	Central Vermont Bulkhead Flatcar, *94*	15	20	[1]
16395	CP Flatcar w/ rail load, *94*	20	25	[1]
16396	Alaska Bulkhead Flatcar, *94*	15	20	[1]
16397	Milwaukee Road I-Beam Flatcar w/ load, *94*	35	40	[1]
16398	C&O Flatcar w/ trailer, *94*	60	70	[1]
16399	Western Pacific I-Beam Flatcar w/ load, *94*	35	40	[1]
16400	PRR Hopper (O27), *88 u, 89*	20	25	[1]
16402	Southern Quad Hopper w/ coal load (SSS), *87*	35	50	[1]
16406	CSX Quad Hopper w/ coal load, *90*	30	35	[1]
16407	B&M Covered Quad Hopper (SSS), *91*	30	40	[1]
(16408)	Union Pacific Hopper "6408" (O27), *90–91 u*	20	25	[1]
16410	MKT Hopper (O27), *92, 93 u*	20	25	[1]
16411	L&N Quad Hopper w/ coal load, *92*	33	38	[1]
16412	C&NW Covered Quad Hopper, *94*	15	20	[1]

		Exc	New	Cond/$
16413	Clinchfield Quad Hopper w/ coal load, *94*	15	20	[1]
16413	(See 52059)			
16414	CCC&StL Hopper (O27), *94*	15	20	[1]
16415	Milwaukee Road Hopper (O27), *94 u*	10	15	[1]
16416	D&RGW Covered Quad Hopper, *95*	20	25	[1]
16417	Wabash Quad Hopper w/ coal load, *95*	20	25	[1]
16418	C&NW Hopper w/ coal load (O27), *95*	15	20	[1]
16420	Western Maryland Quad Hopper w/ coal load (SSS), *95*	30	35	[1]
16421	Western Maryland Quad Hopper w/ coal load (SSS), *95*	30	35	[1]
16422	Western Maryland Quad Hopper w/ coal load (SSS), *95*	30	36	[1]
16423	Western Maryland Quad Hopper w/ coal load (SSS), *95*	30	36	[1]
16424	Western Maryland Covered Quad Hopper (SSS), *95*	30	35	[1]
16425	Western Maryland Covered Quad Hopper (SSS), *95*	30	35	[1]
16426	Western Maryland Covered Quad Hopper (SSS), *95*	30	35	[1]
16427	Western Maryland Covered Quad Hopper (SSS), *95*	30	35	[1]
(16429)	Western Maryland Quad Hoppers w/ coal loads (2) (See 16422,			
(16430)	Georgia Power Quad Hopper w/ coal load "82947", *95 u*		NRS	
16500	Rock Island Bobber Caboose, *87–88*	10	15	[1]
16501	Lehigh Valley SP-Type Caboose, *87*	20	25	[1]
16503	NYC Transfer Caboose, *87*	15	20	[1]
16504	Southern N5C Caboose (SSS), *87*	25	45	[1]
16505	Wabash SP-Type Caboose, *88–91*	10	15	[1]
16506	Santa Fe B/W Caboose, *88*	25	30	[1]
(16507)	Mopar Express SP-Type Caboose "1987", *87–88 u*	40	50	[1]
(16508)	Lionel Lines SP-Type Caboose "6508", *89 u*	15	20	[1]

		Exc	New	Cond/$
16509	D&RGW SP-Type Caboose (SSS), 89	20	25	___[1]
16510	New Haven B/W Caboose, 89	25	30	___[1]
16511	PRR Bobber Caboose, 88 u, 89	10	15	___[1]
16513	Union Pacific SP-Type Caboose, 89	15	25	___[1]
16515	Lionel Lines RailScope SP-Type Caboose, 89	25	30	___[1]
16516	Lehigh Valley SP-Type Caboose, 90	15	25	___[1]
16517	Atlantic Coast Line B/W Caboose, 90	25	30	___[1]
16518	Chessie System B/W Caboose, 90	35	50	___[1]
16519	Rock Island Transfer Caboose, 90	14	18	___[1]
(16520)	"Welcome to the Show" Circus SP-Type Caboose, 89 u	15	25	___[1]
16521	PRR SP-Type Caboose, 90–91	10	15	___[1]
16522	"Chills & Thrills" Circus N5C Caboose, 90–91	10	15	___[1]
16523	Alaska SP-Type Caboose, 91	30	40	___[1]
(16524)	Anheuser-Busch SP-Type Caboose, 89–92 u	30	40	___[1]
16525	D&H B/W Caboose (SSS), 91	35	45	___[1]
16526	Kansas City Southern SP-Type Caboose, 91	20	25	___[1]
16527	Western Pacific Work Caboose, 92		NM	___
(16528)	Union Pacific SP-Type Caboose "6528", 90–91 u	20	25	___[1]
(16529)	Santa Fe SP-Type Caboose "16829", 91	10	15	___[1]
(16530)	Mickey's World Tour SP-Type Caboose "16830", 91, 92 u	15	20	___[1]
16531	Texas &Pacific SP-Type Caboose, 92	20	25	___[1]
16533	C&NW B/W Caboose, 92	25	35	___[1]
16534	Delaware & Hudson SP-Type Caboose, 92	20	25	___[1]
16535	Erie-Lackawanna B/W Caboose, 91 u	35	45	___[1]
16536	Chessie System SP-Type Caboose, 92, 93 u, 94, 95 u	20	27	___[1]
16537	MKT SP-Type Caboose, 92, 93 u	20	25	___[1]
(16538)	L&N B/W Caboose "1041", 92 u	35	40	___[1]

		Exc	New	Cond/$
16538	L&N/Family Lines Steel-sided Caboose w/ smoke (Std. 0), *92*		NM	___
(16539)	WP Steel-sided Caboose w/ smoke "539" (Std. 0) (SSS), *92*	60	75	___[1]
(16541)	Montana Rail Link E/V Caboose w/ smoke "10131", *93*	60	75	___[1]
(16543)	NYC SP-Type Caboose, *93–95*	20	27	___[1]
16544	Union Pacific SP-Type Caboose, *93–95*	25	30	___[1]
16544	(See 16564)			
16546	Clinchfield SP-Type Caboose, *93*	25	30	___[1]
16547	Happy Holidays SP-Type Caboose, *93–95*	33	39	___[1]
16548	Conrail SP-Type Caboose, *93*	25	35	___[1]
16549	Soo Line Work Caboose, *93*	20	30	___[1]
16550	U.S. Navy Searchlight Caboose, *94–95*	20	25	___[1]
16551	Budweiser SP-Type Caboose, *93–94 u*	23	28	___[1]
16552	Frisco Searchlight Caboose, *94*	30	35	___[1]
16553	United Auto Workers SP-Type Caboose, *93 u*		NRS	___
(16554)	GT E/V Caboose w/ smoke "79052", *94*	50	60	___[1]
16555	C&O SP-Type Caboose, *94*	25	30	___[1]
16556	(See 16909)			
16557	Ford SP-Type Caboose, *94 u*	20	25	___[1]
(16558)	Crayola SP-Type Caboose, *94 u, 95*	20	25	___[1]
(16559)	Seaboard CC Caboose "5658", *95*	30	35	___[1]
16560	Chrysler Mopar Caboose, *94 u*	31	36	___[1]
(16561)	Union Pacific CC Caboose "25766", *95*	30	35	___[1]
16562	Reading CC Caboose, *95*	30	35	___[1]
(16563)	Lionel Lines SP-Type Caboose, *95*	25	30	___[1]
16564	Western Maryland CC Caboose (SSS), *95*	30	35	___[1]
16565	Milwaukee Road B/W Caboose, *95*	50	60	___[1]
(16566)	U.S. Army SP-Type Caboose "907", *95*	20	27	___[1]
16570	NdeM E/V Caboose, *96*		NM	___
(16571)	Georgia Power SP-Type Caboose "52789", *95 u*		NRS	___
16578	Lionel Lines SP-Type Caboose, *95 u*	20	27	___[1]
16600	Illinois Central Coal Dump Car, *88*	15	25	___[1]
16601	Canadian National Searchlight Car, *88*	20	25	___[1]

16602	Erie-Lackawanna Coal Dump Car, *87*	15	25	1
16603	Detroit Zoo Giraffe Car (O27), *87*	40	50	1
16604	NYC Log Dump Car, *87*	15	25	1
16605	Bronx Zoo Giraffe Car (O27), *88*	40	45	1
16606	Southern Searchlight Car, *87*	15	25	1
[16606]	Southern TCA Southern Searchlight Car, *88 u*	20	30	1
(16607)	Southern Coal Dump Car "16707" (SSS), *87*	20	30	1
16608	Lehigh Valley Searchlight Car, *87*	25	35	1
16609	Lehigh Valley Derrick Car, *87*	25	35	1
16610	Lionel Track Maintenance Car, *87–88*	14	23	1
16611	Santa Fe Log Dump Car, *88*	15	25	1
16612	Soo Line Log Dump Car, *89*	15	25	1
16613	MKT Coal Dump Car, *89*	15	25	1
16614	Reading Cop and Hobo Car (O27), *89*	28	33	1
16615	Lionel Lines Extension Searchlight Car, *89*	20	30	1
16616	D&RGW Searchlight Car (SSS), *89*	25	35	1
16617	C&NW Boxcar w/ ETD, *89*	21	32	1
16618	Santa Fe Track Maintenance Car, *89*	15	25	1
16619	Wabash Coal Dump Car, *90*	15	25	1
16620	C&O Track Maintenance Car, *90–91*	15	25	1
16621	Alaska Log Dump Car, *90*	20	25	1
16622	CSX Boxcar w/ ETD, *90–91*	20	30	1
16623	MKT DD Boxcar w/ ETD, *91*	20	30	1
16624	NH Cop and Hobo Car (O27), *90–91*	25	35	1
16625	NYC Extension Searchlight Car, *90*	20	30	1
16626	CSX Searchlight Car, *90*	20	30	1
16627	CSX Log Dump Car, *90*	20	25	1
16628	"Laughter" Circus Animated Gondola, *90–91*	40	50	1
16629	"Animal Car" Circus Elephant Car (O27), *90–91*	45	60	1
16630	SP Operating Cowboy Car (O27), *90–91*	25	30	1
16631	RI Boxcar w/ Steam RailSounds, *90*	140	155	1
16632	BN Boxcar w/ Diesel RailSounds, *90*	115	125	1
16633	Great Northern Cop and Hobo Car (O27), *91*		NM	

		Exc	New	Cond/$
16634	WM Coal Dump Car, *91*	20	25	[1]
16635	CP Rail Track Maintenance Car, *91*		NM	
16636	D&RGW Log Dump Car, *91*	20	25	[1]
16637	WP Extension Searchlight Car, *91*	30	35	[1]
16638	Lionelville Circus Operating Animal Car (O27), *91*	75	105	[1]
16639	B&O Boxcar w/ Steam RailSounds, *91*	125	140	[1]
16640	Rutland Boxcar w/ Diesel RailSounds, *91*	125	140	[1]
16641	Toys "R" Us Giraffe Car (O27), *90–91 u*	50	75	[1]
16642	Mickey's World Tour Goofy Car (O27), *91, 92 u*	44	55	[1]
16643	Amtrak Coal Dump Car, *91*		NM	
16644	Amtrak Crane Car, *91, 92 u*	40	50	[1]
16645	Amtrak Searchlight Caboose, *91, 92 u*	30	35	[1]
16646	Railbox Boxcar w/ ETD, *92*		NM	
16649	Railway Express Agency Boxcar w/ Steam RailSounds, *92*	125	155	[1]
16650	NYC "Pacemaker" Boxcar w/ Diesel RailSounds, *92*	125	160	[1]
16651	Circus Operating Clown Car (O27), *92*	32	37	[1]
16652	Lionel Radar Car, *92*	30	38	[1]
16653	Western Pacific Crane Car (SSS), *92*	45	60	[1]
16654	(See 17214)			
(16655)	Steam Tender w/ RailSounds "1993", *93*	135	160	[1]
16656	Burlington Log Dump Car, *92 u*	20	25	[1]
16657	Lehigh Valley Coal Dump Car, *92 u*	20	25	[1]
16658	Erie-Lackawanna Crane Car, *93*	50	60	[1]
16659	Union Pacific Searchlight Car, *93–95*	20	25	[1]
16660	Lionel Fire Car w/ ladders, *93–94*	50	55	[1]
16661	Lionel Flatcar w/ boat, *93*	31	39	[2]
16662	Looney Tunes Operating Bugs Bunny and Yosemite Sam Car (O27), *93–94*	32	36	[1]
16663	Missouri Pacific Searchlight Car, *93*	25	30	[1]
16664	L&N Coal Dump Car, *93*	25	30	[1]
16665	Maine Central Log Dump Car, *93*	25	30	[1]
16666	Lionel Toxic Waste Car, *93–94*	28	37	[1]
16667	Conrail Searchlight Car, *93*	30	35	[1]

		Exc	New	Cond/$
16668	Ontario Northland Log Dump Car, *93*	25	30	___ [1]
16669	Soo Line Searchlight Car, *93*	20	25	___ [1]
16670	Lionel TV Car, *93–94*	25	30	___ [1]
(16673)	Lionel Lines Tender w/ whistle, *94–96*	22	32	___ [1]
16674	Pinkerton Animated Gondola, *94*	33	38	___ [1]
16675	Great Northern Log Dump Car, *94*	25	30	___ [1]
16676	Burlington Coal Dump Car, *94*	25	30	___ [1]
16677	NATO Flatcar w/ Royal Navy submarine, *94*	32	37	___ [1]
16678	Rock Island Searchlight Car, *94*	25	28	___ [1]
16679	U.S. Mail Operating Boxcar, *94*	50	55	___ [1]
16680	Lionel Cherry Picker Car, *94*	26	31	___ [1]
16681	Aquarium Car, *95*	70	90	___ [2]
16682	Lionelville Farms Operating Stock Car (O27), *94*	27	32	___ [1]
16683	Los Angeles Zoo Elephant Car (O27), *94*	26	31	___ [1]
16684	U.S. Navy Crane Car, *94–95*	35	40	___ [1]
16685	Erie Extension Searchlight Car, *95*	35	40	___ [1]
16686	Mickey Mouse and Big Bad Pete Animated Boxcar, *95*	38	43	___ [1]
16687	U.S. Mail Operating Boxcar, *94*	36	45	___ [1]
16688	Lionel Fire Car w/ ladders, *94*	55	75	___ [1]
16689	Lionel Toxic Waste Car, *94*	30	35	___ [1]
16690	Looney Tunes Operating Bugs Bunny and Yosemite Sam Car (O27), *94*	32	37	___ [1]
16701	Southern Tool Car (SSS), *87*	50	65	___ [1]
16702	Amtrak Bunk Car, *91, 92 u*	30	35	___ [1]
16703	NYC Tool Car, *92*	30	35	___ [1]
16704	Lionel TV Car, *94*	30	35	___ [1]
16705	Chesapeake &Ohio Cop and Hobo Car, *95*	30	35	___ [1]
16706	Animal Transport Service Giraffe Car, *95*	30	35	___ [1]
16707	(See 16607)			
16708	C&NW Track Maintenance Car, *95*	25	30	___ [1]
16709	New York Central Derrick Car, *95*	25	30	___ [1]
16710	U.S. Army Operating Missile Car, *95*	42	50	___ [1]
16711	Pennsylvania Searchlight Car, *95*	30	35	___ [1]

		Exc	New	Cond/$
16712	Pinkerton Animated Gondola, *95*	30	35	___1
16713	Great Northern Log Dump Car, *95*	25	30	___1
16714	Burlington Coal Dump Car, *95*	25	30	___1
16717	Jersey Central Crane Car, *96*	—	45	___1
16718	U.S.M.C. Missile Launching Flatcar, *96*		NRS	___1
16800	Lionel Railroader Club Ore Car, *86 u*	80	95	___1
16801	Lionel Railroader Club Bunk Car, *88 u*	35	45	___1
16802	Lionel Railroader Club Tool Car, *89 u*	35	45	___1
16803	Lionel Railroader Club Searchlight Car, *90 u*	30	40	___1
16804	Lionel Railroader Club B/W Caboose, *91 u*	30	45	___1
(16805)	Budweiser Malt Nutrine Reefer "3285", *91–92 u*	75	90	___1
16806	Toys "R" Us Boxcar, *92 u*	36	41	___1
(16807)	H.J. Heinz Reefer "301", *93*	34	39	___1
16808	Toys "R" Us Boxcar, *93 u*	29	34	___1
16829	(See 16529)			
16830	(See 16530)			
(16901)	Lionel Catalog video (VHS), *91 u*	20	25	___1
16903	CP Bulkhead Flatcar w/ pulp load (SSS), *94*	23	28	___1
(16904)	NYC "Pacemaker" TTUX Flatcar set w/ trailers "16905" and "16906", *94*	65	70	___1
16905/16906	NYC "Pacemaker" TTUX Flatcars w/ trailers (See 16904)			
16907	Lionel Flatcar w/ farm tractors, *94*	36	46	___1
(16908)	U.S. Navy Flatcar "04039" w/ submarine "930", *94–95*	50	60	___1
(16909)	U.S. Navy Gondola w/ canisters "16556", *94–95*	15	20	___1
16910	Missouri Pacific Flatcar w/ trailer, *94*	25	30	___1
16911	B&M Flatcar w/ trailer, *94*	24	29	___1
(16912)	CN Maxi-Stack Flatcar set w/ containers "640000" and "640001", *94*	55	60	___1
(16913)/(16914)	CN Maxi-Stack Flatcars w/ containers "640000" and "640001" (See 16912)			
16915	Lionel Lines Gondola (O27), *93–94 u*	8	10	___1
16916	Ford Flatcar w/ trailer, *94 u*	50	60	___1

		Exc	New	Cond/$
(16917)	Crayola Gondola w/ crayons, *94 u*, *95*	8	10	___1
16919	Chrysler Mopar Gondola w/ coil covers, *94 u*	33	39	___1
16920	Lionel Flatcar w/ construction block helicopter, *95*		NM	___
16922	Chesapeake &Ohio Flatcar w/ trailer, *95*	26	31	___1
16923	Lionel Intermodal Service Flatcar w/ wheelchocks, *95*	20	25	___1
16925	New York Central Flatcar w/ trailer, *95*		NRS	___
16926	Frisco Flatcar w/ trailers, *95*	25	30	___1
16927	New York Central Flatcar w/ gondola, *95*	20	25	___1
16928	Soo Line Flatcar w/ dump bin (O27), *95*	15	20	___1
16929	BCRail Gondola w/ cable reels, *95*	20	25	___1
16930	Santa Fe Flatcar w/ wheel load, *95*	20	25	___1
16932	Erie Flatcar w/ rail load, *95*	20	25	___1
16933	Lionel Lines Flatcar w/ automobiles, *95*	37	43	___1
16934	Pennsylvania Flatcar w/ Ertl road grader, *95*	37	42	___1
16935	UP Depressed Flatcar w/ Ertl bulldozer, *95*	37	42	___1
(16936)	Susquehanna Maxi-Stack Flatcar set w/ containers "16937" and "16938", *95*	70	75	___1
16937/16938	Susquehanna Maxi-Stack Flatcars w/ containers (See 16936)			
(16939)	U.S.Navy Flatcar w/ boat "04040", *95*	25	30	___1
16943	Jersey Central Gondola, *96*	—	16	___1
(16944)	Georgia Power Depressed Flatcar w/ transformer "31438", *95 u*		NRS	___
(16945)	Georgia Power Depressed Flatcar w/ cable reels "31950", *95 u*		NRS	___
16952	U.S. Navy Flatcar w/ Ertl helicopter, *96*	30	35	___1
(16953)	NYC Flatcar w/ Red Wing Shoes trailer "1905-95", *95 u*	46	55	___1
17000	(See 17107)			
17002	Conrail 2-bay ACF Hopper (Std. O), *87*	90	100	___1
17003	Du Pont 2-bay ACF Hopper (Std. O), *90*	55	70	___1
17004	MKT 2-bay ACF Hopper (Std. O), *91*	30	40	___1

		Exc	New	Cond/$
17005	Cargill 2-bay ACF Hopper (Std. O), *92*	30	40	___1
17006	Soo Line 2-bay ACF Hopper (Std. O) (SSS). *93*	50	60	___1
(17007)	GN 2-bay ACF Hopper "173872" (Std. O). *94*	32	41	___1
(17008)	D&RGW 2-bay ACF Hopper "10009" (Std. O). *95*	—	32	___1
17100	Chessie System 3-bay ACF Hopper (Std. O). *88*	40	50	___1
17101	Chessie System 3-bay ACF Hopper (Std. O). *88*	40	50	___1
17102	Chessie System 3-bay ACF Hopper (Std. O). *88*	40	50	___1
17103	Chessie System 3-bay ACF Hopper (Std. O). *88*	40	50	___1
17104	Chessie System 3-bay ACF Hopper (Std. O), *88*	40	50	___1
17105	Chessie System 3-bay ACF Hopper (Std. O). *95*	40	50	___1
17107	Sclair 3-bay ACF Hopper (Std. O), *89*	100	110	___1
17108	Santa Fe 3-bay ACF Hopper (Std. O), *90*	60	70	___1
17109	N&W 3-bay ACF Hopper (Std. O), *91*	25	33	___1
17110	Union Pacific Hopper w/ coal load (Std. O). *91*	29	38	___1
17111	Reading Hopper w/ coal load (Std. O), *91*	29	38	___1
17112	Erie-Lack. 3-bay ACF Hopper (Std. O). *92*	30	40	___1
17113	LV Hopper w/ coal load (Std. O), *92–93*	29	38	___1
17114	Peabody Hopper w/ coal load (Std. O), *92–93*	55	65	___1
(17118)	Archer Daniels Midland 3-bay ACF Hopper "60029" (Std. O). *93*	35	45	___1
(17120)	CSX Hopper w/ coal load "295110" (Std. O). *94*	30	40	___1
(17121)	ICG Hopper w/ coal load "72867" (Std. O). *94*	34	45	___1
(17122)	RI 3-bay ACF Hopper "800200" (Std. O). *94*	32	42	___1

		Exc	New	Cond/$
(17123)	Cargill Covered Grain Hopper "844304" (Std. O). *95*	35	45	___ [1]
(17124)	Archer Daniels Midland 3-bay ACF Hopper "50224" (Std. O). *95*	35	45	___ [1]
(17125)	Goodyear 3-bay ACF Hopper (Std. O), *95*		NM	___
17200	Canadian Pacific Boxcar (Std. O), *89*	55	60	___ [1]
17201	Conrail Boxcar (Std. O), *87*	55	65	___ [1]
17202	Santa Fe Boxcar w/ Diesel RailSounds (Std. O), *90*	105	115	___ [1]
17203	Cotton Belt DD Boxcar (Std. O), *91*	37	42	___ [1]
17204	Missouri Pacific DD Boxcar (Std. O), *91*	31	36	___ [1]
17207	C&IM DD Boxcar (Std. O), *92*	35	40	___ [1]
17208	Union Pacific DD Boxcar (Std. O), *92*	38	43	___ [1]
(17209)	B&O DD Boxcar "296000" (Std. O), *93*	36	41	___ [1]
(17210)	Chicago & Illinois Midland Boxcar "16021" (Std. O), *92 u*	30	40	___ [1]
(17211)	Chicago & Illinois Midland Boxcar "16022" (Std. O), *92 u*	30	40	___ [1]
(17212)	Chicago & Illinois Midland Boxcar "16023" (Std. O), *92 u*	30	40	___ [1]
(17213)	Susquehanna Boxcar "501" (Std. O), *93*	35	40	___ [1]
17214	Railbox Boxcar w/ Diesel RailSounds (Std. O), *93*	125	145	___ [1]
(17216)	PRR DD Boxcar "60155" (Std. O), *94*	39	44	___ [1]
(17217)	New Haven "State of Maine" Boxcar "45003" (Std. O), *95*	30	40	___ [1]
(17218)	BAR "State of Maine" Boxcar "2184" (Std. O), *95*	30	40	___ [1]
17219	Tazmanian Devil 40th Birthday Boxcar (Std. O), *95*	40	50	___ [1]
17220	Pennsylvania Boxcar (Std. O), *96*	30	41	___ [1]
17221	NYC Boxcar (Std. O), *96*	30	41	___ [1]
17222	Western Pacific Boxcar (Std. O), *96*	30	41	___ [1]
17300	Canadian Pacific Reefer (Std. O), *89*	55	65	___ [1]
17301	Conrail Reefer (Std. O), *87*	50	60	___ [1]
17302	Santa Fe Reefer w/ ETD (Std. O), *90*	50	60	___ [1]
(17303)	C&O Reefer "7890" (Std. O), *93*	30	40	___ [1]

		Exc	New	Cond/$
(17304)	Wabash Reefer "26269" (Std. O), *94*	31	41	[1]
(17305)	Pacific Fruit Express Reefer "459400" (Std. O), *94*	30	40	[1]
(17306)	Pacific Fruit Express Reefer "459401" (Std. O), *94*	28	37	[1]
(17307)	Tropicana Reefer "300" (Std. O), *95*	30	40	[1]
(17308)	Tropicana Reefer "301" (Std. O), *95*	30	40	[1]
(17309)	Tropicana Reefer "302" (Std. O), *95*	30	40	[1]
(17310)	Tropicana Reefer "303" (Std. O), *95*	30	40	[1]
17311	Railway Express Agency Reefer (Std. O), *96*	36	40	[1]
17400	CP Rail Gondola w/ coal load (Std. O), *89*	50	55	[1]
17401	Conrail Gondola w/ coal load (Std. O), *87*	50	60	[1]
17402	Santa Fe Gondola w/ coal load (Std. O), *90*	36	45	[1]
(17403)	Chessie System Gondola w/ coil covers "371629" (Std. O), *93*	34	39	[1]
(17404)	Illinois Central Gulf Gondola w/ coil covers "245998" (Std. O), *93*	33	38	[1]
(17405)	Reading Gondola w/ coil covers "24876" (Std. O), *94*	35	40	[1]
(17406)	PRR Gondola w/ coil covers "385405" (Std. O), *95*	35	40	[1]
17500	CP Flatcar w/ logs (Std. O), *89*	45	50	[1]
17501	Conrail Flatcar w/ stakes (Std. O), *87*	46	55	[1]
17502	Santa Fe Flatcar w/ trailer (Std. O), *90*	70	85	[1]
17503	NS Flatcar w/ trailer (Std. O), *92*	60	70	[1]
17504	NS Flatcar w/ trailer (Std. O), *92*	60	70	[1]
17505	NS Flatcar w/ trailer (Std. O), *92*	60	70	[1]
17506	NS Flatcar w/ trailer (Std. O), *92*	60	70	[1]
17507	NS Flatcar w/ trailer (Std. O), *92*	60	70	[1]
17508	BN I-Beam Flatcar w/ load (Std. O), *92*		NM	
17509	Southern car w/ load (Std. O), *92*		NM	
(17510)	NP Flatcar w/ logs "51200" (Std. O), *94*	30	35	[1]
(17511)	WM Flatcars w/ logs, set of 3 (Std. O), *95*	—	250	[1]
17512	WM Flatcar w/ logs (Std. O), *95*	50	60	[1]
17513	WM Flatcar w/ logs (Std. O), *95*	50	60	[1]

		Exc	New	Cond/$
17514	WM Flatcar w/ logs (Std. O), *95*	50	60	___1
17515	Norfolk Southern Flatcar w/ tractors (Std. O), *95*	50	60	___1
17600	NYC Wood-sided Caboose (Std. O), *87 u*	55	70	___1
17601	Southern Wood-sided Caboose (Std. O), *88*	55	65	___1
17602	Conrail Wood-sided Caboose (Std. O), *87*	100	120	___1
17603	Rock Island Wood-sided Caboose (Std. O), *88*	36	50	___1
17604	Lackawanna Wood-sided Caboose (Std. O), *88*	43	48	___1
17605	Reading Wood-sided Caboose (Std. O), *89*	42	47	___1
17606	NYC Steel-sided Caboose w/ smoke (Std. O), *90*	65	75	___1
17607	Reading Steel-sided Caboose w/ smoke (Std. O), *90*	60	65	___1
17608	C&O Steel-sided Caboose w/ smoke (Std. O), *91*	75	85	___1
17610	Wabash Steel-sided Caboose w/ smoke (Std. O), *91*	55	65	___1
(17611)	NYC Wood-sided Caboose "6003" (Std. O), *90 u, 91*	55	65	___1
17612	NKP Steel-sided Caboose w/ smoke (FF no. 6) (Std. O), *92*	60	70	___1
(17613)	Southern Steel-sided Caboose w/ smoke "7613" (Std. O), *92*	60	70	___1
17615	Northern Pacific Wood-sided Caboose w/ smoke (Std. O), *92*	60	70	___1
17617	D&RGW Steel-sided Caboose (Std. O), *95*	80	95	___1
17618	Frisco Wood-sided Caboose (Std. O), *95*	70	80	___1
17870	LCCA East Camden & Highland Boxcar (Std. O), *87 u*	70	75	___1
(17871)	TTOS NYC Flatcar w/ Kodak and Xerox trailers "81487", *87 u*	260	345	___1
(17872)	TTOS Anaconda Ore Car "81988", *88 u*	75	110	___1
17873	LCCA Ashland Oil 3-D Tank Car, *88 u*	50	60	___1
(17874)	LOTS MILW Log Dump Car "59629", *88 u*	100	140	___1

		Exc	New	Cond/$
(17875)	LOTS PHD Boxcar "1289", *89 u*	80	100	___1
17876	LCCA Columbia Newberry & Laurens Boxcar (Std. O), *89 u*	60	70	___1
(17877)	TTOS MKT 1-D Tank Car "3739469", *89 u*	55	70	___1
17878	Gadsden Pacific Magma Ore Car w/ load, *89 u*	75	80	___1
(17879)	TCA Valley Forge Dining Car "1989", *89 u*	65	75	___1
17880	LCCA D&RGW Wood-sided Caboose (Std. O), *90 u*	70	80	___1
17881	Gadsden Pacific Phelps-Dodge Ore Car w/ load, *90 u*	40	50	___1
(17882)	LOTS B&O DD Boxcar w/ ETD "298011", *90 u*	70	80	___1
(17883)	TCA New Georgia RR Passenger Car "1990", *90 u*	50	60	___1
17884	TTOS Columbus & Dayton Terminal Boxcar (Std. O), *90 u*	50	70	___1
17885	Artrain 1-D Tank Car, *90 u*	80	95	___1
17886	Gadsden Pacific Cyprus Ore Car w/ load, *91 u*	40	45	___1
17887	LCCA Conrail Flatcar w/ Armstrong Tile trailer (Std. O), *91 u*	55	70	___1
17888	LCCA Conrail Flatcar w/ Ford New Holland trailer (Std. O), *91 u*	70	90	___1
(17889)	TTOS SP Flatcar w/ trailer "15791" (Std. O), *91 u*	55	70	___1
(17890)	LOTS CSX Auto Carrier "151161", *91 u*	95	110	___1
17891	Artrain Grand Trunk Boxcar, *91 u*	80	100	___1
(17892)	LCCA Conrail Flatcars w/ trailers (Std O) (See 17887, 17888)			
[17893]	LCAC BAOC 1-D Tank Car "914", *91 u*	—	90	___1
(17894)	TTOS Southern Pacific Tractor, *91 u*	20	25	___1
(17895)	LCCA Tractor, *91 u*	15	20	___1
(17896)	LCCA Lancaster Lines Tractor, *91 u*	25	30	___1
[17897]	VTC Passenger Cars (See 7692)			

		Exc	New	Cond/$
(17898)	TCA Wabash Reefer "21596", *92 u*	46	55	___[1]
(17899)	LCCA NASA Unibody Tank Car "190" (Std. O), *92 u*	70	75	___[1]
17900	Santa Fe Unibody Tank Car (Std. O), *90*	39	49	___[1]
17901	Chevron Unibody Tank Car (Std. O), *90*	36	45	___[1]
17902	NJ Zinc Unibody Tank Car (Std. O), *91*	36	45	___[1]
17903	Conoco Unibody Tank Car (Std. O), *91*	36	45	___[1]
17904	Texaco Unibody Tank Car (Std. O), *92*	36	45	___[1]
17905	Archer Daniels Midland Unibody Tank Car (Std. O), *92*	36	45	___[1]
(17906)	SCM Unibody Tank Car "78286" (Std. O), *93*	50	60	___[1]
17908	Marathon Oil Unibody Tank Car (Std. O), *95*	50	60	___[1]
17909	Hooker Chemicals Unibody Tank Car (Std. O), *96*	50	55	___[1]
(18000)	PRR 0-6-0 "8977" 89, *91*	580	660	___[2]
(18001)	Rock Island 4-8-4 "5100", *87*	365	430	___[2]
(18002)	NYC 4-6-4 "785", *87 u*	660	750	___[2]
(18003)	Delaware Lackawanna & Western 4-8-4 "1501", *88*	350	435	___[1]
(18004)	Reading 4-6-2 "8004", *89*	295	320	___[2]
(18005)	NYC 4-6-4 "5340" w/ display case, *90*	990	1350	___[2]
(18006)	Reading 4-8-4 "2100", *89 u*	690	760	___[2]
(18007)	Southern Pacific 4-8-4 "4410", *91*	570	730	___[2]
(18008)	Disneyland 35th Anniversary 4-4-0 "4" w/ display case, *90*	235	285	___[1]
(18009)	NYC 4-8-2 "3000", *90 u, 91*	740	820	___[2]
(18010)	Pennsylvania 6-8-6 "6200", *91–92*	1400	1750	___[2]
(18011)	Chessie System 4-8-4 "2101", *91*	740	860	___[1]
(18012)	NYC 4-6-4 "5340", *90*	1000	1250	___[1]
(18013)	Disneyland 35th Anniversary 4-4-0 "4", *90*	210	265	___[1]
(18014)	Lionel Lines 2-6-4 "8014", *91*	130	180	___[1]
(18016)	Northern Pacific 4-8-4 "2626", *92*	435	520	___[1]
(18018)	Southern 2-8-2 "4501", *92*	920	1000	___[1]
18021	(See 18030)			
(18022)	Pere Marquette 2-8-4 "1201", *93*	520	620	___[1]

		Exc	New	Cond/$
(18023)	Western Maryland Shay "6", *92*	1750	2300	[1]
(18024)	Sears T&P 4-8-2 "907" w/ display case, *92 u*	900	1000	[1]
(18025)	T&P 4-8-2 "907" (See 18024), *92 u*			
(18026)	Smithsonian NYC Dreyfuss 4-6-4 "5450" (2-rail), *92 u*		NRS	
(18027)	NYC Dreyfuss 4-6-4 "5450" (3-rail), *93 u*	—	2650	[1]
(18028)	Smithsonian Pennsylvania 4-6-2 "3768" (2-rail), *93 u*		NRS	
(18029)	NYC Dreyfuss 4-6-4 "5454" (3-rail) w/ operating roller base, *93 u*	2500	2950	[1]
(18030)	Frisco 2-8-2 "4100", *93 u*	740	820	[2]
(18031)	Bundesbahn BR-50 2-10-0 (2-rail), *93 u*		NRS	
(18034)	Santa Fe 2-8-2 "3158", *94*	530	640	[1]
(18035)	Reichsbahn BR-50 2-10-0 (2-rail), *93 u*		NRS	
(18036)	French BR-50 2-10-0 (2-rail), *93 u*		NRS	
(18040)	N&W 4-8-4 "612", *95*	1100	1200	[2]
(18041)	Boston &Albany 4-6-4 "619", *95*		NM	
(18042)	Boston &Albany 4-6-4 "618", *95*	450	500	[1]
(18043)	Chesapeake &Ohio 4-6-4 "490", *95*	1050	1250	[2]
(18044)	Southern 4-6-2 "1390", *96*	300	340	[1]
(18046)	Wabash 4-6-4 "700", *96*	450	495	[1]
(18090)	LCCA D&RGW 4-6-2 "1990", *90 u*	345	420	[1]
(18100)	Santa Fe F-3 A Unit "8100" (See 11711)			
(18101)	Santa Fe F-3 B Unit "8101" (See 11711)			
(18102)	Santa Fe F-3 A Unit Dummy "8102" (See 11711)			
(18103)	Santa Fe F-3 B Unit Dummy "8103", *91 u*	280	325	[1]
(18104)	Great Northern F-3 A Unit Dummy "366A" (See 11724)			
(18105)	Great Northern F-3 B Unit Dummy "370B" (See 11724)			
(18106)	Great Northern F-3 A Unit Dummy "351C" (See 11724)			
(18107)	D&RGW Alco PA-1 ABA set "6001" and "6002", *92*	940	1150	[1]
(18108)	Great Northern F-3 B Unit "371B", *93*	115	140	[1]
(18109)	Erie Alco A Unit "725A" (See 11734)			

		Exc	New	Cond/$
(18110)	Erie Alco B Unit "725B" (See 11734)			
(18111)	Erie Alco A Unit Dummy "736A" (See 11734)			
(18112)	TCA F-3 A Unit "40" (See 11737)			
(18113)	TCA F-3 B Unit (See 11737)			
(18114)	TCA F-3 A Unit Dummy "40" (See 11737)			
(18115)	Santa Fe F-3 B Unit, *93*	105	140	___[1]
(18116)	Erie-Lackawanna Alco PA-1 AA set "858" and "859", *93*	480	580	___[1]
(18117)/(18118)	Santa Fe F-3 AA set "200", *93*	350	400	___[1]
(18119)/(18120)	UP Alco AA set "8119" and "8120", *94*	250	300	___[1]
(18121)	Santa Fe F-3 B Unit "200A", *94*	95	125	___[1]
(18122)	Santa Fe F-3 B Unit "200B", *95*	185	210	___[1]
(18123)	ACL F-3 A Unit "342" (See 11903)			
(18124)	ACL F-3 B Unit "342B" (See 11903)			
(18125)	Atlantic Coast Line F-3 A Unit Dummy "343" (See 11903)			
(18200)	Conrail SD-40 "8200", *87*	235	275	___[1]
(18201)	Chessie System SD-40 "8201", *88*	265	320	___[1]
(18202)	Erie-Lackawanna SD-40 Dummy "8459", *89 u*	145	170	___[1]
(18203)	CP Rail SD-40 "8203", *89*	250	330	___[1]
(18204)	Chessie System SD-40 Dummy "8204", *90 u*	155	180	___[1]
(18205)	Union Pacific Dash 8-40C "9100", *89*	260	325	___[2]
(18206)	Santa Fe Dash 8-40B "8206", *90*	250	275	___[1]
(18207)	Norfolk Southern Dash 8-40C "8689", *92*	285	335	___[1]
(18208)	BN SD-40 Dummy "8586", *91 u*	155	180	___[1]
(18209)	CP Rail SD-40 Dummy "8209", *92 u*	195	210	___[1]
(18210)	Illinois Central SD-40 "6006", *93*	275	300	___[1]
(18211)	Susquehanna Dash 8-40B "4002", *93*	215	250	___[1]
(18212)	Santa Fe Dash 8-40B Dummy "8212", *93*	175	200	___[1]
(18213)	Norfolk Southern Dash 8-40C "8688", *94*	320	355	___[1]
(18214)	CSX Dash 8-40C "7500", *94*	415	465	___[1]
(18215)	CSX Dash 8-40C "7643", *94*	290	320	___[1]
(18216)	Conrail SD-60M "5500", *94*	380	425	___[1]
(18217)	Illinois Central SD-40 "6007", *94*	260	285	___[1]

		Exc	New	Cond/$
(18218)	Susquehanna Dash 8-40B "4004", *94*	275	300	[1]
(18219)	C&NW Dash 8-40C "8501", *95*	395	420	[1]
(18220)	C&NW Dash 8-40C "8502", *95*	300	335	[1]
(18221)	D&RGW SD-50 "5512", *95*	425	475	[1]
(18222)	D&RGW SD-50 "5517", *95*	350	425	[1]
(18223)	Milwaukee Road SD-40 "154", *95*	340	390	[1]
(18224)	Milwaukee Road SD-40 "155", *95*	300	350	[1]
(18300)	PRR GG-1 "8300", *87*	560	660	[2]
(18301)	Southern FM Trainmaster "8301", *88*	310	360	[2]
(18302)	GN EP-5 "8302" (FF no. 3), *88*	200	250	[1]
(18303)	Amtrak GG-1 "8303", *89*	350	400	[2]
(18304)	Lackawanna MU Car set, Powered and Dummy "2401" and "2402", *91*	550	620	[1]
(18305)	Lackawanna MU Car set, Dummies "2400" and "2403", *92*	300	350	[1]
(18306)	PRR MU Car set, Powered and Dummy "4574" and "483", *92*	360	440	[1]
(18307)	PRR FM Trainmaster "8699", *94*	300	350	[1]
(18308)	PRR GG-1 "4866", *92*	400	480	[1]
(18309)	Reading FM Trainmaster "863", *93*	275	300	[1]
(18310)	PRR MU Car set, Dummies "484" and "485", *93*	300	375	[1]
(18311)	Disney EP-5 "8311", *94*	210	265	[1]
(18313)	Pennsylvania GG-1 "4907", *96*	300	360	[2]
(18400)	Santa Fe Vulcan Rotary Snowplow "8400", *87*	160	210	[1]
(18401)	Workmen Handcar, *87–88*	37	48	[1]
18402	Lionel Lines Burro Crane, *88*	80	95	[1]
(18403)	Santa Claus Handcar, *88*	33	38	[1]
(18404)	San Francisco Trolley "8404", *88*	90	150	[2]
18405	Santa Fe Burro Crane, *89*	70	80	[1]
18406	Lionel Track Maintenance Car, *89, 91*	46	60	[1]
(18407)	Snoopy and Woodstock Handcar, *90–91*	44	55	[1]
(18408)	Santa Claus Handcar, *89*	30	45	[1]
18410	PRR Burro Crane, *90*	100	110	[1]
18411	Canadian Pacific Fire Car, *90*	90	110	[1]
18412	Union Pacific Fire Car, *91*		NM	

		Exc	New	Cond/$
(18413)	Charlie Brown and Lucy Handcar, *91*	28	55	[1]
(18416)	Bugs Bunny and Daffy Duck Handcar, *92–93*	105	115	[1]
18417	Lionel Gang Car, *93*	75	95	[1]
(18419)	Lionelville Electric Trolley "8419", *94*	90	110	[1]
(18421)	Sylvester and Tweety Handcar, *94*	45	60	[1]
(18422)	Santa and Snowman Handcar, *94*	40	50	[1]
(18423)	On-Track Step Van, *95*	37	46	[1]
(18424)	On-Track Pick-up Truck, *95*	38	47	[1]
(18425)	Goofy and Pluto Handcar, *95*	40	50	[1]
(18426)	Santa and Snowman Handcar, *95*	40	50	[1]
(18429)	Workmen Handcar, *96*	—	36	[1]
(18500)	Milwaukee Road GP-9 "8500" (FF no. 2), *87*	200	225	[1]
(18500)	(See 18550)			
(18501)	WM NW-2 "8501" (FF no. 4), *89*	280	330	[1]
(18502)	Lionel Lines 90th Anniversary GP-9 "1900", *90*	135	160	[1]
(18503)	Southern Pacific NW-2 "8503", *90*	275	300	[1]
(18504)	Frisco GP-7 "504" (FF no. 5), *91*	200	230	[1]
(18505)	NKP GP-7 Powered and Dummy set "400" and "401" (FF no. 6), *92*	295	370	[1]
(18506)	CN Budd RDC Powered and Dummy set "D202" and "D203", *92*	220	265	[1]
(18507)	CN Budd RDC Baggage "D202" (See 18506)			
(18508)	CN Budd RDC Passenger Dummy "D203" (See 18506)			
(18510)	CN Budd RDC Passenger Dummy "D200" (See 18512)			
(18511)	CN Budd RDC Passenger Dummy "D250" (See 18512)			
(18512)	CN Budd RDC Dummies set "D200" and "D250", *93*	225	275	[1]
(18513)	NYC GP-7 "7420", *94*	165	190	[1]
(18514)	Missouri Pacific GP-7 "4124", *95*	175	200	[1]
(18550)	JCPenney MILW GP-9 "8500" w/ display case, *87 u*		NRS	

		Exc	New	Cond/$
(18551)	JCPenney Susquehanna RS-3 "8809" w/ display case, *89 u*	180	200	___[1]
(18552)	JCPenney DM&IR SD-18 "8813" w/ display case, *90 u*	175	200	___[1]
(18553)	Sears UP GP-9 "150" w/ display case, *91 u*	160	185	___[1]
(18554)	JCPenney GM&O RS-3 "721" w/ display case, *92–93 u*	165	190	___[1]
(18555)	Sears C&IM SD-9 "52", *92 u*	175	200	___[1]
(18556)	Sears Chicago & Illinois Midland Caboose and Freight Car set, *92 u*	140	155	___[1]
(18557)	Chessie System 4-8-4 "2101" w/ display case for export, *92 u*		NRS	___
(18558)	JCPenney MKT GP-9 "91" w/ display case, *94 u*	200	225	___[1]
(18600)	ACL 4-4-2 "8600", *87 u*	75	90	___[1]
(18601)	Great Northern 4-4-2 "8601", *88*	80	95	___[1]
(18602)	PRR 4-4-2 "8602", *87*	90	100	___[1]
(18604)	Wabash 4-4-2 "8604", *88–91*	75	90	___[1]
(18605)	Mopar Express 4-4-2 "1987", *87–88 u*	80	125	___[1]
(18606)	NYC 2-6-4 "8606", *89*	155	175	___[2]
(18607)	Union Pacific 2-6-4 "8607", *89*	130	155	___[1]
(18608)	D&RGW 2-6-4 "8608" (SSS), *89*	125	150	___[1]
(18609)	Northern Pacific 2-6-4 "8609", *90*	150	175	___[1]
(18610)	Rock Island 0-4-0 "8610", *90*	165	190	___[1]
(18611)	Lionel Lines 2-6-4 "8611" (SSS), *90*	130	150	___[1]
(18612)	C&NW 4-4-2 "8612", *89*	75	90	___[1]
(18613)	NYC 4-4-2 "8613", *89 u*	85	110	___[1]
(18614)	Circus Train 4-4-2 "1989", *89 u*	90	115	___[1]
(18615)	GTW 4-4-2 "8615", *90*	75	90	___[1]
(18616)	Northern Pacific 4-4-2 "8616", *90 u*	85	110	___[1]
(18617)	Adolphus III 4-4-2, *89–92 u*	100	125	___[1]
(18618)	B&O 4-4-2 "8618", *91*		NM	___
(18620)	Illinois Central 2-6-2 "8620", *91*	175	200	___[1]
(18621)	Western Pacific 0-4-0 "8621", *92*		NM	___
(18622)	Union Pacific 4-4-2 "8622", *90–91 u*	75	95	___[1]
(18623)	Texas & Pacific 4-4-2 "8623", *92*	80	110	___[1]

		Exc	New	Cond/$
(18625)	Illinois Central 4-4-2 "8625", *91 u*	80	110	[1]
(18626)	Delaware & Hudson 2-6-2 "8626", *92*	175	200	[1]
(18627)	C&O 4-4-2 "8627" or "8633", *92, 93 u, 94, 95 u*		NRS	
(18628)	MKT 4-4-2 "8628", *92, 93 u*	75	90	[1]
(18630)	C&NW 4-6-2 "2903", *93*	325	360	[1]
(18632)	NYC 4-4-2 "8632", *93–95*		NRS	
(18633)	Union Pacific 4-4-2 "8633", *93–95*	75	100	[1]
(18633)	(See 18627, 18637)			
(18635)	Santa Fe 2-6-4 "8625", *93*	205	220	[1]
(18636)	B&O 4-6-2 "5300", *94*	300	325	[1]
(18637)	United Auto Workers 4-4-2 "8633", *93 u*		NRS	
(18638)	Norfolk & Western 2-6-4 "638", *94*	175	225	[1]
(18639)	Reading 4-6-2 "639", *95*	125	150	[1]
(18640)	Union Pacific 4-6-2 "8640", *95*	125	150	[1]
(18641)	Ford 4-4-2 "8641", *94 u*	75	100	[1]
(18642)	Lionel Lines 4-6-2 "8642", *95*	125	150	[1]
(18689)	(See 18207)			
(18700)	Rock Island 0-4-0T "8700", *87–88*	40	50	[1]
(18702)	V&TRR 4-4-0 "8702" (SSS), *88*	125	150	[1]
(18704)	Lionel Lines 2-4-0 "8704", *89 u*	40	50	[1]
(18705)	"Neptune" 0-4-0T "8705", *90–91*	40	50	[1]
(18706)	Santa Fe 2-4-0 "8706", *91*	40	50	[1]
(18707)	Mickey's World Tour 2-4-0 "8707", *91, 92 u*	60	75	[1]
(18709)	Lionel Employee Learning Center "Blue Engine" 0-4-0T, *92 u*	—	170	[1]
(18710)	Southern Pacific 2-4-0 "2000", *93*	35	45	[1]
(18711)	Southern 2-4-0 "2000", *93*	35	45	[1]
(18712)	Jersey Central 2-4-0 "2000", *93*	35	45	[1]
(18713)	Chessie System 2-4-0 "1993", *94–95*	35	45	[1]
(18716)	Lionelville Circus 4-4-0 "8716", *90–91*	100	125	[1]
(18800)	Lehigh Valley GP-9 "8800", *87*	100	120	[1]
(18801)	Santa Fe U36B "8801", *87*	100	120	[1]
(18802)	Southern GP-9 "8802" (SSS), *87*	115	140	[1]
(18803)	Santa Fe RS-3 "8803", *88*	105	125	[1]
(18804)	Soo Line RS-3 "8804", *88*	100	120	[1]
(18805)	Union Pacific RS-3 "8805", *89*	85	105	[1]

		Exc	New	Cond/$
(18806)	New Haven SD-18 "8806", *89*	110	130	____1
(18807)	Lehigh Valley RS-3 "8807", *90*	100	125	____1
(18808)	ACL SD-18 "8808", *90*	100	125	____1
(18809)	Susquehanna RS-3 "8809" (See 18551), *89 u*			
(18810)	CSX SD-18 "8810", *90*	100	135	____1
(18811)	Alaska SD-9 "8811", *91*	125	175	____1
(18812)	Kansas City Southern GP-38 "4000", *91*	120	150	____1
(18813)	DM&IR SD-18 "8813" (See 18552), *90 u*			
(18814)	D&H RS-3 "8814" (SSS), *91*	115	155	____1
(18815)	Amtrak RS-3 "1815", *91, 92 u*	100	135	____1
(18816)	C&NW GP-38-2 "4600", *92*	130	160	____1
(18817)	UP GP-9 "150" (See 18553), *91 u*			
(18818)	Lionel Railroader Club GP-38-2 "1992", *92 u*	125	145	____1
(18819)	L&N GP-38-2 "4136", *92*	160	210	____1
(18820)	WP GP-9 "8820" (SSS), *92*	140	165	____1
(18821)	Clinchfield GP-38-2 "6005", *93*	120	145	____1
(18822)	Gulf, Mobile & Ohio RS-3 "721" (See 18554), *92–93 u*			
(18823)	Chicago & Illinois Midland SD-9 "52" (See 18555), *92 u*			
(18824)	Montana Rail Link SD-9 "600", *93*	145	170	____1
(18825)	Soo Line GP-38-2 "4000" (SSS), *93*	130	155	____1
(18826)	Conrail GP-7 "5808", *93*	125	150	____1
(18827)	"Happy Holidays" RS-3 "8827", *93*	160	210	____1
(18830)	Budweiser GP-9 "1947", *93–94 u*	125	170	____1
(18831)	SP GP-20 "4060", *94*	130	150	____1
(18832)	PRR RSD-4 "8446", *95*	125	140	____1
(18833)	Milwaukee Road RS-3 "2487", *94*	125	145	____1
(18834)	C&O SD-28 "8834", *94*	105	145	____1
(18835)	NYC RS-3 "8223" (SSS), *94*	170	195	____1
(18836)	CN/Grand Trunk GP-38-2 "5800", *94*	180	210	____1
(18837)	"Happy Holidays" RS-3 "8837", *94–95*	135	170	____1
(18838)	Seaboard RSC-3 "1538", *95*	115	150	____1
(18840)	U.S. Army GP-7 "1821", *95*	105	135	____1
(18841)	Western Maryland GP-20 "27" (SSS), *95*	125	160	____1
(18842)	Bessemer & Lake Erie SD-38 "868", *95 u*		NRS	____
(18843)	Great Northern RS-3 "197", *96*	125	155	____1

		Exc	New	Cond/$
(18844)	NdeM GP-38 "9288", *96*		NM	
(18890)	LOTS UP RS-3 "8805", *89 u*	125	150	[1]
(18900)	PRR Diesel Switcher "8900", *88 u, 89*	30	40	[1]
(18901)/(18902)	PRR Alco AA set "8901" and "8902", *88*	125	150	[1]
(18903)/(18904)	Amtrak Alco AA set "8903" and "8904", *88–89*	100	150	[1]
(18905)	PRR 44-tonner "9312", *92*	110	130	[1]
(18906)	Erie-Lackawanna RS-3 "8906", *91 u*	130	165	[1]
(18907)	Rock Island 44-tonner "371", *93*	125	150	[1]
(18908)/(18909)	NYC Alco AA set "8908" and "8909", *93*	100	115	[1]
(18910)	CSX Diesel Switcher "8910", *93*	30	35	[1]
(18911)	UP Diesel Switcher "8911", *93*	30	35	[1]
(18912)	Amtrak Diesel Switcher "8912", *93*	30	35	[1]
(18913)	Santa Fe Alco A Unit "8913", *93–94*	60	75	[1]
(18915)	WM Alco A Unit "8915", *93*	55	70	[1]
(18916)	WM Alco A Unit Dummy "8916", *93*	35	40	[1]
18917	Soo Line NW-2, *93*	75	85	[1]
(18918)	B&M NW-2 "8918", *93*	75	90	[1]
(18919)	Santa Fe Alco A Unit Dummy "8919", *93–94*	30	40	[1]
(18920)	Frisco NW-2 "254", *94*	70	80	[1]
(18921)	C&NW NW-2 "1017", *94*	70	80	[1]
(18922)	New Haven Alco A Unit "8922", *94*	60	80	[1]
(18923)	New Haven Alco A Unit Dummy "8923", *94*	65	70	[1]
(18924)	Illinois Central Diesel Switcher "8924", *94–95*	30	35	[1]
(18925)	D&RGW Diesel Switcher "8925", *94–95*	30	35	[1]
(18926)	Reading Diesel Switcher "8926", *94–95*	30	35	[1]
(18927)	U.S. Navy NW-2 "65-00637", *94–95*	65	75	[1]
(18928)	C&NW NW-2 Calf, *95*	45	50	[1]
(18929)	B&M NW-2 Calf, *95*	45	50	[1]
(18930)	Crayola Diesel Switcher, *94 u, 95*	30	35	[1]
(18931)	Chrysler Mopar NW-2 "1818", *94 u*	65	80	[1]
(18932)	Jersey Central NW-2 "8932", *96*	—	70	[1]

		Exc	New	Cond/$
(18933)	Jersey Central NW-2 Calf "8933", *96*	—	70	1
(18934)/(18935)	Reading Alco AA set "300" and "304", *95*	80	100	1
(18936)	Amtrak Alco A Unit "8936", *95*	—	90	1
(18937)	Amtrak Alco A Unit Dummy "8937", *95*	—	45	1
(18938)	U.S. Navy NW-2 Calf, *95*	45	50	1
(18943)	Georgia Power NW-2 "1960", *95 u*		NRS	
19000	Blue Comet Dining Car, *87 u*	70	90	1
19001	Southern Dining Car, *87 u*	70	95	1
19002	Pennsylvania Dining Car, *88 u*	35	55	1
19003	Milwaukee Road Dining Car, *88 u*	35	55	1
19010	B&O Dining Car, *89 u*	38	60	1
(19011)	Lionel Lines Baggage Car "9011", *93*	200	250	1
(19015)	Lionel Lines Passenger Car "9015", *91*	95	115	1
(19016)	Lionel Lines Passenger Car "9016", *91*	95	115	1
(19017)	Lionel Lines Passenger Car "9017", *91*	95	115	1
(19018)	Lionel Lines Observation Car "9018", *91*	95	115	1
(19019)	SP Baggage Car "9019", *93*	125	175	1
(19023)	SP Passenger Car "9023", *92*	110	130	1
(19024)	SP Passenger Car "9024", *92*	110	130	1
(19025)	SP Passenger Car "9025", *92*	110	130	1
(19026)	SP Observation Car "9026", *92*	110	130	1
(19027)	Reading Baggage Car "9027", *92*		NM	
(19031)	Reading Passenger Car "9031", *92*		NM	
(19032)	Reading Passenger Car "9032", *92*		NM	
(19033)	Reading Observation Car "9033", *92*		NM	
(19038)	Adolphus Busch Observation Car, *92–93 u*	—	80	1
(19039)	Pere Marquette Baggage Car, *93*	—	70	1
(19040)	Pere Marquette Passenger Car "1115", *93*	—	70	1
(19041)	Pere Marquette Passenger Car "1116", *93*	—	70	1
(19042)	Pere Marquette Observation Car "36", *93*	—	70	1
(19047)	Baltimore & Ohio Combination Car "9047", *96*	—	45	1
(19048)	Baltimore & Ohio Passenger Car "9048", *96*	—	45	1
(19049)	Baltimore & Ohio Dining Car "9049", *96*	—	45	1

		Exc	New	Cond/$
(19050)	Baltimore & Ohio Observation Car "9050", *96*	—	45	[1]
(19100)	Amtrak Baggage Car "9100", *89*	90	110	[1]
(19101)	Amtrak Combination Car "9101", *89*	90	110	[1]
(19102)	Amtrak Passenger Car "9102", *89*	90	110	[1]
(19103)	Amtrak Vista Dome Car "9103", *89*	75	95	[1]
(19104)	Amtrak Dining Car "9104", *89*	90	110	[1]
(19105)	Amtrak Full Vista Dome Car "9105", *89 u*	115	135	[1]
(19106)	Amtrak Observation Car "9106", *89*	90	110	[1]
(19107)	SP Full Vista Dome Car, *90 u*	70	80	[1]
(19108)	N&W Full Vista Dome Car "576", *91 u*	90	100	[1]
(19109)	Santa Fe Baggage Car "3400", *91*	125	175	[1]
(19110)	Santa Fe Combination Car "3500", *91*	125	175	[1]
(19111)	Santa Fe Dining Car "601", *91*	125	175	[1]
(19112)	Santa Fe Passenger Car, *91*	125	175	[1]
(19113)	Santa Fe Vista Dome Observation Car, *91*	125	175	[1]
(19116)	Great Northern Baggage Car "1200", *92*	90	100	[1]
(19117)	Great Northern Combination Car "1240", *92*	90	100	[1]
(19118)	Great Northern Passenger Car "1212", *92*	90	100	[1]
(19119)	Great Northern Vista Dome Car "1322", *92*	90	100	[1]
(19120)	Great Northern Observation Car "1192", *92*	90	100	[1]
(19121)	Union Pacific Vista Dome Car "9121", *92 u*	95	110	[1]
(19122)	D&RGW California Zephyr Baggage Car, *93*	100	125	[1]
(19123)	D&RGW California Zephyr "Silver Bronco" Vista Dome Car, *93*	100	125	[1]
(19124)	D&RGW California Zephyr "Silver Colt" Vista Dome Car, *93*	100	125	[1]
(19125)	D&RGW California Zephyr "Silver Mustang" Vista Dome Car, *93*	100	125	[1]
(19126)	D&RGW California Zephyr "Silver Pony" Vista Dome Car, *93*	100	125	[1]

		Exc	New	Cond/$
(19127)	D&RGW California Zephyr Vista Dome Observation Car, *93*	100	125	___[1]
(19128)	Santa Fe Full Vista Dome Car "507", *92 u*	180	195	___[1]
(19129)	Illinois Central Full Vista Dome Car "9129", *93*	95	110	___[1]
(19130)	Lackawanna Passenger Cars, set of 4, *94*	330	440	___[1]
(19131)	Lackawanna Baggage Car "2000" (See 19130)			
(19132)	Lackawanna Dining Car "469" (See 19130)			
(19133)	Lackawanna Passenger Car "260" (See 19130)			
(19134)	Lackawanna Observation Car "789" (See 19130)			
(19135)	Lackawanna Combination Car "425", *94*	95	110	___[1]
(19136)	Lackawanna Passenger Car "211", *94*	95	110	___[1]
(19137)	New York Central Roomette Car, *95*	90	110	___[1]
(19138)	Santa Fe Roomette Car, *95*	95	120	___[1]
(19139)	Norfolk & Western Baggage Car "577", *95*	100	125	___[1]
(19140)	Norfolk & Western Combination Car "494", *95*	100	125	___[1]
(19141)	Norfolk & Western Dining Car "495", *95*	100	125	___[1]
(19142)	Norfolk & Western Passenger Car "538", *95*	100	125	___[1]
(19143)	Norfolk & Western Passenger Car "537", *95*	100	125	___[1]
(19144)	Norfolk & Western Observation Car "582", *95*	100	125	___[1]
(19145)	Chesapeake & Ohio Combination Car "1403", *96*	—	90	___[1]
(19146)	Chesapeake & Ohio Passenger Car "1623", *96*	—	90	___[1]
(19147)	Chesapeake & Ohio Passenger Car "1803", *96*	—	90	___[1]
(19150)	Chesapeake & Ohio Observation Car "2504", *96*	—	90	___[1]
(19153)	Chesapeake & Ohio Passenger Cars, set of 4, *96*	—	360	___[1]

		Exc	New	Cond/$
(19159)	Norfolk & Western Passenger Cars, set of 4, *95 u*	400	500	___ [1]
19200	Tidewater Southern Boxcar, *87*	10	18	___ [1]
19201	Lancaster & Chester Boxcar, *87*	55	70	___ [1]
19202	PRR Boxcar, *87*	39	50	___ [1]
19203	D&TS Boxcar, *87*	10	18	___ [1]
19204	Milwaukee Road Boxcar (FF no. 2), *87*	25	33	___ [1]
19205	Great Northern DD Boxcar (FF no. 3), *88*	27	36	___ [1]
19206	Seaboard System Boxcar, *88*	15	18	___ [1]
19207	CP Rail DD Boxcar, *88*	15	18	___ [1]
19208	Southern DD Boxcar, *88*	15	18	___ [1]
19209	Florida East Coast Boxcar, *88*	15	18	___ [1]
19210	Soo Line Boxcar, *89*	17	20	___ [1]
19211	Vermont Railway Boxcar, *89*	17	20	___ [1]
19212	PRR Boxcar, *89*	19	22	___ [1]
19213	SP&S DD Boxcar, *89*	17	20	___ [1]
19214	Western Maryland Boxcar (FF no. 4), *89*	27	32	___ [1]
19215	Union Pacific DD Boxcar, *90*	17	20	___ [1]
19216	Santa Fe Boxcar, *90*	15	18	___ [1]
19217	Burlington Boxcar, *90*	15	18	___ [1]
19218	New Haven Boxcar, *90*	15	18	___ [1]
19219	Lionel Lines 1900-1906 Boxcar w/ Diesel RailSounds, *90*	140	175	___ [1]
19220	Lionel Lines 1926-1934 Boxcar, *90*	30	35	___ [1]
19221	Lionel Lines 1935-1937 Boxcar, *90*	30	35	___ [1]
19222	Lionel Lines 1948-1950 Boxcar, *90*	30	35	___ [1]
19223	Lionel Lines 1979-1989 Boxcar, *90*	30	35	___ [1]
19228	Cotton Belt Boxcar, *91*	18	20	___ [1]
19229	Frisco Boxcar w/ Diesel RailSounds (FF no. 5), *91*	100	125	___ [1]
19230	Frisco DD Boxcar (FF no. 5), *91*	28	33	___ [1]
19231	TA&G DD Boxcar, *91*	17	20	___ [1]
19232	Rock Island DD Boxcar, *91*	17	20	___ [1]
19233	Southern Pacific Boxcar, *91*	15	18	___ [1]
19234	NYC Boxcar, *91*	60	75	___ [1]
19235	MKT Boxcar, *91*	60	75	___ [1]
19236	NKP DD Boxcar (FF no. 6), *92*	25	35	___ [1]

		Exc	New	Cond/$
19237	C&IM Boxcar, *92*	15	20	___ [1]
19238	Kansas City Southern Boxcar, *92*	17	22	___ [1]
19239	Toronto, Hamilton & Buffalo DD Boxcar, *92*	15	20	___ [1]
19240	Great Northern DD Boxcar, *92*	15	20	___ [1]
19241	Mickey Mouse 60th Anniversary Hi-cube Boxcar, *91 u*	135	160	___ [1]
19242	Donald Duck 50th Anniversary Hi-cube Boxcar, *91 u*	135	160	___ [1]
(19243)	Clinchfield Boxcar "9790", *91 u*	42	47	___ [1]
(19244)	L&N Boxcar "9791", *92*	29	34	___ [1]
19245	Mickey's World Tour Hi-cube Boxcar, *92 u*	55	65	___ [1]
19246	Disney World 20th Anniversary Hi-cube Boxcar, *92 u*	60	75	___ [1]
(19247)	6464 Series Boxcars, 1st Edition, set of 3, *93*	270	315	___ [1]
(19248)	Western Pacific Boxcar "6464", *93*	90	105	___ [1]
(19249)	Great Northern Boxcar "6464", *93*	90	105	___ [1]
(19250)	M&StL Boxcar "6464", *93*	90	105	___ [1]
(19251)	Montana Rail Link DD Boxcar "10001", *93*	20	25	___ [1]
19254	Erie Boxcar (FF no. 7), *93*	25	30	___ [1]
19255	Erie DD Boxcar (FF no. 7), *93*	26	31	___ [1]
19256	Goofy Hi-cube Boxcar, *93*	38	47	___ [1]
(19257)	6464 Series Boxcars, 2nd Edition, set of 3, *94*	165	190	___ [1]
(19258)	Rock Island Boxcar "6464", *94*	35	45	___ [1]
(19259)	Western Pacific Boxcar "6464100", *94*	45	65	___ [1]
(19260)	Western Pacific Boxcar "6464100", *94*	45	65	___ [1]
19261	Perils of Mickey Hi-cube Boxcar I, *93*	50	55	___ [1]
19262	Perils of Mickey Hi-cube Boxcar II, *93*	37	41	___ [1]
19263	NYC DD Boxcar (SSS), *94*	35	40	___ [1]
19264	Perils of Mickey Hi-cube Boxcar III, *94*	41	46	___ [1]
19265	Mickey Mouse 65th Anniversary Hi-cube Boxcar, *94*	45	50	___ [1]
(19266)	6464 Series Boxcars, 3rd Edition, set of 3, *95*	115	120	___ [2]
(19267)	NYC "Pacemaker" Boxcar "6464125", *95*	40	45	___ [1]

		Exc	New	Cond/$
(19268)	Missouri Pacific Boxcar "6464150", *95*	41	46	1
(19269)	Rock Island Boxcar "6464", *95*	34	39	1
19270	Donald Duck 60th Anniversary Hi-cube Boxcar, *95*	45	50	1
19271	Minnie Mouse Hi-cube Boxcar, *95*	45	50	1
(19272)	6464 Series Boxcars, 4th edition, set of 3, *96*	115	120	1
(19273)	BAR "State of Maine" Boxcar "6464275", *96*	—	36	1
(19274)	Southern Pacific "Overnight" Boxcar "6464225", *96*	—	36	1
(19275)	Pennsylvania Boxcar "6464", *96*	—	36	1
19300	PRR Ore Car, *87*	19	24	1
19301	Milwaukee Road Ore Car, *87*	20	25	1
19302	Milwaukee Road Quad Hopper w/ coal load (FF no. 2), *87*	25	35	1
19303	Lionel Lines Quad Hopper w/ coal load, *87 u*	24	34	1
19304	GN Covered Quad Hopper (FF no. 3), *88*	32	36	1
19305	Chessie System Ore Car, *88*	15	20	1
19307	B&LE Ore Car w/ load, *89*	15	20	1
19308	GN Ore Car w/ load, *89*	15	20	1
19309	Seaboard Covered Quad Hopper, *89*	15	20	1
19310	L&C Quad Hopper w/ coal load, *89*	22	33	1
19311	SP Covered Quad Hopper, *90*	15	20	1
19312	Reading Quad Hopper w/ coal load, *90*	19	28	1
19313	B&O Ore Car w/ load, *90–91*	16	21	1
19315	Amtrak Ore Car w/ load, *91*	15	20	1
19316	Wabash Covered Quad Hopper, *91*	19	28	1
19317	Lehigh Valley Quad Hopper w/ coal load, *91*	60	75	1
19318	NKP Quad Hopper w/ coal load (FF no. 6), *92*	30	35	1
19319	Union Pacific Covered Quad Hopper, *92*	20	25	1
19320	PRR Ore Car w/ load, *92*	22	27	1
19321	B&LE Ore Car w/ load, *92*	22	27	1
19322	C&NW Ore Car w/ load, *93*	22	27	1

		Exc	New	Cond/$
19323	Detroit & Mackinac Ore Car w/ load, *93*	22	27	1
19324	Erie Quad Hopper w/ coal load (FF no. 7), *93*	30	35	1
19400	Milwaukee Road Gondola w/ cable reels (FF no. 2), *87*	25	35	1
19400	(See 51701)			
19401	GN Gondola w/ coal load (FF no. 3), *88*	26	31	1
19402	GN Crane Car (FF no. 3), *88*	48	70	1
19403	WM Gondola w/ coal load (FF no. 4), *89*	25	30	1
19404	Trailer Train Flatcar w/ WM trailers (FF no. 4), *89*	34	39	1
19405	Southern Crane Car, *91*	50	80	1
19406	West Point Mint Car, *91 u*	50	80	1
19408	Frisco Gondola w/ coil covers (FF no. 5), *91*	31	37	1
19409	Southern Flatcar w/ stakes, *91*	20	25	1
19410	NYC Gondola w/ canisters, *91*	50	60	1
19411	NKP Flatcar w/ Sears trailer (FF no. 6), *92*	60	70	1
19412	Frisco Crane Car, *92*	50	65	1
19413	Frisco Flatcar w/ stakes, *92*	20	25	1
19414	Union Pacific Flatcar w/ stakes (SSS), *92*	20	25	1
(19415)	Erie Flatcar w/ trailer "7200" (FF no. 7), *93*	28	37	1
(19416)	ICG TTUX Flatcar set w/ trailers "19417" and "19418" (SSS), *93*	110	130	1
19417/19418	ICG TTUX Flatcars w/ trailers (See 19416)			
19419	Charlotte Mint Car, *93*	32	40	1
19420	Lionel Lines Vat Car, *94*	25	30	1
19421	Hirsch Brothers Vat Car, *95*	25	30	1
19500	Milwaukee Road Reefer (FF no. 2), *87*	35	45	1
19502	C&NW Reefer, *87*	36	41	1
19503	Bangor & Aroostook Reefer, *87*	34	39	1
19504	Northern Pacific Reefer, *87*	22	26	1
19505	Great Northern Reefer (FF no. 3), *88*	44	55	1
19506	Thomas Newcomen Reefer, *88*	20	25	1
19507	Thomas Edison Reefer, *88*	20	25	1
19508	Leonardo da Vinci Reefer, *89*	21	26	1
19509	Alexander Graham Bell Reefer, *89*	20	25	1
19510	PRR Stock Car (FARR no. 5), *89 u*	29	32	1

		Exc	New	Cond/$
19511	WM Reefer (FF no. 4), *89*	27	32	___[1]
19512	Wright Brothers Reefer, *90*	20	25	___[1]
19513	Ben Franklin Reefer, *90*	19	24	___[1]
19515	Milwaukee Road Stock Car (FF no. 2), *90 u*	27	32	___[1]
19516	George Washington Reefer, *89 u, 91*	15	20	___[1]
19517	Civil War Reefer, *89 u, 91*	14	18	___[1]
19518	Man on the Moon Reefer, *89 u, 91*	15	20	___[1]
19519	Frisco Stock Car (FF no. 5), *91*	28	33	___[1]
19520	CSX Reefer, *91*	20	25	___[1]
19522	Guglielmo Marconi Reefer, *91*	20	25	___[1]
19523	Dr. Robert Goddard Reefer, *91*	22	28	___[1]
19524	Delaware & Hudson Reefer (SSS), *91*	30	35	___[1]
19525	Speedy Alka Seltzer Reefer, *91 u*	40	45	___[1]
19526	Jolly Green Giant Reefer, *91 u*	26	34	___[1]
19527	Nickel Plate Road Reefer (FF no. 6), *92*	30	40	___[1]
19528	Joshua L. Cowen Reefer, *92*	30	40	___[1]
19529	A.C. Gilbert Reefer, *92*	27	32	___[1]
19530	Rock Island Stock Car, *92 u*	35	40	___[1]
19531	Rice Krispies Reefer, *92 u*	30	45	___[1]
(19532)	Hormel Reefer "901", *92 u*	30	40	___[1]
19535	Erie Reefer (FF no. 7), *93*	30	35	___[1]
19536	Soo Line REA Reefer (SSS), *93*	24	29	___[1]
19537	Kellogg's Corn Flakes Reefer, *93*		NM	___
(19538)	Hormel Reefer "102", *94*	29	34	___[1]
19539	Heinz Reefer, *94*	29	34	___[1]
(19599)	Old Glory Reefers, set of 3, *89 u, 91*	48	55	___[1]
19600	Milwaukee Road 1-D Tank Car (FF no. 2), *87*	40	50	___[1]
19601	North American 1-D Tank Car (FF no. 4), *89*	37	42	___[1]
19602	Johnson 1-D Tank Car (FF no. 5), *91*	27	36	___[1]
19603	GATX 1-D Tank Car (FF no. 6), *92*	34	44	___[1]
19604	Goodyear 1-D Tank Car (SSS), *93*	36	41	___[1]
19605	Hudson's Bay 1-D Tank Car (SSS), *94*	35	40	___[1]
19651	Santa Fe Tool Car, *87*	23	28	___[1]
19652	Jersey Central Bunk Car, *88*	20	25	___[1]
19653	Jersey Central Tool Car, *88*	21	26	___[1]
19654	Amtrak Bunk Car, *89*	22	27	___[1]

		Exc	New	Cond/$
19655	Amtrak Tool Car, *90–91*	22	27	[1]
19656	Milwaukee Road Bunk Car w/ smoke, *90*	45	55	[1]
19657	Wabash Bunk Car w/ smoke, *91–92*	50	60	[1]
19658	Norfolk & Western Tool Car, *91*	25	30	[1]
19700	Chessie System E/V Caboose, *88*	55	65	[1]
19701	Milwau E/V Caboose (FF no. 3), *88*	40	50	[1]
19702	PRR N5C Caboose, *87*	40	50	[1]
19703	Great Northern E/V Caboose (FF no. 3), *88*	55	65	[1]
19704	WM E/V Caboose w/ smoke (FF no. 4), *89*	50	60	[1]
19705	CP Rail E/V Caboose w/ smoke, *89*	50	55	[1]
(19706)	UP E/V Caboose w/ smoke "9706", *89*	60	65	[1]
19707	SP Work Caboose w/ searchlight and smoke, *90*	85	100	[1]
(19708)	Lionel Lines B/W Caboose "1990", *90*	60	65	[1]
19709	PRR Work Caboose w/ smoke, *89, 91*	60	75	[1]
19710	Frisco E/V Caboose w/ smoke (FF no. 5), *91*	60	65	[1]
19711	Norfolk Southern E/V Caboose w/ smoke, *92*	60	70	[1]
19712	PRR N5C Caboose, *91*	55	65	[1]
19714	NYC Work Caboose w/ searchlight and smoke, *92*	80	95	[1]
(19715)	DM&IR E/V Caboose "C-217", *92 u*	60	70	[1]
(19716)	Illinois Central E/V Caboose w/ smoke "9405", *93*	60	70	[1]
(19717)	Susquehanna B/W Caboose "0121", *93*	45	55	[1]
(19718)	Chicago & Illinois Midland E/V Caboose "74", *92 u*	40	50	[1]
(19719)	Erie B/W Caboose "C-300" (FF no. 7), *93*	55	65	[1]
19720	Soo Line E/V Caboose (SSS), *93*	50	60	[1]
(19721)	GM&O E/V Caboose "2956", *93 u*	60	70	[1]
19723	Disney E/V Caboose, *94*	44	55	[1]
(19724)	MKT E/V Caboose "125", *94 u*	55	65	[1]
19726	NYC B/W Caboose (SSS), *95*	55	65	[1]
(19727)	Pennsylvania N5C Caboose "477938", *96*	—	45	[1]
19800	Circle L Ranch Operating Cattle Car, *88*	95	135	[1]

		Exc	New	Cond/$
19801	Poultry Dispatch Chicken Car, *87*	40	60	___ [1]
19802	Carnation Milk Car, *87*	85	110	___ [1]
19803	Reading Ice Car, *87*	46	55	___ [1]
19804	Wabash Operating Hopper, *87*	29	38	___ [1]
19805	Santa Fe Operating Boxcar, *87*	30	40	___ [1]
19806	PRR Operating Hopper, *88*	32	41	___ [1]
19807	PRR E/V Caboose w/ smoke, *88*	50	60	___ [1]
19808	NYC Ice Car, *88*	50	60	___ [1]
19809	Erie-Lackawanna Operating Boxcar, *88*	30	40	___ [1]
19810	Bosco Milk Car, *88*	110	135	___ [1]
19811	Monon Brakeman Car, *90*	45	50	___ [1]
19813	Northern Pacific Ice Car, *89 u*	49	60	___ [1]
19815	Delaware & Hudson Brakeman Car, *92*	46	55	___ [1]
(19816)	Madison Hardware Operating Boxcar "190991", *91 u*	155	185	___ [1]
19817	Virginian Ice Car, *94*	40	50	___ [1]
(19818)	Dairymen's League Milk Car "788", *94*	80	95	___ [1]
19819	Poultry Dispatch Car (SSS), *94*	55	65	___ [1]
(19820)	Die-cast Metal Tender w/ RailSounds II, *95–96*		CP	___
(19821)	UP Opera, *95*	40	50	___ [1]
19822	Pork Dispatch Car, *95*	38	48	___ [1]
19823	Burlington Ice Car, *94 u, 95*	40	50	___ [1]
19825	EMD Generator Car, *96*	55	65	___ [1]
19900	Toy Fair Boxcar, *87 u*	100	125	___ [1]
19901	"I Love Virginia" Boxcar, *87*	27	38	___ [1]
19902	Toy Fair Boxcar, *88 u*	100	125	___ [1]
19903	Christmas Boxcar, *87 u*	40	50	___ [1]
19904	Christmas Boxcar, *88 u*	41	55	___ [1]
19905	"I Love California" Boxcar, *88*	18	22	___ [1]
19906	"I Love Pennsylvania" Boxcar, *89*	18	22	___ [1]
19907	Toy Fair Boxcar, *89 u*	100	125	___ [1]
19908	Christmas Boxcar, *89 u*	33	43	___ [1]
19909	"I Love New Jersey" Boxcar, *90*	20	25	___ [1]
19910	Christmas Boxcar, *90 u*	28	33	___ [1]
19911	Toy Fair Boxcar, *90 u*	95	120	___ [1]
19912	"I Love Ohio" Boxcar, *91*	20	25	___ [1]

		Exc	New	Cond/$
19913	Christmas Boxcar for Lionel Employees, *91 u*	250	300	___[1]
19914	Toy Fair Boxcar, *91 u*	100	125	___[1]
19915	"I Love Texas" Boxcar, *92*	20	25	___[1]
19916	Christmas Boxcar for Lionel Employees, *92 u*	250	300	___[1]
19917	Toy Fair Boxcar, *92 u*	120	145	___[1]
19918	Christmas Boxcar, *92 u*	75	95	___[1]
19919	"I Love Minnesota" Boxcar, *93*	25	30	___[1]
(19920)	Lionel Visitor's Center Boxcar, *92 u*	35	45	___[1]
19921	Christmas Boxcar for Lionel Employees, *93 u*	225	270	___[1]
19922	Christmas Boxcar, *93*	38	47	___[1]
19923	Toy Fair Boxcar, *93 u*	110	165	___[1]
19924	Lionel Railroader Club Boxcar, *93 u*	30	40	___[1]
19925	Learning Center Boxcar for Lionel Employees, *93 u*	200	250	___[1]
19926	"I Love Nevada" Boxcar, *94*	19	24	___[1]
(19927)	Lionel Visitor's Center Boxcar "1993", *93 u*	27	36	___[1]
19928	Christmas Boxcar for Lionel Employees, *94 u*	200	250	___[1]
19929	Christmas Boxcar, *94*	30	40	___[1]
19930	Lionel Railroader Club Quad Hopper w/ coal load, *94 u*	32	37	___[1]
19931	Toy Fair Boxcar, *94 u*	100	145	___[1]
19932	Lionel Visitor's Center Boxcar, *94 u*	27	36	___[1]
19933	"I Love Illinois" Boxcar, *95*	20	25	___[1]
(19934)	Lionel Visitor's Center Boxcar "1995", *95 u*	30	40	___[1]
(19935)	Lionel Railroader Club 1-D Tank Car "1995", *95 u*	28	37	___[1]
19937	Toy Fair Boxcar, *95 u*	100	150	___[1]
19938	Christmas Boxcar, *95*	22	29	___[1]
19939	Christmas Boxcar for Lionel Employees, *95 u*	245	310	___[1]
19941	"I Love Colorado" Boxcar, *95*	20	25	___[1]

		Exc	New	Cond/$
19942	"I Love Florida" Boxcar, *96*	20	25	[1]
(19960)	LOTS Western Pacific Boxcar "1952" (Std. 0), *92 u*	75	95	[1]
19961	Gadsden Pacific Inspiration Consolidated Copper Company Ore Car w/ load, *92 u*	40	45	[1]
(19962)	Southwest TTOS SP 3-bay ACF Hopper "496035" (Std. 0), *92 u*	75	100	[1]
(19963)	TTOS Union Equity 3-bay ACF Hopper "86892" (Std. 0), *92 u*	55	65	[1]
(19964)	U.S. JCI Senate Boxcar, *92 u*	75	100	[1]
(21029)	World of Little Choo Choo set, *94 u, 95*	40	50	[1]
21596	(See 17898)			
(23000)	Operating Base Smithsonian NYC Dreyfuss Hudson (2-rail), *92 u*		NRS	
(23001)	Operating Base NYC Dreyfuss Hudson (3-rail), *93 u*		NRS	
(23002)	Operating Base NYC Hudson, *92 u, 93–94*	—	110	[1]
(23003)	Operating Base PRR B-6 Switcher, *92 u, 93–94*	—	110	[1]
(23004)	Operating Base NP 4-8-4, *92 u, 93–94*	—	110	[1]
(23005)	Operating Base Reading T-1, *92 u, 93–94*	—	110	[1]
(23006)	Operating Base Chessie System T-1, *92 u, 93–94*	—	110	[1]
(23007)	Operating Base SP Daylight, *92 u, 93–94*	—	110	[1]
(23008)	Operating Base NYC L-3 Mohawk, *92 u, 93–94*	—	110	[1]
(23009)	Operating Base PRR S-2 Turbine, *92 u, 93–94*	—	110	[1]
(23010)	Left Remote Switch 31" "3010" (O), *95*		CP	
(23011)	Right Remote Switch 31" "3011" (O), *95*		CP	
(23012)	Operating Base F-3 ABA Diesels, *92 u, 93–94*	—	110	[1]
24876	(See 17405)			

		Exc	New	Cond/$
25766	(See 16561)			
26269	(See 17304)			
DX26925	(See 12810)			
31438	(See 16944)			
31950	(See 16945)			
(33000)	Lionel Lines RailScope GP-9 "3000", *88–90*	185	260 ____[1]	
(33002)	RailScope B&W TV, *88–90*	50	75 ____[1]	
(33004)	NYC RailScope GP-9 "3004", *90*		NM ____	
(33005)	Union Pacific RailScope GP-9 "3005", *90*		NM ____	
33621	(See 12909)			
[38356]	LOTS Dow Chemical 3-D Tank Car, *87*	75	100 ____[1]	
45003	(See 17217)			
50224	(See 17124)			
50240	(See 52067)			
51200	(See 17510)			
(51220)	NYC "Imperial Castle" Passenger Car, *93 u*		NRS ____	
(51221)	NYC "Niagara County" Passenger Car, *93 u*		NRS ____	
(51222)	NYC "Cascade Glory" Passenger Car, *93 u*		NRS ____	
(51223)	NYC "City of Detroit" Passenger Car, *93 u*		NRS ____	
(51224)	NYC "Imperial Falls" Passenger Car, *93 u*		NRS ____	
(51225)	NYC "Westchester County" Passenger Car, *93 u*		NRS ____	
(51226)	NYC "Cascade Grotto" Passenger Car, *93 u*		NRS ____	
(51227)	NYC "City of Indianapolis" Passenger Car, *93 u*		NRS ____	
(51228)	NYC "Manhattan Island" Observation Car, *93 u*		NRS ____	
(51229)	NYC Dining Car "680", *93 u*		NRS ____	
(51230)	NYC Baggage Car "5017", *93 u*		NRS ____	
(51231)	NYC "Century Club" Passenger Car, *93 u*		NRS ____	
(51232)	NYC "Thousand Islands" Observation Car, *93 u*		NRS ____	
(51233)	NYC Dining Car "684", *93 u*		NRS ____	
(51234)	NYC Baggage Car "5020", *93 u*		NRS ____	
(51235)	NYC "Century Tavern" Passenger Car, *93 u*		NRS ____	
(51236)	NYC "City of Toledo" Passenger Car, *93 u*		NRS ____	
(51237)	NYC "Imperial Mansion" Passenger Car, *93 u*		NRS ____	
(51238)	NYC "Imperial Palace" Passenger Car, *93 u*		NRS ____	
(51239)	NYC "Cascade Spirit" Passenger Car, *93 u*		NRS ____	

		Exc	New	Cond/$
(51240)	NYC Dining Car "681", *93 u*		NRS	_____
(51241)	NYC "City of Chicago" Passenger Car, *93 u*		NRS	_____
(51242)	NYC "Imperial Garden" Passenger Car, *93 u*		NRS	_____
(51243)	NYC "Imperial Fountain" Passenger Car, *93 u*		NRS	_____
(51244)	NYC "Cascade Valley" Passenger Car, *93 u*		NRS	_____
(51245)	NYC Dining Car "685", *93 u*		NRS	_____
51300	Shell Semi-scale 1-D Tank Car "8124", *91*	—	145	_____[1]
(51301)	Lackawanna Semi-scale Reefer "7000", *92*	—	395	_____[1]
(51401)	PRR Semi-scale Boxcar "100800", N/A, *91*	—	135	_____[1]
(51402)	C&O Semi-scale Stock Car "95250", *92*	—	225	_____[1]
51501	B&O Semi-scale Hopper "532000", *91*	—	115	_____[1]
51701	NYC Semi-scale Caboose "19400", *91*	—	160	_____[1]
(51702)	PRR N-8 Caboose "478039", *91–92*	—	295	_____[1]
52000	Detroit-Toledo TCA Flatcar w/ trailer, *92 u*	80	100	_____[1]
52001	NETCA B&M Quad Hopper w/ coal load, *92 u*	50	75	_____[1]
[52002]	VTC Passenger Cars (See 7692)			
52003	Ozark TCA "Meet Me in St. Louis" Flatcar w/ trailer, *92 u*	—	540	_____[1]
[52004]	LCAC Algoma Central Gondola w/ coil covers "9215", *92 u*	80	100	_____[1]
[52005]	LCAC Canadian National F-3 B Unit "9517", *93 u*		NRS	_____
[52006]	LCAC CP Boxcar "930016" (Std. O), *93 u*		NRS	_____
[52007]	NLOE Long Island RS-3 "1552", *92 u*	130	165	_____[1]
(52008)	TCA Bucyrus Erie Crane Car "1993X", *93 u*	60	75	_____[1]
(52009)	Sacramento Valley TTOS Western Pacific Boxcar "64641993", *93 u*	55	60	_____[1]
(52010)	TTOS Weyerhaeuser DD Boxcar "838593" (Std. O), *93 u*	65	80	_____[1]
52011	Gadsden Pacific Tucson, Cornelia & Gila Bend Ore Car w/ load, *93 u*	30	40	_____[1]
52013	Artrain Norfolk Southern Flatcar w/ trailer (Std. O), *92 u*	200	300	_____[1]

		Exc	New	Cond/$
(52014)	LOTS BN TTUX Flatcar set w/ N&W trailers "637500A" and "637500B", *93 u*	205	270	___[1]
52016	NETCA B&M Gondola w/ coil covers, *93 u*	50	60	___[1]
52018	Lakes & Pines TCA 3M Boxcar, *93 u*	—	540	___[1]
[52019]	NLOE Long Island Boxcar "8393", *93 u*	35	55	___[1]
[52020]	NLOE Long Island B/W Caboose "8393", *93 u*	60	80	___[1]
(52021)	TTOS Weyerhaeuser Tractor and Trailer, *93 u*	20	25	___[1]
52022	TTOS Union Pacific Boxcar, *93 u*	—	720	___[1]
(52023)	LCCA D&TS 2-bay ACF Hopper "2601" (Std. O), *93 u*	55	60	___[1]
52024	Artrain Conrail Auto Carrier, *93 u*	85	100	___[1]
(52025)	LCCA Madison Hardware Tractor and Trailer, *93 u*	23	27	___[1]
[52026]	NLOE Long Island Flatcar w/ Grumman trailer "8394", *94 u*	250	350	___[1]
52027	Gadsden Pacific Pinto Valley Mine Ore Car w/ load, *94 u*	30	35	___[1]
(52028)	TTOS Ford Cars, set of 3, *94 u*	55	65	___[1]
(52029)	TTOS Ford 1-D Tank Car "12" (O27), *94 u*	—	205	___[1]
(52030)	TTOS Ford Gondola "4023", *94 u*		NRS	___
(52031)	TTOS Ford Hopper "1458" (O27), *94 u*		NRS	___
(52032)	TTOS Ford 1-D Tank Car "14" w/ Kughn inscription (O27), *94 u*	90	125	___[1]
(52033)	Wolverine TTOS Lionel Lines Tractor and Trailer (See 52040)			
(52034)	Wolverine TTOS Grand Trunk Flatcar "52040" (See 52040)			
(52035)	TCA Yorkrail GP-9 "1750", shell only, *94 u*	40	50	___[1]
(52036)	TCA 40th Anniversary B/W Caboose, *94 u*	50	60	___[1]
(52037)	TCA Yorkrail GP-9 "1754", *94 u*	125	150	___[1]

		Exc	New	Cond/$
(52038)	LCCA Southern Hopper w/ coal load "360794" (Std. O), *94 u*	60	65	___[1]
(52039)	LCCA "Track 29" Bumper, *94 u*	—	18	___[1]
52040	Wolverine TTOS GTW Flatcar w/ Lionel Lines Tractor and Trailer, *94 u*	65	70	___[1]
(52041)	LOTS BN TTUX Flatcar set w/ Conrail trailers "637500D" and "637500E", *94 u*	100	140	___[1]
(52042)	LOTS BN TTUX Flatcar w/ CN trailer "637500C", *94 u*	60	65	___[1]
[52043]	NETCA LL Bean Boxcar "1994", *94 u*	60	75	___[1]
[52045]	TCA Penn Dutch Milk Car "61052", *94 u*	—	120	___[1]
(52046)	TTOS ACL Boxcar "16247", *94 u*	—	115	___[1]
(52047)	Southwest TTOS Cotton Belt Wood-sided Caboose w/ smoke "1921" (Std. O), *93–94 u*	80	85	___[1]
(52048)	LOTS CN Tractor and Trailer "197993", *94 u*	43	48	___[1]
52049	Artrain BN Gondola w/ coil covers, *94 u*	75	100	___[1]
[52050]	Schuylkill Haven Borough Day SP-Type Caboose "1994", *94 u*	—	45	___[1]
(52051)	TCA Baltimore &Ohio "Sentinel" Boxcar "6464095", *95 u*	65	70	___[1]
[52052]	TCA 40th Anniversary Boxcar, *94 u*	—	90	___[1]
52053	TTOS Carail Boxcar, *94 u*	75	90	___[1]
52054	Carail Boxcar, *94 u*		NRS	___
(52055)	LCCA Sovex Tractor and Trailer, *94 u*	26	33	___[1]
(52056)	LCCA Southern Tractor and Trailer "206502", *94 u*	22	28	___[1]
(52057)	TTOS Western Pacific Boxcar "64641995", *95 u*	80	100	___[1]
(52058)	Central California TTOS Santa Fe Boxcar "64641895", *95 u*	42	60	___[1]
(52059)	Eastern TCA Clinchfield Quad Hopper w/ coal load "16413", *94 u*	150	200	___[1]
[52060]	VTC Tender w/ whistle "7694", *94 u*		NRS	___
[52061]	NLOE Long Island Stern's Pickle Products Vat Car "8395", *95 u*		NRS	___

		Exc	New	Cond/$
(52062)	TCA "Skytop" Observation Car "1995", *95 u*	—	250	___1
(52063)	TCA New York Central "Pacemaker" Boxcar "6464125", *95 u*		NRS	___
(52064)	TCA Missouri Pacific Boxcar "6464150", *95 u*	—	430	___1
(52066)	Trainmaster Tractor and Trailer, *94 u*	—	185	___1
(52067)	LOTS Burlington Ice Car "50240", *95 u*	—	70	___1
(52068)	Toy Train Parade TTOS Contadina Boxcar "16245", *94 u*	—	45	___1
52069	Carail Tractor and Trailer, *94 u*	—	70	___1
52070	Knoebel's Boxcar, *95 u*	—	70	___1
52071	Gadsden Pacific Copper Basin Railway Ore Car w/ load, *95 u*		NRS	___
[52072]	NLOE Grumman Tractor, *94 u*		NRS	___
(52073)	Southwest TTOS Pacific Fruit Express Reefer "459402" (Std. O), *95 u*	—	65	___1
(52074)	LCCA Iowa Beef Packers Reefer "197095" (Std. O), *95 u*	—	50	___1
52075	United Auto Workers Boxcar, *95 u*	—	100	___1
[52076]	NLOE Long Island Observation Car "8396", *96 u*		NRS	___
(52077)	Pacific Northwest TCA Great Northern Hi-cube Boxcar "9695", *95 u*		CP	___
(52078)	TTOS Southern Pacific SD-9 "5366", *96 u*	—	315	___1
(52079)	TTOS SP B/W Caboose "1996", *96 u*		NRS	___
[52080]	NETCA Boston & Maine Flatcar w/ trailer "91095", *95 u*		NRS	___
52082	Steamtown Lackawanna Boxcar, *95 u*		NRS	___
(52084)	TTOS Union Pacific I-Beam Flatcar w/ load "16380", *95 u*		NRS	___
(52085)	TCA Full Vista Dome Car "1996", *96 u*	—	155	___1
(52086)	Canadian TTOS Pacific Great Eastern Boxcar "64641972", *96 u*	—	60	___1
(52087)	TTOS New Mexico Central Boxcar "64641996", *96 u*	—	60	___1

		Exc	New	Cond/$
[52088]	Desert TCA 25th Anniversary On-Track Step Van. *96 u*		NRS	_____
52089	Gadsden Pacific SMARRCO Ore Car w/ load, *96 u*		NRS	_____
(52090)	LCCA Pere Marquette DD Boxcar (Std. O), *96 u*	—	60	_____ [1]
(52091)	LCCA Lenox Tractor and Trailer, *95 u*		NRS	_____
(52092)	LCCA Iowa Interstate Tractor and Trailer, *95 u*		NRS	_____
(52093)	Lone Star TCA Boxcar "6464696", *96 u*		NRS	_____
52097	Artrain Chessie System Reefer, *95 u*		NRS	_____
52789	(See 16571)			
59629	(See 17874)			
60029	(See 17118)			
60155	(See 17216)			
61052	(See 52045)			
72867	(See 17121)			
78286	(See 17906)			
79052	(See 16554)			
81487	(See 17871)			
81988	(See 17872)			
82947	(See 16430)			
86892	(See 19963)			
[87010]	LCAC CN Express Reefer, *87 u*		NRS	_____
[88011]	LCAC CN Wood-sided Caboose (Std. O), *88 u*		NRS	_____
91095	(See 52080)			
95250	(See 51402)			
100800	(See 51401)			
151161	(See 17890)			
173872	(See 17007)			
190991	(See 19816)			
197095	(See 52074)			
197993	(See 52048)			
206502	(See 52056)			
245998	(See 17404)			
295110	(See 17120)			
296000	(See 17209)			
298011	(See 17882)			

360794	(See 52038)		
371629	(See 17403)		
385405	(See 17406)		
459400	(See 17305)		
459401	(See 17306)		
45940	(See 52073)		
477938	(See 19727)		
478039	(See 51702)		
496035	(See 19962)		
532000	(See 51501)		
610584	(See 12827)		
637500A/B	(See 52014)		
637500D/E	(See 52041)		
637500C	(See 52042)		
640000	(See 16912)		
640001	(See 16912)		
680441	(See 12910)		
800200	(See 17122)		
838593	(See 52010)		
844304	(See 17123)		
[900013] LCAC CN Flatcar w/ trailers, *90 u*		NRS	___
[930016] (See 52006)			
3739469 (See 17877)			
6106888 (See 16252)			
No Number Amtrak Passenger set, *89, 89 u*		720	900 ___[1]
No Number Baltimore & Ohio set, *94, 96*			NRS ___[1]
No Number C&NW Passenger set, *93*		450	540 ___[1]
No Number Chesapeake & Ohio set, *95–96*			NRS ___[1]
No Number D&RGW "California Zephyr" set, *92, 93*		1250	1450 ___[1]
No Number Erie-Lackawanna Passenger set, *93, 94*		1100	1150 ___[1]
No Number Erie set (FF no. 7), *93*		450	540 ___[1]
No Number Frisco set (FF no. 5), *91*		450	495 ___[1]
No Number Great Northern "Empire Builder" set, *92, 93*		860	990 ___[1]
No Number Great Northern set (FF no. 3), *88*		405	450 ___[1]

	Exc	New	Cond/$
No Number Illinois Central "City of New Orleans" set, *85, 87, 93*	1150	1350	___¹
No Number Illinois Central set, *91–92, 95*	270	295	___¹
No Number Lionel Lines Madison Car set, *91, 93*	540	630	___¹
No Number The Mint set, *79 u, 80–83, 84 u, 86 u, 87, 91 u, 93*	1100	1250	___¹
No Number Milwaukee Road set (FF no. 2), *87, 90 u*	405	450	___¹
No Number Missouri Pacific set, *95*		NRS	___¹
No Number Norfolk & Western Passenger set, *94*	360	430	___¹
No Number Norfolk & Western "Powhatan Arrow" Passenger set, *95*		NRS	___¹
No Number Nickel Plate Road set (FF no. 6), *92*	450	540	___¹
No Number New Haven set, *94–95*		NRS	___¹
No Number Northern Pacific set, *90–92*	225	295	___¹
No Number New York Central set, *89, 91*	270	315	___¹
No Number Pennsylvania set, *87–90, 95*	270	315	___¹
No Number Pere Marquette set, *93*	810	900	___¹
No Number SP Daylight Steam set, *90, 92, 93*	920	1100	___¹
No Number Santa Fe "Super Chief" set, *91, 91 u, 92 u, 93, 95*	1650	2000	___¹
No Number Union Pacific set, *94*	500	590	___¹
No Number Wabash set (FF no. 1), *86, 87*	920	1100	___¹
No Number Western Maryland set (FF no. 4), *89*	405	475	___¹

O GAUGE CLASSICS

1-263E	Lionel Lines "Blue Comet" 2-4-2 (See 51004)
44E	(See 51100)
350E	Lionel Lines "Hiawatha" 4-4-2 (See 51000)
882	Lionel Lines Combination Car (See 51000)
883	Lionel Lines Passenger Car (See 51000)
884	Lionel Lines Observation Car (See 51000)
892	(See 51202)
893	(See 51203)
894	(See 51204)

895	(See 51205)		
1612	Lionel Lines Passenger Car (See 51004)		
1613	Lionel Lines Passenger Car (See 51004)		
1614	Lionel Lines Baggage Car (See 51004)		
1615	Lionel Lines Observation Car (See 51004)		
8814	(See 51400)		
8816	(See 51500)		
8817	(See 51700)		
8820	(See 51800)		
(51000)	Milwaukee Road "Hiawatha" set, *88 u*	—	720 ___ [1]
(51001)	Lionel no. 44 Freight Special set, *89*	—	520 ___ [1]
(51004)	Blue Comet set, *91*	—	1400 ___ [1]
(51100)	Lionel Lines Electric "44E" (See 51001), *89*		
(51201)	Rail Chief Passenger Cars, set of 4, *90*	—	590 ___ [1]
(51202)	Lionel Lines Combination Car "892" (See 51201)		
(51203)	Lionel Lines Passenger Car "893" (See 51201)		
(51204)	Lionel Lines Passenger Car "894" (See 51201)		
(51205)	Lionel Lines Observation Car "895" (See 51201)		
(51400)	Lionel Lines Boxcar "8814" (See 51001), *89*		
(51500)	Lionel Lines Hopper "8816" (See 51001), *89*		
(51700)	Lionel Lines Caboose "8817" (See 51001), *89*		
(51800)	Lionel Lines Searchlight Car "8820" (See 51001), *89*		

STANDARD GAUGE CLASSICS

1-44	(See 13805)
1-214	(See 13605)
1-215	(See 13303)
1-318E	Lionel Lines Electric (See 13001)
1-381E	(See 13102)
1-384E	(See 13101)

1-390E	(See 13100)
1-400E	(See 13103)
1-408E	(See 13107)
1-4390	American Flyer "West Point" Baggage Car (See 13003)
1-4391	American Flyer "Academy" Passenger Car (See 13003)
1-4392	American Flyer "Army/Navy" Observation Car (See 13003)
1-4689	(See 13109)
2-390E	(See 13106)
2-400E	(See 13108)
7E	(See 13104)
8	(See 13803)
9	(See 13803)
126	(See 13801)
183	(See 13413)
184	(See 13414)
185	(See 13415)
200	(See 13900)
201	(See 13901)
323	(See 13400)
324	(See 13401)
325	(See 13402)
326	(See 13416)
327	(See 13417)
328	(See 13418)
437	(See 13804)
1115	(See 13800)
1217	(See 13702)
1412	(See 13404)
1413	(See 13405)
1414	(See 13407)
1416	(See 13406)
1420	(See 13409)
1421	(See 13410)
1422	(See 13411)

		Exc	New	Cond/$
1423	(See 13425)			
1512	(See 13300)			
1513	(See 13600)			
1517	(See 13700)			
1520	(See 13200)			
2412	(See 13421)			
2413	(See 13422)			
2414	(See 13423)			
2416	(See 13424)			
4400C	(See 51900)			
5130	Lionel Lines Flatcar w/ lumber (See 13001)			
5140	Lionel Lines Reefer (See 13001)			
5150	Lionel Lines "Shell" Tank Car (See 13001)			
5160	Lionel Lines Caboose (See 13001)			
(13001)	1-318E Freight Express Train set, *90–91*	—	1150	___[1]
(13002)	Fireball Express set, *90 u*	—	1150	___[1]
(13003)	American Flyer "Mayflower" Passenger Car set, *92*	—	1350	___[1]
(13100)	Lionel Lines 2-4-2 "1-390E", *88 u*	—	730	___[1]
(13101)	Lionel Lines 2-4-0 "1-384E", *89 u*	—	780	___[1]
(13102)	Lionel Lines Electric "1-381E", *89 u*	—	1050	___[1]
(13103)	Lionel Lines "Blue Comet" 4-4-4 "1-400E", *90*	—	1450	___[1]
(13104)	Lionel Lines "Old #7" 4-4-0 "7E", *90*	—	720	___[1]
(13106)	Lionel Lines "Fireball Express" 2-4-2 "2-390E" (See 13002)			
(13107)	Lionel Lines Electric "1-408E", *91*	—	1050	___[1]
(13108)	Lionel Lines 4-4-4 "2-400E", *91*	—	1300	___[1]
(13109)	American Flyer "Mayflower" Electric "1-4689", *92*	—	990	___[1]
(13200)	Lionel Lines Searchlight Car "1520", *89 u*	—	130	___[1]
(13300)	Lionel Lines Gondola "1512", *89 u*	—	90	___[1]
(13303)	Lionel Lines Sunoco Tank Car "1-215", *92*	—	180	___[1]
(13400)	Lionel Lines Baggage Car "323", *88 u*	—	180	___[1]
(13401)	Lionel Lines Passenger Car "324", *88 u*	—	180	___[1]
(13402)	Lionel Lines Observation Car "325", *88 u*	—	180	___[1]

		Exc	New	Cond/$
(13403)	Lionel Lines State Passenger Car set, *89 u*	—	1350	___1
(13404)	Lionel Lines "California" Passenger Car "1412" (See 13403)			
(13405)	Lionel Lines "Colorado" Passenger Car "1413" (See 13403)			
(13406)	Lionel Lines "New York" Observation Car "1416" (See 13403)			
(13407)	Lionel Lines "Illinois" Passenger Car "1414", *90*	—	540	___1
(13408)	Lionel Lines "Blue Comet" Passenger Car set, *90*	—	1250	___1
(13409)	Lionel Lines "Faye" Passenger Car "1420" (See 13408)			
(13410)	Lionel Lines "Westphal" Passenger Car "1421" (See 13408)			
(13411)	Lionel Lines "Tempel" Observation Car "1422" (See 13408)			
(13412)	Lionel Lines "Old #7" Passenger Car set, *90*	—	720	___1
(13413)	Lionel Lines Combination Car "183" (See 13412)			
(13414)	Lionel Lines Passenger Car "184" (See 13412)			
(13415)	Lionel Lines Observation Car "185" (See 13412)			
(13416)	Lionel Lines "New Jersey" Baggage Car "326" (See 13002)			
(13417)	Lionel Lines "Connecticut" Passenger Car "327" (See 13002)			
(13418)	Lionel Lines "New York" Observation Car "328" (See 13002)			
(13420)	Lionel Lines State Passenger Car set, *91*	—	1600	___1
(13421)	Lionel Lines "California" Passenger Car "2412" (See 13420)			
(13422)	Lionel Lines "Colorado" Passenger Car "2413" (See 13420)			

		Exc	New	Cond/$
(13423)	Lionel Lines "Illinois" Passenger Car "2414", *92 u*	—	540	___1
(13424)	Lionel Lines "New York" Observation Car "2416" (See 13420)			
(13425)	Lionel Lines "Barnard" Passenger Car "1423", *91 u*	—	540	___1
(13600)	Lionel Lines Cattle Car "1513", *89 u*	—	110	___1
13601	Season's Greetings Boxcar, *89 u*	—	120	___1
13602	Season's Greetings Boxcar, *90 u*	—	115	___1
13604	Season's Greetings Boxcar, *91 u*	—	135	___1
(13605)	Lionel Lines Boxcar "1-214", *92*	—	180	___1
(13700)	Lionel Lines Caboose "1517", *89 u*	—	125	___1
(13702)	Lionel Lines Caboose "1217", *91*	—	155	___1
(13800)	Lionelville Passenger Station "1115", *88 u*	200	250	___1
(13801)	Lionelville Station "126", *89 u*	—	205	___1
(13802)	Lionel Runabout Boat, *90*	—	430	___1
(13803)	Lionel Racing Automobiles "8" and "9", *91*	—	850	___1
(13804)	Lionelville Switch Tower "437", *91*	—	225	___1
(13805)	Lionel Racing Boat "1-44", *91*	—	430	___1
(13807)	Racing Automobiles Straight Track, *91 u*		NRS	___
(13808)	Racing Automobiles Inner Radius Curve Track, *91 u*		NRS	___
(13809)	Racing Automobiles Outer Radius Curve Track, *91 u*		NRS	___
(13900)	Electric Rapid Transit Trolley "200", *89 u*	—	335	___1
(13901)	Electric Rapid Transit Trolley Trailer "201", *89 u*	—	160	___1
(51900)	Signal Bridge and Control Panel "4400C", *89 u*	—	305	___1

Section 5
MODERN ERA 1996–2000
Lionel LLC Production

(2162)	Automatic Crossing Gate and Signal "262", *70–87, 94, 96-99*	CP ____
(2180)	Road Signs (16) "307", *77–99*	CP ____
(2181)	Telephone Pole set "150", *77–99*	CP ____
(2283)	Die-cast illuminated bumpers "260", *84–99*	CP ____
(2709)	Rico Station kit, *81–99*	CP ____
(2716)	Short Extension Bridge, *88–99*	CP ____
(2900)	Lockon, *70–99*	CP ____
(2901)	Track Clips (12) (027), *71–99*	CP ____
(2905)	Lockon and Wire, *74–99*	CP ____
(2909)	Smoke Fluid, *70–99*	CP ____
(2927)	Maintenance kit, *70, 78–96-99*	CP ____
(2985)	The Lionel Train Book, *86–99*	CP ____
(5014)	Half-Curved Track 27" (027), *70–99*	CP ____
(5019)	Half-Straight Track (027), *70–99*	CP ____
(5020)	90° Crossover (027), *70–99*	CP ____
(5021)	Left Manual Switch 27" (027), *70–99*	CP ____
(5022)	Right Manual Switch 27" (027), *70–99*	CP ____
(5023)	45° Crossover (027), *70–99*	CP ____
(5024)	35" Straight Track (027), *88–99*	CP ____
(5033)	Curved Track 27" (027), *79–99*	CP ____
(5038)	Straight Track (027), *79–99*	CP ____
(5041)	Insulator Pins (12) (027), *70–99*	CP ____
(5042)	Steel Pins (12) (027), *70–99*	CP ____
(5049)	Curved Track 42" (027), *88–99*	CP ____
(5113)	Curved Track 54" (027), *79–99*	CP ____
(5121)	Left Remote Switch 27" (027), *70–99*	CP ____
(5122)	Right Remote Switch 27" (027), *70–99*	CP ____
(5149)	Remote Uncoupling Section (027), *70–99*	CP ____
(5165)	Right Remote Switch 72" (0), *87–99*	CP ____
(5166)	Left Remote Switch 72" (0), *87–99*	CP ____
(5167)	Right Remote Switch 72" (027), *88–99*	CP ____

		Exc	New	Cond/$
(5168)	Left Remote Switch 42" (027), *88–99*		CP	____
(5500)	Straight Track 10" (O), *71–99*		CP	____
(5501)	Curved Track 31" (O), *71–99*		CP	____
(5504)	Half-Curved Track 31" (O), *83–99*		CP	____
(5505)	Half-Straight Track (O), *83–99*		CP	____
(5523)	40" Straight Track (O), *88–99*		CP	____
(5530)	Remote Uncoupling Section (O), *81–99*		CP	____
(5540)	90° Crossover (O), *81–99*		CP	____
(5543)	Insulator Pins (12) (O), *70–99*		CP	____
(5545)	45° Crossover (O), *83–99*		CP	____
(5551)	Steel Pins (12) (O), *70–99*		CP	____
(5554)	Curved Track 54" (O), *90–99*		CP	____
(5572)	Curved Track 72" (O), *79–99*		CP	____
(18250)	BNSF SD70 "9870", *99*		CP	____
(11735)	NYC Flyer Freight set "1735WS", *96–99*		CP	____
(11748)	Amtrak Alco Passenger set, *96*		NRS	____
(11809)	Lionel Village Trolley Company set "1809" (O), *96–97*	—	80	____
(11826)	Zenith/Sears Freight set, *95–96 u*	—	810	____
(11828)	NJ Transit Passenger set, *96 u*	—	245	____
11833	NJ Transit GP-38 Passenger set, *97*	250	270	____
(11837)	UP GP-9 Unit Train set, *97*	—	680	____
(11838)	AT&SF Warhorse Hudson Freight set, *97*	—	1150	____
(11839)	SP&S 4-6-2 Steam Freight set, *97*	—	305	____
11843	Boston & Maine GP9 A-B-A Diesel Locomotive set, "2381", "2380", "2389", *98*	—	650	____
11844	Union Pacific Die-cast Ore Cars 4-pack, *98*	—	275	____
11849	1998 Lionel Centennial Series Reefer Cars 4-pack, *98*	—	160	____
11863	Southern Pacific GP9, *98*	—	275	____
11864	New York Central GP9, *98*	—	275	____
(11900)	SF Special Freight set "1900WS" (O), *96–97*	—	160	____
(11905)	US Coast Guard set, *96*	—	195	____
(11909)	N&W J 4-8-4 Warhorse set, *96*	—	800	____
(11910)	Lionel Lines set (027), *96*	—	155	____
(11912)	"57" Switcher Service Exclusive, *96*	—	430	____

		Exc	New	Cond/$
(11913)	SP GP-9 Freight set, *97*	—	425	___
(11914)	NYC GP-9 Freight set, *97*	—	425	___
(11918)	Conrail SD-20 Service Exclusive "X1144" (SSS), *97*	—	310	___
(11919)	Lionel Docksider set "1919" (O), *97*	—	80	___
(11920)	Port of Lionel City Dive Team set "1920", *97*	—	220	___
(11921)	Lionel Lines Freight set "1113WS", *97*	—	160	___
(11929)	AT&SF Warbonnet Passenger set "1929W", *97–99*		CP	___
(11930)	Warbonnet Passenger 2-pack "2404-05", *97–99*	—	80	___
(11931)	Chessie Flyer Freight set "1931S" (O), *97–99*		CP	___
11933	Dodge Ram Motorsports set, *96u*	—	245	___
(11934)	Virginian Rectifier Freight set, *97–99*	—	385	___
(11935)	Lionel NYC Flyer Freight set, *97*	—	140	___
11936	Little League Baseball Steam set, *97*	245	270	___
11939	SP&S 4-6-2 Steam Freight set, *97*	—	305	___
11940	Southern Pacific SD40 Warhorse Coal set, *98*	—	750	___
11944	Lionel Lines 4-4-2 Steam Freight set, *98*	—	165	___
(11956)	UP GP-9 "2380", "2381" (Powered and Dummy), *97*	—	450	___
11957	Mobil Oil Steam Special set, *97u*		NRS	___
11971	D&H 4-4-2 Steam Freight set, *98*	—	140	___
11972	ARR GP-7 Train set, *98–99*		CP	___
11974	Station Accessory set, *98*	—	30	___
11975	Freight Accessory Pack, *98*	—	40	___
11976	Factory Selection set, *98u*	—	145	___
11977	NP 4-pack Freight Cars, *98*	—	225	___
11979	N&W 4-4-2 Steam Freight set, *98*	—	85	___
11981	1998 Holiday Trolley set, *98*	—	81	___
11982	NJ Transit Ore Car set, *98u*	—	243	___
(11983)	Farmrail Agricultural set, *99*		CP	___
(11984)	Corvette GP-7 set, *99*		CP	___
(11988)	NYC Firecar "18444" and Instruction Car "19853" set, *99*		CP	___
(12705)	Lumber Shed kit "832K", *88–99*		CP	___
(12706)	Barrel Loader Building kit, *87–99*		CP	___

		Exc	New	Cond/$
(12707)	Billboards (3), *87–99*	—	6	___
(12709)	Banjo Signal "140", *87–91, 95–99*		CP	___
(12711)	Water Tower kit, *87–99*		CP	___
(12713)	Automatic Gateman "145", *87–88, 94–99*		CP	___
(12714)	Crossing Gate "252", *87–91, 93–96-99*		CP	___
(12715)	Illuminated Bumpers "261", *87–96-99*		CP	___
(12717)	Non-illuminated Bumpers (3), *87–99*		CP	___
(12718)	Barrel Shed kit, *87–98*	—	9	___
(12726)	Grain Elevator kit, *88–91, 94–98*	—	30	___
(12727)	Semaphore "159", *89–98*	—	37	___
(12730)	Girder Bridge "314", *88–99*		CP	___
(12731)	Station Platform "158", *88–99*		CP	___
(12732)	Coal Bag "206", *88–99*		CP	___
(12733)	Watchman Shanty kit, *88–98*	—	9	___
(12734)	Passenger/Freight Station, *89–99*		CP	___
(12737)	Whistle Shed "118", *88–99*	—	41	___
(12740)	Genuine Wood Logs "2740", *97*	—	3	___
(12742)	Gooseneck Lamps "58", *89–99*		CP	___
(12743)	Track Clips (12) (O), *89–99*		CP	___
(12744)	Rock Piers (2) "920-5", *89–92, 94–99*		CP	___
(12745)	Barrel Pack (6), *89–99*		CP	___
(12746)	Operating/Uncoupling Track (O27), *89–99*		CP	___
(12748)	Illuminated Passenger Platform "157", *89–99*	—	24	___
(12754)	Graduated Trestle set (22) "110", *89–99*		CP	___
(12755)	Elevated Trestle set (10) "111", *89–99*		CP	___
(12759)	Floodlight Tower "195", *90–99*		CP	___
(12770)	Arch-Under Bridge "332", *90–99*		CP	___
(12772)	Truss Bridge w/ Flasher and Piers "318", *90–99*		CP	___
(12773)	Freight Platform kit, *90–98*	—	17	___
(12774)	Lumber Loader kit, *90–99*		CP	___
(12795)	Lionel Cable Reels "40-15", *97–98*	—	5	___
(12804)	Highway Lights "72", *92–99*		CP	___
(12812)	Illuminated Freight Station "133", *93–99*		CP	___
(12832)	Block Target Signal "253", *93–98*	—	32	___
(12838)	Crate Load (2), *93–97*	—	4	___
(12839)	Grade Crossing (2), *93–98*	—	4	___

(12840)	Uncoupling Straight Track, *99*		CP ___
(12841)	Insulated Straight Track (O27), *93–99*		CP ___
(12843)	Die-cast Metal Sprung Trucks (2), *93–99*		CP ___
(12844)	Coil Covers (2) (O), *93–98*	—	8 ___
(12847)	Animated Ice Depot "352", *97–99*	—	85 ___
(12852)	Die-cast Intermodal Trailer Frame, *94–99*	—	6 ___
(12853)	Coil Covers (2) (Std. O), *94–98*	—	11 ___
(12866)	PowerHouse Power Supply, *94–99*		CP ___
(12867)	PowerMaster Power Distribution Center, *94 u, 95–96-99*		CP ___
(12868)	CAB-1 Remote Controller, *94 u, 95–99*		CP ___
(12873)	Operating Sawmill "464", *95–97*	—	105 ___
(12874)	Classic Street Lamps "71", *94–99*		CP ___
(12883)	Dwarf Signal "148", *95–99*		CP ___
(12884)	Truck Loading Dock kit, *96–98*	—	21 ___
(12885)	40-watt Control System, *94 u, 96–99*		CP ___
(12886)	Floodlight Tower "395", *95–98*	—	49 ___
(12888)	Railroad Crossing Flasher "154", *95–99*		CP ___
(12889)	Operating Windmill "453", *95–98*	—	57 ___
(12890)	Big Red Control Button, *94 u, 95–96-99*		CP ___
(12892)	Automatic Flagman "1045", *92–98*	—	40 ___
(12893)	PowerMaster Power Adapter Cable, *94 u, 95–99*		CP ___
(12894)	Signal Bridge "452", *95–99*		CP ___
(12895)	Double-track Signal Bridge "450", *95–99*		CP ___
(12896)	Tunnel Portals (2) "920-2", *96–99*		CP ___
(12897)	Engine House kit, *96–98*	—	30 ___
(12898)	Flagpole "89", *96–97*	—	6 ___
(12899)	Searchlight Tower "496", *95–98*	—	30 ___
(12900)	Crane kit "6828-100", *96–98*	—	11 ___
(12901)	Shovel kit "6827-100", *96–98*	—	11 ___
(12903)	Diesel Horn Shed "114", *95–98*	—	40 ___
(12904)	Coaling Station kit, *95–98*	—	30 ___
(12905)	Factory kit, *96–98*	—	33 ___
(12906)	Maintenance Shed kit, *96–98*	—	33 ___
(12911)	TrainMaster Command Base, *95–99*		CP ___
(12912)	Oil Pumping Station "457", *95–98*	—	72 ___
(12914)	SC-1 Switch and Accessory Controller, *95–98*		CP ___

		Exc	New	Cond/$
(12915)	Log Loader "164", 96	—	160	_____
(12916)	Water Tower "138", 96–97	—	85	_____
(12917)	Animated Switch Tower "445", 97–98	—	88	_____
(12925)	O Gauge O42 Curved Track Section, 96–99		CP	_____
(12926)	Globe Street Lamps "64", 96–99		CP	_____
(12927)	Yard Light "65", 96–99		CP	_____
(12929)	Rail-truck Loading Dock, 96–98	—	74	_____
(12931)	Electrical Substation, 96	—	32	_____
(12932)	Laimbeer Packaging Tractor & Trailer set, 96	—	14	_____
(12936)	SP Intermodal Crane "292", 97	—	210	_____
(12937)	NS Intermodal Crane "292", 97	—	210	_____
(12938)	PS PowerStation—PowerHouse set, 97–99		CP	_____
(12939)	PG PowerGrid—PowerHouse set, 97		NM	_____
(12943)	Illuminated Station Platform, 97–99		CP	_____
(12944)	Sunoco Oil Derrick "455", 97	—	105	_____
(12945)	Sunoco Pumping Oil Station "457", 97	—	80	_____
(12948)	Bascule Bridge "313", aluminum, 97	—	270	_____
(12949)	Billboard set "310", 97–99		CP	_____
(12951)	Airplane Hangar kit "837K", 97–98	—	35	_____
(12952)	Big L Diner kit "838K", 97	—	28	_____
(12953)	Linex Gas Tall Oil Tank "840K", 97	—	13	_____
(12954)	Linex Gas Wide Oil Tank "839K", 97	—	13	_____
(12955)	Road Runner & Wile E. Coyote Ambush Shack "145", 97	—	65	_____
(12958)	Industrial Water Tower "193", 97–98	—	57	_____
(12960)	Rotary Radar Antenna "197", 97	—	32	_____
(12961)	Lionel News Stand w/ diesel horn "114", 97	—	41	_____
(12962)	LL Passenger Service Train Whistle "118", 97–98	—	41	_____
(12964)	Donald Duck Radar Antenna "197", 97	—	65	_____
(12965)	Goofy Rotary Beacon "494", 97	—	55	_____
(12966)	Lionel Rotary Aicraft Beacon "494", 97		NRS	_____
(12968)	Girder Bridge Building kit "841K", 97	—	24	_____
(12969)	TrainMaster Command set, 97–98	—	139	_____
(12974)	Blinking-light Billboard "410", 97–99		CP	_____
(12975)	"Steiner" Victorian Building kit "842K", 97–98	—	43	_____

		Exc	New	Cond/$
(12976)	"Dobson" Victorian Building kit "843K", 97–98	—	43	_____
(12977)	"Kindler" Victorian Building kit "844K", 97–98	—	43	_____
(12982)	Culvert Loader, 98	—	190	_____
(12983)	Culvert Unloader (Conventional Version), 99		CP	_____
(12983)	Culvert Unloader (Command Control Version), 99		CP	_____
(12987)	Intermodal 3-pack, 98	—	19	_____
(12989)	Lionel Logo Tractor-Trailer, 98	—	16	_____
(12991)	Linex Gas Tractor-Tanker, 98	—	16	_____
(15002)	Chesapeake & Ohio Waffle-sided Boxcar, 96	—	29	_____
(15003)	Green Bay & Western Waffle-sided Boxcar, 96	—	29	_____
(15100)	Amtrak Passenger Car, 96–97	—	41	_____
(15107)	Amtrak Vista Dome Car, 96	—	41	_____
(15108)	Northern Pacific Vista Dome Car, 96	—	41	_____
(15112)	AT&SF Coach Albuquerque, "2405", 97	—	41	_____
(15113)	AT&SF Vista Dome Culebra, "2404", 97	—	41	_____
(15117)	Annie Passenger Coach, surprised face, 97–98	—	28	_____
(15118)	Clarabel Passenger Coach, smiling face, 97-98	—	28	_____
(15149)	Conrail Flatcar w/Blum coal shovel, 98		NRS	_____
(16098)	Amtrak Passenger Car, 96–97	—	41	_____
(16099)	Amtrak Vista Dome Car, 96–97	—	41	_____
(16150)	Sunoco 1-D Tank Car "6315", 97	—	36	_____
(16152)	Sunoco 3-D Tank Car "6415", 97	—	32	_____
(16153)	AEC Reactor Fluid "6315-1" SD Tank Car, 97	—	45	_____
(16154)	AEC Reactor Fluid "6315-2" SD Tank Car, 97	—	45	_____
(16155)	AEC Reactor Fluid "6315-3" SD Tank Car, 97	—	45	_____
(16160)	Atomic Energy Commission Tank Car w/ reactor fluid "6515", 98	—	55	_____

		Exc	New	Cond/$
(16173)	Harold the Helicopter Flatcar, *98*	—	41	_____
(16180)	Tabasco Single-Dome Tank Car, *98*	—	36	_____
(16181)	Biohazard Tank Car with Lights, *98*	—	62	_____
(16187)	Linex 3D Tank Car "6425", *99*		CP	_____
(16188)	Kodak SD Tank Car "6515", *99*		CP	_____
(16196)	Lava Lite SD Tank Car "9968", *99*		CP	_____
(16272)	1997 Christmas Boxcar "9700", *97*	—	32	_____
(16274)	Marvin the Martian Boxcar "9700", *97*	—	39	_____
(16284)	Galveston Wharves Boxcar "9700", *98*	—	37	_____
(16285)	Savannah State Docks Boxcar "9700", *98*	—	37	_____
(16291)	1998 Christmas Boxcar, *98*	—	38	_____
(16419)	Tennessee Central Hopper, *96*	—	20	_____
(16431)	Lionel Corporation 2-Bay Hopper "6456-1", *96*	—	23	_____
(16432)	Lionel Corporation 2-Bay Hopper "6456-2", *96*	—	23	_____
(16433)	Lionel Corporation 2-Bay Hopper "6456-3", *96*	—	23	_____
(16434)	LV 2-bay Hopper "6456", "TLDX", *97*	—	27	_____
(16438)	Frisco 4-Bay Covered Hopper "87538", *98*		NRS	_____
(16439)	Southern 4-Bay Covered Hopper "87538", *98*		NRS	_____
(16441)	Four Bay New York Central Hopper "6464", *99*		CP	_____
(16581)	Union Pacific Illuminated Caboose, *96*	—	41	_____
(16585)	LL Illuminated Caboose "6257", *97*		NM	_____
(16586)	SP Illuminated Caboose "6357", *97*	—	45	_____
(16593)	Lionel Belt Line Caboose "6257", *98*	—	39	_____
(16594)	Lionel Caboose "6357", *98*	—	39	_____
(16673)	Whistle Tender, *96–97*	—	32	_____
(16719)	Exploding Boxcar, *96*	—	41	_____
(16720)	Lionel Lines Searchlight Car "3650", *96–97*	—	49	_____
(16724)	Mickey and Friends Submarine Car, *96*	—	45	_____
(16725)	Rhino Transport Car, *97*	—	36	_____
(16726)	US Army Fire Ladder Car, *96*	—	55	_____
(16737)	Warner Bros. Road Runner and Wile E. Coyote ACME Gondola "3444", *96*	—	45	_____
(16738)	Warner Bros. Pepe Le Pew and Penelope Boxcar "3370", *96*	—	45	_____

(16739)	Warner Bros. Foghorn Leghorn Poultry Car "6434", *96*	—	49 _____
(16740)	Lionel Corporation Mail Car "3428", *96*	—	45 _____
(16741)	Union Pacific Illuminated Bunk Car, *97*	—	36 _____
(16742)	Trout Ranch Aquarium Car "3435", *96*	—	41 _____
(16747)	Breyer Animated Horsecar "6473", *97*	—	31 _____
(16748)	US Forest Service Log-Dump Car "3361", *97*	—	38 _____
(16749)	Midget Mines Ore-Dump Car "3479", *97*	—	38 _____
(16750)	Lionel City Aquarium Car "3436", *97*	—	32 _____
(16751)	WLNL Channel 7-AIREX Sports TV Car "3545", *97*	—	41 _____
(16752)	Warner Bros. Marvin the Martian Missile-Launching Flatcar "6655", *97*	—	49 _____
(16754)	Warner Bros. Porky Pig and Instant Martians "6805", *97*	—	55 _____
(16755)	Warner Bros. Daffy Duck Animated Balloon Car "3470", *97*	—	65 _____
(16760)	Pluto and Cats Animated Gondola "3444", *97*	—	46 _____
(16765)	Bureau of Land Management Log Car "3351", *98*	—	38 _____
(16766)	Bureau of Land Management Ore Car "3479", *98*	—	38 _____
(16767)	New York Central Ice Docks Ice Car "6352", *98*	—	56 _____
(16776)	Lionel Holiday Railsounds Boxcar, *98*	—	175 _____
(16777)	Lionel Cola Animated Car and Platform, *98*	—	105 _____
(16782)	Bethlehem Ore Dumpcar "3479", *99*		CP _____
(16783)	Westside Lumber Log Dumpcar "3351", *99*		CP _____
(16784)	Pratt's Hollow Seed Dumpcar "3479", *99*		CP _____
(16785)	Happy Holidays Music Reefer "5700", *99*		CP _____
(16789)	Easter Operating Boxcar "9700", *99*		CP _____
(16790)	UP Crowsounds Stock Car "3356", *99*		CP _____
(16791)	NY City Lights Boxcar "9700", *99*		CP _____
(16792)	Constellation Boxcar "9600", *99*		CP _____

(16793)	Animated Glow-in-the-Dark Alien Boxcar "9700", *99*		CP _____
(16794)	Wicked Witch Halloween Boxcar "9700", *99*		CP _____
(16795)	Elf Chasing Rudolph Gondola "6462", *99*		CP _____
(16796)	Snowman Loading Ice Car "6352", *99*		CP _____
(16924)	Lionel Corporation Trailer-on-Flatcar "6424", *96*	—	32 _____
(16946)	C&O F9 Well Car "3840", *96*	—	35 _____
(16951)	Southern I-Beam Flatcar w/ load "9823", *97*	—	38 _____
(16954)	NYC Flatcar w/ Ertl scraper "6424", *96*	—	38 _____
(16955)	AT&SF Flatcar w/ Ertl Challenger, *96*	—	36 _____
(16957)	Lionel Depressed-Center Flatcar w/ Ertl Case 4WD tractor "6461", *96*	—	38 _____
(16958)	Lionel Flatcar w/ Ertl New Holland loader, *96*	—	36 _____
(16963)	Lionel Corporation Flatcar "6411", *96–97*	—	38 _____
(16964)	Lionel Corporation Gondola "6462", *97*	—	23 _____
(16967)	Lionel Depressed-Center Flatcar w/ transformer "6461", *96*	—	32 _____
(16968)	Lionel Aviation Depressed-Center Flatcar w/ General Hospital LifeFlight Ertl helicopter "6461", *96*	—	45 _____
(16969)	Flatcar w/ Beechcraft Bonanza "6411", *96*	—	55 _____
(16970)	LA County Flatcar w/ motorized LA County Lifeguard powerboat "6424", *96*	—	45 _____
(16972)	P&LE Gondola "6462", *97*	—	23 _____
(16975)	Lionel Doublestack set "6480", 2 well cars, *97*	—	80 _____
(16978)	MILW Flatcar "6424" w/ P&H shovel kit, *97*	—	36 _____
(16980)	Warner Bros. Speedy Gonzales Missile Flatcar "6823", *97*	—	32 _____
(16982)	BC Rail Bulkhead Flatcar w/ wood load "9823", *97*	—	38 _____
(16983)	PRR F9 Well Car w/ cable reels "6983", *97*	—	45 _____
(17009)	New York Central 2-bay ACF Hopper (Std O), *96*	—	41 _____

		Exc	New	Cond/$
(17010)	Government du Canada ACF 2-bay Covered Hopper "7000" (Std O), *98*	—	45	____
(17011)	NP ACF 2-bay Covered Hoppers "75052" (Std O), *98*	—	45	____
(17012)	Government du Canada ACF 2-bay Covered Hopper "7001" (Std O), *98*		45	____
(17013)	NYC Graffiti 2-bay Coverd Hopper "7000" (Std O), *99*		CP	____
(17014)	Graffiti 2-bay Covered Hopper (Std O), *99*		CP	____
(17127)	Delaware & Hudson 3-bay Hopper (Std O), *96*	—	45	____
(17128)	Chesapeake & Ohio 3-bay Hopper (Std O), *96*	—	45	____
(17129)	WM 3-bay Hopper w/ coal load "9300" (Std O), *97*	—	45	____
(17132)	PRR 3-bay SCF Hopper "260815" (Std O), *98*	NRS		____
(17133)	BNSF ACE 3-bay Covered Hopper "403698" (Std O), *98*	NRS		____
(17135)	BNSF ACF 3-bay Covered Hopper with ETD (Std O), *98*	NRS		____
(17223)	Milwaukee Road DD Boxcar (Std O), *96*	—	49	____
(17224)	Central of Georgia Boxcar "9464-197" (Std O), *97*	—	35	____
(17225)	Penn Central Boxcar "9464-297" (Std O), *97*	—	35	____
(17226)	Milwaukee Road Boxcar "9464-397" (Std O), *97*	—	35	____
(17227)	UP DD Boxcar "9200" (Std O), *97*	—	49	____
(17231)	Wisconsin Central Double-door Boxcar w/ Auto Frames "9200" (Std O), *98*	—	62	____
(17232)	Southern Pacific/Union Pacific Merger Double-door Boxcar "9200" (Std O), *98*	—	62	____
(17233)	Western Pacific Caboose "9464-198" (Std O), *98*	—	57	____
(17234)	Port Huron & Detroit Boxcar "9464-298" (Std O), *98*	—	57	____
(17235)	Boston & Maine Boxcar "9464-398" (Std O), *98*	—	57	____

(17239)	AT&SF Texas Chief Boxcar "9464-1" (Std O), *97*		NRS ____
(17240)	AT&SF Super Chief Boxcar "9464-2" (Std O), *97*		NRS ____
(17241)	AT&SF El Capitan Boxcar "9464-3" (Std O), *97*		NRS ____
(17242)	AT&SF Grand Canyon Boxcar "9464-4" (Std O), *97*		NRS ____
(17243)	NP Boxcar "8722" (Std O), *98*		NRS ____
(17244)	Santa Fe Chief Boxcar (Std O), *98*	—	45 ____
(17245)	C&O Boxcar with Chessie Kitten (Std O), *98*	—	45 ____
(17246)	NYC Pacemaker Rolling Stock 4-pack (Std O), *98*	—	215 ____
(17247)	NYC 9464 Boxcar "174940" (Std O), *98*		NRS ____
(17248)	NYC 9464 Boxcar "174945" (Std O), *98*		NRS ____
(17249)	NYC 9464 Boxcar "174949" (Std O), *98*		NRS ____
(17251)	BNSF Modern Boxcar "103277" (Std O), *99*		CP ____
(17252)	N&S Modern Boxcar "564824" (Std O), *99*		CP ____
(17253)	CSX Modern Boxcar "141756" (Std O), *99*		CP ____
(17254)	Union Pacific Modern Boxcar "551967" (Std O), *99*		CP ____
(17255)	Chevy Modern Double-door Boxcar "9200" (Std O), *99*		CP ____
(17257)	Atlantic Coast Line Boxcar "9464" (Std O), *99*		CP ____
(17258)	D&H Boxcar "9464" (Std O), *99*		CP ____
(17259)	MKT Boxcar "9464" (Std O), *99*		CP ____
(17314)	Pacific Fruit Express Reefer "9800-198" (Std O), *98*	—	43 ____
(17315)	Pacific Fruit Express Reefer "9800-298" (Std O), *98*	—	43 ____
(17316)	NP Reefer "98583" (Std O), *98*		NRS ____
(17317)	PRR Reefer FGE "91904" (Std O), *96–98*		NRS ____
(17407)	NKP Gondola w/ scrap load (Std O), *96*	—	41 ____
(17408)	Cotton Belt Gondola w/ scrap load "9820" (Std O), *97*	—	41 ____
(17455)	Carail Flatcar w/ trailer (Std O), *98*		NRS ____

		Exc	New	Cond/$
(17516)	T&P Flatcar w/ 2 Beechcraft Bonanzas "9823" (Std O), *97*	—	49	___
(17517)	WP Flatcar w/ Ertl Caterpillar Frontloader "9823" (Std O), *97*	—	45	___
(17518)	PRR Flatcar w/ 2 Corgi Mack trucks "9823" (Std O), *97*	—	55	___
(17522)	Flatcar with Plymouth Prowler (Std O), *98*	—	60	___
(17527)	Flatcar with Pair of Dodge Vipers (Std O), *98*	—	68	___
(17529)	AT&SF Flatcar "90010" w/ Ford milk truck (Std O), *99*		CP	___
(17533)	MTTX Ford Flatcar w/ auto frames (Std O), *99*		CP	___
(17534)	Diamond T Flat "9823" w/ Mack trucks (Std O), *99*		CP	___
(17536)	Route 66 Flatcar w/ 2 luxury coupes "9823-3" (Std O), *99*		CP	___
(17537)	Route 66 Flatcar w/ 2 touring coupes "9823-4" (Std O), *99*		CP	___
(17550)	BN Center Beam Flatcar w/ lumber load "6216" (Std O), *99*		CP	___
(17551)	NYC Flatcar with NYC Pickups (Std O), *99*		CP	___
(17620)	NP Wood-sided Caboose "1746" (Std O), *98*		NRS	___
(17624)	Conrail Extended-vision Caboose "6900" (Std O), *99*		CP	___
(17625)	Burlington Northern Steel-sided Caboose "7606" (Std O), *99*		CP	___
(17910)	Sunoco Unibody Tank Car "7900" (Std O), *97*	—	41	___
(17913)	J.M. Huber Tankcar (Std O), *98*	—	53	___
(17914)	Englehard Tank Car (Std O), *98*	—	53	___
(18045)	"777" Commodore Vanderbilt, *96*	—	1050	___
(18049)	N&W Warhorse 4-8-2 "600", *96*	—	770	___
(18050)	JC Penney 4-6-2 Steam "2055", *96*	425	475	___
(18052)	"238E" Pennsylvania Torpedo, *97*	—	630	___
(18053)	Berkshire Steam Locomotive 2-8-4 "726", *97*	—	940	___
(18054)	NYC Switcher 0-4-0 "1665", black, *97*	—	205	___

		Exc	New	Cond/$
(18056)	"763E" NYC J1-e Hudson Steam Locomotive and Vanderbilt Tender, 97	—	990	
(18057)	Century Steam Locomotive 6-8-6 "671", 97	—	1100	
(18058)	Hudson Steam Locomotive 4-6-4 "773", 97	—	1100	
(18059)	Western Maryland Baby Pacific 4-6-2 Locomotive "209", 98		NM	
(18062)	AT&SF 4-6-4 Hudson L/T "3447", 97		NRS	
(18063)	NYC Commodore Vanderbilt 4-6-4, 99		CP	
(18064)	New York Central 4-8-2 Mohawk L-3A Steam Engine w/ Tender "3005", 98		1100	
(18067)	Commodore Vanderbilt Special Edition, 97	1700	1800	
(18070)	Western Maryland Baby Pacific 4-6-2 Locomotive "208", 98		NM	
(18071)	Southern Pacific Daylight Locomotive "4449", 98	—	900	
(18072)	Lionel Lines Torpedo Engine w/ Tender, 98	—	650	
(18079)	NYC Mikado 2-8-2 "1967", 99		CP	
(18080)	Denver & Rio Grande Mikado 2-8-2 "1210", 99		CP	
(18082)	NYC Hudson 4-6-4 "5404", 99		CP	
(18083)	C&O Hudson 4-6-4 "305", 99		CP	
(18084)	Santa Fe Hudson 4-6-4 "305", 99		CP	
(18085)	NH Pacific 4-6-2 "1334", 99		CP	
(18086)	NYC Pacific 4-6-2 "4929", 99		CP	
(18087)	Santa Fe Pacific 4-6-2 "3448", 99		CP	
(18088)	SP Pacific 4-6-2 "1407", 99		CP	
(18089)	CNJ Camelback 4-6-0 "771", 99		CP	
(18091)	PRR Camelback 4-6-0 "821", 99		CP	
(18092)	SP Camelback 4-6-0 "2283", 99		CP	
(18093)	C&NW Camelback 4-6-0 "3006", 99		CP	
(18097)	CNJ Camelback 4-6-0 "770", 99		CP	
(18098)	PRR Camelback 4-6-0 "820", 99		CP	
(18099)	SP Camelback 4-6-0 "2282", 99		CP	
(18128)	Santa Fe F-3 A Unit "2343", 96	—	710	
(18129)	Santa Fe F-3 B Unit w/ RS II, 96	—	710	
(18130)	Santa Fe F-3 Diesel Locomotive AB set, 96	—	630	
(18131)	NP F-3 AB set, "2390A", "2390C", 97	—	540	

		Exc	New	Cond/$
(18134)	Santa Fe F-3 A Unit Dummy "2343", *97*	—	205	___
(18135)	NYC F-3 AA Diesel "2333", *97*		CP	___
(18136)	AT&SF F-3 B Unit w/ Railsounds "2343C", *97*	—	230	___
(18140)	Milwaukee Road F3 A-B Diesel Locomotive "75A", *98*	—	500	___
(18145)	NP F-3 A Unit "2390A", *97*		NRS	___
(18146)	NP F-3 B Unit "2390C", *97*		NRS	___
(18147)	NP F-3 AB Units "2390A, 2390C", *97*	—	540	___
(18149)	Union Pacific Veranda Gas Turbine "61", *98*		CP	___
(18154)	Deluxe Santa Fe FT AB "168", *98*		CP	___
(18157)	Santa Fe FT AB "158", *98*		CP	___
(18160)	New York Central Deluxe FT AB "1603", "2403", *98*		CP	___
(18163)	New York Central FT AB Unit, "1600", "2400", *98*		CP	___
(18191)	WP F-3 A-A, *98*	—	610	___
(18192)	WP F3 A Non-powered, *98*		NRS	___
(18197)	WP F3 B Unit "2355C", *99*		CP	___
(18198)	WP F3 B Unit "2355C" Command Control, *99*		CP	___
(18226)	GE Dash 9 Diesel Locomotive, *97*	—	465	___
(18228)	SP Dash 9 "8228", black, red nose, *97*	—	520	___
(18231)	BNSF Dash 9 Diesel Locomotive Deluxe "739", *98*		NRS	___
(18232)	SOO Line SD-60 Diesel "5500", *97*	—	630	___
(18233)	BNSF Dash 9 Diesel Locomotive "745", *98*		NM	___
(18235)	BNSF Dash 9 Diesel Locomotive 2-pack "739", "740", *98*		NM	___
(18238)	Conrail SD70 "4145", *99*		CP	___
(18239)	Southern Pacific SD40 Warhorse Diesel Engine "7333", *98*		NM	___
(18241)	BN SD70 "9413", *99*		CP	___
(18245)	PRR Alco PA-1 AA "5750", *99*		CP	___
(18248)	PRR Alco PB-1 "5750B", *99*		CP	___
(18251)	CSX SD60 "8701", *99*		CP	___
(18260)	Conrail SD70 "4144", *99*		CP	___
(18261)	BN SD60 "9412", *99*		CP	___

		Exc	New	Cond/$
(18262)	BNSF SD70 "9869", *99*		CP	
(18263)	CSX SD60 "8700", *99*		CP	
(18264)	SD70M Southern Pacific "8238", *99*		CP	
(18265)	SD70M Southern Pacific "9803", *99*		CP	
(18314)	Century Pennsylvania GG-1 "2332", *96*	—	1000	
(18319)	New Haven EP-5 (Rectifier), *99*		CP	
(18321)	CNJ Trainmaster "2341", *99*		CP	
(18322)	Lackawanna Trainmaster "2321", *99*		CP	
(18427)	Tie-Jector "55", *97*	—	60	
(18430)	Crew Car, *96*	—	49	
(18431)	Trolley Car, *96–97*	—	55	
(18433)	Mickey and Minnie Handcar, *96–97*	—	55	
(18434)	Porky and Petunia Handcar, *96*	—	55	
(18436)	Dodge Ram Track Inspection Vehicle, *97*	—	65	
(18438)	Pennsylvania High-rail Vehicle "49", *98*	—	60	
(18439)	Union Pacific High-rail Maintenance Vehicle, *98*	—	68	
(18440)	NJ Transit High-rail Inspection Vehicle, *98*	—	61	
(18445)	NYC Fire Car, *98*		NRS	
(18446)	GN Rotary Snowplow "58", *99*		CP	
(18447)	Executive Inspection Vehicle, *99*		CP	
(18515)	Lionel Steel Vulcan Diesel "57" (SSS), *96*	—	500	
(18562)	SP GP-9 "2380", *96*	—	245	
(18563)	NYC GP-9 "2380", *96*	—	245	
(18564)	CP GP-9 "2380", *97*	—	205	
(18565)	Milwaukee GP-9 "2338", *97*	—	255	
(18566)	CR SD-20 "8495" (SSS), *97*		NRS	
(18567)	PRR GP-9 "2028", *97*	—	255	
(18569)	Chicago Burlington & Quincy GP-9 Diesel "2380", *98*	—	300	
(18573)	Santa Fe GP-9 Diesel Freight "2380", *98*	—	170	
(18574)	Milwaukee Road GP-20 "975", *98*	—	305	
(18575)	Custom Series I GP-9 "2398", *98*	—	345	
(18576)	Southern Pacific GP-9 Non-powered B Unit "2385", *98*	—	170	
(18577)	New York Central GP-9 Non-powered B Unit "2385", *98*	—	175	

		Exc	New	Cond/$
(18579)	Milwaukee GP-9 Non-powered "2384", 99		CP	___
(18580)	Pennsylvania GP-9 B Unit "2027", 98	—	172	___
(18582)	Seaboard NW-2 Switcher, 98	—	445	___
(18583)	AEC-57 Switcher, 98	—	220	___
(18585)	Centennial SD40 "1999", 99		CP	___
(18595)	D&H RS-11 (Traditional) "5002", 99		CP	___
(18596)	D&H RS-11 (Command Control) "5001", 99		CP	___
(18597)	NYC RS-11 (Traditional) "8011", 99		CP	___
(18598)	NYC RS-11 (Command Control) "8010", 99		CP	___
(18653)	B&A 4-6-2 Pacific "2044", 97	—	205	___
(18654)	SP 4-6-2 Pacific "2044", 97	—	235	___
(18660)	Canadian National 4-6-2 Steam Locomotive w/ Tender "2044", 98	—	240	___
(18661)	Norfolk & Western 4-6-2 Steam Locomotive w/ Tender "2044", 98	—	240	___
(18662)	Pennsylvania 0-4-0 Switcher, 98	—	245	___
(18681)	PRR 4-4-2 Steam Engine "460", 99		CP	___
(18684)	LRRC Pacific 4-6-2 "1999", 99		CP	___
(18719)	Thomas the Tank Engine 0-6-0 "1", 97-98	—	110	___
(18722)	Percy the Tank Engine "6", 99		CP	___
(18845)	D&RGW RS-3 "5204", 97	—	150	___
(18846)	1997 Lionel Centennial Series GP-9 Diesel Locomotive, 98	—	314	___
(18847)	Santa Fe H-12-44 Switcher "9087", 99		CP	___
(18848)	Phantom II, 99		CP	___
(18858)	1998 Lionel Centennial GP-20 Diesel Engine "1998", 98	—	314	___
(18860)	The Pratt's Hollow Collection I: The Phantom, 98	—	345	___
(18864)	Southern Pacific GP-9 B Unit "2386", 98	—	177	___
(18865)	New York Central GP-9 B Unit "2386", 98	—	177	___
(18877)	Milwaukee Road GP-9 "2383", 98	—	300	___
(18870)	Pennsylvania GP-9 Diesel "2029", 98	—	300	___
(18872)	Wabash GP-7 3-unit set "453, 454, 455", 99		CP	___
(18876)	C&NW H-12-44 Switcher "1053", 99		CP	___
(18877)	Union Pacific GP-9 Non-powered "2399", 99		CP	___
(18878)	Alaska GP-7 "1803", 99		CP	___

		Exc	New	Cond/$
(18879)	B&O GP-9 "5616", *99*		CP	___
(18881)	Custom GP-9 "5616", *99*		CP	___
(18892)	Burlington GP-9 "2328", *99*		CP	___
(18937)	Non-powered Amtrak FA-2 ALCO, *96–97*	—	55	___
(18939)	Union Pacific NW-2 Diesel Switcher set, *96*	—	170	___
(18948)	Port of Lionel City Alco FB-2 "2030B", *97*	—	75	___
(18949)	NYC NW-2 "622", black, *97*		NM	___
(18951)	Erie NW-2 "6220", black, *97*		NM	___
(18952)	AT&SF Alco PA-1 "2000", *97*	—	220	___
(18953)	NYC Alco PA-1 "2000", *97*	—	255	___
(18959)	NYC NW-2 Switcher "622", *97*		NRS	___
(18961)	Erie Alco PA-1"850", *98*		NM	___
(18965)	Santa Fe Alco PB1, *98*	—	384	___
(18966)	New York Central Alco BP1 "20008", *98*	—	284	___
(18971)	Santa Fe Alco A Unit (Non-powered) "211", *98*	—	74	___
(18972)	Rock Island Alco FA AA, *98*	—	530	___
(18975)	Southern 44-Ton Switcher "1955", *99*		CP	___
(19056)	NYC Heavyweight Baggage Car, *96*		NRS	___
(19057)	NYC Heavyweight Willow Run Coach, *96*		NRS	___
(19058)	NYC Heavyweight Willow Trail Coach, *96*		NRS	___
(19059)	NYC Heavyweight Seneca Valley Observation, *96*		NRS	___
(19060)	Pullman Heavyweight set, *96*	—	325	___
(19061)	Wabash Railway Passenger set, *97*	—	340	___
(19062)	Wabash Railway City of Columbia Coach "2361", *97*		NRS	___
(19063)	Wabash Railway City of Danville Coach "2362", *97*		NRS	___
(19064)	Wabash REA Baggage Car "2360", *97*		NRS	___
(19065)	Wabash Windy City Observation "2363", *97*		NRS	___
(19066)	Commodore Vanderbilt Pullman Heavyweight 2-pack, *97*	—	180	___
(19067)	Comm. Vanderbilt Willow River Pullman "2543", *97*		NRS	___
(19068)	Comm. Vanderbilt Willow Valley Pullman "2544", *97*		NRS	___

		Exc	New	Cond/$
(19069)	Pullman Baby Madison set "9500-02", *97*	—	170	___
(19070)	Baby Madison REA/Combo "9501", *97*		NRS	___
(19071)	Baby Madison Laurel Gap Coach "9500", *97*		NRS	___
(19072)	Baby Madison Laurel Summit Coach "9500", *97*		NRS	___
(19073)	Baby Madison Catskill Valley Observation "9502", *97*		NRS	___
(19074)	Legends of Lionel Madison set, *97*	—	340	___
(19075)	Lionel Legends Mazzone Coach "2621", *97*		NRS	___
(19076)	Lionel Legends Caruso Coach "2624", *97*		NRS	___
(19077)	Lionel Legends Raphael Coach "2652", *97*		NRS	___
(19078)	Lionel Legends Cowen Observation "2600", *97*		NRS	___
(19079)	NYC Heavyweight Passenger Car set, *97*	—	360	___
(19080)	NYC Heavyweight REA Baggage Car "2564", *97*		NRS	___
(19081)	NYC Heavyweight Park Place Coach "2565", *97*		NRS	___
(19082)	NYC Heavyweight Star Beam Coach "2566", *97*		NRS	___
(19083)	NYC Heavyweight Hudson Valley Observation "2566", *97*		NRS	___
(19087)	C&O Heavyweight Passenger Car 4-pack "2571-74", *97*	—	360	___
(19088)	C&O Heavyweight Baggage Car "2571", *97*		NRS	___
(19089)	C&O Heavyweight Sleeper Car "2572", *97*		NRS	___
(19090)	C&O Heavyweight Diner Car "2573", *97*		NRS	___
(19091)	C&O Heavyweight Observation Car "2574", *97*		NRS	___
(19093)	Commodore Vanderbilt Heavyweight Sleeper Cars 2-pack, *98*	—	190	___
(19094)	Comm. Vanderbilt Niagara Falls Sleeper, *98*		NRS	___
(19095)	Comm. Vanderbilt Highland Falls Sleeper, *98*		NRS	___
(19096)	Legends of Lionel Madison Cars 2-pack, *98*	—	180	___
(19097)	Legends of Lionel Bonnano Coach, "2653", *98*		NRS	___
(19098)	Legends of Lionel Pagano Coach, "2654", *98*		NRS	___

(19148)	C&O Chessie Club Coach "1903", *96*		NRS ____
(19149)	C&O Gadsby Kitchen Pass./Diner "1950", *96*		NRS ____
(19151)	Norfolk & Western Duplex Roomette car, *96*	—	105 ____
(19152)	Union Pacific Duplex Roomette Car, *96*	—	105 ____
(19154)	Atlantic Coast Line Passenger Cars set, *96*	—	405 ____
(19155)	ACL Passenger/Combo "101", *96*		NRS ____
(19156)	ACL Talladega Diner, *96*		NRS ____
(19157)	ACL Moultrie Coach, *96*		NRS ____
(19158)	ACL Observation "256", *96*		NRS ____
(19160)	Super Chief REA Baggage Car, *96*		NRS ____
(19161)	Super Chief Silver Sky Coach, *96*		NRS ____
(19162)	Super Chief Silver Mesa Vista Dome, *96*		NRS ____
(19163)	Super Chief Silver Rail Observation, *96*		NRS ____
(19164)	Chesapeake & Ohio Passenger Cars, *96*	—	200 ____
(19165)	Super Chief set, *96*	—	405 ____
(19166)	NP Vista Dome set, *97*	—	180 ____
(19167)	NP Pullman "2571", *97*		NRS ____
(19168)	NP Pullman "2571", *97*		NRS ____
(19169)	NP Pullman "2570", *97*		NRS ____
(19170)	NP Pullman "2571", *97*		NRS ____
(19171)	NYC Streamlined Passenger set "2570-75", *97*	—	405 ____
(19176)	AT&SF Indian Arrow Diner "2572", *97*		NRS ____
(19177)	AT&SF Grass Valley Coach "2573", *97*		NRS ____
(19178)	AT&SF Citrus Valley Coach "2574", *97*		NRS ____
(19179)	AT&SF Vista Heights "2575", *97*		NRS ____
(19180)	AT&SF Surfliner Passenger set "2572-75", *97*	—	320 ____
19181	GN Prairie View Vista Dome "1394", *98*	—	NRS ____
19182	GN River View Vista Dome "1395", *98*	—	NRS ____
(19183)	Great Northern Empire Builder Vista Dome Cars 2-pack, *98*	—	250 ____
(19184)	Milwaukee Passenger set 4-pack, *99*		CP ____
(19276)	"6464" Boxcar Series V "19277-79", *96*	—	110 ____
(19277)	Rutland Boxcar "6464-300" (Series V), *96*	35	38 ____
(19278)	B&O Boxcar "6464-325" (Series V), *96*	—	32 ____

		Exc	New	Cond/$
(19279)	Central of Georgia "6464-375" (Series V), *96*	—	32	___
(19280)	Mickey's Wheat Hi-cube Boxcar, *96*	—	60	___
(19281)	Mickey's Carrots Hi-cube Boxcar, *96*	—	60	___
(19282)	Santa Fe "Super Chief" Boxcar "6464-196", *96*	—	37	___
(19283)	Erie Boxcar "6464-296", *96*	—	37	___
(19284)	Northern Pacific Boxcar "6464-396", *96*	—	37	___
(19285)	Bangor and Aroostook "State of Maine" Boxcar "6464-275", *96*	—	37	___
(19286)	Warner Bros. "All Abirrrrd" Boxcar, *96*	—	49	___
(19287)	NYC/PC Merger Boxcar "6464-125X", *97*	70	125	___
(19288)	PRR/CR Merger Boxcar "6464-200X", *97*	70	125	___
(19289)	Monon "Hoosier Line" Boxcar "6464", *97*	—	29	___
(19290)	Seaboard "Silver Meteor" Boxcar "6464", *97*	—	29	___
(19291)	GN Boxcar "6464-397", dark green, *97*	—	29	___
(19292)	"6464" Boxcar Series VI "19293-95", *97*	—	120	___
(19293)	MKT Boxcar "6464-350" (Series VI), *97*	35	45	___
(19294)	B&O Boxcar "6464-400" (Series VI), *97*	35	50	___
(19295)	NH Boxcar "6464-425" (Series VI), *97*	35	50	___
(19325)	N&W 4-bay Hopper w/ coal "6446-1", *97*	—	90	___
(19326)	N&W 4-bay Hopper w/ coal "6446-2", *96*	—	90	___
(19327)	N&W 4-bay Hopper w/ coal "6446-3", *96*	—	90	___
(19328)	N&W 4-bay Hopper w/ coal "6446-4", *96*	—	90	___
(19329)	N&W 4-bay Hopper w/ coal "6436", *97*	—	90	___
(19338)	Cotton Belt 4-bay Hopper 2-pack, *99*		CP	___
(19339)	Cotton Belt 4-bay Hopper 2-pack "64469", *99*		CP	___
(19340)	Cotton Belt 4-bay Hopper 2-pack "64470", *99*		CP	___
(19423)	Circle-L Racing Flatcar w/ stock cars "6424", *96*	—	37	___
(19424)	Edison Electric Dep. Center Flatcar with transformer "6461", *97*	—	41	___
(19427)	Evans Auto Loader "6414", *99*		CP	___
(19428)	Evans Boat Loader "6414", *99*		CP	___
(19429)	Culvert Gondola "35621", *98–99*		CP	___

(19430)	AT&SF Flatcar w/ Beechcraft Bonanza "6411", *98*	—	55 _____
(19438)	Standard O Christmas Gondola, *98*	—	41 _____
(19439)	Flatcar with Safes, *98*	—	42 _____
(19440)	Flatcar with FedEx Trailer, *98*	—	38 _____
(19441)	Lobster Vat Car, *98*	—	41 _____
(19444)	Flatcar with VW Bug, *98*	—	66 _____
(19445)	Borden Milk Tank Car "520", *99*		CP _____
(19446)	Pittsburg Paint Vat Car, *99*		CP _____
(19447)	Mama's Baked Beans Vat Car, *99*		CP _____
(19448)	Easter Gondola w/ Candy "6462", *99*		CP _____
(19449)	Liquified Gas Tank Car "6469", *99*		CP _____
(19450)	Barrel Ramp Car "6343", *99*		CP _____
(19451)	Wheel Car "6262", *99*		CP _____
(19454)	PRR Flatcar with Gondola "6424", *99*		CP _____
(19459)	Valentine Gondola w/ candy "6462", *99*		CP _____
(19474)	L&N Flatcar w/ die-cast trailer frames, *99*		CP _____
(19478)	Culvert Gondola "6342", *99*		CP _____
(19540)	Broken Arrow Ranch Stock Car "3356", *97*	—	41 _____
(19607)	Sunoco 1-D Tank Car "6315", *96*	—	37 _____
(19611)	Gulf Oil Single-dome Tank Car "6315", *98*	—	36 _____
(19612)	Gulf Oil 3-dome Tank Car "6425", *98*	—	31 _____
(19621)	Centennial SD Tank Car "6015-1", *99*		CP _____
(19622)	Centennial SD Tank Car "6015-2", *99*		CP _____
(19623)	Centennial SD Tank Car "6015-3", *99*		CP _____
(19624)	Centennial SD Tank Car "6015-4", *99*		CP _____
(19660)	Lionel Mint Car, *98*	—	45 _____
(19663)	Pratt's Hollow Bunk Car "5717", *99*		CP _____
(19667)	Wellspring Gold Bullion Car, *99*		CP _____
(19669)	King Tut Museum Car "9660", *99*		CP _____
(19728)	N&W Bay Window Caboose, *96*	—	90 _____
(19732)	AT&SF B/W Caboose "6517", *96*	—	65 _____
(19733)	New York Central Caboose "6357", *96*	—	45 _____
(19734)	Southern Pacific Caboose "6357", *96*	—	45 _____
(19736)	PRR N5c Caboose "6417" "Buffalo Zone", tuscan, *97*	—	45 _____

		Exc	New	Cond/$
(19737)	Lackawanna Searchlight Caboose "2420", 97	—	120	
(19739)	NYC Wood-sided Caboose "6907", 97	—	90	
(19741)	Pennsylvania N5C Caboose "6417", 98	—	57	
(19742)	Erie Bay Window Caboose w/ Caboose Talk "C301", 98	—	162	
(19750)	1998 Holiday Music Bay Window Caboose, 98	—	162	
(19751)	PRR Caboose N5C PRR "492418", 98		NRS	
(19752)	NP Bay Window Caboose "407", 98		NRS	
(19754)	NYC 7606 Caboose "20112", 98		NRS	
(19755)	Centennial Porthole Caboose, 99		CP	
(19756)	Lionel Lines Bay Window Caboose, 99		CP	
(19774)	LRRC Caboose Porthole "1999", 99		CP	
(19824)	US Army Target Launcher, 96	—	46	
(19827)	NYC Operating Boxcar, 97	—	45	
(19828)	C&NW Animated Stock Car and Stockyard "3356", 96–97	—	125	
(19830)	US Mail Operating Boxcar "3428", 97	—	45	
(19831)	GM Generator Car w/ power pole and wire "3530", 97	—	75	
(19832)	Lionel Cola Ice Car "6352", 97	—	49	
(19833)	Railsounds II Tender "2426RS", 97	—	215	
(19834)	LL 6-Wheel Crane Car "2460", 97	—	75	
(19835)	FedEx Animated Boxcar "3464X", 97	—	45	
(19837)	Bucyrus 6-wheel Crane Car "2460", 98u	—	80	
(19845)	Command Control Aquarium Car "3435", 98	—	240	
(19846)	Animated Giraffe Car "3376C", 98	—	220	
(19855)	Christmas "Aquarium" Car, 98	—	48	
(19856)	Mermaid Transport, 98	—	48	
(19857)	NYC Fire Instruction Car "19853", 98–99		CP	
(19858)	Lionelville Operational Searchlight Car "19584", 99		CP	
(19859)	REA Steam R/S Boxcar "6267", 99		CP	
(19860)	Conrail Diesel R/S Boxcar "169671", 99		CP	
(19864)	Animated Ostrich Boxcar "9700", 99		CP	
(19867)	Operational Poultry Dispatch Car "3434", 99		CP	

(19868)	Shark Aquarium Car "3435", *99*		CP	____
(19869)	Alien Aquarium Car "3435", *99*		CP	____
(19877)	Operating Barrel Car, *99*		CP	____
(19878)	Operating Helium Tank Flatcar "3362", *99*		CP	____
(19882)	Sanderson Farms Poultry Car "3434", *99*		CP	____
(19943)	"I Love Arizona" Boxcar, *96*	—	29	____
(19944)	Lionel Visitor's Center Tank Car, *96 u*	—	30	____
(19945)	Holiday Boxcar, *96*	—	29	____
(19947)	Lionel Corporation Toy Fair Boxcar "9700", *96 u*	NRS		____
(19948)	Visitors Center Flatar w/ trailer, *96*	NRS		____
(19949)	"I Love NY" Boxcar "9700", *97*	—	37	____
(19950)	"I Love Montana" Boxcar "9700", *97*	—	29	____
(19951)	"I Love Massachusetts" Boxcar "9700", *98*	—	37	____
(19952)	"I Love Indiana" Boxcar, "9700", *98*	—	37	____
(19957)	Ambassadore Caboose "1997", *97*	—	275	____
(19965)	LRRC Aquarium Car "3435", *99*		CP	____
(19966)	LRRC Gondola "9820" (Std O), *98*	NRS		____
(19967)	Kids Club Animated Gondola, *98*	NRS		____
(19968)	"I Love Maine" Boxcar "9700", *99*		CP	____
(19969)	"I Love Vermont" Boxcar "9700", *99*		CP	____
(19970)	"I Love New Hampshire" Boxcar "9700", *99*		CP	____
(19971)	"I Love Rhode Island" Boxcar "9700", *99*		CP	____
(19981)	Lionel Centennial Boxcar "1998-1", *99*		CP	____
(19982)	Lionel Centennial Boxcar "1998-2", *99*		CP	____
(19983)	Lionel Centennial Boxcar "1998-3", *99*		CP	____
(19984)	Lionel Centennial Boxcar "1998-4", *99*		CP	____
(21750)	Nickel Plate Rolling Stock 4-pack, *98*	—	189	____
(21751)	PRR Rolling Stock 4-pack, *98*	—	189	____
(21752)	Conrail Unit Trailer Train set, *98*	—	618	____
(21753)	1998 Service Station Fire Rescue Train set, *98*	—	450	____
(21754)	BNSF 3-bay Covered Hopper 2-pack, *98*	—	90	____
(21755)	4-bay Covered Hoppers 2-pack, *98*	—	98	____
(21756)	Overstamped 6464-style Boxcars 2-pack, *98*	—	89	____
(21757)	UP Freight Car set, *98*	—	197	____
(21758)	Bethlehem Steel Service Station Exclusive "44", *99*		CP	____

		Exc	New	Cond/$
(21759)	Canadian Pacific F3 Passenger set, *99*		CP	___
(21761)	B&M Boxcar set 4-pack, *99*		CP	___
(21763)	New Haven Freight set, *99*		CP	___
(21766)	ACL Passenger Car set 2-pack, *99*		CP	___
(21769)	Centennial SD Tank Car set 4-pack, *99*		CP	___
(21770)	NYC Reefer set 4-pack, *99*		CP	___
(21771)	D&RGW Stock Car set 4-pack, *99*		CP	___
(21774)	Custom Series Consist II 3-pack "6424", *99*		CP	___
(21775)	Lionel Train Wreck Recovery set, *99*		CP	___
(21779)	Seaboard Freight Car set, *99*		CP	___
(21780)	NYC Aluminum Pass Car set 2-pack, *99*		CP	___
(21900)	Union Civil War Train set, *99*		CP	___
(21901)	Confederate Civil War Train set, *99*		CP	___
(21914)	Lionel Lines Freight set, *99*		CP	___
(21916)	Lionel Village Trolley, *99*		CP	___
(21917)	N&W Freight set, *99*		CP	___
(21920)	Amtrak "Talgo" Passenger set, *99*		CP	___
(21925)	Thomas Tank Engine Island of Sodor Train set, *99*		CP	___
(21956)	New York Central Freight set "5412", *99*		CP	___
(22902)	Quonset Hut, *98*	—	31	___
(22907)	Die-cast Girder Bridge, *98–99*		CP	___
(22910)	Gilbert Tractor-Trailer, *98*	—	16	___
(22914)	PowerHouse Lockon, *98–99*		CP	___
(22915)	Municipal Building, *98–99*		CP	___
(22916)	190-watt Power Accessory System, *98*		NM	___
(22918)	The Lionel Locomotive Backshop, *98*	—	600	___
(22919)	ElectroCouplers kit for GP9, *98–99*		CP	___
(22920)	Steam Service Siding, *98*		NM	___
(22922)	SP Intermodal Crane, *98*	—	250	___
(22929)	Lionel Factory, *98*		NM	___
(22931)	Die-cast Cantilever Signal Bridge, *98–99*		CP	___
(22932)	High-tension Metal Wire Tower, *98*		NM	___
(22933)	Section Gang House, *98*		NM	___
(22934)	Walkout Cantilever Signal, *98–99*		CP	___
(22935)	Hot Box Detector, *98*		NM	___
(22936)	3-piece Coaling Tower, *98*	—	70	___

		Exc	New	Cond/$
(22938)	High-tension Plastic Tower, *98*	NM		___
(22939)	Transformer Substation, *98*	NM		___
(22940)	Mast Signal, *98–99*	CP		___
(22942)	Accessories Box, *98–99*	CP		___
(22944)	Automatic Operating Semaphore, *98–99*	CP		___
(22945)	Block Target Signal, *98–99*	CP		___
(22946)	Automatic Crossing Gate and Railroad Crossing Signal, *98–99*	CP		___
(22947)	Auto Crossing Gate, *98–99*	CP		___
(22948)	Gooseneck Street Lamps, set of 2, *98–99*	CP		___
(22949)	Highway Lights, set of 4, *98–99*	—	24	___
(22950)	Classic Street Lamps, set of 3, *98–99*	CP		___
(22951)	Dwarf Signal, *98–99*	CP		___
(22952)	Classic Billboard, set of 3, *98–99*	CP		___
(22953)	Linex Gasoline Tall Oil Tank, *98*	NM		___
(22954)	Linex Gasoline Wide Oil Tank, *98*	NM		___
(22955)	ElectroCouplers kit for J class Tender and B&A Tender, *98–99*	CP		___
(22956)	ElectroCouplers kit for Switcher/NW2, *98*	NM		___
(22957)	ElectroCouplers kit for F3, *98–99*	CP		___
(22958)	ElectroCouplers kit for Dash 9, *98–99*	CP		___
(22960)	TrainMaster Command Basic Upgrade kit, *98–99*	CP		___
(22961)	Standard GP-9 B Unit Upgrade kit, *98–99*	CP		___
(22962)	Deluxe GP-9 B Unit Upgrade kit (with Black Trucks), *98–99*	CP		___
(22963)	RailSounds Upgrade kit w/ Steam Railsounds, *98–99*	CP		___
(22964)	RailSounds Upgrade kit w/ Diesel Railsounds, *98–99*	CP		___
(22965)	Command Control Culvert Loader, *98*	—	290	___
(22966)	Track Pack no. 1, *98–99*	CP		___
(22967)	Track Pack no. 2, *98–99*	CP		___
(22968)	Track Pack no. 3, *98–99*	CP		___
(22969)	Track Pack no. 4, *98–99*	CP		___
(22972)	Bascule Bridge, black, *98–99*	—	300	___
(22973)	Lionel Corp Tractor-Trailer, *98*	—	16	___

		Exc	New	Cond/$
(22979)	GP-9 B Unit Deluxe Upgrade kit (with Silver Trucks), *98–99*		CP	____
(22980)	TCC SC-2 Switch Controller, *99*		CP	____
(22982)	ZW Postwar Celebration Series Controller and Transformer set, *98*		NM	____
(22983)	Powerhouse Power Supply Units, *99*		CP	____
(22990)	Route 66 Autos on Flatcar 4-pack, *99*		CP	____
(22993)	Route 66 Sinclair/Dino Cafe, *99*		CP	____
(22997)	Oil Drum Loader, *99*		CP	____
(22998)	Triple Action Magnetic Crane, *99*		CP	____
(22999)	Sound Dispatching Station, *99*		CP	____
(23010)	Left Remote Switch 31" "3010" (O), *96–99*		CP	____
(23011)	Right Remote Switch 31" "3011" (O), *96–99*		CP	____
(26200)	NP Boxcar "18211", *98*		NRS	____
(26201)	Operation Lifesaver Boxcar, *98*	—	38	____
(26205)	Rocky and Bullwinkle Boxcar "9700", *99*		CP	____
(26206)	Curious George Boxcar "9700", *99*		CP	____
(26208)	Vapor Records Boxcar no. 2, *98*	—	50	____
(26214)	Lionel Stamp Boxcar *98u*	—	95	____
(26215)	Glow-in-the-Dark AEC Boxcar, *98*	—	38	____
(26216)	Cheerios Boxcar "9700", *98*		NRS	____
(26222)	Penn Central Boxcar "125962", *99*		CP	____
(26223)	FEC Boxcar "5027", *99*		CP	____
(26224)	D&H Boxcar "9700", *99*		CP	____
(26228)	Vapor Records Holiday Boxcar "9700", *98u*	—	75	____
(26230)	Glow-in-the-Dark Boxcar II "9700", *99*		CP	____
(26232)	Martin Guitar Lumber Boxcar "9823", *99*		CP	____
(26234)	NYC Boxcar "9700", *99*		CP	____
(26235)	Valentine Boxcar "9700", *99*		CP	____
(26236)	Aircraft Boxcar "9700", *99*		CP	____
(26237)	Boy Scout Boxcar "9700", *99*		CP	____
(26238)	Detroit Historical Museum Boxcar "9700", *99*		CP	____
(26239)	M.A.D.D Boxcar "9700", *99*		CP	____
(26240)	Starter set RailBox Boxcar "9700", *99*		CP	____
(26241)	Starter set Norfolk & Western "9700", *99*		CP	____
(26242)	D.A.R.E Boxcar "9700", *99*		CP	____
(26243)	Lionel Christmas Boxcar "9700", *99*		CP	____

(26244)	Woody Woodpecker Box Car "9700", *99*	CP	
(26256)	Salvation Army Charity Boxcar "9700", *99*	CP	
(26271)	Glow-in-the-Dark AEC Boxcar "9700-glo", *99*	CP	
(26503)	AT&SF High-Cupola Caboose "7606R", *97*	NRS	
(26513)	NYC Emergency Caboose "26505", *99*	CP	
(26528)	PRR Square Window Caboose "6257", *99*	CP	
(26530)	LL Square Window Caboose "6257", *99*	CP	
(26709)	Flatcar w/ Psychedelic Psubmarine "6511", *99*	CP	
(26710)	Southern Railroad Carsounds Stockcar, *99*	CP	
(26713)	Shay Log Car 3-pack "9823", *99*	CP	
(26905)	Bethlehem Steel Gondola w/ canisters "6462", *98*	—	25
(26906)	Southern Pacific Flatcar w/ Corgi '57 Chevy "9823", *98*	—	50
(26908)	T.T.U.X. w/Apple trailers "6300", *98*	—	75
(26913)	E. St. Louis Gondola "9820", *98*	—	41
(26926)	Union Pacific Die-cast Ore Car, *98*	NRS	
(26927)	Union Pacific Die-cast Ore Car, *98*	NRS	
(26928)	Union Pacific Die-cast Ore Car, *98*	NRS	
(26929)	Union Pacific Die-cast Ore Car, *98*	NRS	
(26936)	Die-cast Tank Car 4-pack, *98*	—	445
(26937)	Die-cast Hopper 4-pack, *98*	—	445
(26947)	Gulf Die-cast Tank Car, *98*	—	110
(26948)	P&LE Die-cast Hopper, *98*	—	110
(26949)	NP Flatcar w/ Trailer "6424-2017", *98*	NRS	
(26950)	NP Flatcar w/ Trailer "6424-2016", *98*	NRS	
(26951)	TTX Flatcar w/ PRR Trailer "475185", *98*	NRS	
(26971)	16-wheel Depressed Flatcar with Steel Load, *98*	—	165
(26972)	Animated Pony Express Gondola, *98*	—	38
(26973)	Getty Die-cast Tank Cars 3-pack, *98*	—	330
(26974)	Getty Die-cast GETX Tank Car "4003", *98*	NRS	
(26975)	Getty Die-cast GETX Tank Car "4004", *98*	NRS	
(26976)	Getty Die-cast GETX Tank Car "4005", *98*	NRS	
(26977)	Sinclair Die-cast Tank Cars 3-pack, *98*	—	330
(26978)	Sinclair Tank Car UTLX "64026", *98*	NRS	
(26979)	Sinclair Tank Car UTLX "64027", *98*	NRS	

		Exc	New	Cond/$
(26980)	Sinclair Tank UTLX "64028", *98*		NRS	_____
(26981)	Gulf Die-cast Tank Car 2-pack, *99*		CP	_____
(26985)	B&O Die-cast Hoppers 2-pack "235154", *99*		CP	_____
(26991)	Lionelville Ladder Firecar, Dept #2, *99*		CP	_____
(28000)	C&NW Hudson 4-6-4 "3005", *99*		CP	_____
(28007)	NYC Hudson 4-6-4 "5406", *99*		CP	_____
(28008)	C&O Hudson 4-6-4 "306", *99*		CP	_____
(28009)	Santa Fe Hudson 4-6-4 "3463", *99*		CP	_____
(28011)	C&O 2-6-6-6 Allegheny Steam "1601", *99*		CP	_____
(28013)	NH Pacific 4-6-2 "1335", *99*		CP	_____
(28014)	NYC Pacific 4-6-2 "4930", *99*		CP	_____
(28015)	Santa Fe Pacific 4-6-2 "3449", *99*		CP	_____
(28016)	Southern Pacific 4-6-2 "1408", *99*		CP	_____
(28020)	Lionel Lines Pacific 4-6-2 "3344", *99*		CP	_____
(28022)	West Side Lumber Shay "800", *99*		CP	_____
(28028)	Virginian 2-6-6-6 Allegheny Steam "1601", *99*		CP	_____
(28801)	Lionel Lines 44-ton Switcher, *99*		CP	_____
(29003)	PRR Madison Cars 4-pack, *98*	—	350	_____
(29007)	NYC Heavyweight Passenger set 2-pack, *98*	—	169	_____
(29008)	NYC Heavyweight Diner "383", *98*		NRS	_____
(29009)	NYC Heavyweight Combo Car "Van Twiller", *98*		NRS	_____
(29010)	C&O Heavyweight Passenger set 2-pack, *99*		CP	_____
(29086)	Madison set 3-pack, *99*		CP	_____
(29090)	Lionel Liontech Madison Car "2656", *99*		CP	_____
(29122)	Erie-Lackawanna F3 A-B Passenger set, *99*		CP	_____
(29129)	Texas Special Passenger set 4-pack, *99*		CP	_____
(29134)	WP Passenger set 4-pack, *99*		CP	_____
(29139)	Lionel Kughn Madison Car "2655", *99*		CP	_____
(29200)	LRRC Boxcar "9700", *98*		NRS	_____
(29202)	Santa Fe Map Boxcar "6464", *97 u*	—	70	_____
(29203)	Maine Central Boxcar "6464-597", *97 u*	—	27	_____
(29204)	Century Club Boxcar "1900-2000", *97*	630	1000	_____
(29205)	MM Railroad Hi-cube Boxcar "9555", *97*	—	60	_____
(29209)	6464 Boxcar Assortment, *98*	—	110	_____
(29210)	GN Boxcar "6464-50", *98*	—	3	_____
(29211)	B&M Boxcar "6464-450", *98*		NRS	_____

		Exc	New	Cond/$
(29212)	Timken Boxcar "6464-500", *98*		NRS	___
(29213)	AT&SF Grand Canyon Route 6464 Boxcar "6464-198", *98*	—	38	___
(29214)	Southern Railway 6464 Boxcar "6464-298", *98*		NRS	___
(29215)	Canadian Pacific 6464 Boxcar "6464-398", *98*		NRS	___
(29218)	Vapor Records Boxcar "6464-496", *97 u*	—	100	___
(29220)	1997 Lionel Centennial Series Hi-cube Boxcar 4-car set, *97*	—	225	___
(29221)	1997 Centennial Series Hi-cube Boxcar "9697-1", *97*		NRS	___
(29222)	1997 Centennial Series Hi-cube Boxcar "9697-2", *97*		NRS	___
(29223)	1997 Centennial Series Hi-cube Boxcar "9697-3", *97*		NRS	___
(29224)	1997 Centennial Series Hi-cube Boxcar "9697-4", *97*		NRS	___
(29225)	H.O.R.D.E. Music Festival Boxcar, *97*	75	90	___
(29226)	Century Club Berkshire Boxcar, *97*	80	100	___
(29227)	Century GG-1 Boxcar, *98u*	—	100	___
(29229)	Vapor Records Holiday Car, *98u*	—	75	___
(29231)	Animated Halloween Boxcar, *98*	—	42	___
(29232)	Lenny the Lion Hi-cube, *98*	—	61	___
(29233)	CR Overstamp PC Boxcar "6464-598", *98*		NRS	___
(29234)	CR Overstamp Erie Boxcar "6464-698", *98*		NRS	___
(29250)	Phoebe Snow boxcar "6464-199", *99*		CP	___
(29251)	BN Boxcar "6464-299", *99*		CP	___
(29252)	CP Boxcar "6464-399", *99*		CP	___
(29257)	Southern Boxcar "9464-199", *99*		CP	___
(29258)	Reading Boxcar "9464-299", *99*		CP	___
(29259)	NP Bicentennial Boxcar "9464-399", *99*		CP	___
(29265)	Maine Central Boxcar "6565", *99*		CP	___
(29266)	Frisco Boxcar "6565", *99*		CP	___
(29267)	6464 Boxcar Assortment, *99*		CP	___
(29268)	Rio Grande Boxcar "6565", *99*		CP	___
(29268)	Overstamp 2-pack "6464", *99*		CP	___
(29271)	Lionel Cola Tractor-Trailer, *98*	—	16	___

(29281)	Post-merger Boxcar "6464", 99		CP ___
(29282)	Overstamp 3-pack "6464", 99		CP ___
(29861)	Post-merger Boxcar Conrail Overstamped CNJ & LV 2-pack set, 99		CP ___
(32900)	DC Billboard Lionel, 99		CP ___
(32902)	Construction Signs, 99		CP ___
(32904)	Lionel Hell Gate Bridge, 99		CP ___
(32905)	Lionel Irvington Factory, 99		CP ___
(32919)	Animated Maiden Rescue, 99		CP ___
(32920)	Animated Pylon w/ Airplane, 99		CP ___
(32921)	Electric Coaling Station, 99		CP ___
(32922)	Highway Signs, 99		CP ___
(32923)	Accessory Transformer, 36-watt, 99		CP ___
(32929)	Icing Station with Santa, 99		CP ___
(32930)	ZW Controller w/ 2 190-watt transformers, 99		CP ___
(32960)	Hindenburger Cafe, 99		CP ___
(32961)	Route 66 U.F.O. Cafe, 99		CP ___
(32988)	No. 192 Railroad Control Tower, 99		CP ___
(32989)	No. 464 Sawmill, 99		CP ___
(32990)	Linex Oil Derrick, 99		CP ___
(32991)	WLLC Radio Station, 99		CP ___
(36000)	Route 66 Flatcar with 2 red sedans, 98	—	50 ___
(36001)	Route 66 Flatcar with 2 wagons, 98	—	50 ___
(36002)	Pratt's Hollow Passenger Cars 4-pack, 98		CP ___
(36006)	Uranium Flatcar "6508", 99		CP ___
(36016)	Flatcar with propellers, 98	—	70 ___
(36020)	Flatcar "TT-6424" w/ auto frames, 99		CP ___
(36021)	Alaska Flatcar w/ airplane "6424", 99		CP ___
(36026)	Flatcars w/ J.B. Hunt trailers 2-pack, 99		CP ___
(36029)	SP Auto Carrier "516712", 99		CP ___
(36030)	Troublesome Truck "1", 99		CP ___
(36031)	Troublesome Truck "2", 99		CP ___
(36900)	Depressed-center Flatcar w/ backshop load, 99		CP ___
(38100)	Texas Special F3 AB set "2245", 99		CP ___
(38103)	Texas Special F3 "2245", 99		CP ___
(38150)	Platinum Ghost "2333", 99		CP ___

(38153)	Spirit of the Century "2333", *99*		CP _____
(39104)	Phoebe Snow Stationsounds Car, *99*		CP _____
(39105)	Milwaukee Road Hiawatha Stationsounds Car, *99*		CP _____
(39109)	Spirit of the Century Aluminum Car 4-pack, *99*		CP _____
(51502)	Lionel Steel Ore Car "6486-3", *96*	—	120 _____
(51503)	Die-cast Ore Car "6486", *96*	—	85 _____
(51504)	Die-cast Ore Car "6486", *96*	—	85 _____
(51600)	Lionel Lines Depressed-center Flatcar w/ transformer load "6418", *96*	—	150 _____
No Number	Rock Island Rocket set, *96*		NM _____
No Number	"773" Hudson and Madison cars, *97*		NM _____
No Number	GE AC4400 Diesel Locomotive set, *97*		NM _____
No Number	Lionel Lines Command-equipped Log Car "3361", *97*		NM _____
No Number	Lionel Lines Command-equipped Searchlight Car "6520", *97*		NM _____
No Number	FEC Flatcar w/ Ertl dump truck "6434", *98*		NM _____
No Number	Lionel Const. Depressed Flatcar w/ Ertl Uniloader "6461", *98*		NM _____
No Number	Pacific Fruit Express Reefer "459403", *98*		NM _____

Section 6
UNCATALOGED CLUB CARS
AND SPECIAL PRODUCTION

ARTRAIN

___	**9486**	GTW "I Love Michigan" Boxcar, *87*
___	**17885**	Artrain 1-D Tank Car, *90*
___	**17891**	Grand Trunk Boxcar, *91*
___	**52013**	Norfolk Southern Flatcar w/ trailer (Std. O), *92*
___	**52024**	Conrail Auto Carrier, *93*
___	**52049**	Burlington Northern Gondola w/ coil covers, *94*
___	**52097**	Chessie System Reefer, *95*
___	**19425**	CSX Flatcar w/ trailer, *97*
___		Union Pacific Bunk Car, *97*
___		Southern Pacific Caboose, *98*

CHICAGOLAND RAILROAD CLUB

___	**(52081)**	C&NW Boxcar "6464555", *96*
___	**(52102)**	Santa Fe E/V Caboose "999556" w/ black roof, *96*
___	**(52103)**	Santa Fe E/V Caboose "999758" w/ red roof, *96*
___	**(52101)**	BN Maxi-Stack Flatcar w/ containers "64287", *97*
___	**(52120)**	Shedd Aquarium Car "3435-557", *98*
___	**(52148)**	REA/Santa Fe Boxcar "52148-558", *99*
___	**(52171)**	UP Time Zone Boxcar "52171-561", *98*
___	**(52170)**	SP Daylight Boxcar "52170-562", *99*

CLASSIC TOY TRAINS

___	**(52126)**	MILW Boxcar w/ CTT logo "21027", *97*

INLAND EMPIRE TRAIN COLLECTORS ASSOC. (IETCA)

___	**[1979]**	IETCA Boxcar, *79*
___	**[1980]**	IETCA SP-Type Caboose, *80*
___	**[1981]**	IETCA Quad Hopper, *81*

UNCATALOGED CLUB CARS AND SPECIAL PRODUCTION

____ [1982]   IETCA 3-D Tank Car, *82*
____ [1983]   IETCA Reefer, *83*
____ [7518]   IETCA Carson City Mint Car, *84*
____ [1986]   IETCA Bunk Car, *86*

LIONEL CENTRAL OPERATING LINES (LCOL)

____ [1981]   LCOL Boxcar, *81*
____ [9184]   Erie B/W Caboose, *82*
____ [6508]   Canadian Pacific Crane Car, *83*
____ [5724]   Pennsylvania Bunk Car, *84*
____ [9475]   D&H "I Love NY" Boxcar, *85*
____ [1986]   LCOL Work Caboose, shell only, *86*

LIONEL COLLECTORS ASSOC. OF CANADA (LCAC)

____ [9718]   Canadian National Boxcar, *79*
____ [9413]   Napierville Junction Boxcar, *80*
____ [8103]   Toronto, Hamilton & Buffalo Boxcar, *81*
____ [8204]   Algoma Central Boxcar, *82*
____ [6100]   Ontario Northland Covered Quad Hopper, *82*
____ [830005]   Canadian National Boxcar, *83*
____ [5710]   Canadian Pacific Reefer, *83*
____ [840006]   Canadian Wheat Board Covered Quad Hopper, *84*
____ [8507]/[8508]   Canadian National F-3 AA, shells only, *85*
____ [5714]   Michigan Central Reefer, *85*
____ [86009]   Canadian National Bunk Car, *86*
____ [87010]   Canadian National Express Reefer, *87*
____ [88011]   Canadian National Wood-sided Caboose (Std. O), *88*
____ [8912]   Canada Southern Operating Hopper, *89*
____ [900013]   Canadian National Flatcar w/ trailers, *90*
____ [17893]   BAOC 1-D Tank Car "914", *91*
____ [52004]   Algoma Central Gondola w/ coil covers "9215", *92*
____ [52005]   Canadian National F-3 B Unit "9517", *93*
____ [52006]   Canadian Pacific Boxcar "930016" (Std. O), *93*

LIONEL COLLECTORS CLUB OF AMERICA (LCCA)

LCCA National Convention Cars

___	[9701]	Baltimore & Ohio DD Boxcar, *72*
___	9727	TA&G Boxcar, *73*
___	9118	Corning Covered Quad Hopper, *74*
___	9155	Monsanto 1-D Tank Car, *75*
___	9212	Seaboard Coast Line Flatcar w/ trailers, *76*
___	X9259	Southern B/W Caboose, *77*
___	9728	Union Pacific Stock Car, *78*
___	9733	Airco Boxcar w/ tank, *79*
___	9358	Sands of Iowa Covered Quad Hopper, *80*
___	(8068)	Rock Island GP-20 "1980", *80*
___	9435	Central of Georgia Boxcar, *81*
___	9460	D&TS DD Boxcar, *82*
___	6112	Commonwealth Edison Quad Hopper w/ coal load, *83*
___	7403	LNAC Boxcar, *84*
___	(6567)	Illinois Central Gulf Crane Car "100408", *85*
___	6323	Virginia Chemicals 1-D Tank Car, *86*
___	17870	East Camden & Highland Boxcar (Std. O), *87*
___	17873	Ashland Oil 3-D Tank Car, *88*
___	17876	Columbia, Newberry & Laurens Boxcar (Std. O), *89*
___	17880	D&RGW Wood-sided Caboose (Std. O), *90*
___	(18090)	D&RGW 4-6-2 "1990", *90*
___	17887	Conrail Flatcar w/ Armstrong Tile trailer (Std. O), *91*
___	17888	Conrail Flatcar w/ Ford New Holland trailer (Std. O), *91*
___	(17899)	NASA Unibody Tank Car "190" (Std. O), *92*
___	(29232)	Lenny the Lion Hi-cube, signed by Lenny Dean, *99*
___	(52023)	D&TS 2-bay ACF Hopper "2601" (Std. O), *93*
___	(52038)	Southern Hopper w/ coal load "360794" (Std. O), *94*
___	(52074)	Iowa Beef Packers Reefer "197095" (Std. O), *95*
___	(52090)	Pere Marquette DD Boxcar "71996" (Std. O), *96*
___	(52110)	CStPM&O Boxcar "71997" (Std. O), *97*
___	(Not Assigned)	Amtrak Express Baggage Boxcar "71998" (Std. O), *98*
___	(Not Assigned)	Fort Worth & Denver Boxcar "8277" (Std O), *99*

UNCATALOGED CLUB CARS AND SPECIAL PRODUCTION

LCCA Meet Specials

____	**[6014-900]**	Frisco Boxcar (O27), *75–76*
____	**[No Number]**	Lionel Lines Tender only, *76–77*
____	**[9142]**	Republic Steel Gondola w/ canisters, *77–78*
____	**[9036]**	Mobilgas 1-D Tank Car (O27), *78–79*
____	**[9016]**	Chessie System Hopper (O27), *79–80*
____	**6483**	Jersey Central SP-Type Caboose, *82*

Other LCCA Production

____	**[9771]**	Norfolk & Western Boxcar, *77*
____	**[9739]**	D&RGW Boxcar, *78*
____	**(17895)**	LCCA Tractor, *91*
____	**(17896)**	Lancaster Lines Tractor, *91*
____	**(52025)**	Madison Hardware Tractor and Trailer, *93*
____	**(52039)**	"Track 29" Bumper, *94*
____	**(52055)**	SOVEX Tractor and Trailer, *94*
____	**(52056)**	Southern Tractor and Trailer "206502", *94*
____	**(52091)**	Lenox Tractor and Trailer, *95*
____	**(52092)**	Iowa Interstate Tractor and Trailer, *95*
____	**(52131)**	LCCA Blue Airplane
____	**(52138)**	LCCA Orange Airplane
____	**(52100)**	LCCA Station Platform, *98*
____	**(52107)**	On-Track Pickup Truck, orange, *96*
____	**(52108)**	On-Track Step Van, blue, *96*

LIONEL OPERATING TRAIN SOCIETY (LOTS)

LOTS National Convention Cars

____	**[9414]**	Cotton Belt Boxcar, *80*
____	**[3764]**	Kahn Boxcar, *81*
____	**[80948]**	Michigan Central Boxcar, *82*
____	**[6111]**	L&N Covered Quad Hopper, *83*
____	**[121315]**	Pennsylvania Hi-cube Boxcar, *84*
____	**[303]**	Stauffer Chemical 1-D Tank Car, *85*
____	**[6211]**	C&O Gondola w/ canisters, *86*
____	**[38356]**	Dow Chemical 3-D Tank Car, *87*
____	**(17874)**	Milwaukee Road Log Dump Car "59629", *88*

UNCATALOGED CLUB CARS AND SPECIAL PRODUCTION

___	**(17875)**	PHD Boxcar "1289", *89*
___	**(17882)**	B&O DD Boxcar w/ ETD "298011", *90*
___	**(18890)**	Union Pacific RS-3 "8805", *90*
___	**(17890)**	CSX Auto Carrier "151161", *91*
___	**(19960)**	Western Pacific Boxcar "1952" (Std. O), *92*
___	**(52014)**	BN TTUX Flatcar set w/ N&W trailers "637500A/B", *93*
___	**(52041)**	BN TTUX Flatcar set w/ Conrail trailers "637500D/E", *94*
___	**(52067)**	Burlington Ice Car "50240", *95*
___	**(16812)**	Grand Trunk 2-bay ACF Hopper "16812" (Std. O), *96*
___	**(16813)**	Pennsylvania Power & Light Co. Hopper w/ coal load (Std. O), *97*
___		Santa Fe Reefer, *98*
___		GM&O DD Boxcar, "24580", *98*

Other LOTS Production

___	[1223]	Seattle & North Coast Hi-cube Boxcar, *86*
___	**(52042)**	BN TTUX Flatcar w/ CN trailer "637500C", *94*
___	**(52048)**	Canadian National Tractor and Trailer "197993", *94*

LIONEL CENTURY CLUB (LCC)

___	**(29204)**	Lionel Century Club Boxcar "1900-2000", *96*
___	**(29226)**	Lionel Century Club Berkshire Boxcar, *97*
___	**(29227)**	Lionel Century Club GG-1 Boxcar, *98*

LIONEL RAILROADER CLUB (LRRC)

___	**0780**	LRRC Boxcar, *82*
___	**0781**	LRRC Flatcar w/ trailers, *83*
___	**0784**	LRRC Covered Quad Hopper, *84*
___	**0782**	LRRC 1-D Tank Car, *85*
___	**16800**	LRRC Ore Car, *86*
___	**16801**	LRRC Bunk Car, *88*
___	**16802**	LRRC Tool Car, *89*
___	**16803**	LRRC Searchlight Car, *90*
___	**16804**	LRRC B/W Caboose, *91*
___	**(18818)**	LRRC GP-38-2 "1992", *92*

UNCATALOGED CLUB CARS AND SPECIAL PRODUCTION

	19924	LRRC Boxcar, *93*
	19930	LRRC Quad Hopper w/ coal load, *94*
	(12875)	LRRC Tractor and Trailer, *94*
	(19935)	LRRC 1-D Tank Car "1995", *95*
	(19940)	LRRC Vat Car, *96*
	(12921)	LRRC Illuminated Station Platform, *95*
	(29200)	LRRC Lionel Corporation Boxcar "9700", *96*
	(19953)	LRRC Lionel Corporation Boxcar "6464-97", *97*
	(19937)	LRRC Flatcar w/ Inside Track Trailer "1997", *97*
	(29200)	LRRC Boxcar "9700", *98*
	(19966)	LRRC Gondola "9820" (Std O), *98*
	(19965)	LRRC Aquarium Car "3435", *99*
	(18684)	LRRC Pacific 4-6-2 "1999", *99*
	(19774)	LRRC Porthole Caboose "1999", *99*
	(19775)	LRRC Stock Car, *99*
	(19473)	LRRC Log Dump Car, *99*

LIONEL RAILROAD CLUB—MILWAUKEE

| | [52116] | MILW Flatcar w/ tractor and trailer, *97* |
| | (Not Assigned) | Milwaukee Road DD Boxcar "194798", *98* |

NASSAU LIONEL OPERATING ENGINEERS (NLOE)

	[8389]	Long Island Boxcar, *89*
	[8390]	Long Island Covered Quad Hopper, *90*
	[8391A]	Long Island Bunk Car, *91*
	[8391B]	Long Island Tool Car, *91*
	[8392]	Long Island 1-D Tank Car, *92*
	[52007]	Long Island RS-3 "1552", *93*
	[52019]	Long Island Boxcar "8393", *93*
	[52020]	Long Island B/W Caboose "8393", *93*
	[52026]	Long Island Flatcar w/ Grumman trailer "8394", *94*
	[52072]	Grumman Tractor, *94*
	[52061]	Long Island Stern's Pickle Products Vat Car "8395", *95*
	[52076]	Long Island Observation Car "8396", *96*

UNCATALOGED CLUB CARS AND SPECIAL PRODUCTION

___ **(52122)** NLOE Meenan Oil 1-D Tank Car "8397" (Std O.)
___ Long Island Flatcar w/ Grumman trailer "8398", *98*

ST. LOUIS LIONEL RAILROAD CLUB (ST. LOUIS LRRC)

___ **(52099)** MP Flatcar w/ St. Louis LRRC trailer, *96*
___ **(52117)** Wabash Flatcar w/ REA tractor and trailer, *97*

TRAIN COLLECTORS ASSOCIATION (TCA)

TCA National Convention Cars

___ **6464-1970** TCA Chicago Boxcar, *70*
___ **6464-1971** TCA Disneyland Boxcar, *71*
___ **6315** TCA Pittsburgh 1-D Tank Car, *72*
___ **(9123)** TCA Dearborn Auto Carrier "1973" (3-tier), *73*
___ **9864** TCA Seattle Reefer, *74*
___ **9774** TCA Orlando Southern Belle Boxcar, *75*
___ **(9779)** TCA Philadelphia Boxcar "9700-1976", *76*
___ **7812** TCA Houston Stock Car, *77*
___ **9611** TCA Boston Hi-cube Boxcar, *78*
___ **9319** TCA Silver Jubilee Mint Car, *79*
___ **(9544)** TCA Chicago Observation Car "1980", *80*
___ **(0511)** TCA St. Louis Baggage Car "1981", *81*
___ **(7205)** TCA Denver Combination Car "1982", *82*
___ **(7206)** TCA Louisville Passenger Car "1983", *83*
___ **(7212)** TCA Pittsburgh Passenger Car "1984", *84*
___ **5734** TCA REA Reefer, *85*
___ **(8476)** TCA 4-6-4 "5484", *85*
___ **6926** TCA New Orleans E/V Caboose, *86*
___ **(17879)** TCA Valley Forge Dining Car "1989", *89*
___ **(17883)** New Georgia Railroad Passenger Car "1990", *90*
___ **(17898)** Wabash Reefer "21596", *92*
___ **(52008)** Bucyrus Erie Crane Car "1993X", *93*
___ **(11737)** TCA 40th Anniversary F-3 ABA set "40", *93*
___ **(52035)** Yorkrail GP-9 "1750", shell only, *94*
___ **(52036)** TCA 40th Anniversary B/W Caboose, *94*

____	**(52037)**	Yorkrail GP-9 "1754", *94*
____	**(52062)**	TCA "Skytop" Observation Car "1995", *95*
____	**(52085)**	TCA Full Vista Dome Car "1996", *96*
____	**(52105)**	TCA City of Phoenix Diner "1997", *97*
____		TCA "City of Providence" Passenger Car "1998", *98*
____		TCA Mass. Central Maxi-stack "5100-01", *98*
____	**(Not Assigned)**	TCA City of San Francisco Baggage Car "1999", *99*

TCA Museum-Related Cars

____	**[9771]**	Norfolk & Western Boxcar, *77*
____	**[1018-1979]**	Mortgage Burning Hi-cube Boxcar, *79*
____	**[7780]**	TCA Museum Boxcar, *80*
____	**[7781]**	Hafner Boxcar, *81*
____	**[7782]**	Carlisle & Finch Boxcar, *82*
____	**[7783]**	Ives Boxcar, *83*
____	**[7784]**	Voltamp Boxcar, *84*
____	**[7785]**	Hoge Boxcar, *85*
____	**[5731]**	L&N Reefer, *90*
____	**[52045]**	Penn Dutch Milk Car "61052", *94*
____	**[52052]**	TCA 40th Anniversary Boxcar, *94*
____	**(52051)**	Baltimore & Ohio "Sentinel" Boxcar "6464095", *95*
____	**(52063)**	NYC "Pacemaker" Boxcar "6464125", *95*
____	**(52064)**	Missouri Pacific Boxcar "6464150", *95*
____	**(16811)**	Rutland Boxcar "5477096", *96*
____		Penn Dutch Grain Operating Boxcar "9028", *96*
____	**(52118)**	Rio Grande Boxcar "5477097", *97*
____	**(Not Assigned)**	L&N Share the Freedom Boxcar "5477099", *98*

TCA Bicentennial Special Set

____	**1973**	TCA Bicentennial Observation Car, *76*
____	**1974**	TCA Bicentennial Passenger Car, *76*
____	**1975**	TCA Bicentennial Passenger Car, *76*
____	**1976**	TCA Bicentennial U36B, *76*

UNCATALOGED CLUB CARS AND SPECIAL PRODUCTION

Atlantic Division TCA

____ [9788] Lehigh Valley Boxcar, *78*

____ [9186] Conrail N5C Caboose, *79*

____ [1980] Atlantic Division Flatcar w/ trailers, *80*

____ [6101] Burlington Northern Covered Quad Hopper, *82*

____ [9466] Wanamaker Boxcar, *83*

____ [9193] Budweiser Vat Car, *84*

____ [No Number] Pennsylvania Reading Seashore Bunk Car, *85*

Desert Division TCA

____ [52088] Desert Division 25th Anniversary On-Track Step Van, *96*

Dixie Division TCA

____ (52127) TCA Dixie Division 10th Anniversary Southern 3-bay Hopper "360997", *98*

Eastern Division TCA

____ (52059) Clinchfield Quad Hopper w/ coal load "16413", *94*

Eastern Division TCA—Washington, Baltimore and Annapolis Chapter

____ [9740] Chessie System Boxcar, *76*

____ [9783] B&O "Time-Saver" Boxcar, *77*

____ [9771] Norfolk & Western Boxcar, *78*

____ [9412] Richmond, Fredericksburg, & Potomac Boxcar, *79*

Ft. Pitt Division TCA

____ [1984-30X] Heinz Ketchup Boxcar, *84*

Great Lakes Division TCA

____ [9740] Chessie System Boxcar, *76*

____ [1983] Churchill Downs Boxcar, *83*

____ [1983] Churchill Downs Reefer, *83*

Great Lakes Division TCA—Detroit-Toledo Chapter

____ [9730] CP Rail Boxcar, *76*

____ [9119] Detroit & Mackinac Covered Quad Hopper, *77*

____ [9401] Great Northern Boxcar, *78*

UNCATALOGED CLUB CARS AND SPECIAL PRODUCTION

____ **[9272]** New Haven B/W Caboose, *79*
____ **[8957]** Burlington Northern GP-20, *80*
____ **[8958]** Burlington Northern GP-20 Dummy, *80*
____ **52000** Detroit-Toledo Division Flatcar w/ trailer, *92*

Great Lakes Division TCA—Three Rivers Chapter
____ **[9113]** Norfolk & Western Quad Hopper, *76*

Great Lakes Division TCA—Western Michigan Chapter
____ **[9730]** CP Rail Boxcar, *74*

Lake & Pines Division TCA
____ **52018** 3-M Boxcar, *93*

Lone Star Division TCA
____ **[7522]** New Orleans Mint Car w/ coin, *86*
____ **(52093)** Lone Star Division Boxcar "6464696", *96*

Lone Star Division TCA—North Texas Chapter
____ **[9739]** D&RGW Boxcar, *76*
____ **[9184]** Erie B/W Caboose, *77*
____ **[9119]** Detroit & Mackinac Covered Quad Hopper, *78*
____ **[No Number]** Texas Special F-3 A Unit, shell only, *81*
____ **[No Number]** Texas Special F-3 B Unit, shell only, *82*

METCA
____ **[10]** Jersey Central F-3 A Unit, shell only, *71*
____ **[9754]** New York Central "Pacemaker" Boxcar, *76*
____ **[9272]** New Haven B/W Caboose, *79*

Midwest Division TCA
____ **[9725]** Midwest Division Stock Car "00002", *75*
____ **[7600]** Frisco "Spirit of '76" N5C Caboose "00003", *76*
____ **[4]** C&NW F-3 A Unit, shell only, *77*
____ **[00005]** Midwest Division Covered Quad Hopper, *78*
____ **[9872]** PFE Reefer "00006", *79*

UNCATALOGED CLUB CARS AND SPECIAL PRODUCTION

____ **[1287]** C&NW Reefer, *84*
____ **[1988]** Illinois Central Boxcar, *88*

Midwest Division TCA Museum Express

____ **9785]** Conrail Boxcar, *77*
____ **[9264]** Illinois Central Gulf Covered Quad Hopper, *78*
____ **[9786]** Chicago & North Western Boxcar, *79*
____ **[9289]** Chicago & North Western N5C Caboose, *80*

NETCA

____ **[1203]** Boston & Maine NW-2, shell only, *72*
____ **[9753]** Maine Central Boxcar, *75*
____ **[9768]** Boston & Maine Boxcar, *76*
____ **[9181]** Boston & Maine N5C Caboose, *77*
____ **[9400]** Conrail Boxcar, *78*
____ **[9785]** Conrail Boxcar, *78*
____ **[9415]** Providence & Worcester Boxcar, *79*
____ **[9423]** NYNH&H Boxcar, *80*
____ **[9445]** Vermont Northern Boxcar, *81*
____ **[5710]** Canadian Pacific Reefer, *82*
____ **[5716]** Vermont Central Reefer, *83*
____ **[6124]** Delaware & Hudson Covered Quad Hopper, *84*
____ **[8051]** Hood's Milk Boxcar, *86*
____ **52001** Boston & Maine Quad Hopper w/ coal load, *92*
____ **52016** Boston & Maine Gondola w/ coil covers, *93*
____ **[52043]** L.L. Bean Boxcar "1994", *94*
____ **[52080]** B&M Flatcar w/ trailer "91095", *95*

Ozark Division TCA—Gateway Chapter

____ **[9068]** Reading Bobber Caboose, *76*
____ **[9601]** Illinois Central Gulf Hi-cube Boxcar, *77*
____ **[9767]** Railbox Boxcar, *78*
____ **[5700]** Oppenheimer Reefer, *81*
____ **52003** "Meet Me In St. Louis" Flatcar w/ trailer, *92*

UNCATALOGED CLUB CARS AND SPECIAL PRODUCTION

Pacific Northwest Division TCA

____ **[No Number]** Pacific Northwest Division F-3 AA, shells only, *74*

____ **(52077)** Great Northern Hi-cube Boxcar "9695", *95*

Rocky Mountain Division TCA

____ **1971-1976** Rocky Mountain Division Reefer, *76*

Sacramento—Sierra Chapter TCA

____ **[9723]** Western Pacific Boxcar, *73*

____ **[9705]** D&RGW Boxcar, *75*

____ **[9301]** US Mail Operating Boxcar, *76*

____ **[9730]** CP Rail Boxcar, *77*

____ **[9785]** Conrail Boxcar, *78*

____ **[9726]** Erie-Lackawanna Boxcar, *79*

____ **[9414]** Cotton Belt Boxcar, *80*

____ **[9427]** Bay Line Boxcar, *81*

____ **[9444]** Louisiana Midland Boxcar, *82*

____ **[9452]** Western Pacific Boxcar, *83*

____ **[6401]** Virginian B/W Caboose, *84*

____ **[No Number]** Lionel Lines Tender, shell only, *84*

Southern Division TCA

____ **[1976]** Florida East Coast F-3 ABA, shells only, *76*

____ **[9287]** Southern N5C Caboose, *77*

____ **[9403]** Seaboard Coast Line Boxcar, *78*

____ **[9405]** Chattahoochie Boxcar, *79*

____ **[9352]** Trailer Train Flatcar w/ Circus trailers, *80*

____ **[9443]** Florida East Coast Boxcar, *81*

____ **[6111]** L&N Covered Quad Hopper, *83*

____ **[9471]** ACL Boxcar, *84*

____ **[9482]** Norfolk & Southern Boxcar, *85*

____ **[1986]** Southern Division Bunk Car, *86*

____ **[16606]** Southern Searchlight Car, *88*

TOY TRAIN OPERATING SOCIETY (TTOS)

TTOS National Convention Cars

____	**6076**	Santa Fe Hopper (O27), *70*
____	**9512**	TTOS Summerdale Junction Passenger Car, *74*
____	**9520**	TTOS Phoenix Combination Car, *75*
____	**9526**	TTOS Snowbird Observation Car, *76*
____	**9535**	TTOS Columbus Baggage Car, *77*
____	**9678**	TTOS Hollywood Hi-cube Boxcar, *78*
____	**9347**	TTOS Niagara Falls 3-D Tank Car, *79*
____	**9868**	TTOS Oklahoma City Reefer, *80*
____	**[9326]**	Burlington Northern B/W Caboose, *82*
____	**[9355]**	Delaware & Hudson B/W Caboose, *82*
____	**[9361]**	Chicago & North Western B/W Caboose, *82*
____	**[9382]**	Florida East Coast B/W Caboose, *82*
____	**[9883]**	TTOS Phoenix Reefer, *83*
____	**[1984]**	TTOS Sacramento Northern Boxcar, *84*
____	**[1985]**	TTOS Snowbird Covered Quad Hopper, *85*
____	**6582**	TTOS Portland Flatcar w/ wood load, *86*
____	**(17871)**	NYC Flatcar w/ Kodak and Xerox trailers "81487", *87*
____	**(17872)**	Anaconda Ore Car "81988", *88*
____	**(17877)**	MKT 1-D Tank Car "3739469", *89*
____	**17884**	Columbus & Dayton Terminal Boxcar (Std. O), *90*
____	**(17889)**	Southern Pacific Flatcar w/ trailer "15791" (Std. O), *91*
____	**(19963)**	Union Equity 3-bay ACF Hopper "86892" (Std. O), *92*
____	**(52010)**	Weyerhaeuser DD Boxcar "838593" (Std. O), *93*
____	**(52029)**	Ford 1-D Tank Car "12" (O27), *94*
____	**(52030)**	Ford Gondola "4023", *94*
____	**(52031)**	Ford Hopper "1458" (O27), *94*
____	**(52057)**	Western Pacific Boxcar "64641995", *95*
____	**(52087)**	New Mexico Central Boxcar "64641996", *96*

TTOS Division Cars

____	**(52009)**	Sacramento Valley Division Western Pacfic Boxcar "64641993", *93*
____	**52040**	Wolverine Division GTW Flatcar w/ LL tractor and trailer, "52033", *94*

UNCATALOGED CLUB CARS AND SPECIAL PRODUCTION

___	**(52058)**	Central California Division Santa Fe Boxcar "64641895", *95*
___	**(52086)**	Canadian Division Pacific Great Eastern Boxcar "64641972", *96*
___	**(52113)**	Northeastern Division Genesee & Wyoming RR 3-bay ACF Hopper "10000" (Std O), *97*
___	**52114**	NYC Flatcar w/ Gleason and Sasib trailers, *97*
___	**(15149)**	Conrail Flatcar w/Blum coal shovel, *98*

Southwest Division TTOS Cal-Stewart

___	**(19962)**	Southern Pacific 3-bay ACF Hopper "496035" (Std. O), *92*
___	**(52047)**	Cotton Belt Wood-sided Caboose w/ smoke "1921" (Std. O), *93–94*
___	**(52073)**	Pacific Fruit Express Reefer "459402" (Std. O), *95*
___	**(52098)**	National Bureau of Standards Boxcar (Std O), *96*
___	**(52121)**	Mobilgas Tank Car "238" (Std O), *97*
___	**(Not Assigned)**	Pacific Fruit Express Reefer "459403" (Std O), *98*

Other TTOS Production

___	**[1983]**	TTOS Phoenix 3-D Tank Car, *83*
___	**(17894)**	Southern Pacific Tractor, *91*
___	**(52021)**	Weyerhaeuser Tractor and Trailer, *93*
___	**52022**	Union Pacific Boxcar, *93*
___	**(52032)**	Ford 1-D Tank Car "14" w/ Kughn inscription (O27), *94*
___	**(52046)**	ACL Boxcar "16247", *94*
___	**52053**	TTOS Carail Boxcar, *94*
___	**(52068)**	Toy Train Parade TTOS Contadina Boxcar "16245", *94*
___	**(52084)**	Union Pacific I-Beam Flatcar w/ load "16380", *95*
___	**(52078)**	Southern Pacific SD-9 "5366", *96*
___	**(52079)**	Southern Pacific B/W Caboose "1996", *96*

TTOS Gadsden Pacific Ore Cars

___	**17878**	Magma Ore Car w/ load, *89*
___	**17881**	Phelps-Dodge Ore Car w/ load, *90*
___	**17886**	Cyprus Ore Car w/ load, *91*
___	**19961**	Inspiration Consolidated Copper Co. Ore Car w/ load, *92*

UNCATALOGED CLUB CARS AND SPECIAL PRODUCTION

____	**52011**	Tucson, Cornelia & Gila Bend Ore Car w/ load, *93*
____	**52027**	Pinto Valley Mine Ore Car w/ load, *94*
____	**52071**	Copper Basin Railway Ore Car w/ load, *95*
____	**52089**	SMARRCO Ore Car w/ load, *96*
____	**(52124)**	EPSW Ore Car w/ load, *97*

VIRGINIA TRAIN COLLECTORS (VTC)

____	**[7679]**	VTC Boxcar, *79*
____	**[7681]**	VTC N5C Caboose, *81*
____	**[7682]**	VTC Covered Quad Hopper, *82*
____	**[7683]**	Virginia Fruit Express Reefer, *83*
____	**[7684]**	Vitraco 3-D Tank Car, *84*
____	**[7685]**	VTC Boxcar, *85*
____	**[7686]**	VTC GP-7, *86*
____	**[7692-1]**	VTC Baggage Car (O27), *92*
____	**[7692-2]**	VTC Combination Car (O27), *92*
____	**[7692-3]**	VTC Dining Car (O27), *92*
____	**[7692-4]**	VTC Passenger Car (O27), *92*
____	**[7692-5]**	VTC Vista Dome Car (O27), *92*
____	**[7692-6]**	VTC Passenger Car (O27), *92*
____	**[7692-7]**	VTC Observation Car (O27), *92*
____	**[52060]**	VTC Tender w/ whistle "7694", *94*

Section 7
LARGE SCALE 1987–1999

1	(See 85120)
3	(See 85115)
4	(See 85117)
5	(See 85121)
8	(See 85122)
100	(See 85100)
101	(See 85101, 85124)
112	(See 85112)
400	(See 87400)
401	(See 87401)
404	(See 87404)
485	(See 85006)
486	(See 85007)
700	(See 87700)
701	(See 87701, 87724)
709	(See 87709)
712	(See 85008, 87712)
722	(See 85013)
2003	(See 85003)
2004	(See 85005)
5000	(See 55000, 85000)
5001	(See 85001)
5102	(See 85102)
5103	(See 85103)
5104	(See 85104)
5105	(See 85105)
5106	(See 85106)
5107	(See 85107)
5108	(See 85108)
5109	(See 85109)
5110	(See 85110)
5111	(See 85111)
5113	(See 85113)
5114	(See 85114)

		Exc	New	Cond/$
6000	(See 86000)			
6001	(See 86001)			
6002	(See 86002)			
6003	(See 86003)			
6004	(See 86004)			
6005	(See 86005)			
7402	(See 87402)			
7403	(See 87403)			
7405	(See 87405)			
7406	(See 87406)			
7407	(See 87407)			
7500	(See 87500)			
7501	(See 87501)			
7502	(See 87502)			
7503	(See 87503)			
7504	(See 87504)			
7508	(See 87508)			
7702	(See 87702)			
7703	(See 87703)			
7704	(See 87704)			
7705	(See 87705)			
7706	(See 87706)			
7707	(See 87707)			
7708	(See 87708)			
7711	(See 87711)			
7713	(See 87713)			
7716	(See 87716)			
7800	(See 87800)			
7806	(See 87806)			
7808	(See 87808)			
(55000)	Lionel Lines RailScope 0-4-0T "5000", *88–90*	150	230	_____
(81000)	Gold Rush Special set, *87–90*	—	160	_____
(81001)	Thunder Mountain Express set, *88–89*	—	200	_____
(81002)	Frontier Freight set, *88–89*	—	175	_____
(81003)	Great Northern set, *90*		NM	_____
(81004)	North Pole Railroad set, *89–91*	—	165	_____

		Exc	New	Cond/$
(81006)	Union Pacific Limited set, *90–91*	100	220	_____
(81007)	Disney Magic Express set, *90*	—	250	_____
(81008)	Walt Disney World set, *91*		NM	_____
(81011)	Thomas the Tank Engine set, *93 u*	110	130	_____
(81014)	James & Troublesome Trucks set, *94–95*	85	130	_____
(81016)	Thomas the Tank Engine Deluxe set, *94–95*	—	180	_____
(81017)	Ornament Express set, *94–95*	—	150	_____
(81019)	1998 Large Scale Christmas set, *98*	—	165	_____
(81050)	Gold Rush Special set w/ mailer, *87 u*		NRS	_____
(81051)	Spiegel PRR set, *87 u*		NRS	_____
(81054)	Gold Rush Special set w/o transformer, *90 u*		NRS	_____
(81057)	North Pole Railroad set w/ mailer, *90 u*		NRS	_____
(81059)	JCPenney Thomas the Tank Engine set, *94 u*	125	150	_____
(81061)	Thomas the Tank Engine set, *95*	—	130	_____
(81064)	Gold Rush set, *99*		NM	_____
(82000)	Straight Track, *87–98*	—	3	_____
(82001)	Curved Track 4.3', *87–98*	—	3	_____
(82002)	Straight Track, box of 4, *87–99*		CP	_____
(82003)	Curved Track 4.3', box of 4, *87–99*		CP	_____
(82004)	Curved Track 5.3', *88–99*		CP	_____
(82006)	35" Straight Track, *88–98*	—	12	_____
(82007)	Right Remote Switch, *89–96*		CP	_____
(82008)	Left Remote Switch, *89–96*		CP	_____
(82010)	Thomas Track Pack, *94–95*	—	40	_____
(82011)	Thomas Left Manual Switch, *94–95*	—	18	_____
(82012)	Thomas Right Manual Switch, *94–95*	—	18	_____
(82013)	Thomas Curved Track 4.3', box of 4, *94–95*	—	9	_____
(82014)	Thomas Straight Track, box of 4, *94–95*	—	9	_____
(82015)	Right Manual Switch, *95–97*	—	40	_____
(82016)	Left Manual Switch, *95–97*	—	40	_____
(82101)	Lockon w/ wires, *88–97*	—	5	_____
(82102)	Conversion Rail Joiners (6), *88–96*		CP	_____

		Exc	New	Cond/$
(82103)	Conversion Knuckle Couplers (2), *88–91*	—	5	___
(82104)	Water Tower kit, *88–89*	—	50	___
(82105)	Engine House kit, *88–89*	—	125	___
(82106)	Watchman Shanty kit, *88–89*	—	65	___
(82107)	Passenger and Freight Station kit, *88–89*	—	100	___
(82108)	Manual Uncoupler, *88–97*		CP	___
(82109)	Brass Pins (12), *88–97*	—	2	___
(82110)	Lumber Shed kit, *89*	—	65	___
(82111)	Freight Platform kit, *89*	—	90	___
(82112)	Figure set (6), *89–99*		CP	___
(82115)	RailSounds Control Box, *90–95*	—	20	___
(82115)	Wooden Vehicle Assortment, *89*		NM	___
(82116)	DC Converter Box, *91 u, 92–96*		CP	___
(82116)	1936 Ford Pickup, *89*		NM	___
(82117)	Crossing Gate and Signal, *91*		NM	___
(82117)	1928 Ford Model A Coupe, *89*		NM	___
(82118)	1936 Ford "Woody" Station Wagon, *89*		NM	___
(82120)	Thomas Sound System, *94–95*	—	5	___
(82121)	Thomas Play Pack, *94–95*	—	70	___
(82122)	Thomas Building Pack, *94–95*	—	27	___
(85000)	Seaboard System GP-9 "5000", *90–91*	—	315	___
(85001)	Conrail GP-7 "5001", *90–91*	—	315	___
(85003)	BN GP-20 "2003", *91 u, 92–94*	—	365	___
(85005)	BN GP-20 Dummy "2004", *92–94*	—	225	___
(85006)	Union Pacific GP-20 "485", *93–95*	—	265	___
(85007)	Union Pacific GP-20 Dummy "486", *93–95*	—	235	___
(85008)	Santa Fe GP-9 "712", *95*		NM	___
(85013)	Santa Fe GP-9 Dummy "722", *95*		NM	___
(85014)	Pennsylvania GP-9 Diesel, "7151", *98*		CP	___
(85015)	Milwaukee Road GP-20 Diesel, "971", *98*		CP	___
(85100)	Pennsylvania 0-6-0T "100", *87*	—	110	___
(85101)	D&RG 0-6-0T "101", *87–90*	—	100	___
(85102)	New York Central 4-4-2 "5102", *88*	150	200	___
(85103)	Santa Fe 4-4-2 "5103", *88*	—	200	___
(85104)	Santa Fe 0-4-0T "5104", *88–89*	—	90	___

		Exc	New	Cond/$
(85105)	Pennsylvania 0-4-0T "5105", *88–89*	—	90	___
(85106)	Chessie System 4-4-2 "5106", *89*	—	190	___
(85107)	Great Northern 4-4-2 "5107", *89*	—	200	___
(85108)	B&O 0-4-0T "5108", *89*	—	95	___
(85109)	Canadian Pacific 0-6-0T "5109", *89*	—	100	___
(85110)	PRR 4-4-2 "5110", *90, 94–95*	160	350	___
(85111)	Great Northern 0-4-0T "5111", *90*		NM	___
(85112)	RI&P 0-6-0T "112", *90*		NM	___
(85113)	Union Pacific 0-4-0T "5113", *90–91*	—	100	___
(85114)	North Pole Railroad 0-4-0T "5114", *89–91*	—	105	___
(85115)	Disneyland 0-6-0T "3", *90*	—	110	___
(85117)	Disney World 0-6-0T "4", *91*		NM	___
(85120)	Thomas the Tank Engine 0-6-0T "1", *93 u, 94–95*	—	65	___
(85121)	James the Red Engine 2-6-0 "5", *94–95*	—	70	___
(85122)	Ornament Express 0-6-0T "8", *94–95*	—	75	___
(85124)	D&RG 0-6-0T "101", *95*	—	40	___
(86000)	PRR Passenger Car "6000", *88–89*	—	65	___
(86001)	PRR Observation Car "6001", *88–89*	—	65	___
(86002)	Union Pacific Passenger Car "6002", *90–91*	—	65	___
(86003)	Union Pacific Observation Car "6003", *90–91*	—	65	___
(86004)	Disney World Passenger Car "6004", *91*		NM	___
(86005)	Disney World Observation Car "6005", *91*		NM	___
(86006)	"Annie" Passenger Car, *93 u, 94–95*		NRS	___
(86007)	"Clarabel" Passenger Car, *93 u, 94–95*		NRS	___
87000	New York Central Boxcar, *89*	—	45	___
87001	Pennsylvania Boxcar, *88*	—	45	___
87002	Santa Fe Boxcar, *88*	—	45	___
87003	Great Northern Boxcar, *89*	—	45	___
87004	Southern Boxcar, *90*	—	50	___
87005	Northern Pacific Boxcar, *90*	—	50	___
87006	Christmas Boxcar, *89 u*	—	75	___
87007	Christmas Boxcar, *90 u*	—	80	___
87009	Western Pacific Boxcar, *91*	—	50	___

		Exc	New	Cond/$
87013	Christmas Boxcar, *95*	—	35	____
(87015)	Christmas Boxcar, *96*	—	45	____
(87016)	Union Pacific Boxcar, "507406", *98*	—	40	____
(87017)	Large Scale Christmas Boxcar, "9700", *98*	—	40	____
(87021)	Happy Holidays 1999 Boxcar, *99*		CP	____
87100	Union Pacific PFE Reefer, *88*	—	50	____
87101	Pennsylvania Reefer, *88*	—	50	____
87102	Chesapeake & Ohio Reefer, *89*	—	50	____
87103	Tropicana Reefer, *90*	—	55	____
87104	Gerber Reefer, *90*	—	55	____
87105	Seaboard Reefer, *89*	—	50	____
87107	A&P Reefer, *91*	—	60	____
87108	Pacific Fruit Express Reefer, *95*	—	35	____
87109	Santa Fe Reefer, *95*	—	35	____
(87110)	Pennsylvania Reefer, "91910", *98*	—	48	____
87200	Buford & Roscoe Handcar, *89–90*	—	70	____
87201	Milwaukee Road Ore Car, *89*	—	35	____
87202	Chessie System Ore Car, *89*	—	35	____
87203	Santa & Snowman Handcar, *90*	—	85	____
87204	Northern Pacific Ore Car, *90*	—	40	____
87205	Pennsylvania Ore Car, *90*	—	40	____
87207	Mickey & Donald Handcar, *91, 95*	—	75	____
87208	Wile E. Coyote & Roadrunner Handcar, *92*	—	100	____
87210	Santa Fe Ore Car, *95*	—	40	____
(87400)	PRR Gondola "400", *87*	—	35	____
(87401)	D&RG Gondola "401", *87–90*	—	30	____
(87402)	Santa Fe Gondola "7402", *88*	—	35	____
(87403)	New York Central Gondola "7403", *88*	—	35	____
(87404)	Disneyland Gondola "404", *90*	—	40	____
(87405)	Chessie System Gondola "7405", *89*	—	35	____
(87406)	Southern Gondola "7406", *89*	—	35	____
(87407)	MKT Gondola "7407", *90*	—	40	____
(87410)	Ornament Express Gondola w/ ornaments, *94–95*		NRS	____
(87411)	"Troublesome Trucks" Gondola, *94–95*	—	20	____
(87500)	D&RG Flatcar "7500", *88*	—	35	____
(87501)	Pennsylvania Flatcar "7501", *88*	—	35	____

		Exc	New	Cond/$
(87502)	Santa Fe Flatcar "7502", *88–89*	—	30	
(87503)	ICG Flatcar "7503", *89*	—	30	
(87504)	Union Pacific Flatcar "7504", *89*	—	30	
87505	Soo Line Flatcar w/ logs, *90*	—	45	
87507	Great Northern Flatcar, *90*		NM	
(87508)	Merry Christmas Lines Flatcar, *89–91*	—	35	
87600	Alaska Tank Car, *89*	—	55	
87601	Santa Fe Tank Car, *89*	—	50	
87602	Gulf Tank Car, *90*	—	55	
87603	Borden Tank Car, *90*	—	55	
87604	Shell Tank Car, *91*	—	65	
87612	Santa Fe Tank Car, *95*	—	40	
(87700)	Pennsylvania Caboose "700", *87*	—	50	
(87701)	D&RG Caboose "701", *87–90*	—	50	
(87702)	Santa Fe Caboose "7702", *88*	—	45	
(87703)	New York Central Caboose "7703", *88*	—	45	
(87704)	Santa Fe Bobber Caboose "7704", *88–89*	—	40	
(87705)	Great Northern Caboose "7705", *89*	—	50	
(87706)	Chessie System Caboose "7706", *89*	—	50	
(87707)	B&O Bobber Caboose "7707", *89*	—	40	
(87708)	Canadian Pacific Bobber Caboose "7708", *89*	—	45	
(87709)	Disneyland Caboose "709", *90*	—	50	
(87010)	CN LCAC Reefer, *96*	—	150	
(87711)	Great Northern Bobber Caboose "7711", *90*		NM	
(87712)	RI&P Caboose "712", *90*		NM	
(87713)	Pennsylvania Caboose "7713", *90*	—	50	
(87716)	North Pole Railroad Bobber Caboose "7716", *89–91*	—	45	
(87722)	Ornament Express Bobber Caboose, *94–95*		NRS	
(87724)	D&RG Caboose "701", *95*	—	20	
(87800)	NYC Searchlight Car "7800", *89–90*	—	85	
87802	Conrail Boxcar w/ ETD, *90–91*	—	70	
87803	Seaboard Boxcar w/ ETD, *90–91*	—	70	
(87806)	REA Boxcar w/ Steam RailSounds, *91*		NM	
(87808)	Union Pacific Searchlight Car "7808", *95*		NRS	
87809	Railbox Boxcar, *95*		NRS	

Section 8
LIONEL CATALOGS 1945–1999

			Exc	New
____ **1945** Consumer Catalog	8½" x 11"	4 pages		NRS
____ **1946** Consumer Catalog	8⅜" x 11¼"	20 pages	50	75
____ **1947** Consumer Catalog	11¼" x 7⅝"	32 pages	30	45
____ **1948** Consumer Catalog	11¼" x 8"	36 pages	30	45
____ **1949** Consumer Catalog	11¼" x 8"	40 pages	75	100
____ **1950** Consumer Catalog	11¼" x 8"	44 pages	45	75
____ **1951** Consumer Catalog	11¼" x 7¾"	36 pages	25	45
____ **1952** Consumer Catalog	11¼" x 7¾"	36 pages	20	35
____ **1953** Consumer Catalog	11¼" x 7⅝"	40 pages	20	30
____ **1954** Consumer Catalog	11¼" x 7⅝"	44 pages	20	30
____ **1955** Consumer Catalog	11¼" x 7⅝"	44 pages	20	30
____ **1956** Consumer Catalog	11¼" x 7⅝"	40 pages	12	24
____ **1957** Consumer Catalog	11¼" x 7½"	52 pages	10	20
____ **1958** Consumer Catalog	11¼" x 7⅝"	56 pages	10	15
____ **1959** Consumer Catalog	11" x 8½"	56 pages	10	15
____ **1960** Consumer Catalog	11" x 8⅜"	56 pages	6	10
____ **1961** Consumer Catalog	8½" x 11"	72 pages	6	10
____ **1962** Consumer Catalog	8½" x 11"	100 pages	8	12
____ **1963** Consumer Catalog	8⅜" x 10⅞"	56 pages	4	6
____ **1964** Consumer Catalog	8⅜" x 10⅞"	24 pages	4	6
____ **1965** Consumer Catalog	8½" x 10⅞"	40 pages	4	6
____ **1966** Consumer Catalog	10⅞" x 8⅜"	40 pages	4	6
____ **1967** Same Catalog as 1966			4	6
____ **1968** Consumer Catalog	8½" x 11"	8 pages	4	6
____ **1969** Consumer Catalog	11" x 8½"	8 pages	3	5
____ **1970** Consumer Catalog w/ foldout poster	8½" x 11"	8 pages	3	5
____ **1971** Consumer Catalog	8½" x 11"	12 pages	3	5
____ **1972** Consumer Catalog	8½" x 11"	16 pages	3	5
____ **1973** Consumer Catalog	8½" x 11"	16 pages	2	4
____ **1974** Consumer Catalog	8½" x 11"	20 pages	2	4
____ **1975** Consumer Catalog	8½" x 11"	24 pages	2	4
____ **1976** Consumer Catalog	8½" x 11"	24 pages	2	4
____ **1977** Consumer Catalog	8½" x 11"	24 pages	2	4

				Exc	New
____	**1978** Consumer Catalog	8½" x 11"	24 pages	2	4
____	**1979** Consumer Catalog	8½" x 11"	24 pages	2	4
____	**1980** Consumer Catalog	8½" x 11"	28 pages	2	4
____	**1981** Consumer Catalog	5½" x 7"	32 pages	1	2
____	**1982** Traditional Series Consumer Catalog	8½" x 11"	20 pages	2	4
____	**1982** Collector Series Consumer Catalog	8½" x 11"	12 pages	2	4
____	**1983** Traditional Series Consumer Catalog	8½" x 11"	20 pages	2	3
____	**1983** Collector Series Consumer Catalog	8½" x 11"	16 pages	2	3
____	**1984** Traditional Series Consumer Catalog	8½" x 11"	20 pages	2	3
____	**1984** Collector Series Consumer Catalog	8½" x 11"	16 pages	2	3
____	**1985** Traditional Series Consumer Catalog	8½" x 11"	20 pages	2	3
____	**1985** Collector Series Consumer Catalog	8½" x 11"	12 pages	2	3
____	**1986** Traditional Series Consumer Catalog	8½" x 11"	16 pages	2	3
____	**1986** Collector Series Consumer Catalog	8½" x 11"	16 pages	2	3
____	**1986** Stocking Stuffers Brochure	8½" x 11"	4 pages	2	3
____	**1987** Consumer Catalog	8½" x 11"	40 pages	3	4
____	**1987** Large Scale Brochure	11" x 8½"	6 pages	1	2
____	**1987** Stocking Stuffers Brochure	8½" x 11"	4 pages	2	3
____	**1988** Consumer Catalog	8½" x 11"	40 pages	2	3
____	**1988** Large Scale Catalog	8½" x 11"	16 pages	1	2
____	**1988** Classics Brochure	8½" x 11"	4 pages	1	2
____	**1988** Hiawatha Brochure	8½" x 11"	4 pages	2	3
____	**1988** Stocking Stuffers Flyer	8½" x 11"	1 page	2	3

				Exc	New
____ **1989** Pre-Toy Fair Consumer Catalog	8½" x 11"	20 pages		2	3
____ **1989** Toy Fair Consumer Catalog	8½" x 11"	28 pages		2	3
____ **1989** Pre-Toy Fair Classics Brochure	8½" x 11"	4 pages		1	2
____ **1989** Toy Fair Classics Brochure	8½" x 11"	4 pages		1	2
____ **1989** Large Scale Catalog	8½" x 11"	20 pages		1	2
____ **1989** Stocking Stuffers Brochure	8½" x 11"	4 pages		2	3
____ **1990** Book 1 Consumer Catalog	8½" x 11"	20 pages		2	4
____ **1990** Book 2 Consumer Catalog	8½" x 11"	36 pages		2	3
____ **1990** Large Scale Catalog	8½" x 11"	16 pages		1	2
____ **1990** Stocking Stuffers Brochure	8½" x 11"	6 pages		2	3
____ **1991** Book 1 Consumer Catalog	8½" x 11"	24 pages		2	4
____ **1991** Book 2 Consumer Catalog	8½" x 11"	60 pages		2	3
____ **1991** Stocking Stuffers Brochure	8½" x 11"	6 pages		2	3
____ **1992** Book 1 Consumer Catalog	8½" x 11"	32 pages		2	4
____ **1992** Book 2 Consumer Catalog	8½" x 11"	48 pages		2	3
____ **1992** Stocking Stuffers Brochure	8½" x 11"	8 pages		2	3
____ **1993** Book 1 Consumer Catalog	8½" x 11"	32 pages		2	4
____ **1993** Book 2 Consumer Catalog	8½" x 11"	52 pages		2	3
____ **1993** Stocking Stuffers 1994 Spring Releases Catalog	8½" x 11"	28 pages		2	3
____ **1994** Consumer Catalog	8½" x 11"	64 pages		3	4

				Exc	New
____	**1994** Thomas the Tank Engine Catalog	8½" x 11"	8 pages	1	2
____	**1994** Trainmaster Transformer Catalog	8½" x 11"	8 pages	1	2
____	**1994** Stocking Stuffers/ 1995 Spring Releases Catalog	8½" x 11"	32 pages	2	3
____	**1994** Preschool Brochure	8½" x 11"	4 pages	1	2
____	**1994** Crayola Brochure	8½" x 11"	4 pages	1	2
____	**1994** Gift Collection Catalog	8½" x 11"	12 pages	1	2
____	**1995** Consumer Catalog	8½" x 11"	88 pages	3	4
____	**1995** Stocking Stuffers/ 1996 Spring Releases Catalog	8½" x 11"	32 pages	2	3
____	**1996** Consumer Catalog	8½" x 11"	24 pages	2	3
____	**1996** Consumer Catalog illustrated	10" x 8"	24 pages	2	3
____	**1996** Accessories Catalog	10" x 8"	32 pages	2	3
____	**1997** Heritage Catalog	10" x 8"	12 pages	2	3
____	**1997** Century Club Catalog	10" x 8"	16 pages	2	3
____	**1997** Classic I Catalog	10" x 8"	24 pages	2	3
____	**1997** Classic II Catalog	10" x 8"	36 pages	2	3
____	**1997** Lionel Brochure	10" x 8"	4 pages	2	3
____	**1997** Fall '97 Heritage II Catalog	10" x 8"	12 pages	2	3
____	**1998** Classic Catalog	8½" x 9"	76 pages	2	3
____	**1998** Heritage Catalog	11" x 8½"	24 pages	2	3
____	**1998** Legendary Trains Catalog	10⅞" x 8½"	64 pages	2	3
____	**1998** Gilbert American Flyer Trains Brochure	8½" x 11"	4 pages		CP
____	**1999** Classic Trains Catalog Volume 1	8¼" x 10½"	64 pages		CP
____	**1999** Classic Trains Catalog Volume 2	8¼" x 10½"	44 pages		CP
____	**1999** Heritage Catalog	11" x 8½"	24 pages		CP

ABBREVIATIONS
Pocket Guide Descriptions

A	diesel A unit	**elec.**	electric
AA	two diesel A units	**electr.**	electronic
AAR	Association of American Railroads (truck type)	**EP-5**	electric type locomotive
		ETD	end-of-train device
AC	alternating current	**Exp.**	express
acc.	accessory	**ext.**	extended
ACF	hopper type	**E/V**	extended vision
Alco	diesel type	**F-3**	diesel type
Alco A	diesel type	**F.A.O.S.**	F A O Schwarz
Alco FA-2A	diesel type	**FARR**	Famous American Railroad Series
Alco FA-2B	diesel type		
Anniv.	Anniversary	**FF**	Fallen Flag Series
appro.	approaches	**Flat.**	flatcar
auto.	automatic	**FM**	Fairbanks-Morse
B	diesel B unit	**GG-1**	electric type locomotive
Bag.	baggage	**GE**	switcher type
Bldg.	building	**Gen.**	General, steam type
Blvd.	boulevard	**Gon.**	gondola
Box.	boxcar	**GP-7**	diesel type
b/w	black and white	**GP-9**	diesel type
B/W	bay window	**GP-20**	diesel type
bump.	bumper(s)	**GP-35**	diesel type
Cab.	caboose	**GP-38-2**	diesel type
cata.	catalog	**Hi-cube**	boxcar type
CC	center cupola	**Hop.**	hopper
cent.	central	**HS**	heat-stamped
chem.	chemical	**illum.**	illuminated
con.	connection	**ins.**	insulated, insulator
cont.	control	**lett.**	lettering
Conv.	conversion	**litho.**	lithographed
CP	current production	**low-cup.**	low-cupola
C.V.	Commodore Vanderbilt	**maint.**	maintenance
Dash 8	diesel type	**man.**	manual
Dash 9	diesel type	**MB**	multi-block door
DC	direct current	**mech.**	mechanical
DD	double-door	**merch.**	merchandise
dep.	depressed	**MU**	multiple unit (commuter cars)
d.p.d.t.	double-pole, double-throw switches		
		N5C	caboose type
dir.	direct	**N8**	caboose type
dum.	dummy	**NBA**	National Basketball Assoc.
dz.	dozen		

NHL	National Hockey League		**St.**	state
NM	not manufactured		**Sta.**	station
NW-2	diesel type		**Std.**	Standard gauge (2⅛" between outside rails)
O	Lionel gauge (1¼" between outside rails)		**Std. O**	Standard O (scale length and dimension)
OO	Lionel Gauge (¾" between outside rails)		**Steam**	steam engine
Obs.	observation		**str.**	straight
oper.	operating		**Sup.**	super
or.	orange		**S/W**	square window
pass.	passenger		**Switch.**	switcher
pc(s).	piece(s)		**Tdr.**	tender
port.	porthole		**TOFC**	flatcar type
pow.	power, powered		**TT**	TruTrack
pr.	pair		**TTUX**	flatcar type
Pull.	Pullman		**Trk.**	track
Quad	quad hopper		**Trans.**	transformer
Rad.	radius		***u* or uncat.**	uncataloged
R.C.	remote control		**U36B**	diesel type
RDC	diesel-powered passenger unit		**U36C**	diesel type
rect.	rectifier		**V. D.**	Vista Dome
rectifier	electric type locomotive		**w/**	with
Reefer	refrigerator car		**w/o**	without
Refrig.	refrigerator		**whl.**	wheel
rem.	remote		**1-D**	one dome
rnd.	round		**2-D**	two dome
RS	rubber-stamped		**3-D**	three dome
RS-3	diesel type			
RSC-3	diesel type			
RSD-4	diesel type			
SB	single-block door			
SD-9	diesel type			
SD-18	diesel type			
SD-24	diesel type			
SD-28	diesel type			
SD-38	diesel type			
SD-40	diesel type			
SD-50	diesel type			
SD-60M	diesel type			
sec.	section			
SP	caboose type			
spec.	special			
SSS	Service Station Special			

Railroad Name Abbreviations

ACL	Atlantic Coast Line
ACY	Akron, Canton and Youngstown
ALASK	Alaska Railroad
AT&SF (ATSF)	Atchison, Topeka, and Santa Fe
B&A	Boston & Albany
BAOC	British American Oil Co.
BAR	Bangor and Aroostook
B&LE	Bessemer and Lake Erie
B&M	Boston and Maine
BN	Burlington Northern
B&O	Baltimore and Ohio
C&A	Chicago and Alton
C&IM	Chicago & Illinois Midland
CB&Q (CBQ)	Chicago, Burlington, and Quincy
CCC&StL	Cleveland, Cincinnati, Chicago and St. Louis
CN	Canadian National
CNJ	Central of New Jersey
C&NW (CNW)	Chicago and North Western
C&O	Chesapeake and Ohio
CP	Canadian Pacific
CRI&P	Chicago, Rock Island, and Peoria
CSt PM&O	Chicago, St. Paul, Minneapolis and Omaha
D&H	Delaware and Hudson
DL&W	Delaware, Lackawanna, and Western
DM&IR	Duluth, Missabe, and Iron Range
D&RG	Denver and Rio Grande
D&RGW	Denver and Rio Grande Western
DT&I	Detroit, Toledo, and Ironton
D&TS	Detroit and Toledo Shore Line
EJ&E	Elgin, Joliet, and Eastern
EMD	Electro-Motive Division
Erie-Lack.	Erie-Lackawanna
FEC	Florida East Coast
GM&O	Gulf, Mobile, and Ohio
GN	Great Northern
GTW	Grand Trunk Western
IC	Illinois Central
ICG	Illinois Central Gulf

IETCA	Inland Empire Train Collectors Association
L&C	Lancaster and Chester
Lack	Lackawanna
LCAC	Lionel Collectors Association of Canada
LCCA	Lionel Collectors Club of America
LCOL	Lionel Central Operating Lines
LL	Lionel Lines
L&N	Louisville and Nashville
LNAC	Louisville, New Albany, and Corydon
LOTS	Lionel Operating Train Society
LRRC	Lionel Railroader Club
LV	Lehigh Valley
MD&W	Minnesota, Dakota, and Western
METCA	New York Metropolitan Division TCA
MKT	Missouri, Kansas, Texas (KATY)
MNS (MN&S)	Minneapolis, Northfield, and Southern
MP (MoPac)	Missouri Pacific
MPA	Maryland and Pennsylvania (Ma and Pa)
MILW	Milwaukee Road
M&StL	Minneapolis and St. Louis
NC&StL	Nashville, Chattanooga, and St. Louis
NdeM	Nacionales de Mexico Railway
NETCA	New England Division Train Collectors Association
NH	New Haven
NKP	Nickel Plate Road
NLOE	Nassau Lionel Operating Engineers
NP	Northern Pacific
N&W	Norfolk and Western
NYC	New York Central
NYNH&H	New York, New Haven, and Hartford
ON	Ontario Northland
PC	Penn Central
P&E	Peoria and Eastern
PFE	Pacific Fruit Express
PHD	Port Huron and Detroit
P&LE	Pittsburgh and Lake Erie
PRR	Pennsylvania Railroad
REA	Railway Express Agency

RF&P	Richmond, Fredericksburg, and Potomac
RI	Rock Island
RI&P	Rock Island and Peoria
SCL	Seaboard Coast Line
SMARRCO	San Manuel Arizona Railroad Company
SP	Southern Pacific
SP&S	Spokane, Portland, and Seattle
SUNX	Sunoco
TA&G	Tennessee, Alabama, and Georgia
TCA	Train Collectors Association
T&P	Texas and Pacific
TP&W	Toledo, Peoria, and Western
TTOS	Toy Train Operating Society
UP	Union Pacific
USMC	United States Marine Corps
VTC	Virginia Train Collectors
V&TRR	Virginia and Truckee Railroad
Wab.	Wabash
W&ARR (W&A)	Western and Atlantic Railroad
WB&A	Washington, Baltimore, and Annapolis Chapter TCA
WM	Western Maryland
WP	Western Pacific

NOTES

NOTES

NOTES

NOTES

GREENBERG'S®
Great Train and Collectible Shows
Saturday 11 a.m. to 5 p.m. and Sunday 11 a.m. to 4 p.m.;
Two-day admission: $6 adults/$2 ages 6-12.

For more information about the Greenberg Show nearest you, send a SASE to Greenberg Shows, Inc., 7566 Main Street, Sykesville, MD 21784 or phone 410-795-7447, fax 410-549-2553, or visit our home page at www.greenbergshows.com. Changes may occur due to circumstances beyond our control.

— October through December, 1999 —

NORCROSS, GA	*North Atlanta Trade Center*	**Oct. 2-3**
STONY BROOK, NY	*State University of NY at Stony Brook*	**Oct. 9-10**
PENNSAUKEN, NJ	*South Jersey Expo Center*	**Nov. 6-7**
MONROEVILLE, PA	*Pittsburgh ExpoMart*	**Nov. 13-14**
EDISON, NJ	*New Jersey Convention and Expo Center*	**Nov. 20-21**
NOVI, MI	*Novi Expo Center ($6 incl p)*	**Nov. 20-21**
DANBURY, CT	*O'Neill Ctr.,Western CT State Univ.*	**Nov. 27-28**
TIMONIUM, MD	*Maryland State Fairgrounds*	**Dec. 4-5**
WILMINGTON, MA	*Shriners Auditorium*	**Dec. 4-5**
FT. WASHINGTON, PA	*Ft. Washington Expo Center*	**Dec. 11-12**
CHARLOTTE, NC	*Charlotte Merchandise Mart*	**Dec. 18-19**
CLEVELAND, OH	*Cleveland Convention Center*	**Dec. 18-19**

— January through August, 2000 —

NORCROSS, GA	*North Atlanta Trade Center*	**Jan. 8-9**
VIRGINIA BEACH, VA	*Virginia Beach Convention Center*	**Jan. 8-9**
JACKSONVILLE, FL	*Greater Jacksonville Fairgrounds*	**Jan. 15-16**
LEBANON, PA	*Lebanon Valley Expo Center*	**Jan. 15-16**
CHANTILLY, VA	*Capital Expo Center*	**Jan. 22-23**
COLUMBUS, OH	*Franklin County Veterans Memorial*	**Jan. 22-23**
TAMPA, FL	*Florida State Fairgrounds*	**Jan. 22-23**
COLLINSVILLE, IL	*Gateway Center*	**Jan. 29-30**
POMPAO BEACH, FL	*The Omni, Broward Community College*	**Jan. 29-30**
FT. WASHINGTON, PA	*Ft. Washington Expo Center*	**Feb. 5-6**
STONY BROOK, NY	*State University of NY at Stony Brook*	**Feb. 12-13**
UPPER MARLBORO, MD	*The Show Place Arena*	**Feb. 12-13**
NILES, OH	*Eastwood Expo Center*	**Feb. 19-20**
MONROEVILLE, PA	*Pittsburgh Expo Mart*	**Feb. 26-27**
PENNSAUKEN, NJ	*South Jersey Expo Center*	**Mar. 4-5**
EDISON, NJ	*New Jersey Convention & Expo Center*	**Mar. 11-12**
TIMONIUM, MD	*Maryland State Fairgrounds*	**Mar. 18-19**
HACKENSACK, NJ	*Fairleigh-Dickinson University*	**Mar. 25-26**
WILMINGTON, MA	*Shriners Auditorium*	**Apr. 1-2**
MONROEVILLE, PA	*Pittsburgh ExpoMart*	**July 8-9**
CHANTILLY, VA	*Capital Expo Center*	**July 15-16**
PENNSAUKEN, NJ	*South Jersey Expo Center*	**July 29-30**
TIMONIUM, MD	*Maryland State Fairgrounds*	**Aug. 5-6**
EDISON, NJ	*New Jersey Convention & Expo Center*	**Aug. 12-13**

Greenberg Auctions

All Greenberg auctions are held at the location below. The preview is at 8 a.m., and the auction at 9 a.m.

SYKESVILLE, MD	*Sykesville-Freedom Fire Company*	**Oct. 9, 1999**
	Community Building	**Apr. 8, 2000**
		July 8, 2000
		Oct. 14, 2000